GLOBAL GOVERNANCE FUTURES

Global Governance Futures addresses the crucial importance of thinking through the future of global governance arrangements. It considers the prospects for the governance of world order approaching the middle of the twenty-first century by exploring today's most pressing and enduring health, social, ecological, economic, and political challenges. Each of the expert contributors considers the drivers of continuity and change within systems of governance and how actors, agents, mechanisms, and resources are and could be mobilized.

The aim is not merely to understand state, intergovernmental, and non-state actors. It is also to draw attention to those underappreciated aspects of global governance that push understanding beyond strictures of traditional conceptualizations and offer better insights into the future of world order.

The book's three parts enable readers to appreciate better the sum of forces likely to shape world order in the near and not-so-near future:

- "Planetary" encompasses changes wrought by continuing human domination of the earth; war; current and future geopolitical, civilizational, and regional contestations; and life in and between urban and non-urban environments.
- "Divides" includes threats to human rights gains; the plight of migrants; those who have and those who do not; persistent racial, gender, religious, and sexual-orientation-based discrimination; and those who govern and those who are governed.
- "Challenges" involves food and health insecurities; ongoing environmental degradation and species loss; the current and future politics of international assistance and data; and the wrong turns taken in the control of illicit drugs and crime.

Designed to engage advanced undergraduate and graduate students in international relations, organization, law, and political economy as well as a general audience, this book invites readers to adopt both a backward- and forward-looking view of global governance. It will spark discussion and debate as to how dystopic futures might be avoided and change agents mobilized.

Thomas G. Weiss is Presidential Professor of Political Science at the CUNY Graduate Center, New York; he is also Distinguished Fellow, Global Governance, at the Chicago Council on Global Affairs and Eminent Scholar at Kyung Hee University, Korea.

Rorden Wilkinson is Professor of International Political Economy and Pro Vice-Chancellor, Education and Student Experience, at the University of New South Wales, Sydney, Australia.

GLOBAL GOVERNANCE FUTURES

Edited by
Thomas G. Weiss and
Rorden Wilkinson

 Routledge
Taylor & Francis Group

LONDON AND NEW YORK

First published 2022
by Routledge
2 Park Square, Milton Park, Abingdon, Oxon OX14 4RN

and by Routledge
52 Vanderbilt Avenue, New York, NY 10017

Routledge is an imprint of the Taylor & Francis Group, an informa business

© 2022 selection and editorial matter, Thomas G. Weiss and Rorden Wilkinson; individual chapters, the contributors

British Library Cataloguing-in-Publication Data
A catalogue record for this book is available from the British Library

Library of Congress Cataloging-in-Publication Data
Names: Weiss, Thomas G. (Thomas George), 1946- editor. |
   Wilkinson, Rorden, 1970- editor.
Title: Global governance futures / edited by Thomas G. Weiss and Rorden Wilkinson
   Description: Abingdon, Oxon ; New York, NY : Routledge, 2022. |
   Includes bibliographical references and index.
Identifiers: LCCN 2021013610 (print) | LCCN 2021013611 (ebook) |
   ISBN 9780367689711 (hardback) | ISBN 9780367689735 (paperback) |
   ISBN 9781003139836 (ebook) Subjects: LCSH: International cooperation.
Classification: LCC JZ1308 .G56 2022 (print) | LCC JZ1308 (ebook) |
   DDC 341.201/13—dc23 LC record available at https://lccn.loc.gov/2021013610
   LC ebook record available at https://lccn.loc.gov/2021013611

ISBN: 9780367689711 (hbk)
ISBN: 9780367689735 (pbk)
ISBN: 9781003139836 (ebk)

Doi: 10.4324/9781003139836

Typeset in Times New Roman
by Apex CoVantage, LLC

CONTENTS

Illustrations

Figures

Tables

CONTRIBUTORS

Editors

Thomas G. Weiss is Presidential Professor of Political Science, the CUNY Graduate Center; Co-Chair, Cultural Heritage at Risk Project, J. Paul Getty Trust; Distinguished Fellow, Global Governance, The Chicago Council on Global Affairs; and Eminent Scholar, Kyung Hee University, Korea. He was President of the International Studies Association and its 2016 Distinguished IO (international organization) Scholar; 2016 Andrew Carnegie Fellow; and Research Director of the International Commission on Intervention and State Sovereignty. His most recent authored books include *The "Third" UN: How a Knowledge Ecology Helps the UN Think* (2021, with Tatiana Carayannis), *Rethinking Global Governance* (2019, with Rorden Wilkinson), *Would the World Be Better without the UN?* (2018), *Humanitarianism, War, and Politics: Solferino to Syria and Beyond* (2018, with Peter J. Hoffman), *What's Wrong with the United Nations and How to Fix It* (2016), and *Humanitarian Intervention: Ideas in Action* (2016).

Rorden Wilkinson is Professor of International Political Economy and Pro Vice-Chancellor, Education and Student Experience at the University of New South Wales, Sydney, Australia. He has held professorial and leadership positions at the University of Manchester and the University of Sussex and visiting appointments at Brown University, Wellesley College, and the Australian National University. He researches broadly in the areas of global governance, international trade, and international development. His recent books include *Rethinking Global Governance* (2019, with Thomas G. Weiss), *What's the Point of International Relations?* (2017, with Jan Selby and Synne L. Dyvik), and *What's Wrong with the WTO and How to Fix It* (2014). He and Thomas G. Weiss are editors of *International Organization and Global Governance* (second edition, 2018) and founding editors of the Routledge "Global Institutions Series."

Contributors

Adriana Erthal Abdenur is a Brazilian policy expert and Executive Director of Plataforma CIPÓ, an independent institute dedicated to issues of climate, governance, and peace in Latin America and the Caribbean. She is Policy Fellow at the United Nations University's Center for Policy Research and Adjunct Lecturer in International Affairs at Sciences-Po, Paris. In addition to the UN Committee for Development Policy (CDP), she is a member of the Climate Governance Commission and the Strategic Advisory Board of the Weathering Risk initiative on Climate and Security.

Michele Acuto is Professor of Urban Politics and Director of the Connected Cities Lab at the University of Melbourne, where he also is Associate Dean (Research) in the Faculty of Architecture, Building, and Planning. His research explores the interplay between global and urban governance, the dynamics of urban development, and the role of information in urban policy-making. He previously worked at the University of Oxford, University College London, and Australian National University, and outside academia for the International Campaign to Ban Landmines, the World Bank, and the European Commission, mainly focusing on how cities shape the global governance of infectious disease, international development, and climate change.

Alexander Betts is Professor of Forced Migration and International Affairs, William Golding Senior Fellow in Politics at Brasenose College, and Associate Head (Doctoral and Research Training) of the Social Science Division at the University of Oxford. Between 2014 and 2017, he served as Director of the Refugee Studies Centre. His research focuses on the politics and economics of refugee assistance, with a focus on Africa. His recent books include *Refuge: Transforming a Broken Refugee Regime* (2017, with Paul Collier), which was named as one the *Economist*'s books of the year for 2017. He is a World Economic Forum Young Global Leader and was named by *Foreign Policy* as one of the top 100 global thinkers of 2016, and his TED Talks have been viewed by over three million people. His latest single-authored book is *The Wealth of Refugees: How Displaced People Can Build Economies* (2021).

Madeline Carr is Professor of Global Politics and Cybersecurity at University College London and Director of the UK-wide Research Institute in Sociotechnical Cyber Security, which looks at the human and organizational factors of cybersecurity. She is also Director of the Digital Technologies Policy Lab, which supports policy-making to adapt to the pace of change, and Deputy Director of the Centre for Doctoral Training in Cybersecurity and of REPHRAIN – a research consortium focusing on protecting citizens online. Her research focuses on the implications of emerging technology for national and global security, international order, and global governance. Her publications cover cyber norms, multi-stakeholder Internet governance, the future of the insurance sector in the Internet of Things (IoT), cybersecurity and international law, and the public/private partnership in national cybersecurity strategies. She is a member of the World Economic Forum Global Council on the IoT.

Jennifer Clapp is Canada Research Chair in Global Food Security and Sustainability and Professor in the School of Environment, Resources, and Sustainability at the University of Waterloo. She has published widely on the global governance of problems that arise at the intersection of the global economy, food security and food systems, and the natural environment. Her recent books include *Food* (2020), *Speculative Harvests: Financialization, Food, and Agriculture* (2018, with S. Ryan Isakson), and *Hunger in the Balance: The New Politics of International Food Aid* (2012). She is a member of the High-Level Panel of Experts on Food Security and Nutrition of the UN Committee on World Food Security.

Peter Dauvergne is Professor of International Relations at the University of British Columbia, specializing in global environmental politics. His recent books include *AI in the Wild: Sustainability in the Age of Artificial Intelligence* (2020), *Will Big Business Destroy Our Planet?* (2018), and *Environmentalism of the Rich* (2016 – winner of the American Political Science Association's Michael Harrington Book Award).

Natalia Escobar-Pemberthy is Assistant Professor of International Relations and Global Governance in the Department of International Business at Universidad EAFIT in Medellín (Colombia), Research Associate for the Center for Governance and Sustainability at the University of Massachusetts Boston, and Sustainability Fellow at the Yale University Office of Sustainability. Her research focuses on environmental governance, particularly on the implementation of global environmental conventions and their linkages to the Sustainable Development Goals.

Rosemary Foot is Professor and Senior Research Fellow in the Department of Politics and International Relations, University of Oxford, an Emeritus Fellow of St. Antony's College, Oxford, and a Research Associate of Oxford's China Centre. In 1996, she was elected a Fellow of the British Academy. Her research interests and publications cover security relations in the Asia-Pacific, human rights, Asian regional institutions, China and regional and world order, and China-US relations. Author or editor of 13 books, her latest authored volume is *China, the UN, and Human Protection: Beliefs, Power, Image* (2020).

Thomas Hanson is Diplomat in Residence at the Alworth Institute for International Affairs at the University of Minnesota Duluth and Bigelow Teacher in Residence in the Department of Political Science at Carleton College. He is also Chair of the Minnesota Committee on Foreign Relations and Co-Chair of the Minnesota China Business Council. Hanson is a former US foreign service officer with the Department of State who has worked on the Foreign Relations Committees of the US Senate and House of Representatives; he also served as Director for NATO and European Affairs at the Atlantic Council of the United States in Washington, DC.

Stephen Hopgood is Professor of International Relations at SOAS, University of London. He is co-editor of *Human Rights Futures* (2017, with Jack Snyder and Leslie Vinjamuri) and the author of *The Endtimes of Human Rights* (2013) and *Keepers of the Flame: Understanding Amnesty International* (2006). Among his recent publications are "When the Music Stops: Humanitarianism in a Post-Liberal World Order" (2019, in *Journal of Humanitarian Affairs*) and "For a Fleeting Moment: The Short Happy Life of Modern Humanism" (2020, in *Humanitarianism and Human Rights: A World of Difference?*).

David Hulme is Professor of Development Studies at the Global Development Institute, University of Manchester, and Chair Professor in International Development at the College of International Development and Global Agriculture at the China

Agricultural University. At Manchester, he is CEO of the Effective States and Inclusive Development (ESID) and the Future DAMS Research Centres. For more than 30 years, he has researched on poverty and inequality in Asia, Africa, and the Pacific, with a specialization on Bangladesh. Recent books include *Should Rich Nations Help the Poor?* (2016) and *Global Poverty* (second edition, 2015).

Maria Ivanova is Associate Professor of Global Governance at the John W. McCormack Graduate School of Policy and Global Studies and Director of the Center for Governance and Sustainability at the University of Massachusetts Boston. Her work focuses on the performance of international institutions, the implementation of international environmental agreements, and sustainability. She has published extensively about the history and performance of international environmental institutions, including *The Untold Story of the World's Leading Environmental Institution: UNEP at Fifty* (2021). Ivanova's current work examines national performance on global environmental conventions and informs policy at the national and international level. From 2014 to 2018, she served on the Scientific Advisory Board of the UN Secretary-General and chairs the Board of UN University's Institute for Advanced Study of Sustainability. She was also a coordinating lead author for the policy chapter of the fifth *Global Environmental Outlook* (GEO-5).

Aarti Krishnan is Hallsworth Research Fellow at the Global Development Institute, University of Manchester. She is an economist working at the nexus of environment, trade, and development. Her areas of expertise include value-chain analysis, green industrial policy, and sustainable digital development. Prior to her current post, she worked as a commodity derivate market analyst and a researcher at the Overseas Development Institute. Her research spans countries in Asia and Africa as well a breadth of sectors including food, retail, and light manufacturing.

Jose Tomas Llanos is Research Fellow in Privacy-Aware Cloud Ecosystems in the Department of Science, Technology, Engineering and Public Policy, University College London; he was previously Research Fellow at the British Institute of International and Comparative Law in the Big Data and Market Power Project and Lecturer in Competition Law at the School of Law of King's College London. A consultant for the Organisation for Economic Co-operation and Development in the digital economy, he has experience in interdisciplinary research, having worked with computer scientists to develop a blockchain-based technology capable of enforcing provisions through smart contracts and flagging potential data protection breaches. His research interests revolve around the legal foundations of data protection, the legal status of privacy-enhancing technologies, the implementation of data-protection-by-design principles, and abridging the knowledge and operational gap between law and computer science.

Kishore Mahbubani – a veteran diplomat, student of philosophy, and author of eight books – is Distinguished Fellow at the Asia Research Institute, National University of Singapore, where he was the founding dean of the Lee Kuan Yew School of Public

Policy (2004–2017). A former permanent representative of Singapore to the UN who twice was president of the Security Council, he writes and speaks on the rise of Asia, geopolitics, and global governance. His books and articles in the *New York Times*, *Washington Post*, *Financial Times*, and *Foreign Affairs* have earned him global recognition as "the muse of the Asian century." He is a member of the American Academy of Arts and Sciences, and his latest book is *Has China Won?* (2020).

Daniel Pejic is Research Fellow in International Urban Migration and PhD Researcher in the Connected Cities Lab at the University of Melbourne. His research explores the concept of city agency in global governance and sits at the intersection of international relations and urban politics. His current focus is on the role of cities as actors in global migration governance and the rescaling of the politics of migration. He has also held a number of professional research roles and leadership positions, working to communicate and translate evidence into policy for non-profit organizations as well as federal, state, and local governments in Australia.

Anne Roemer-Mahler is Associate Professor in International Relations and Deputy Director of the Centre for Global Health Policy at the University of Sussex. Her research interests are in the politics of global health and global health security, and she has worked extensively on the role of pharmaceutical companies in global health security. More recently, her research has turned to health security in Africa and the role of China in global health governance. She has been involved in various interdisciplinary research projects, including on the development of the Africa Centres for Disease Control and Prevention, health security in Tanzania, and stigmatizing skin diseases in Ethiopia, Rwanda, and Sudan.

Rachel Rosenberg is a Master of Global Policy Studies candidate at the LBJ School of Public Policy at the University of Texas at Austin and a research affiliate with Innovations for Peace and Development, an interdisciplinary experiential learning lab. She studies international development with a focus on gender and development assistance. She also has experience studying, working, and volunteering in Latin America.

Mónica Serrano is Professor of International Relations at El Colegio de México and a member of the international faculty of the doctorate program on organized crime at the University of Milan. She was previously Executive Director of the Global Centre for the Responsibility to Protect and is on the Board of Directors of the Academic Council on the United Nations System. Her research focuses on the international relations of Latin America and North America, with particular reference to international institutions, human rights, security, and transnational crime. She is the author of numerous articles and book chapters and co-editor of *Transnational Organised Crime and International Security* (2002), *Human Rights Regimes in the Americas* (2009), *Transitional Justice in Latin America and Eastern Europe* (2012), *Mexico's Security Failure* (2012), and *The International Politics of Human Rights: Rallying to the R2P Cause?* (2014).

Laura J. Shepherd is Australian Research Council Future Fellow and Professor of International Relations at the University of Sydney, Australia. Much of her research relates to the gendered logics and effects of peace and security governance, often under the auspices of the UN's Women, Peace and Security Agenda. She has published widely on topics related to gender, peace, and security. Her most recent book is *Narrating the Women, Peace and Security Agenda* (2021). She maintains a keen interest in pedagogy and popular culture, and she blogs occasionally for *The Disorder of Things*.

Robbie Shilliam is Professor of International Relations at the Johns Hopkins University. He is most recently author of *Decolonizing Politics* (2021) and co-editor of the *Routledge Handbook of Postcolonial Politics* (2018, with Olivia Rutazibwa).

Laura Sjoberg is British Academy Global Professor of Politics and International Relations at Royal Holloway, University of London, and Professor of Political Science at the University of Florida. She specializes in gender, international relations, and international security, with work on war theory and women's political violence. Her work has been published in more than four dozen journals of politics, international relations, gender studies, geography, and law. She is author or editor of 15 books, including, most recently, *Gender and Civilian Victimization* (2019, with Jessica Peet) and *International Relations' Last Synthesis* (2019, with J. Samuel Barkin).

Catherine Weaver is Associate Dean for Student and Associate Professor at the LBJ School of Public Affairs at the University of Texas at Austin, where she co-directs Innovations for Peace and Development, an interdisciplinary experiential learning lab. She is the author of *Hypocrisy Trap: The World Bank and the Poverty of Reform* (2008), in addition to numerous journal articles, edited books, chapters, and policy reports. Her newest work focuses on transparency in international aid and bureaucratic representation in global governance.

ACKNOWLEDGEMENTS

We began thinking about this volume at least a decade and a half ago; it formed part of early discussions about what became our Routledge "Global Institutions Series," which by the end of 2020 had some 165 titles in print or production, many in a second or third edition. Earlier, when we approached the 10th anniversary of our collaboration, we put together a two-part proposal for books about international organization and global governance: a comprehensive introduction for new and general readers and a cutting-edge volume for specialists and advanced graduate students.

The first project was a mammoth undertaking with more than 50 chapters, but it was by design to be economically viable for classroom use. The result, *International Organization and Global Governance*, appeared in 2014, with an expanded second edition in 2018. A third edition will appear in 2023. We never totally forgot the second project, but our wish list of authors and topics was filed in Dropbox until 2019, when we were invited to organize a research conference at the Fudan Institute for Advanced Study in Social Sciences, Shanghai, China. The outbreak of COVID-19, however, forced the cancellation of that conference but did little to dissipate the head of steam the project had gathered. We are grateful to Sujian Guo – acting Dean of the Fudan Institute for Advanced Study in Social Sciences and Professor of Political Science and Director of the Center for US–China Policy Studies at San Francisco State University – and his team for organizing the Shanghai conference that was cancelled as the first phase of the pandemic played out.

The pandemic altered not only world politics but also the emphases in many of the chapters. Indeed, it has given us some sense of what a truly global crisis means, one that disrupts everything from working or shopping to visiting parents or other countries, from attending schools or weddings to organizing classes or holidays via Teams and Zoom. In the midst of an economic calamity and fears about additional waves of COVID-19, it is hard to imagine that we need to make the case for rethinking global problem-solving. But we do. At the same time, global governance during and immediately after the pandemic will not constitute the totality of forces shaping world order now or in the future – a case for which we make in the first chapter of this book.

We were pleased when Rob Sorsby encouraged us to move ahead with this edited collection. Routledge promptly sent the proposal to referees. We were delighted when, not too long thereafter, eight glowing endorsements for the proposal came back, along with useful suggestions. The feedback from those reviews helped us refine aspects of the book, modify chapters, and add authors; in the meantime, our own thinking had evolved so that we also had our own ideas about additions and subtractions. The pages assembled here represent recommendations from all sides.

For two editors who have long worked at the coalface of what it is that we imagine as global governance, the continuing combination of this term's ubiquity and imprecision is a source of frustration and professional embarrassment. However, it is not for a lack of trying on our part.[1] This volume represents an even more ambitious undertaking – namely, to ask other analysts to think with us about the shape of world politics and order over the next quarter century and how it will be managed and governed. These pages do not advance a unified view of global governance into the future – it would be folly to do so. What we have done is bring together a series of first-rate minds to focus on where we are and where we could and should be headed.

The text would not have come together without support from Giovanna Kuele, the managing editor for the Routledge series and an advanced PhD candidate in political science at The City University of New York's Graduate Center. Merrow Le, now a senior education insights officer in the portfolio of the Pro Vice-Chancellor Education and Student Experience (PVCESE) at the University of New South Wales (UNSW), and Emma Murrell, Executive Assistant to the PVCESE at UNSW, deftly kept us organized across many time zones throughout the course of the project.

Tom appreciates the time that he was able to devote to this volume on sabbatical leave from the CUNY Graduate Center and in residence at the Chicago Council on Global Affairs. Rorden did so while juggling a transglobal move from the University of Sussex to UNSW and taking up a new role leading the university's educational portfolio including the response to COVID-19.

Almost two decades of collaborating closely on this and many other projects has been fruitful and rewarding. This book has made us especially nostalgic for earlier collaborations because long car journeys, airways, and conferences – fueled occasionally with fine wine and craft beer – were replaced by digital communications and a 15-hour-plus time difference. We would like to claim, in particular, that Priscilla Read and Claire Annesley have been patient in dealing with each respective spouse's usual workaholic tendencies to produce an insightful volume about global governance. We are grateful and acknowledge their support in the midst of a pandemic; they're nice people to be hunkered down with.

Mistakes, as always, are our own.

T.G.W. and R.W.
Chicago and Sydney
February 2021

Note

1 In chronological order, see Thomas G. Weiss and Rorden Wilkinson, "Rethinking Global Governance: Complexity, Authority, Power, Change," *International Studies Quarterly* 58, no. 2 (2014): 207–215; "Global Governance to the Rescue: Saving International Relations?," *Global Governance* 20, no. 1 (2014): 19–36; "Introduction" and "Change and Continuity in Global Governance," *Ethics & International Affairs* 29, no. 4 (2015): 391–395 and 397–406; "Global Governance Beyond IR," in *International Relations Theory Today*, ed. Ken Booth and Toni Erskine (Cambridge: Polity Press, 2016), 217–230; "Continuity and Change in Global Governance," in *Rising Powers, Global Governance, and Global Ethics*, ed. Jamie Gaskarth (London: Routledge, 2015), 41–56; "The Globally Governed – Everyday Global Governance," *Global Governance* 24, no. 3 (2018): 193–210; *International Organization and Global Governance*, 2nd ed. (London: Routledge, 2018); and *Rethinking Global Governance* (Cambridge: Polity Press, 2019).

ABBREVIATIONS

ABM	Anti-Ballistic Missile Treaty
AfD	Alternative für Deutschland [Alternative for Germany]
AI	artificial intelligence
AIIB	Asian Infrastructure Investment Bank
ASEAN	Association of Southeast Asian Nations
AU	African Union
BASIC	Brazil, South Africa, India, and China
BAT	Baidu, Alibaba, and Tencent
BEPS	base erosion and profit shifting
BHN	basic health needs
BPA	Beijing Platform for Action
BRI	Belt and Road Initiative
BRICS	Brazil, Russia, India, China, and South Africa
BWIs	Bretton Woods institutions
CBD	Convention on Biological Diversity
CBDR	common but differentiated responsibilities
CBM	confidence-building measures
CCRT	Catastrophe Containment and Relief Trust
CDC	Centers for Disease Control and Prevention
CEO	chief executive officer
CEPI	Coalition for Epidemic Preparedness Innovations
CFCs	chlorofluorocarbons
CFS	Committee on World Food Security
CGIAR	Consultative Group on International Agricultural Research
CIA	Central Intelligence Agency
CITES	Convention on International Trade in Endangered Species of Wild Flora and Fauna
CMS	Convention on Migratory Species
CND	Commission on Narcotic Drugs
COP	Conference of the Parties
CPTPP	Comprehensive and Progressive Agreement for a Trans-Pacific Partnership
CRS	Congressional Research Service
CSCE	Conference on Security and Cooperation in Europe
CSM	Civil Society Mechanism
CSR	corporate social responsibility
DAC	Development Assistance Committee [OECD]
DEA	Drug Enforcement Agency
DESA	Department of Economic and Social Affairs
DoJ	Department of Justice
DPD	Data Protection Directive

DRC	Democratic Republic of the Congo
DSSI	Debt Services Suspension Initiative
EAEU	Eurasian Economic Union
EMDEs	emerging markets and developing economies
EU	European Union
FAO	Food and Agriculture Organization
FBI	Federal Bureau of Investigation
FDA	Food and Drug Administration
FDI	foreign direct investment
FERPA	Family Educational Rights and Privacy Act
FIES	Food Insecurity Experience Scale
FOCAC	Forum on China-Africa Co-operation
FSC	Forest Stewardship Council
FSS	Food System Summit
G7	Group of Seven
G8	Group of Eight
G18	Group of 18
G20	Group of 20
G77	Group of 77
GAFA	Google, Amazon, Facebook, Apple
GAP	Good Agricultural Practices
GAVI	Global Alliance on Vaccination and Immunization
GDP	gross domestic product
GDPR	General Data Protection Regulation
GEP	global environmental politics
GFATM	Global Fund to Fight AIDS, Tuberculosis and Malaria
GHG	greenhouse gas
GRI	Global Reporting Initiative
HCFCs	hydrochlorofluorocarbons
HDI	Human Development Index
HIPPA	Health Information Portability and Accountability Act
HLP	High-Level Panel of Eminent Persons
IAEA	International Atomic Energy Agency
IATI	International Aid Transparency Initiative
ICAO	International Civil Aviation Organization
ICC	International Criminal Court
ICRC	International Committee of the Red Cross
ICT	information communication technologies
IDCR	International Drug Control Regime
IDGs	International Development Goals
IEA	International Energy Agency
IFAD	International Fund for Agricultural Development
IGAD	Intergovernmental Authority for Development
IGC	Intergovernmental Consultations on Asylum, Refugees, and Migration
IHL	international humanitarian law

IHR	International Health Regulations
ILO	International Labour Organization
IMF	International Monetary Fund
INCB	International Narcotics Control Board
INF	Intermediate-Range Nuclear Forces Treaty
IO	international organization
IOM	International Organization for Migration
IoT	Internet of Things
IP	intellectual property
IPCC	Intergovernmental Panel on Climate Change
IPE	international political economy
IR	international relations
IRD	Integrated Rural Development
ITU	International Telecommunications Union
IUCN	International Union for the Conservation of Nature
LGBTQ+	lesbian, gay, bisexual, transgender, and queer
LICs	low-income countries
LMICs	lower-middle-income countries
LMOs	living modified organisms
LSD	lysergic acid diethylamide
MDGs	Millennium Development Goals
MPI	Multidimensional Poverty Index
MSC	Marine Stewardship Council
MSF	Médecins Sans Frontières [Doctors Without Borders]
MUNS	Multilateralism and the United Nations System
NAM	Non-Aligned Movement
NATO	North Atlantic Treaty Organization
NDB	New Development Bank
NGO	non-governmental organization
NSA	National Security Agency
ODA	official development assistance
OECD	Organisation for Economic Co-operation and Development
OHCHR	Office of the High Commissioner for Human Rights
OSCE	Organization for Security and Co-operation in Europe
OWG	Open Working Group
P5	permanent five members of the UN Security Council
PETs	privacy-enhancing technologies
PPP	purchasing power parity
PPM	parts per million
PRC	People's Republic of China
PRSP	poverty reduction strategy paper
PSM	Private Sector Mechanism
QUAD	Quadrennial Security Dialogue
R&D	research and development
RCEP	Regional Comprehensive Economic Partnership

RCPs	Regional Consultative Processes
RSPO	Roundtable on Sustainable Palm Oil
RTRS	Round Table on Responsible Soy
SADC	Southern African Development Community
SAP	structural adjustment programs
SARS	severe acute respiratory syndrome
SCO	Shanghai Cooperation Organization
SDGs	Sustainable Development Goals
SDI	Slum Dwellers International
SDRs	Special Drawing Rights
SIA	Security Identities Alliance
SIDS	Small Island Developing States
SSA	sub-Saharan Africa
START	Strategic Arms Reduction Treaty
SUVs	sport utility vehicles
TANs	transnational advocacy networks
TNC	transnational corporation
UCLG	United Cities and Local Governments
UNACLA	United Nations Advisory Committee of Local Authorities
UNAIDS	Joint United Nations Programme on HIV/AIDS
UNCCD	United Nations Convention to Combat Desertification
UNCED	United Nations Conference on Environment and Development
UNCHE	United Nations Conference on the Human Environment
UNCLOS	United Nations Conference on the Law of the Sea
UNCTAD	United Nations Conference on Trade and Development
UNDP	United Nations Development Programme
UNEP	United Nations Environment Programme
UNESCO	United Nations Educational, Scientific and Cultural Organization
UNFCCC	United Nations Framework Convention on Climate Change
UNFF	United Nations Forum on Forests
UNFPA	United Nations Population Fund
UNHCR	[Office of the] United Nations High Commissioner for Refugees
UNICEF	United Nations Children's Fund
UNIDO	United Nations Industrial Development Organization
UNISDR	United Nations Office for Disaster Risk Reduction
UNODC	United Nations Office on Drugs and Crime
UNRRA	United Nations Relief and Rehabilitation Agency
UNRWA	United Nations Relief and Works Agency for Palestine Refugees in the Near East
UNSW	University of New South Wales
UNU	United Nations University
USACS	United States Alien Control Services
USAID	United States Agency for International Development
USSR	Union of Soviet Socialist Republics
WEF	World Economic Forum

WFP	World Food Programme
WHO	World Health Organization
WIPO	World Intellectual Property Organization
WMO	World Meteorological Organization
WTO	World Trade Organization

CONTENTS

Making sense of global governance futures

Thomas G. Weiss and Rorden Wilkinson

The year 2020 began gloomily, though there was little to suggest that it would stand out from the long-run ebb and flow of world politics. Decades-old growth in trade was being eroded by tensions between the leading commercial powers, particularly the United States and China. The United Kingdom's divorce from the EU had yet to be finalized. Washington, Beijing, and others were at loggerheads over the use of Huawei products in national infrastructure projects as well as over pro-democracy protests in Hong Kong. Long-standing tensions between the United States and Iran were exacerbated by the drone-strike killing of Qasem Soleimani – the commander of the Iranian Islamic Revolutionary Guards Quds force. Australia was suffering from some of the worst bush fires in recent history. And long-standing corruption investigations in South Africa had culminated in an arrest warrant being issued for former president Jacob Zuma while he was in Cuba for medical treatment.

While these events and many others were cause for concern, they did not suggest that 2020 would be exceptional. Yet, in the space of a few weeks, the complexion of world politics and everyday life changed. On 30 January 2020, the World Health Organization (WHO) declared that the spread of a novel coronavirus first detected in Wuhan, China – what became known as "COVID-19" – was a public health emergency of international concern. This was upgraded on 11 March 2020 to a pandemic – by definition a global crisis. By the end of 2020, some 75 million cases had occurred with more than 1.75 million deaths.[1] The Americas were by far

DOI: 10.4324/9781003139836-1

the hardest hit continents, with the United States and Brazil recording the highest number of infections and rates of mortality. Significant outbreaks had also affected Europe, South and Southeast Asia, and the eastern Mediterranean. In less than a year, COVID-19 had gone from an also-ran influenza to a global catalyst for change, with the months that followed reaping further and increasing misery.

The pandemic not only threatened lives and killed weak and vulnerable people worldwide, but its myriad consequences and the fledgling responses to mitigate its spread exerted significant governance effects on all aspects of life on the planet. The initial reaction from most countries was to close borders and restrict domestic travel. In highly affected areas, severe lockdowns restricted movement outside of personal homes to essential matters. The dramatic reduction in social interactions and the introduction of physical distancing and additional hygiene measures had a significant positive effect on the virus' spread in those countries where effective processes were put in place. In others, where the response was equivocal – including Brazil, the United States, India, and the United Kingdom – the virus ran amuck. The announcement of an effective vaccine in the waning days of 2020 provided a moment of rare respite and optimism.

Irrespective of the national measures, globally the aggregate consequences of COVID-19 were severe. In the first months of the pandemic, xenophobia increased markedly, particularly toward people of East Asian origin. The global airline and hospitality industries all but collapsed, along with national and international tourism. The supply of goods, including essential foodstuffs and medicines, was disrupted globally and nationally. Panic purchasing ensued. Industries collapsed as workers stayed home. The fall in demand for goods and services generated pressure on employers to lay off staff. Those governments that could underwrote the temporary furloughing of employees to cushion some of the damage wrought by falling demand. For others, the lack of capacity or political will for public intervention generated additional pressure on already vulnerable populations. Globally, housing markets initially teetered on the edge of collapse, and the number of people deferring or defaulting on mortgage payments and rents increased. The price of oil temporarily plummeted to below $0. Universities faced substantial financial challenges in the face of disruption to national and international student recruitment and returns. The shift to remote working created significant demand for technological goods and services. Video conferencing and algorithms shaped not only the delivery and consumption of education but also the nature of work, social interactions, the flow of information, and understandings of domestic and international politics.

These were not the only consequences of the virus's first blush. Stock market values fell sharply across the globe before the move to remote working and the search for effective vaccines drove the price of technology and pharmaceutical shares skyward. Those that were able bought heavily in these markets and took advantage of otherwise depressed stock prices to expand their portfolios. Property markets, too, though suffering significant initial contractions, boomed in suburban and rural areas, fueled by stamp duty holidays, favorable prices, lower population densities, and the longer-run prospects of remote working and learning. The inevitable consequence of these and other financial movements was an increase in the wealth of the already rich and a very different experience for those in the middle or already living at the margins. Similar patterns played out in access to health care, essential foodstuffs, and even leisure, as they did once effective vaccines became available. In sum, the responses to the virus generated by governments and market movements combined to exert some of the biggest and most dramatic govern-ance effects in centuries. COVID-19 had become – for a discernible time, at least – global governance and generated many of its discontents.

The onset and immediate aftermath of the pandemic inevitably became the focus of journalistic, scholarly, and policy analyses. Yet, no matter how significant its effects, the global governance of COVID-19 will not constitute the totality of forces shaping world order, now or in the future. Although global crises on the scale – or greater – than COVID-19 cannot be discounted, in the next quarter century we are likely to continue to confront unprecedented economic, political, social, ecological, and health changes – arising from and independent of the pandemic. Our modest effort, and that of the other contributors to this volume, is to offer some of what we consider the most significant emerging and enduring issues that will also shape the world order to come and the forces involved in its governance. As we collectively note, the changes wrought by continuing human domination of the planet; war; current and future geopolitical, civilizational, and regional contestations; life in and between urban and non-urban environments; the endur-ing divides between those who govern and those who are governed, and those that have and those that do not; persistent racial, gender, religious, and sexual-orientation-based discriminations, among many others; the plight of migrants worldwide and the threats to the human rights gains of the modern era; and the challenges of food and health insecur-ities, ongoing environmental degradation and species loss, the current and future politics of international assistance, and the wrong turns taken in the control of illicit drugs, among other international regimes, will bring as many challenges as they do opportunities.

Our endeavor is to understand and interrogate the *problématique* of future global governance in light of recent developments and the themes we detect in those areas that we have chosen to highlight. Our aim is not merely to understand what state, intergov-ernmental, and non-state actors – the traditional fare of global governance – will do. While state-based responses are clearly important, they are not – and indeed never have been – the whole story, as COVID-19 has illustrated only too well. Our purpose is more broadly conceived: to understand the forces large and small, the systems of governance, the enduring divides, and the primary challenges that will shape life on our planet into the middle of the twenty-first century and beyond. We seek to mobilize our current under-standing of contemporary forces to appreciate how the world is likely to be governed and ordered as well as to comprehend how adjustments can be made to improve prospects for the survival and meaningful advancement of humanity and the planet. We do this through the lens of a rearticulated understanding of global governance.

Thus, our objective in this chapter is to provide a framework for making sense of what is to come. We do so by offering an understanding of global governance that wrests it from the strictures of traditional conceptualizations and enables us to appre-ciate better the sum of forces likely to shape world order in the near and not-so-near future. We achieve this by setting out a series of conceptual markers to help better understand future global governance and the alternative possibilities that may and could be realized. We draw attention to the need to account for the underappreciated temporal and spatial aspects of global governance; we consider the role of a wider variety of actors – including those we call the "missing middle"; and we highlight the impact that global governance has and may have on those whose relationship with its outcomes is most intimate but also often underappreciated.

Global governance futures: A framework for thinking

One way to imagine the global governance of the future is to start with the global governance of today: its constitution, organizational form, and inner logic. Yet, to do so is not without problems. These problems arise because of the lack of both a clear understanding of global governance and a common consensus about what it could and should be. For some, global governance is merely old wine in new bottles – an alternative expression for the actions and activities of international organizations. For others, it is a descriptor for a global stage packed with ever more actors, a call to arms for a better world, and an attempt to control the pernicious aspects of accelerating economic and social change. For others still, it is a synonym for world government, a pejorative term, and a hegemonic plot to advance the interests of a murky global elite.

Our contention is different. We see considerable analytical value in the term. Our assertion, however, is that to be able to think about the global governance of the future, we first have to acknowledge and overcome eight problems that have come to be baked into its current meaning and that restrict its utility to comprehend not only the governance of today but also eras past and future. These problems are:

1 the overly strong association between global governance and the problems and possibilities of international organization in the late twentieth and early twenty-first centuries;

2 the lack of a comprehensive identification and explanation of the structure of global authority that accounts not just for grand patterns of command and control but also how regional, national, and local systems intersect with and push against that structure;

3 an ignorance of myriad ways that power is exercised within such a system, how interests are articulated and pursued, and the kind of ideas and discourses from which power and interests draw substance as well as help establish, maintain, and perpetuate the system;

4 misunderstandings of what propels changes *in* and transformations *of* systems of global governance that focus on the causes, consequences, and drivers of continuity and change, not just today but over extended periods in the past and the future;

5 an unwillingness to ask questions about systems and instances of global governance through time to explore the mechanisms, machineries, institutions, rules, norms, ideas, interests, and material capabilities that have governed world orders in times before and after our own;

6 an assumption that the "global" preceding "governance" is necessarily planetary in scale, which risks ignoring the forces involved in the governance – for example, of the Silk Road, ancient empires, and colonial regimes, among many others – and the indelible marks left by those systems on the governance of world order today and tomorrow;

7 too little an appreciation of the output end of the global governance equation – what is produced, the effects that are generated, the impact of systems and expressions of global governance on everyday lives, and the feedback loops that exist between aspects of global governance and those whose lives are affected by it; and

8 a neglect of those directly and indirectly involved in the production of global governance, not just those identified as the "global governors" but also the professionals, service teams, and individuals at work behind the scenes whose combined activities contribute to creating, sustaining, disrupting, and dismantling world orders – what we call the "missing middle."

To appreciate how these shortcomings came to be part of conventional understandings and how they inhibit our capacity to look forward to global governance of the future, we need to recover the genesis of the term "global governance." The term "global governance" emerged from academic and policy responses to a series of real-world events in the late 1980s and early 1990s. These responses sought to understand the forces at play on the world stage that had led to the end – and were in evidence in the aftermath – of the Cold War. Early works on global governance were also concerned with identifying and enhancing the prospects for a better world order after a half century in which East-West rivalry had crowded out many a progressive global public policy initiative; thinking through how feminist analyses could be brought to bear in a subject where they had previously found little traction; and understanding the transformative potential of grassroots resistance and civil society movements.[2] Global governance was, as a result, a concept imbued with possibility – one that was expressly concerned with understanding change, complexity, and alternative futures – but it was also born from a narrow moment in time.

In their pioneering collection *Governance without Government*, James Rosenau and Ernst Czempiel charted a pathway for thinking about how the world was governed and ordered in the post-Cold War world. They chose to focus not only on the state and its intergovernmental entanglements but also hidden, in-between, emerging, and non-state sources of governance and authority. Elsewhere, the policy-oriented Commission on Global Governance led by Sonny Ramphal and Ingmar Carlsson focused on the normative possibilities of the newly emerging world order. At the same time, others were thinking about the future world order under the auspices of the Multilateralism and the United Nations System (MUNS) project – coordinated by Robert W. Cox and sponsored by the United Nations University (UNU).[3] Indeed, a proliferation of works emerged keen to shine new light on the possibilities of and prospects for the new world order.[4] Such was its appeal that by the time of the 1995 publication of the commission's report, *Our Global Neighbourhood*, the term "global governance" had gained considerable traction and was being used as a forward-focused optic in academic and policy-making circles.

These early works, and the events they sought to understand, paved the way for a raft of works about growing global complexity, the management of globalization, and the challenges confronting international institutions.[5] What they did not do, however, was settle on a common understanding or a clear path for inquiry. As Lawrence Finkelstein noted, ambiguity was a design feature of early works on global governance as scholars sought to understand the changing dynamics of global politics in the aftermath of the end of the Cold War. His complaint, however, was that far from being helpful, this ambiguity rendered global governance "virtually anything."[6]

Cox and his colleagues choose to define global governance as "the procedures and practices which exist at the world (or regional) level for the management of political, economic and social affairs." While this definition also appeared rather elastic, it came with an important caveat:

> One hypothetical form of [global] governance (world government or world empire) can be conceived as having a hierarchical form of coordination, whether centralized (unitary) or decentralized (federal). The other form of coordination would be non-hierarchical, and this we would call multilateral.[7]

What was instructive about Cox's definition was the liberty it gave to thinking about global governance. Cox and his colleagues were clearly concerned with thinking about the normative possibilities of one element of global governance – multilateralism. But they also left open the understanding that global governance could, had, and would take many and varied forms. This, in turn, opened the way for thinking about global governance through time by focusing on how world orders were managed and arranged in different eras, and this clarified some of the issues about which Finkelstein complained. That said, Cox's definition and the challenge of understanding global governance through historical time and social space are not widely explored by others in the literature. They are, however, key elements of our call for rethinking the analytical utility of global governance.[8]

As global governance gained traction and interest both in and beyond the academy, subtle changes in conceptualization emerged. Some of these changes were driven by scholars adapting understandings of global governance to account for important earlier work that had run out of steam, no longer captured the attention of a new generation, or had hit conceptual hurdles that had proven tricky to surmount.[9] For others, the term was manipulated to account for newly noted but seldom satisfactorily explained phenomenon.[10] As Joseph Barrata observed, during the 1990s, "the new expression, 'global governance,' emerged as an acceptable term in debate on international organization for the desired and practical goal of progressive efforts, in place of 'world government.'" He continued, noting that scholars Michael Barnett and Raymond Duvall observed only a decade after the expression had come into use that "the idea of global governance has attained near-celebrity status. . . [it] has gone from the ranks of the unknown to one of the central orienting themes in the practice and study of international affairs."[11]

> wished to avoid using a term that would harken back to the thinking about world government in the 1940s, which was largely based on fear of atomic bombs and too often had no practical proposals for the transition short of a revolutionary act of the united peoples of the world.[12]

This growth in interest was not without problems. Subtle changes moved global governance away from a concern with appreciating complexity, change, and possibility on a worldwide scale to a narrower focus on collective efforts to identify, comprehend, and address problems and processes that went beyond the capacities of individual states in the post-Cold War period. As a result, global governance became overly associated with the capacity of, and the desire for, intergovernmental arrangements – sometimes working hand in glove with non-governmental actors, sometimes not – to provide government-like services in the absence of anything like a world government. Debates became reified between supporters and detractors of international institutions in fields ranging from health and conflict prevention to trade and development. In short, global governance had ceased to be analytically useful and instead had become a proxy descriptor whose meaning had become ever narrower as its usage increased. The result was to dull the edges of the term's analytical utility.

Another, darker turn also emerged. While global governance continued to carry with it the hopes and fears of many inside and outside the academy at the turn of the millennium, it had also been captured by more conspiratorial forces who chose to interweave the term with discourses about global elites and cabals with little basis in fact and often with highly racialized tones – as was much in evidence in some of the proclamations of those who stormed the US Capitol building on 6 January 2021. The result was that global governance had – in a few short decades – shifted from a genuine attempt to understand and affect the changing map of authority worldwide to a new way of talking about international organization and, to a lesser extent, conspiracy theories in the post-Cold War era.

Why do these changes in meaning matter? The future of international organizations and other expressions of intergovernmental cooperation are important – conceptually and otherwise – as we have argued previously,[13] and synonyms can provide a useful shorthand for talking about broad phenomena. Moreover, many students are interested in classes on international organization because they are fascinated by these institutionalized sites of discord and collaboration, often hoping to embark on careers in international public service. As we think about the future, it is important not to ignore the experiments of the last century and a half;[14] we should not dismiss the relevance or irrelevance of the mandates and activities of international organizations or the perceptions and forces that drive conspiratorial thinking. Nonetheless, such restricted understandings reduce analytical utility. They stifle the capacity to ask broader questions about how world order is governed – now, in the past, and in the future. To focus only on burgeoning forms of intergovernmentalism at the turn of the twentieth century would, for instance, fail to do more than glance briefly at the significant role of imperialism, social Darwinism, and industrialization. Equally, to stress contemporary criticism (during the Trump administration in the United States, for instance) of international organizations would falsify interpretations of today's global governance and the world order that it shapes.

Our contention is that, to enhance its analytical utility, global governance must move beyond a singular association with alterations in international organization in the late twentieth and early twenty-first centuries. The complexities of the post-Cold War era are concrete expressions of global governance at that moment in time, but earlier formations have been different, as future ones will be in epochs to come; they are driven by ideas, interests, and forces that vary and evolve.[15] To be useful, an inquiry into global governance has to identify and explain the often contested[16] structures of global authority in play at any given moment; it must account not just for grand patterns of command and control but also for how regional, national, and local systems intersect with and push against that structure. It needs to involve an investigation into the myriad ways that power is exercised within such a system, how interests are articulated and pursued, and the kind of ideas and discourses from which power and interests draw substance as well as which help establish, maintain, and perpetuate the system. It should account for less and more substantial changes *in* and *of* the system and probe the causes, consequences, and drivers of change and continuity, not just today but over extended periods in the past and into the future. And, crucially, it must account for the outcomes of systems of governance at all levels. Only then will we be able to understand better "global governance as it has been, is, and may become"[17] as well as provide reasonable answers to questions about "how the world hangs together."[18]

What is required to realize the analytical potential of global governance? The first part of the answer is to tackle global complexity in a more satisfactory fashion, to not be afraid to disaggregate by issue and by context, and then to try to fit what we find back together into a better explanatory whole. We should not only describe who the principal actors are and how they connect to one another but also how a particular outcome has resulted, why and on what grounds authority is effectively or poorly exercised, and who and what has been lost or excluded. We should examine the consequences of new forms of organization and determine what adjustments might enhance their utility to meet existing, new, or changing objectives. Important as well are subtler understandings and a better appreciation of the differing characteristics of actors, institutions, and governance machineries and their significance when those with varying natures and capabilities come together or clash.

We also should give greater prominence to the way that power of various types is exercised. State capabilities clearly matter, but so, too, does the way that formal and informal institutions mediate relations between states and the way that goods and services are exchanged and managed. When the numbers and kinds of actors proliferate, when states exert less control over markets, and when complex relations exist among various actors and markets, questions of power are less straightforward. For instance, we should probe more than the relationship between the birth of the current system of global governance and US preponderant power, and we should look beyond Washington's crucial role in the creation of the first and second generations of universal intergovernmental bodies to explore other elements of structural power. We should also reflect on institutional expressions and social groups, epistemic communities and policy networks, financial decision-making, and changing capabilities among other actors.[19]

A final task is the need to understand fully the ideas and interests that drive the machineries of governance that we have, how they arose and developed, and how they subsequently permeated and modified the international system at all levels.[20] Here, ideas themselves are essential, as are the value systems upon which they rest and inform, the discourses in which they are embedded, the interests to which they speak, and other elements of symbolic power of which they are part. So too are the entrepreneurs and despots who generate ideas, the networks through which they are disseminated, the ways that various institutions mediate core messages, and the processes through which they are translated into forms of organization and policy delivery. So far, we have failed to adequately link ideas to global governance, to tease out what works and why.

Global governance through time

Without a concerted effort to press forward our understanding of the complexities of global governance, the way that authority and power are exercised, and the ideational and material aspects of world order, we risk not only misunderstanding but also underestimating our capacity to make meaningful adjustments to that order and its governance. In short, our task is far from finished. As noted, Cox's distinction between forms of global governance provides a fruitful way to remove some of the restraints that its association with the post-Cold War moment thus far has imposed. To be useful, our view of global governance must go beyond its *contemporary* manifestations and their emergence from a specific and very recent historical juncture.

One way to think about global governance over time is to evaluate prevailing ideas about world order at any given moment. In the two-dimensional and static view of the Westphalian order as essentially an interstate system, pointing to the organizing principle of anarchy tells us little about why the world has been organized that way, or why we should strive to understand what existed before. Such an approach takes us into well-charted territory, but our way of journeying through it – if we focus on questions of how and why the world is organized – is different and potentially provides additional insights.

One reason for the emergence of the interstate system, as the broad framework that governs the world, was a response to ideas that – in the European world, at least – sought to move away from a form of governance in which papal authority was supreme to one in which various secular and non-secular rulers exercised sovereignty over discrete geographic units. While ideas of self-determination found their first expression here, the move from papacy to state was not necessarily in the interests of those populations who were subjected to previous or subsequent forms of governance. Nor did it end the influence of the papacy – or religious institutions more generally – in the global governance of that time or extinguish ideas about the subjugation of peoples beyond notional national borders as a "legitimate" product of that global governance.

Other agents that contributed to how the world was governed until that point – such as mercenary armies and city-states, to name but two – fell into desuetude, but new actors emerged to play more central roles. Eric Hobsbawm's *The Age of Empire*[21] emphasized, for instance, the actions and activities of private enterprises – which in many cases started off as "privateer" ventures and became the nationally sanctioned "companies" of European empires – and their roles in extending imperialism as a worldwide system of order and governance. Thus, asking questions about the rush to empire enables us to see the role of such actors as the British and Dutch East India companies. It also helps to distinguish between the kind of global governance that existed before and during the accumulation of European imperial power (as well as the brutal forms of governance experienced by colonized peoples) and the versions that existed once the scramble for territory subsided and the world map had settled into areas well demarcated by colonial acquisition, expansion, and interests.

Our usual disciplinary route into thinking about how the world was organized and ordered in the nineteenth century is to examine how the balance of power was institutionalized among the major European states through the Holy Alliance and the Concert of Europe.[22] Yet this perspective merely tells us of efforts to avoid costly and catastrophic wars in Europe among ruling elites, not how the world was governed. Absent are understandings of the competing imperialisms that were the dominant framework for nineteenth-century global governance along with differing ideas about the subjugation of non-European peoples and the colonization of apparently uninhabited lands (treated as *terra nullius* irrespective of indigenous populations). Also missing are the ways that this dominant form of organization and its ideas were challenged – both ideationally and physically – which, in turn, eroded the bases of competing imperialisms and helped set in motion wholesale changes in global governance.

Craig Murphy's examination of international public unions as the forerunners of the intergovernmental elements of contemporary global governance illustrates the crucial importance of testing the framework of global governance as an approach to understanding how the world was ordered in historical periods other than just in the post-Cold War moment.[23] The utility of Murphy's work lies in his willingness to connect changes in the form and function of contemporary global governance with the onset, consolidation, and acceleration of another global dynamic that mainstream international relations (IR) has always found difficult to comprehend – the onset of the Industrial Revolution and the spread of capitalist production and organization.

A few other analysts have peered through these economic and social lenses as a starting point for thinking about how the world is and was organized and governed in earlier times.[24] They have contributed to our understanding of the world authority structures that we have, but they do not – attempts to historicize these approaches notwithstanding[25] – fully explore the kinds of questions that a deep dive into the historical manifestations of global governance demands. John M. Hobson's exploration of the contributions of non-Western civilizations and non-European forms of organization to the contemporary world is a good example of important insights into thinking about historical and contemporary aspects of global governance, but it also illustrates the work that remains.[26]

If the need to understand change and new horizons in the immediate post-Cold War era drove us to pose questions about global governance, it should also encourage us to ask similar questions about earlier epochs and find satisfactory, or at least better, answers than we have fashioned to date. Yet wrenching global governance from the contemporary moment and applying it historically is, by itself, insufficient. Any shift should also help inform and anticipate tomorrow. The future-oriented value lies in treating global governance as an appropriate set of questions that enable us to work out how the world is, was, will, or could be governed and how changes in grand and not-so-grand patterns of governance occurred, are or will be occurring, and *ought* to occur. These questions, in turn, need to be pursued in areas of critical concern and wherein we have a long-run understanding that highlights likely trends, and precisely in those areas that our contributors address in the following chapters.

Global governance across space

Wresting our comprehension of global governance from the grip of presentism is not the only pressing requirement. We also need to rescue it from an obligatory association with the planet as the distinguishing spatial and conceptual element. Investigating the manner that systems combine to organize, manage, govern, and arrange the world does not demand that those arrangements be planetary in scale. Indeed, in eras prior to our own, forms of global governance have been less than planetary in their reach and scale. Our reconceptualization requires merely that they curate a good proportion of human-centered activity over large swathes of the understood and imagined worlds.

Two shortcomings have impeded the analytical traction of this aspect of global governance and motivate our line of inquiry. The first is that existing conceptualizations invariably treat "global" as a synonym for "planetary." The second is the lack of familiarity with – or perhaps even a reticence about – what the governance of world order might look like if it is not as encompassing as our own.

As is evident from the previous historical examples, not all world orders have been global. This was as true for the nineteenth-century's inter-imperial order as it was for uneasy arrangements among competing empires in the ancient world. In these and many other cases, the systems of order that orchestrated actions for a large share of humanity were not planetary in coverage – although many individuals at the time may well have imagined that they were. They were world orders nonetheless, and we can identify the systems that lent order to those epochs as forms of global governance. What is different about today's world order is that it is genuinely planetary in scope, and we exist in the first epoch in which such an arrangement has been possible and a reality.

That said, just because we have reached a moment when we can talk of planetary governance does not mean that all future constellations will necessarily be manifest in that way – they could be smaller or more extensive. Although ongoing advances in technology and communications – not to mention climate change and COVID-19 – lead us toward the planet as the logical unit of analysis, moments of retreating global governance have also been evident in times gone by, as they were during the interwar years. Both a technology-driven closeness and the reassertion of centrifugal tendencies are possible.

It is important to note, however, that areas of the globe need not be formally governed to be elements of, or integrated into, a worldwide system. They can also take a position in opposition to, or be (consciously or otherwise) different or excluded from, a dominant system. What is key to our understanding is that such stances are taken in direct response to – and thus inevitably entail a measure of orientation around – a dominant system of world order.

Conceptualizing global governance in this way has considerable utility. It enables us to ask questions about the spatial and substantive arrangements in different (and sometimes competing) systems of world-order management as well as of how areas outside formally orchestrated space relate to relationships of command and control. This has particular pertinence when we think about the evolution of our own order. For example, at its inception Pax Americana was far from global in reach and occupied a space also inhabited by declining empires and a nascent communist system. Later, during the height of the Cold War, the Washington-centered "world" order coexisted alongside a competing Moscow-centered system. Both orders organized life not only within the respective spheres of influence but also affected those areas that formally lay beyond but were nonetheless oriented in relation to the Cold War's dominant powers – for example, countries of the Non-Aligned Movement (NAM) or the Group of 77 (G77). None of the world orders or their systems of management could genuinely be described as "global." All three were, nevertheless, elements of a wider system of global governance based on ideological rivalry and opposition thereto, and it is helpful to conceptualize them as such.

Thus, emphasizing history alone is insufficient for understanding the whole global governance puzzle. We also need to comprehend the implications of real and imagined space. Expanding our conception of global governance across time and space enables us to ask questions about how non-planetary world orders were and are organized as well as how regulatory systems among small settlements governing relations among themselves at the outset of human evolution have developed into systems that define and determine the Anthropocene.

Global governance, up and down

Time and space are not the only elements missing from a more satisfactory under-standing of global governance. Also neglected are interpretations that reflect more accurately two other perspectives that are typically absent from macro views. The first is the "everyday" – that is, accounts of the daily experiences of those across social groups whose lives are affected by the myriad ways that world order is fashioned and governed. The second is "the missing middle," those individuals who create, shape, and produce global governance but whose role is often unseen or overlooked.

These additional optics help us understand not only the complexion and complexity of systems but also their consequences – what we describe elsewhere as the "output end" of the global governance equation. The reasons are relatively simple. Global governance has multiple and varying effects, as the literature suggests. However, these effects are often starker than acknowledged. We should, for instance, consider the effect that international borders have on everyday life – a key technology of governance and a means by which order is lent to the contemporary world. International borders shape relations between communities, and not just those who find themselves bifurcated by them – such as Kurds in Iraq, Iran, Syria, and Turkey or families seeking refuge in the United States from Central America. They also have an impact on those whose commerce and communications require trans-border passage – such as Syrian shepherds in the Israeli-occupied Golan Heights. Likewise, alterations to international borders and rules governing movements across them (of goods, services, information, and people) have a profound impact. The changes wrought by the United Kingdom's departure from the EU – in passing from the Republic of Ireland to Northern Ireland and in traveling to and from the United Kingdom to continental Europe – is a contemporary example. The continuing reverberations of colonial border-making – in the Middle East, Africa, and elsewhere – provide many other illustrations.

It is thus important to reverse the usual direction of the top-down analytical lens of global governance in order to appreciate how systems and expressions of governance are experienced and encountered from the bottom up – that is, from the perspective of the "globally governed."[27] When viewed from this angle, we discover a perspective that is all-too-often absent; we are better able to appreciate how global governance is gendered and racialized; and we are then able to feedback into analyses in ways that have so far been eschewed, or at least overlooked. This, in turn, enables us to lend further precision to thinking about what is required to bring about effective and lasting change.

This perspective begs the question: why do we know so little about global governance in the everyday? We appreciate a great deal about the power of financial markets because the effects of catastrophic financial collapse have animated the work of scholars after every major economic collapse – the 2007/2008 global financial and the COVID-19 crises are only the most recent illustrations. Yet we do not know nearly enough about how precisely global financial decision-making affects daily life. We are, for example, far from understanding the relationships between what transpires in Zurich and London and personal income quakes on the ground for farmers in the Andes or Great Plains or the connections between the speculative actions of traders in global commodity markets and the effects on local spot markets, farming livelihoods, and household economies.[28] The best that we can probably say is that financial and economic crises render the everyday lives of ordinary people more precarious, with those living in the Global South likely to be the most affected.

These shortcomings in knowledge are not confined to our understanding of global financial systems alone. We are equally remiss in failing to comprehend the every-day effects of international assistance programs and crisis responses or of health restrictions put in place in response to an outbreak of infectious diseases and the impact of their subsequent removal on the capacity of communities to reestablish commerce. All too often we have failed to explore how the globally governed have encountered – for good and for ill – global governance. Instead, we have concentrated on the actions and activities of those who govern.

Why are the globally governed so invisible?[29] Conceptually, the close association between the term "global governance" and what international organizations do has overly determined the extent to which the field has proceeded. We tend to read global governance – its history, content, and drivers of change – from the vantage points of Washington, London, Brussels, or Geneva and through the eyes of privileged elites, rather than from communities in Ruhororo (Burundi), Ürümqi (China), or Dili (Timor-Leste). This orientation has concentrated minds on the art of governance as practiced by the powerful rather than on its consequences for recipients. It also reflects the origins and locations of those who study global governance – namely, from countries at the center of global decision-making whose analytical radars are insufficiently tuned to looking at the multiple variables in the governance equation and whose physical distance is far removed from many of the consumers of global governance. In addition, no one has yet confronted sufficiently the enduring legacy of colonial ways of thinking.[30] Studying those on the receiving end of global governance can require the kind of fieldwork and investigation into primary sources for which few IR scholars or prospective students were equipped, even before COVID-19.[31] We have much to learn from anthropologists whose careers are devoted to comprehending the everyday, often in communities far removed in distance and culture from classrooms, library stacks, and data sets.

That said, global governance scholarship is not, in fact, all that different from research in other disciplines. Most social scientists tend to focus on the most visible institutions and individuals at the center of problem-solving and policy-making. They customarily stop short of understanding how power and influence flow to recipients. Most of us, particularly in the digital era, have access to primary documents and interviews at the press of a button. Few have the time, resources, language skills, or courage to run risks in war zones, go to makeshift customs houses abutting contested international borders, build social networks in isolated communities, or wander into volatile borderlands. The result is that our view of global governance is restricted by our privilege and is confined to questions of institutional design and construction and to policy development and delivery.

There are other reasons why we should correct this gaping oversight in our analytical industry. As indicated, much of the practice of governing globally originates in the Global North. This is – to paraphrase Deborah Avant, Martha Finnemore, and Susan Sell – where most of the global governors reside, work, and play.[32] In contrast, many of the recipients of contemporary global governance are in the Global South, and the most acute effects are often experienced by their most vulnerable citizens (women, children, the elderly, and indigenous peoples). This reality does not mean that the effects of, and strong perceptions about, global governance are absent in the Global North. But it does mean that many of the world's most precarious communities have a more intimate daily relationship with global governance than do citizens of states where the global governors reside. Their familiarity comes from the World Bank, the International Monetary Fund (IMF), the Office of the United Nations High Commissioner for Refugees (UNHCR), the WHO, Oxfam, the International Federation of Red Cross and Red Crescent Societies, and Médecins Sans Frontières (MSF). The globally governed encounter not only these recognizable players but also such less visible ones such as transnational criminal networks, faith groups, and financial markets.

Moreover, those populations on the receiving end of global governance seldom have access to, or even a say in, the decision-making whose consequences affect their daily existence. This startling imbalance is especially pronounced when we examine the design and consequences of institutional actions. Indeed, because we as a scholarly community have studied the successes, failures, and impacts of global governance so narrowly, we may have been complicit in prolonging ineffectual systems that ignore recipients and their plights as well as restrict and constrain their agency.

Attenuating these conceptual shortcomings requires removing our blinders and bringing the globally governed to the fore. This appeal is akin to previous clarion calls sounded for the "everyday" to be brought front and center in international relations, international political economy, and peace studies.[33]

At the same time, a broader and potentially richer appreciation of global governance also requires turning our analytical radars toward other individuals who create, shape, and produce global governance – what we call "the missing middle." These often unheard and unheard-of people are the professionals, service teams, and individuals who are involved behind the scenes in making global governance happen, in doing the policy, operational, and support work to move the needle of global governance institutions of all varieties from the local to global levels. Certainly, insights into their effect on global governance can be gleaned from work on epistemic communities, transnational activism and networks, and, more recently, professions in international governance.[34] But even these accounts do not focus on the everyday roles of staff employed to keep the proverbial lights on – whose actions and activities animate the beating heart of global governance.

The members of the missing middle go beyond the relatively absent everyday contributions of professionals and staffers employed in intergovernmental organizations. The missing middle also includes those whose contributions shape the impact of other elements of global governance pertinent to shaping world orders. The computer programmers who develop algorithms that predict and shape behavior are as much a part of contemporary global governance as resident representatives and their support staff in the country and regional offices of the UN system. Equally, mediators and military personnel in war zones play significant roles in shaping global governance. In the same way, the scientists and medical personnel in the response to and developing vaccines for COVID-19 are as much a part of crafting the contemporary world order as mercenaries and privateers were in creating non-Western and European imperial systems.

For those primarily concerned with international organizations, the legions of missing-middle officials are not absent – they feature in interviews, notes about the models of service, and levels of politicization – but they are seldom the cornerstone of reflection. Studies focusing on instances of global governance output – refugee camps, multilateral relief programs, and health emergencies – tend to emphasize the high politics that spawned or impeded initiatives or, alternatively, the beneficiaries on the ground. Analytical attention is rarely on the aid workers, military personnel, and volunteers who make relief programs happen. Similarly, analyses of financial markets stress the consequences of collective investor decision-making and, to a lesser extent, the behavior of individual fund managers. Rarely do everyday investors, market operatives, managers, or technicians appear center stage, let alone in the limelight of analytical attention. Yet global governance cannot and does not occur without them. Otherwise, strategic visions would not be translated into reality, decisions would not be made, actions would not be taken, projects and programs would not be monitored, and standards would not be enforced.[35] In short, we ignore the missing middle, their work, its effects, and those who are subject to the consequences at our peril.

The task at hand

How does all this help us think about the future of global governance? Unlike historical and current events that can be documented and examined, the systems of the future and the outcomes that they might generate have yet to be determined. While "global governance futures" are yet to be created, we nonetheless have challenged our contributors to imagine them – using methods of their choosing – which explains the title of this book.

Those futures will not unfold in a vacuum. Rather, they will be shaped by a combination of events influenced by the past and present, which stand apart from those that have yet to occur. The future remains unknown, but the identification and avoidance of past mistakes is a realizable goal – as each subsequent contribution demonstrates. Understanding global governance's complexity, its manifestations over time and space, those individuals involved in its production, and the experiences of those on the receiving end would enable us to parse the distinctions between significant changes *of* global governance from more marginal changes *in* global governance so that we are able to understand global governance and make a genuine difference.

To do so requires that we understand the systems of the past and the enduring reverberations that are likely to continue. We need to evaluate how gender, war, race, colonial legacy, and the human environment are likely to animate global governance, in familiar as well as new ways. We need to understand where progress has been made – for example, in education, longevity, and other areas – as well as where it has not – for example, in the enduring legacies of colonial administrators, cartographers, and social Darwinists.

The purpose of this edited collection is to consider the prospects for the governance of world order as we approach the middle of the twenty-first century. The chapters explore the consequences of some of today's most pressing problems in order to discern the prospects for improving global governance futures. The essays are designed to complement our edited volume *International Organization and Global Governance*, published by Routledge in its second edition in 2018 – the third will appear in 2023 – which is where readers seeking more foundational elements should begin.

The book has three parts covering what we believe are some of the most fruitful avenues along which to travel toward understanding global governance futures. The first is "Planetary," which includes six essays that encompass global perspectives: the Anthropocene, war, geopolitics, civilizations, regions, and cities. It is often said that the world is more polarized than ever, and so Part II examines five "Divides": human rights, migration, poverty and inequality, race, and people. The third part addresses seven "Challenges" that are present and looming and potentially fatal: food, health, climate, biodiversity, aid, data, and illicit drugs. "Suggested Reading" appears at the end of each chapter, in addition to extensive endnotes, to guide users who wish to pursue additional research.

We have commissioned essays from a stellar and intellectually diverse set of authors. Indeed, one of the strengths of this volume is that its contributors approach topics from distinct perspectives and disciplines, using a range of methods. The variety of approaches is not only helpful but also necessary for anyone interested in probing the problems and prospects of global governance futures as well as keen to avoid the pitfalls created by previous thinking and theorizing in the field. The "About the Contributors" section includes brief biographies on the authors, all of whom have researched and written extensively about the subject matter of their chapters.

Rather than introducing them here, readers will find an overview of each of the parts of the book and the chapters that they contain in a few pages at the outset of each of the book's three main parts. These texts preview the importance of thinking differently about global governance and exploring the futures that may follow. They also lend insight into the arrangement of the chapters and their collective contribution to the task at hand.

Our expectation is that readers will discover the importance of reimagining global governance – namely, its temporal and spatial dimensions as well as its impact on the globally governed and inputs from the missing middle – to understand the possibilities, prospects, opportunities, and pitfalls that lie ahead. In addition, the substantive emphases in separate chapters add additional proof to what the COVID-19 crisis had already revealed: the limits of the current system of global governance. Our collective call is for an ambitious rethinking of global governance possibilities as we move toward the middle of the century to avoid some of the trapdoors that line the way. This book is a modest contribution to that objective.

Suggested reading

Amitav Acharya, ed., *Why Govern? Rethinking Demand and Progress in Global Governance* (Cambridge: Cambridge University Press, 2016).
Deborah D. Avant, Martha Finnemore, and Susan K. Sell, eds., *Who Governs the Globe?* (Cambridge: Cambridge University Press, 2010).
Alice Ba and Matthew J. Hoffmann, eds., *Contending Perspectives on Global Governance: Coherence, Contestation and World Order* (London: Routledge, 2005).
Martin Hewson and Timothy J. Sinclair, eds., *Approaches to Global Governance Theory* (Albany, NY: State University of New York, 1999).
Tana Johnson, *Organizational Progeny: Why Governments Are Losing Control Over the Proliferating Structures of Global Governance* (Oxford: Oxford University Press, 2017).
Kathryn C. Lavelle, *The Challenges of Multilateralism* (New Haven, CT: Yale University Press, 2020).
Mark Mazower, *Governing the World: The History of an Idea* (New York: Penguin, 2012).
Thomas G. Weiss and Rorden Wilkinson, *Rethinking Global Governance* (Cambridge: Polity Press, 2019).

Notes

1 See World Health Organization, "WHO Coronavirus (COVID-19) Dashboard," https://covid19.who.int.
2 See, for example, Mohammed Ayoob, "The New-old Disorder in the Third World," *Global Governance* 1, no. 1 (1995): 59–77; Elisabeth Prügl, "Gender in International Organization and Global Governance: A Critical Review of the Literature," *International Studies Notes* 21, no. 1 (1996): 15–24; Mary K. Meyer and Elisabeth Prügl, eds., *Gender Politics in Global Governance* (New York: Rowman & Littlefield, 1999); Lean Gordenker, "Pluralizing Global Governance: Analytical Approaches and Dimensions," *Third World Quarterly* 16, no. 3 (1995): 357–388; Robert O'Brien, Anne Marie Goetz, Jan Aart Scholte, and Marc Williams, *Contesting Global Governance: Multilateral Economic Institutions and Global Social Movements* (Cambridge: Cambridge University Press, 2000).
3 Yoshikazu Sakamoto, ed., *Global Transformations: Challenges to the State System* (Tokyo: United Nations University Press, 1992); Keith Krause and W. Andy Knight, eds., *State, Society and the UN System: Changing Perspectives on Multilateralism* (Tokyo: United Nations University Press, 1995); Robert W. Cox, ed., *The New Realism: Perspectives on Multilateralism and World Order* (Basingstoke, UK: Macmillan, 1997); Stephen Gill, ed., *Globalization, Democratization and Multilateralism* (London: Macmillan, 1997); Michael G. Schechter, ed., *Future Multilateralism: The Political and Social Framework* (London: Macmillan, 1999), and *Innovation in Multilateralism* (London: Macmillan, 1999). See, also, John Gerard Ruggie, ed., *Multilateralism Matters: The Theory and Praxis of an Institutional Form* (New York: Columbia University Press, 1993); Rorden Wilkinson, *Multilateralism and the World Trade Organisation: The Architecture and Extension of International Trade Regulation* (London: Routledge, 2000); and Edward Newman, Ramesh Thakur, and John Tirman, eds., *Multilateralism Under Challenge? Power, International Order, and Structural Change* (Tokyo: United Nations University Press, 2006).
4 David Goldblatt, Jonathan Perraton, David Held, and Anthony McGrew, *Global Transformations: Politics, Economics, Law* (Cambridge: Polity Press, 1999); and Martin

Hewson and Timothy J. Sinclair, eds., *Approaches to Global Governance Theory* (Albany, NY: State University of New York, 1999).

5 Aseem Prakash and Jeffrey A. Hart, eds., *Globalization and Governance* (London: Routledge, 1999); David Held and Anthony McGrew, eds., *Governing Globalization* (Cambridge: Polity Press, 2002); and Robert W. Cox, "The Crisis of World Order and the Challenge to International Organization," *Cooperation and Conflict* 29, no. 2 (1994): 99–113.

6 Lawrence Finkelstein, "What Is Global Governance?" *Global Governance* 1, no. 3 (1995): 368.

7 Cox, "Introduction," in *The New Realism*, XVI.

8 Thomas G. Weiss and Rorden Wilkinson, *Rethinking Global Governance* (Cambridge: Polity Press, 2019).

9 See, for example, Richard B. Falk and Saul H. Mendlovitz, eds., *A Strategy of World Order*, vols. I-IV (New York: World Law Fund, 1966–67); and Grenville Clark and Louis B. Sohn, *World Peace Through World Law* (Cambridge, MA: Harvard University Press, 1958).

10 Timothy J. Sinclair, *Global Governance* (Cambridge: Polity Press, 2012), 16.

11 Michael Barnett and Raymond Duvall, eds., *Power in Global Governance* (Cambridge: Cambridge University Press, 2005), 1.

12 Joseph Preston Barrata, *The Politics of World Federation*, 2 vols. (Westport, CT: Praeger Publishers, 2004), quote from vol. 2, 534–535.

13 For example, Thomas G. Weiss, *What's Wrong with the United Nations and How to Fix It* (Cambridge: Polity Press, 2008); and Rorden Wilkinson, *What's Wrong with the WTO and How to Fix It* (Cambridge: Polity Press, 2014).

14 Kathryn C. Lavelle, *The Challenges of Multilateralism* (New Haven, CT: Yale University Press, 2020).

15 For one contemporary view of continuity and change see Kishore Mahbubani, "Europe in the 21st Century: Powerful and Powerless," *Global Policy* 11, no. 1 (2020): 143–146.

16 Laura J. Shepherd, "Power and Authority in the Production of United Nations Security Council Resolution 1325," *International Studies Quarterly* 52, no. 2 (2008): 383–404; and Karim Makdisi and Coralie Pison Hindawi, "The Syrian Chemical Weapons Disarmament Process in Context: Narratives of Coercion, Consent, and Everything in Between," *Third World Quarterly* 38, no. 8 (2017): 1691–1709.

17 Martin Hewson and Timothy J. Sinclair, "Preface," in *Approaches to Global Governance Theory*, ed. Martin Hewson and Timothy J. Sinclair (Albany, NY: State University of New York Press, 1999), IX.

18 John Gerard Ruggie, *Constructing the World Polity* (London: Routledge, 1998), 2.

19 Peter M. Haas, "Epistemic Communities and International Policy Coordination," *International Organization* 46, no. 1 (1992): 1–35; Diane Stone, "Governance via Knowledge: Actors, Institutions and Networks," in *Oxford University Press Handbook of Governance*, ed. David Levi-Faur (Oxford: Oxford University Press, 2012), 339–354; and Eric Helleiner and Stefano Pagliari, "The End of an Era in International Financial Regulation? A Post-crisis Research Agenda," *International Organization* 65, no. 1 (2011): 169–200.

20 Louis Emmerij, Richard Jolly, and Thomas G. Weiss, *Ahead of the Curve? UN Ideas and Global Challenges* (Bloomington: Indiana University Press, 2001); Stephen Gill, "Constitutionalizing Inequality and the Clash of Globalizations," *International Studies Review* 4, no. 2 (2002): 47–65; and Martha Finnemore and Kathryn Sikkink, "International Norm Dynamics and Political Change," *International Organization* 52, no. 4 (1998): 887–917.

21 Eric Hobsbawm, *The Age of Empire* (London: Abacus, 1994).

22 Hans J. Morgenthau, *Politics Among Nations: The Struggle for Power and Peace*, 6th ed. (New York: McGraw-Hill, 1995), 481–489.

23 Craig Murphy, *International Organization and Industrial Change: Global Governance Since 1850* (Cambridge: Polity Press, 1994).

24 Christopher Chase-Dunn and Joan Sokolovsky, "Interstate Systems, World Empires and the Capitalist World Economy," *International Studies Quarterly* 27, no. 3 (1983): 357–367.

25 André Gunder Frank and Barry K. Gills, eds., *The World System: Five Hundred Years of Five Thousand* (London: Routledge, 2003).

26 John M. Hobson, *The Eastern Origins of Western Civilization* (Cambridge: Cambridge University Press, 2004).

27 Thomas G. Weiss and Rorden Wilkinson, "The Globally Governed: Everyday Global Governance," *Global Governance* 24, no. 2 (2018): 193–210; and Kate Pincock, Alexander Betts, and Evan Easton-Calabria, *The Global Governed? Refugees as Providers of Protection and Assistance* (Cambridge: Cambridge University Press, 2020).

28 Adrienne Roberts, "Financing Social Reproduction: The Gendered Relations of Debt and Mortgage Finance in Twenty-first-century America," *New Political Economy* 18, no. 1 (2013): 21–42; and Genevieve LeBaron, "The Political Economy of the Household: Neoliberal Restructuring, Enclosures, and Daily Life," *Review of International Political Economy* 17, no. 5 (2010): 889–912.

29 Exceptions are research that tells us something about the receipt of global governance as an unexpected outcome of projects designed for other analytical purposes. For instance, Jim Yong Kim, Joyce V. Millen, Alec Irwin, and John Gershman, eds., *Dying for Growth: Global Inequality and the Health of the Poor* (Monroe, ME: Common Courage Press, 2000); and Ellen Chesler and Terry McGovern, eds., *Women and Girls Rising* (London: Routledge, 2015).

30 Robbie Shilliam, ed., *International Relations and Non-Western Thought: Imperialism, Colonialism and Investigations of Global Modernity* (London: Routledge, 2010).

31 Caroline Nordstrom, *Global Outlaws: Crime, Money, and Power in the Contemporary World* (Los Angeles, CA: University of California Press, 2007).

32 Deborah D. Avant, Martha Finnemore, and Susan K. Sell, eds., *Who Governs the Globe?* (Cambridge: Cambridge University Press, 2010).

33 Juanita Elias and Adrienne Roberts, "Feminist Global Political Economies of the Everyday: From Bananas to Bingo," *Globalizations* 13, no. 6 (2016): 787–800; Laura Sjoberg and Caron E. Gentry, "Introduction: Gender and Everyday/Intimate Terrorism," *Critical Studies on Terrorism* 8, no. 3 (2015): 358–361; Michele Acuto, "Everyday International Relations: Garbage, Grand Designs and Mundane Matters," *International Political Sociology* 8, no. 4 (2014): 345–362; John M. Hobson and Leonard Seabrooke, eds., *Everyday Politics of the World Economy* (Cambridge: Cambridge University Press, 2007); and Roger MacGinty, "Everyday Peace Bottom-up and Local Agency in Conflict-Affected Societies," *Security Dialogue* 45, no. 6 (2014): 548–564.

34 Haas, "Epistemic Communities and International Policy Coordination"; Cecilia Milwertz and Wei Bu, "Non-governmental Organising for Gender Equality in China – Joining a Global Emancipatory Epistemic Community," *International Journal of Human Rights* 11, nos. 1–2 (2007): 131–149; Inderjeet Parmar, "American Foundations and the Development of International Knowledge Networks," *Global Networks* 2, no. 1 (2002): 13–20; Leonard Seabrooke and Lasse Folke Henriksen, eds., *Professional Networks in Transnational Governance* (Cambridge: Cambridge University Press, 2017); and Anne-Marie Slaughter, "Everyday Global Governance," *Daedalus* 132, no. 1 (2003): 83–90.

35 Craig N. Murphy and JoAnne Yates, *The International Organization for Standardization (ISO): Global Governance Through Voluntary Consensus* (London: Routledge, 2009).

PART I
PLANETARY

Introduction

The first part of the book is composed of six chapters that deal with global governance futures from the viewpoint of the planet in its entirety as well as the primary elements of human organization. Each explores a critical dynamic that is crucial to understanding the kind of global governance and world orders that could – and are likely to – emerge in the near and not-so-near future. In combination, they offer a powerful insight into how the primary dynamics and forms of human organization are driving forces of continuity and change.

This first part of the book begins, in Chapter 2, with Peter Dauvergne's powerful account of "Global Governance and the Anthropocene: Explaining the Escalating Global Crisis." His task is to draw attention to the impact of human domination of the planet across the past five centuries and humanity's attempts to address its negative effects as well as what this means for the global governance of the future. He argues that humanity's impact on the environment, particularly during the last half century, has been profound and has resulted in a significant deterioration of the global environment. However, he suggests, today's problems would have been worse without the multilayered architecture we currently have to govern the planetary-scale impact of human beings. His view is not, however, rose tinted. He views the likely solutions for the future that emanate from this system of global governance as uneven, incremental, and patchy. These solutions underestimate the true costs of business as usual and overestimate the true value and potential of the private sector and new technologies. Looking ahead a quarter century, Dauvergne sees some cause for optimism as grassroots activism intensifies, local successes spread, and calls for sweeping reforms grow louder. Equally, as he (inevitably presciently) notes, the world order of the future is likely to be more, rather than less, determined by the lasting effects of the Anthropocene than today.

In Chapter 3, Laura J. Shepherd considers a second major dynamic – whether because of its prevalence or absence – likely to shape the world

DOI: 10.4324/9781003139836-2

order of the future and its governance. Her account focuses on war and "The Governance of Violence and the Violence of Governance." What the International Committee of the Red Cross (ICRC) calls the "laws of war," or "international humanitarian law," is the starting point for contemporary examinations of the governance of armed conflict. The flipside of efforts to "save succeeding generations from the scourge of war" (the aspirational words at the very outset of the UN Charter) reflects a progressive understanding of the impact of previous efforts to mitigate the effects of that bluntest of all policy instruments, the resort to war. As part of what she views as responsible scholarship, Shepherd examines how the governance effects of war – including domination, oppression, and annihilation – are inextricably interwoven into the tapestry of today's world order. Shepherd's concluding reflections concern the possibilities for and limitations of managing violence as well as the violent influences and impacts of global governance itself. Her insights are important and help shape understandings of both how future war may be governed as well as the governance effects that war itself exerts on populations (and particular social groups) and the planet.

Thomas Hanson's reflections on "Geopolitics: Competition in an Age of Shared Global Threats" comprise the fourth chapter of the book and are a natural next port of call. Bringing to bear sharp insights from his own research and teaching as well as his earlier career as a US foreign service officer with postings in Eastern and Western Europe, he explores the complex and thorny topic of geopolitics. After an introduction to this staple of both academic international relations and practical diplomacy, which is older than the state system itself, he dissects the past, current, and future intersections or clashes of interest among today's major geopolitical rivals: the United States, China, and the European Union (EU). No chapter in this book could ignore COVID-19, and Hanson argues that the pandemic accelerated three trends very much in evidence before 2020: a global sustainability crisis, an explosion of new technologies, and shifts in the balance of power. He sees that a witches' brew of crises could either help or hinder cooperation that is essential for improved global governance. Traditional geopolitics emphasized geography, but contemporary non-traditional threats arguably represent even graver dangers, especially climate change and pandemics.

The analysis of geopolitics leads logically to Chapter 5, Kishore Mahbubani's "Civilizations: Fusion or Clash?" Mahbubani begins with a puzzle: many positive aspects of Western civilization have significantly improved the human condition worldwide, but currently populations in the West are depressed about the future. Meanwhile, he argues, the ancient civilizations of China and India have been underperforming over the last two centuries, but their populations are optimistic in imagining the future. Mahbubani outlines what he sees as three key strategic errors committed by the West: an unwillingness to adapt to a changing world order in which it is less dominant than previously; clinging to power in international organizations; and the United States, especially under the Trump administration, challenging China on its own, without its allies. He holds out the possibility – with reversals of the three faulty strategies – for a "fusion" rather than a "clash" of civilizations. Like the chapters preceding his, Mahbubani's reflections tell us much about the likely forces shaping world order, and they encourage us to look beyond the global governance of the West for insights into what is yet to come.

In the penultimate essay in this first part, Rosemary Foot explores the role of "Regions and Regionalism: Confronting New Forms of Connectedness" as a critical dynamic shaping future global governance. Chapter 6 brings to bear her extensive research and teaching in the examination of how regions have been and will increasingly be a promising and productive point of departure for geopolitics in the pursuit of national as well as common interests. Foot explores various forms of connectedness that fuel skeptical views from numerous observers about the role of regions as cooperative mechanisms in a globalizing and globalized world. She nonetheless views regions as having the potential to act as a crucial lever to reverse the more general assault on multilateralism by the new populists and nationalists whose influence was increasing even prior to the additional inward-turning pressures in response to COVID-19. Foot does not foresee the demise of regionalism in the coming decades but rather the emergence of a range of "hybrids," or mixtures, of regional and global institutions as essential features in global governance futures.

Chapter 7 brings the first part of the book to a close. Daniel Pejic and Michele Acuto offer a compelling account of the role of "Cities: Understanding Global Urban Governance" in shaping the world order of the future and its likely governance. With half of the world's population currently living in large urban agglomerations – which will probably increase to 70 percent by mid-century – the acute challenges of cities seem obvious. They are not the usual unit of analysis that jumps to most minds for global problem-solving, even by those who understand that actors besides governments and international organizations are essential players. Pejic and Acuto, however, ask readers to consider that cities are halfway houses that provide a specific location to meld competing local, national, and global agendas amid crosscutting scales of governance. Indeed, they argue that cities may be one of the most effective venues for addressing global governance challenges. The responses, successful and not, to COVID-19 reflect an overwhelmingly urban crisis (the location for 95 percent of cases). In analytical terms, a focus on urban areas also enriches understanding of networked governance across distinct policy domains, including interdependencies and the formal and informal modes of global urban governance.

CONTENTS

Global governance and the Anthropocene

Explaining the escalating global crisis

Peter Dauvergne

Global environmental governance has thickened and deepened over the past half century. There are more than a thousand international environmental agreements in place. Every country has an environmental department or agency, with thick layers of policies enforced from the national to municipal levels. Private environmental governance has proliferated, too. Just about every transnational corporation (TNC) has published sustainability guidelines, established a corporate social responsibility (CSR) unit, and enacted a code of conduct for global suppliers. Countless non-governmental organizations (NGOs) are also now monitoring the performance of corporations, certifying eco-labels and sustainability certificates, and partnering with governments to run nature reserves. Additionally, as has been the case for millennia, communities around the world are continuing to govern the local consumption of water, land, timber, and mineral resources.

This governance of the global environment has done a great deal of good. International agreements have largely eliminated the substances depleting the ozone layer, constrained international trade in hazardous

DOI: 10.4324/9781003139836-3

waste, and saved some species from the brink of extinction. National legislation has improved air quality, established parklands, and protected watersheds. Municipal policies have improved sanitation, garbage disposal, and rates of curbside recycling. CSR programming and new technologies have reduced waste across supply chains and improved the energy efficiency of manufacturing. Certification schemes, such as the Forest Stewardship Council (FSC) and the Marine Stewardship Council (MSC), have created more sustainable options for consumers. Communities have defended ecosystems from poachers, loggers, and miners, as in El Salvador, where an uprising for water rights pushed the national government to ban industrial metal mining. And hundreds of millions of people have replanted trees, cleaned up beaches, and restored native vegetation.

Despite these efforts, the earth is spinning into ever-greater crisis as pollution soars, biodiversity crashes, and climate change intensifies. Why is contemporary global governance failing to deescalate this crisis? What are the prospects of overcoming problems in the future? Could this crisis implode the world order over the course of the twenty-first century?

Answering these questions requires a deep understanding of the origins of today's global environmental crisis. This crisis goes back to at least the beginnings of the Anthropocene in the 1500s, as European imperialists brought deadly diseases and biological havoc to Africa, Latin America, and the Asia-Pacific. The planetary consequences of humans intensified in the 1800s in the wake of the Industrial Revolution and have been accelerating rapidly since the 1950s as economies expand, corporate power grows, and more people consume more of just about everything. Today, humanity is jackhammering the earth with unprecedented ferocity, further degrading and destabilizing ecosystems.

The architecture of contemporary global governance is failing to confront the magnitude, depth, and escalating nature of ecological destruction in the Anthropocene. Governance solutions tend to be weak, patchy, and incremental, treating environmental "problems" in isolation, rather than addressing them as intertwined, mutually reinforcing ecosystems in decline. These solutions, moreover, are underestimating the destructive power of business as usual and overestimating the capacity of technology and private governance to advance global sustainability. Put simply, global governance is doing more to protect the interests of the rich and powerful than safeguard the biological integrity of the earth. This does not mean, however, that the world order is moving inexorably toward a future of chaos as the ecological consequences of the Anthropocene intensify. Even in the face of worldwide crises like the COVID-19 pandemic, resistance to business as usual grew, from climate strikes to the Extinction Rebellion to uprisings by Indigenous Peoples. Increasing numbers of cities, communities, and local groups, moreover, are pushing for more environmentally oriented systems of governance, offering hope that a bottom-up, diffuse movement may be able to stave off ecological collapse.

The chapter begins by surveying the devastation of the Anthropocene, as this is necessary to demonstrate the failure of global governance to confront the origins, scale, and scope of contemporary environmental change. Next, it explains the structure of global environmental governance today, demonstrating how institutional solutions are underestimating the ecological costs of business as usual. Probing deeper, the analysis moves to two especially serious weaknesses of global environmental governance: an overestimation of the effectiveness of corporate self-governance and an overvaluing of new technology. The conclusion reflects on the prospects of bottom-up reforms and grassroots resistance to confront these failures and shift global governance onto a more sustainable trajectory over the coming decades.

The devastation of the Anthropocene

The International Commission on Stratigraphy has not officially declared the end of the Holocene epoch, a geological time period that began nearly 12,000 years ago with the last major ice age. Still, it is now common to describe our current time as the "Anthropocene," or the epoch of humans. An intense debate, however, rages about when this epoch began. The chemist Paul Crutzen and the biologist Eugene Stoermer, who helped popularize the idea of renaming our geological time period to the Anthropocene, were thinking of a start date in the late eighteenth century to reflect the planetary consequences of the Industrial Revolution. More recently, a working group advising the International Commission on Stratigraphy recommended a start date in the middle of the twentieth century to reflect the impact of the testing of nuclear weapons and the acceleration of production and consumption after the 1950s.[1] Yet, although these dates may well make sense in geological terms, they fail to reflect the scope, depth, and origins of the ecological crisis now destabilizing global governance. To see this, as the historian Alfred Crosby argues, we need to step back to see the shattering impact of European imperialism, especially after the 1500s.[2]

Explorers, colonizers, and settlers decimated the social, political, and biological foundations of Oceania, Asia, the Americas, and Africa from 1500 to 1900. Villages were razed, the young and old murdered, and those left alive frequently enslaved or bonded into other forms of enduring servitude. Smallpox, influenza, tuberculosis, and measles killed untold numbers, with 90 percent of some Indigenous communities dying within a generation. The population of the Americas alone fell by around 50 million from 1492 to 1650.[3] Droves of European settlers would then shred the ecology of the "New World" in the eighteenth and nineteenth centuries. Forests were cleared, streams diverted, and wetlands drained. Native animals were hunted into extinction. Pigs, cows, and rats proliferated, as did wheat, barley, and weeds.

The twentieth century saw a further globalization of social and biological harms. Colonization and wars decimated even more of the world's Indigenous Peoples. Meanwhile, over the course of the century, the world population rose from 1.6 to 6.1 billion. The second half of the century saw a "Great Acceleration" in the ecological consequences of the Anthropocene.[4] Mass advertising over this time reengineered cultures toward excessive and wasteful consumption. Industrial agriculture took off, washing away soils, draining water tables, and polluting lands with chemical fertilizers, fungicides, and herbicides. Radioactive fallout and heavy metals contaminated soils. Vast quantities of coal, oil, and natural gas were extracted, with the concentration of carbon dioxide in the atmosphere rising almost 25 percent, from 296 parts per million (PPM) in 1900 to 369 PPM in 2000. Roads were paved, skyscrapers built, and mega-dams constructed. Heavily logged rainforests were burned down to clear lands for cattle, soy, and oil palm. The seas were plundered, too, with once teeming species such as the Atlantic cod virtually wiped out.

The devastation of the Anthropocene has continued to escalate during the twenty-first century. The average surface temperature of the earth is now more than 1°C above pre-1880 levels. Without swift action, the earth could warm by another 2°C–5°C by the end of the twenty-first century, with some regions, such as the Arctic, potentially warming two to three times faster. Such an outcome would cause mass extinctions. Storms would become more frequent, intense, and volatile. Droughts, forest fires, and severe flooding would intensify. Food insecurity would rise. Diseases would travel in new, unpredictable ways. Greater numbers of glaciers would melt, and sea levels would rise many meters, swamping low-lying regions and forcing hundreds of millions of people to flee. If this were to occur, as climate scientist James Hansen has said, "it would be hard to imagine how the planet would be governable."[5]

Climate change, moreover, is but one of many environmental problems spinning the earth into crisis.[6] The global population continues to rise, exceeding 7.8 billion in 2021 and heading toward 10 billion by the middle of the twenty-first century. Consumption is rising even faster as firms extract more resources and churn out more products. The consequences are striking the planet like a tidal wave. The seas are emptying of life, while the quantity of plastics pouring into the oceans is set to double from 2010 to 2025.[7] Industrial agriculture is continuing to homogenize landscapes. Fresh water is growing scarcer by the day, and carcinogens are leaching into drinking water. Persistent organic pollutants and heavy metals are continuing to poison food chains. And biodiversity is continuing to decline as oceans acidify, coral reefs die, and forests vanish.[8] Tellingly, over the past few decades, the earth has been losing a football field of old-growth tropical forests every four to eight seconds.[9]

Why are human beings failing to rein in the escalating destruction of the Anthropocene? One reason is a weak architecture of global environmental governance that is underestimating the costs of business as usual amid the multilayered architecture of governmental and non-governmental institutions, policies, and norms shaping world affairs.[10] Another reason is simply inaction.

The weak architecture of environmental governance

Scholars of global environmental politics (GEP) have long called for the creation of a world environment organization with powers akin to an institution like the World Trade Organization (WTO). The core international environmental institution – the United Nations Environment Programme (UNEP), also known as UN Environment – is a relatively weak body primarily aiming at encouraging dialogue and research. Headquartered in Nairobi, it has a small budget and no real power over states or TNCs. Yet states have managed to negotiate more than 1,300 multilateral and 2,200 bilateral environmental agreements.[11] And some of these agreements, such as the 1997 Montreal Protocol on Substances that Deplete the Ozone Layer, have been highly effective. However, the vast majority of these agreements have only improved management slightly, if at all. States, moreover, have never managed to adopt a specific international agreement to regulate the environmental consequences of TNCs, while general principles for responsible and sustainable corporate conduct, such as the United Nations Global Compact, are nonbinding and voluntary. Indeed, the power of TNCs has been steadily rising in the twentieth-first century as corporations merge, exploit tax havens, capture political parties, and increasingly govern themselves through voluntary mechanisms.[12]

National and municipal regulations have done more to improve local environmental conditions, particularly in wealthier countries and neighborhoods. Governments have set aside parkland and protected lakes and rivers; they have built bike lanes and greenways as well as improved air quality, sanitation, and garbage collection. Yet state governance is clearly failing to resolve the biggest threats to the planet, including climate change, tropical deforestation, biodiversity loss, soil erosion, freshwater depletion, chemical contamination, and overfishing. Many factors underlie this failure. National and subnational policies tend to prioritize economic growth. They tend, as well, to produce incremental and partial gains at best, as with the growing reliance on market incentives, voluntary pledges, and offsetting to solve climate change. Environmental gains in the Global North, meanwhile, have far exceeded those in the Global South, where enforcement of laws tends to be weak and inconsistent. At the same time, domestic environmental policies commonly deflect, rather than solve, problems on a global scale, as when the United Kingdom ships recycled plastics abroad, or Norway exports oil to finance clean energy, or Japan relocates dirty factories overseas, or China imports timber to protect domestic forests.

The architecture of global governance is failing as well to mitigate the shadows of rising consumption. Long, intricate supply chains are casting ecological costs far from the end consumer, both physically and psychologically. These costs include the mining of coltan, cobalt, and rare earth elements to service the electronics industry. They include the corporate takeover of smallholder lands to grow fruits and vegetables for the global marketplace; the drilling of oil and natural gas to make plastics and manufacture consumer products; the clearing of forests for cardboard, packaging, and shipping pallets; and the burning of tropical forests to produce palm oil, which is an ingredient in half of packaged food and hygiene products in a typical high-end supermarket.

Eco-labels offer consumers a way to try to avoid casting harms onto vulnerable ecosystems and marginalized peoples. Yet even prominent certification schemes such as the FSC and the MSC are only reaching a small segment of the global market. Moreover, certification has a poor record when it comes to improving on-the-ground management. One example is the Roundtable on Sustainable Palm Oil (RSPO), which certifies around one-fifth of the world's palm oil as sustainably sourced and produced. Yet most of this certified palm oil comes from Indonesia and Malaysia, where transparency is low and illegality high. Certification has done little, moreover, to reduce unsustainable production of palm oil globally, as firms exploit loopholes, output shifts into illicit supply chains, and demand for non-certified products rises (e.g., for cooking oil in India).[13]

Today's environmental crisis would certainly be worse without the architecture of international organizations and agreements, national and subnational policies, and non-governmental schemes. Yet this architecture is fragmented, uneven, highly politicized, and riddled with vague rules, gaping loopholes, and unenforceable declarations.[14]

Quite evidently, it is not managing to stop this crisis from escalating, and in some ways, it is legitimizing and reinforcing business as usual. A prominent example is the fossil fuel industry, which continues to thrive even in the midst of the climate emergency and despite carbon taxes, decarbonization targets, and commitments such as the 2015 Paris Agreement on climate change. World oil production in 2018 was higher than ever before, the ninth straight year of record-setting output – and "there is no peak oil demand in sight," according to the International Energy Agency.[15] That year natural gas production set a new record, too, up more than 5 percent from 2017. Even coal production went up in 2018, edging back toward its record-setting levels of 2013.[16] The COVID-19 pandemic of 2020–21 did undercut demand for fossil fuels. But demand is set to resurge as economies rebound, and the trajectory before the pandemic should give us pause when business analysts suggest that fossil fuel production may have peaked.[17]

The global automobile industry is continuing to prosper, too, in the face of the escalating climate crisis. Sales of sport utility vehicles (SUVs), in particular, have been soaring, comprising 39 percent of the world auto market in 2018, up from 17 percent in 2000. Heavier, larger, and less fuel efficient, the increase in SUVs was the second biggest cause (after power generation) of rising carbon dioxide emissions from 2000 to 2018. Total carbon pollution in 2018 from SUVs alone exceeded the combined carbon emissions of the Netherlands and the United Kingdom. And total automobile sales are on track to keep rising for decades to come.[18]

Other climate-polluting industries are booming, too, from construction to agriculture, from aviation to heavy industry. With business as usual continuing to gain force, atmospheric carbon dioxide levels set a new record in 2020, exceeding, on average, 417 parts per million in the month of May (up 48 PPM from the start of the century, as measured at Mauna Loa, Hawaii). The concentration of carbon dioxide in the atmosphere is set to keep rising, with most countries still on track for higher emissions for decades to come: a trend set to "lock in severe impacts from climate change" by 2040, according to the International Energy Agency (IEA).[19]

Weak governance institutions and mechanisms, then, are partly to blame for the escalating destruction of the Anthropocene. Also to blame is the growing reliance on corporate self-governance and technology as primary pathways toward global sustainability.

Overestimating the value of corporate self-governance

Since 2005, there has been an upsurge in what TNCs call "aspirational" sustainability commitments, especially among firms with global brands. Typical pledges include "net carbon neutrality," "zero waste to landfill," "100% renewable energy," "100% sustainable sourcing," and "zero deforestation." At the same time, it has become increasingly common for the chief executive officers (CEOs) of these TNCs to claim to be leading a sustainability revolution, arguing that states are now lagging badly, stuck in domestic politics and lacking the necessary power to govern globally.

This latest version of corporate social responsibility still involves feel-good rhetoric and traditional public relations. But it is not greenwashing as usual.[20] Underneath, there are layers of specific undertakings. These include energy efficiency programs; smart packaging policies to reduce waste; internal recycling initiatives; eco-products and eco-labeling; codes of conduct for suppliers; and supply chain tracing and supplier audits. On the surface, this CSR programming would seem to be advancing sustainability; on some measures, it is producing gains. Mining and timber firms are financing community infrastructure. Manufacturers are requiring suppliers to meet stricter safety standards. Retailers are recycling more plastic, paper, and cardboard. Technology firms are increasing the energy efficiency of data centers.

To understand the full consequences, however, we need to ask: "Why have TNCs put this sustainability programming in place?" Partly, it is in response to government regulations, consumer demand for eco-products, and pressure from activists. Yet the main reason why TNCs are deploying sustainability programming is to compete for traditional business advantages. The monitoring and auditing of suppliers is increasing their control over long supply chains, decreasing the risk of product recalls, and protecting the value of brands. Efficiency gains and waste reductions across operations and supply chains are lowering production and transportation costs. Reporting and monitoring schemes are offering critical advantages in the competition for high-quality inputs, which is intensifying as ecosystems degrade. Sustainability savings across supply chains are helping them roll back prices and sell more products. Finally, sustainability programming is helping them increase profits, expand operations, and enhance investor confidence.[21] We see this with Walmart, for instance, which has been leading the charge over the past two decades to use sustainability programming to grow bigger and more powerful. Today, Walmart is by far the world's biggest company, with revenues in fiscal year 2021 of $559 billion – a rise of nearly $400 billion since 2000.[22]

Fundamentally, the goal of CSR programming is sustainability of business, not social justice or sustainability of the planet. It is extending corporate powers to define metrics, self-report findings, and self-govern operations. It is ignoring a growing problem of overconsumption, or "consumption that exceeds the capacity of the earth to regenerate natural systems and retain biological dynamism."[23] It is disregarding the intensifying shadows of consumption, where the costs of overconsumption are disproportionately cast onto marginalized communities, fragile ecosystems, and future generations. It is downplaying the need for social justice and fair earth shares. And it is reinforcing inequality and business wealth. Indicative, the gap between the wealthiest and poorest people is growing by the year, with the top 26 billionaires in 2018 owning as much as the bottom half of humanity.[24]

Relying on TNCs to govern the Anthropocene is like hiring arsonists to be our firefighters. At times, they may well skillfully extinguish a flame or two, but the urge to light new fires never goes away. With this in mind, let's now turn to examine the limits, risks, and dangers of relying on new technology to advance global sustainability. Understanding this is essential because just about every TNC and government is now emphasizing the necessity of technology – and technological breakthroughs – as a way to solve global environmental problems.

Overestimating the value of new technology

Technological advances, as with the CSR programming by TNCs, can bring many benefits for people and the planet. We can see this with the gains in global life expectancy as health care improves: from under 30 years in the mid-1800s to around 73 years today. We also can see this with the importance of electricity, the internet, and cell phones for advancing economic welfare. And we can see this with the value of biodiversity mapping, reforestation, and habitat monitoring for protecting and restoring ecosystems; the environmental benefits of smokestack scrubbers and catalytic converters; and the potential of solar and wind technology to transition economies toward clean energy.[25]

At the same time, technology has brought some of the greatest threats to life. Scientists have given us nuclear, chemical, and biological weapons. And military engineers are now working to further enhance the power of weaponry with artificial intelligence (AI). Commercial technologies have brought great harms, too. Thomas Midgley Jr.'s idea in 1921 to add tetraethyl lead to gasoline ended up poisoning generations of children during the twentieth century. Seven years later Midgley would then concoct a new compound to cool refrigerators – chlorofluorocarbons (CFCs), trademarked as Freon – that would go on to deplete the ozone layer necessary to protect life from ultraviolet radiation from the sun.

No doubt, improving governance of the Anthropocene is going to require new technologies. Yet, without state regulations and strict precautionary measures, relying on technology to fill in the gaps in global governance risks worsening the global environmental crisis. Over time, just about every technology has brought both costs and benefits. We see this proverbial double-edged sword, for instance, with the automobile; it speeds up mobility yet kills 1.3 million people a year. Most technologies, too, end up diffusing with contradictory consequences for sustainability, as with machine learning, which conservationists are using to map biodiversity, TNCs are deploying to ramp up sales, and militaries are integrating into increasingly deadly drones.[26]

The efficiency gains from new technologies, moreover, tend to rebound into even greater extraction and production, frequently intensifying, rather than alleviating, environmental degradation. The history of overfishing is an apt illustration, with driftnets, trawlers, refrigeration, and sonar enabling ever-greater catches even as species after species have been fished out. Other examples can be found in the histories of the mining industry (from blasting to dump trucks), the oil and gas industry (from offshore rigs to fracking), and the logging industry (from chainsaws to bulldozers).

Replacing outdated or harmful technologies tends to bring additional risks and dangers. This was the case when companies switched from using ozone-depleting CFCs to climate-warming hydrochlorofluorocarbons (HCFCs) to meet the timelines and targets of the 1987 Montreal Protocol on Substances that Deplete the Ozone Layer. This is the case, too, as the world invests in solar power and electric cars to try to reduce carbon emissions, a strategy that is stimulating demand for inputs such as lithium as well as adding to the mountains of electronic waste piling up around the world.

Rising sales of consumer technologies run the risk, as well, of further straining global resources and waste sinks. One example, among countless possibilities, is the sale of 1.5 billion smartphones a year, with consumers routinely upgrading as firms design hardware and software for rapid obsolescence, as new features are added, and as developers such as Apple advertise ever-newer models. Without question, these phones are benefiting people. Yet producing so many phones is spurring demand for cobalt and coltan in regions with long histories of human rights and environmental abuses, such as the Democratic Republic of the Congo (DRC). Using so many phones is increasing the energy consumption of data centers, including ones run on coal-fired electricity. And upgrading so many phones is one of the reasons volumes of electronic waste are on track to more than double from 2020 to 2050. There is, as former UNEP executive director Achim Steiner has put it, a "tsunami of e-waste rolling out over the world."[27]

The environmental and social costs of technology, moreover, tend to disperse in highly unequal ways. Those with money and power tend to benefit the most. Those living in the poorest communities tend to benefit the least. Costs also tend to accumulate in the most vulnerable ecosystems and snowball into the future. We see this with e-waste from rich countries piling up in the poorest neighborhoods of Africa. We see this as microplastics pour into the Pacific and Atlantic Oceans. And we see this as persistent organic pollutants "grasshopper" across the planet until settling in the Arctic, poisoning wildlife and the food chains of the Inuit.

There are many reasons why wealthy and powerful people tend to benefit disproportionately from technology. Rich neighborhoods have more political capacity to shift the costs of new technologies into marginalized neighborhoods, as the locations of chemical factories, incinerators, and landfills demonstrate across the United States.[28] Wealthy jurisdictions also have more capacity to export the costs overseas, as is occurring with hazardous waste, recycled plastics, and garbage. The world's most powerful companies, moreover, tend to extract the bulk of the profits from advanced technologies, as has been the case with the globalization of chemical fertilizers, herbicides, and genetically modified seeds. Meanwhile, the poorest countries and people tend to gain the least as new technologies diffuse through the global economy.

Around the world, states and businesses are now calling for a doubling down on technological innovation to deescalate the global environmental crisis. Some environmentalists are jumping aboard, too, such as the group calling themselves "eco-modernists," who are backing accelerated urbanization, industrial agriculture, nuclear power, and aquaculture.[29] Yet great care is necessary to avoid making the crisis worse with technology. There is a long history of inventors misjudging the long-term consequences of technologies. There is an equally long history of commercializing a new technology well before anyone knows if it is safe, from leaded gasoline to CFCs, from sugar-free gum to Teflon pans. Particularly when big profits are at stake, it is common, too, for TNCs to hype new technologies, downplay risks, and then, if evidence of harm does arise, attack critics, spread misinformation, and block reforms, as has been the case for tobacco, oil, and toxic chemicals.[30]

To reiterate, green technology can improve management. Clean energy can help reduce greenhouse gases. Drones can help rangers locate and arrest poachers. Smart tractors can apply pesticides and herbicides more efficiently than conventional tractors. However, technology is never going to fix the flawed architecture of global environmental governance. Technology is an instrument of power and tends to reinforce business as usual, unless strict controls are in place.

Nor is the world going to be able to rely on corporate self-governance to deescalate the global environmental crisis. States are going to be obliged to do far more to regulate TNCs to prevent ecological calamity and a collapse of the world order over the course of this century. Radical economic and political reforms are also going to be necessary to accelerate progress toward the UN's Sustainable Development Goals (SDGs). This is possible. It is even possible we are now seeing the beginnings of such reforms as Indigenous Peoples, communities, and grassroots movements join forces to govern the Anthropocene from below.

Conclusion: Looking toward 2050, resisting the crisis

The deepening ecological crisis of the Anthropocene poses one of the greatest threats to today's world order. Climate disruption alone has the potential to implode economies, cause severe food and water shortages, and displace hundreds of millions of people. Over the next three decades, this could fuel populism, nationalism, and war, as some look to profit from the chaos and others look to blame foreigners.

An escalating planetary crisis, however, may also open up new pathways toward a truly sustainable world order, where earth systems stabilize, societies thrive, and justice prevails. But to move in these directions necessitates a governance architecture that confronts the full scale and scope of destruction in the Anthropocene. Doing so requires confronting the dangers of private governance and technology. And it undoubtedly is going to require a worldwide uprising to demand sustainability and justice.

There are signs this uprising has begun. Students from Sweden to Australia are striking for real action to stop climate change. Citizens are uniting to fight for the environmental rights of future generations, from the movement for water rights in Latin America to the Extinction Rebellion in Western Europe. Farmers across the developing world are organizing to conserve crop diversity and prevent soil erosion. Cities in China and the United States are upgrading waste facilities to reduce greenhouse gas emissions. Women in Africa are uniting to stop poaching in nature reserves. Citizens are self-organizing in Europe to decrease carbon footprints. Indigenous Peoples are joining forces to demand land rights and social justice. Environmental lawyers in Bolivia, Ecuador, and New Zealand are fighting for the rights of nature, so a river or a tree or a mountain has a right to exist beyond its value for humans. Greenpeace activists are shaming global brands into no longer buying conflict gold, unsustainable palm oil, and blood diamonds. Meanwhile, local activists in the Philippines, Colombia, and Brazil are putting their lives on the line to blockade logging roads, open pit mines, and agribusinesses.[31]

The environmentalist Naomi Klein, in her 2019 book *On Fire*, sees a groundswell of resistance to global injustice and unsustainability.[32] Others also see powerful, subterranean forces rising up to contest the inequities and failures of global governance. Craig Kauffman, a political scientist at the University of Oregon, demonstrates how subnational politics in Ecuador has infused the global governance of watershed management with local ideas and norms: a process that he calls "grassroots global governance."[33] This uprising of mass protest and grassroots governance is clearly advancing sustainability. Twenty years ago, who would have thought that cities worldwide would be taking leadership in climate governance? Or who would have thought that El Salvador would ban the industrial mining of gold to protect the water rights of the poor?[34]

This is an exciting, even exhilarating, time for grassroots environmental activism. Nonetheless, it is far too early to celebrate. Confronting business as usual comes with grave risks. States and corporate allies are fighting back, especially against challenges to mining, logging, agribusinesses, and construction projects. Security services are tracking online communications, filming demonstrations, and deploying facial recognition technology to identify protestors.[35] Police are jailing activists, treating them as ecoterrorists and agents of foreign interests.[36] And paramilitaries and corporate hitmen are killing environmental and Indigenous activists, with at least 212 murdered in 2019 alone.[37]

In brief, dismantling and rebuilding the architecture of global environmental governance is not going to be easy. Yet even in the face of brutal crackdowns, resistance to business as usual is continuing to intensify, offering real hope that humanity may be able to move toward governing the Anthropocene sustainably and away from imploding the world order.

Suggested reading

Frank Biermann, *Earth System Governance: World Politics in the Anthropocene* (Cambridge, MA: Massachusetts Institute of Technology Press, 2014).

Dain Bolwell, *Governing Technology in the Quest for Sustainability on Earth* (New York: Routledge, 2019).

Peter Dauvergne, *AI in the Wild: Sustainability in the Age of Artificial Intelligence* (Cambridge, MA: Massachusetts Institute of Technology Press, 2020).

John S. Dryzek and Jonathan Pickering, *The Politics of the Anthropocene* (Oxford: Oxford University Press, 2019).

Peter Newell, *Global Green Politics* (Cambridge: Cambridge University Press, 2019).

Simon Nicholson and Sikina Jinnah, eds., *New Earth Politics: Essays from the Anthropocene* (Cambridge, MA: Massachusetts Institute of Technology Press, 2016).

Notes

1 Paul Crutzen and Eugene F. Stoermer, "Have We Entered the Anthropocene?" *International Geosphere-Biosphere Programme Newsletter* (31 October 2000): 17; Working Group on the "Anthropocene," *Subcommission on Quaternary Stratigraphy*, 21 May 2019, http://quaternary.stratigraphy.org/working-groups/anthropocene.

2 Alfred W. Crosby, *Ecological Imperialism: The Biological Expansion of Europe, 900–1900*, new ed. (Cambridge: Cambridge University Press, 2004).

3 Simon L. Lewis and Mark A. Maslin, "Defining the Anthropocene," *Nature* 519 (12 March 2015): 176.

4 Will Steffen, Paul J. Crutzen, and John R. McNeill, "The Anthropocene: Are Humans Now Overwhelming the Great Forces of Nature?" *AMBIO: A Journal of the Human Environment* 36, no. 8 (2007): 614–622.

5 James Hansen, "James Hansen on Ice Sheets," Video Recording, *YouTube*, December 2015, www.youtube.com/watch?v=Ykn8_ayFqNI.

6 Simon Nicholson and Sikina Jinnah, "Introduction: Living on a New Earth," in *New Earth Politics: Essays from the Anthropocene*, ed. Simon Nicholson and Sikina Jinnah (Cambridge, MA: Massachusetts Institute of Technology Press, 2016), 1–16.

7 Jenna R. Jambeck et al., "Plastic Waste Inputs from Land into the Ocean," *Science* 347 (6223) (2015): 768–771.

8 Gerardo Ceballos, Paul R. Ehrlich, and Rodolfo Dirzo, "Biological Annihilation Via the Ongoing Sixth Mass Extinction Signaled by Vertebrate Population Losses and Declines," *Proceedings of the National Academy of Sciences* 114, no. 30 (2017): E6089–E6096.

9 Mikaela Weisse and Elizabeth Dow Goldman, "The World Lost a Belgium-sized Area of Primary Rainforests Last Year," *World Resources Institute Blog*, 25 April 2019, www.wri. org/blog/2019/04/world-lost-belgium-sized-area-primary-rainforests-last-year.

10 Thomas G. Weiss and Rorden Wilkinson, *Rethinking Global Governance* (Cambridge: Polity Press, 2019).

11 Ronald Mitchell, "International Environmental Agreements Database Project," https://iea. uoregon.edu.

12 Susan George, *Shadow Sovereigns: How Global Corporations Are Seizing Power* (Cambridge: Polity Press, 2015); John Mikler, *The Political Power of Global Corporations* (Cambridge: Polity Press, 2018); Jennifer Clapp, "Mega-Mergers on the Menu: Corporate Concentration and the Politics of Sustainability in the Global Food System," *Global Environmental Politics* 18, no. 2 (2018): 12–33.

13 Peter Dauvergne, "The Global Politics of the Business of 'Sustainable' Palm Oil," *Global Environmental Politics* 18, no. 2 (2018): 34–52.

14 Simon Nicholson and Sikina Jinnah, eds., *New Earth Politics: Essays from the Anthropocene* (Cambridge, MA: Massachusetts Institute of Technology Press, 2016); Ian Angus, *Facing the Anthropocene: Fossil Fuel Capitalism and the Crisis of the Earth System* (New York: New York University Press, 2016). For a balanced assessment of the consequences of the "fragmentation" of environmental governance, see Frank Biermann, Philipp Pattberg, Harro Van Asselt, and Fariborz Zelli, "The Fragmentation of Global Governance Architectures: A Framework for Analysis," *Global Environmental Politics* 9, no. 4 (2009): 14–40.

15 International Energy Agency (IEA), *Oil 2018: Analysis and Forecasts to 2023: Executive Summary* (Paris: Organisation for Economic Co-operation and Development and IEA, 2018), 3; for data on oil production, see International Energy Agency, *Oil 2019: Analysis and Forecasts to 2024: Executive Summary* (Paris: Organisation for Economic Co-operation and Development and IEA, 2019), particularly page 2.

16 BP, *BP Statistical Review of World Energy* (London: BP, 2019), 16, 32, 44.

17 BP, *Energy Outlook: 2020 Edition* (London: BP, 2020).

18 Laura Cozzi and Apostolos Petropoulos, "Commentary: Growing Preference for SUVs Challenges Emissions Reductions in Passenger Car Market," *IEA Newsroom*, 15 October 2019, www.iea.org/newsroom/news/2019/october/growing-preference-for-suvs-challenges-emissions-reductions-in-passenger-car-mark.html; see also International Energy Agency, *World Energy Outlook 2019* (Paris: IEA, 2019).

19 International Energy Agency, "World Energy Outlook 2019 Highlights Deep Disparities in the Global Energy System," *IEA Newsroom*, 13 November 2019, www.iea.org/newsroom/news/2019/november/world-energy-outlook-2019-highlights-deep-disparities-in-the-global-energy-system.html. For an analysis of the greenhouse gas trajectory of the countries within the G20, see *Climate Transparency, Brown to Green: The G20 Transition Towards a Net-Zero Emissions Economy* (Berlin: Climate Transparency, 2019).

20 Michael John Bloomfield, *Dirty Gold: How Activism Transformed the Jewelry Industry* (Cambridge, MA: Massachusetts Institute of Technology Press, 2017); Hamish van der Ven, *Beyond Greenwash: Explaining Credibility in Transnational Eco-Labeling* (Oxford:

Oxford University Press, 2019); and Stefan Renckens, *Private Governance and Public Authority: Regulating Sustainability in a Global Economy* (Cambridge: Cambridge University Press, 2020).

21 Peter Dauvergne and Jane Lister, *Eco-Business: A Big-Brand Takeover of Sustainability* (Cambridge, MA: Massachusetts Institute of Technology Press, 2013).

22 "Fortune Global 500," https://fortune.com/global500.

23 Peter Dauvergne, *Will Big Business Destroy Our Planet?* (Cambridge: Polity Press, 2018), 12.

24 Oxfam, *Public Good or Private Wealth?* (London: Oxfam, 2019), 12.

25 Alec Broers, *The Triumph of Technology: The BBC Reith Lectures 2005* (Cambridge: Cambridge University Press, 2005); Simon Nicholson and Jesse L. Reynolds, "Taking Technology Seriously: Introduction to the Special Issue on New Technologies and Global Environmental Politics," *Global Environmental Politics* 20, no. 3 (2020): 1–8.

26 Peter Dauvergne, *AI in the Wild: Sustainability in the Age of Artificial Intelligence* (Cambridge, MA: Massachusetts Institute of Technology Press, 2020); Peter Dauvergne, "Is Artificial Intelligence Greening Supply Chains? Exposing the Political Economy of Environmental Costs," *Review of International Political Economy* (2020), https://doi.org /10.1080/09692290.2020.1814381.

27 UNEP, "UN Environment Chief Warns of 'Tsunami' of E-waste at Conference on Chemical Treaties," *Sustainable Development Blog*, 5 May 2015, www.un.org/sustainabledevelopment/ blog/2015/05/un-environment-chief-warns-of-tsunami-of-e-waste-at-conference-on-chemical-treaties.

28 Robert D. Bullard, *Dumping in Dixie: Race, Class, and Environmental Quality*, 3rd ed. (New York: Routledge, 2000); David Naguib Pellow, *Garbage Wars: The Struggle for Environmental Justice in Chicago* (Cambridge, MA: Massachusetts Institute of Technology Press, 2004); Ifesinachi Okafor-Yarwood and Ibukun Jacob Adewumi, "Toxic Waste Dumping in the Global South as a Form of Environmental Racism: Evidence from the Gulf of Guinea," *African Studies* 79, no. 3 (2020): 285–304.

29 John Asafu-Adjaye et al., *The Ecomodernist Manifesto* (Oakland, CA: The Breakthrough Institute, 2015); Jonathan Symons, *Ecomodernism: Technology, Politics and the Climate Crisis* (Cambridge: Polity Press, 2019).

30 Naomi Oreskes and Erik M. Conway, *Merchants of Doubt: How a Handful of Scientists Obscured the Truth on Issues from Tobacco Smoke to Global Warming* (London: Bloomsbury, 2011).

31 For a small (and diverse) sampling of the literature demonstrating the growing influence of local environmental actions, see: Rob Atkinson, Thomas Dörfler, and Eberhard Rothfuß, "Self-Organisation and the Co-Production of Governance: The Challenge of Local Responses to Climate Change," *Politics and Governance* 6, no. 1 (2018): 169–179; Craig M. Kauffman and Pamela L. Martin, "Constructing Rights of Nature Norms in the US, Ecuador, and New Zealand," *Global Environmental Politics* 18, no. 4 (2018): 43–62; Mark Cooper, "Governing the Global Climate Commons: The Political Economy of State and Local Action, After the US Flip-Flop on the Paris Agreement," *Energy Policy* 118 (2018): 440–454; Paula Franco Moreira, Jonathan Kishen Gamu, Cristina Yumie Aoki Inoue, Simone Athayde, Sônia Regina da Cal Seixas, and Eduardo Viola, "South–South Transnational Advocacy: Mobilizing Against Brazilian Dams in the Peruvian Amazon," *Global Environmental Politics* 19, no. 1 (2019): 77–98; Todd A. Eisenstadt and Karleen Jones West, *Who Speaks for Nature? Indigenous Movements, Public Opinion, and the Petro-state in Ecuador* (Oxford: Oxford University Press, 2019).

32 Naomi Klein, *On Fire: The (Burning) Case for a Green New Deal* (New York: Simon & Schuster, 2019).

33 Craig M. Kauffman, *Grassroots Global Governance: Local Watershed Management Experiments and the Evolution of Sustainable Development* (Oxford: Oxford University Press, 2016).
34 For an analysis of cities in climate governance, see David J. Gordon, *Cities on the World Stage: The Politics of Global Urban Climate Politics* (Cambridge: Cambridge University Press, 2020). For an analysis of the campaign to ban metal mining in El Salvador, see Rose J. Spalding, "From the Streets to the Chamber: Social Movements and the Mining Ban in El Salvador," *European Review of Latin American and Caribbean Studies* 106 (July–December 2018): 47–74.
35 Peter Dauvergne, "The Globalization of Artificial Intelligence: Consequences for the Politics of Environmentalism," *Globalizations* 18, no. 2 (2021): 285–299.
36 Miriam Matejova, Stefan Parker, and Peter Dauvergne, "The Politics of Repressing Environmentalists as Agents of Foreign Influence," *Australian Journal of International Affairs* 72, no. 2 (2018): 145–162.
37 Global Witness, *Defending Tomorrow: The Climate Crisis and Threats Against Land and Environmental Defenders* (London: Global Witness, 2020), 10.

CONTENTS

War

The governance of violence and the violence of governance

Laura J. Shepherd

Both conceptually and in practice, war is messy. It is hard to define, it is difficult to differentiate – for example, from proximate concepts such as "armed conflict," – and it is difficult to contain within boundaries that are assumed to hold it steady, such as boundaries of time, space, and mortality. The temporality and spatiality of war, moreover, has changed markedly as we occupy an increasingly mediated and entangled world; so too has the deadliness of war-fighting techniques increased over time (glossed as "efficiency" and "precision"), and we are only just now beginning to comprehend and count war-related deaths of non-human animals and environmental elements such as waterways and forests.[1] The scale of such losses must be grappled, in tandem, with the more conventional measures of mortality such as "body count."

This is the backdrop against which I explore the futures of war governance. The governance of war is the focus of multiple interventions by different international organizations, and it manifests in multiple mechanisms and at multiple levels. A long historical perspective renders visible the "laws of armed conflict," standards of international humanitarian law that govern conduct during war, as part of these mechanisms. A more contemporary view, by contrast, makes apparent not only the various ways conceptions of war have changed over time but also expectations

DOI: 10.4324/9781003139836-4

about its governance and the relationship of war governance to conflict prevention, conflict resolution, and post-conflict governance. Moreover, the governance of war does not only "live" or occur in the overt expression or application of power and authority – in what we might think of as the "implementation" of governance mechanisms – but its reproduction and the conditions of its legitimacy can also be traced through the discourses and practices that articulate and (at least temporarily) stabilize its various meanings. This chapter engages briefly with histories of war's conceptualization and governance as a prelude to an examination of how war is and might be governed in contemporary global politics. The first part elaborates the institutional context of war's governance and the frameworks and laws that support governance interventions. The second part of the chapter offers some critical insights into war's governance and dimensions of war and governance, together and separately, that have historically been understudied or overlooked entirely, including the operation of gendered power and the effects of ongoing colonial violence. The third part explores present innovations in the study and practice of war to foreshadow futures of war governance. A brief conclusion offers reflections about the possibilities and limitations of governing violence and the violence of governance itself.

Institutions of war's governance

Cicero (106–43 BCE) purportedly said, "inter arma leges silent": during war, laws fall silent.[2] However, the "silence" of law – the presumed inapplicability of "peacetime" legal strictures and institutions – does not mean that war is without mechanisms of governance, as law and governance are distinct. Where law creates binding obligation, governance is blurrier and more diffuse, relating to the (formal and informal, tacit and explicit) organization and regulation of human life.[3] Both are applicable to war, and throughout history numerous institutions and architectures have developed to manage war and mitigate its effects. From the earliest surviving records of Middle Eastern and Mediterranean societies, it is clear that governance institutions (in the broadest sense, including diplomacy and the formation of treaties) enabled peaceful interactions and exchange in ancient times, with covenants guaranteed by spiritual belief and ritual practice.[4] Around 1400 BCE, for example, there were agreements in place between Egypt and Sumeria governing the treatment of prisoners of war, and there are copious texts from Asia dating back to 200 BCE and earlier that describe the rules of armed conflict.[5] In the period of classical antiquity, there is evidence that Chinese, Greek, and Roman political systems contained numerous norms relating to the necessity for war to have a just cause, for clear rituals to be undergone in the commencement and conclusion of war, and for the right of neutrality and certain constraints to be honoured in the conduct of war.[6]

Moving forward through time, the Congress of Vienna in 1814 and the Hague Conferences in 1899 and 1907 attempted to put in place machinery to resolve disputes peacefully and maintain peace.[7] The expression – in word and in deed – of respect for norms, and more formal frameworks of war's governance, conditioned the development of various institutions in contemporary world politics that seek to prevent war and secure peace. In this light, war's governance consists of "activities backed by shared goals,"[8] where the goal is to minimize, or – if necessary – regulate, harm.

In the first instance, harm is minimized through the normative and legal prohibition against waging war in the contemporary international system, enshrined within the Charter of the United Nations, which is a powerful instrument of global governance. Chapter I of the UN Charter requires that member states seek to resolve conflict by peaceful means in the first instance, with or without the support and direction of the UN Security Council, which Chapter V specifies is the entity charged with "primary responsibility for the maintenance of international peace and security." Thus, in accordance with Article 39 of Chapter VII, war may only be waged lawfully under the auspices of the Council:

> The Security Council shall determine the existence of any threat to the peace, breach of the peace, or act of aggression and shall make recommendations, or decide what measures shall be taken in accordance . . . to maintain or restore international peace and security.

This governance structure is intended to ensure that UN member states explore a peaceful resolution to conflicts that emerge and resort to war only when all other measures are exhausted. Obviously, this codification of *jus ad bello* pertains only to the governance of interstate war; civil wars, "asymmetric wars," and other forms of "new wars" challenge the state-centric conventional logics of war governance and draw attention to different possibilities for, and vectors of, harm.[9]

International humanitarian law (IHL), or *jus in bello*, seeks to minimize harms experienced during war; it is "that branch of public international law that seeks to moderate the conduct of armed conflict and to mitigate the suffering that it causes."[10] As another institution of war's governance, IHL attempts to regulate war, in accordance with four core principles: "distinction, military necessity, unnecessary suffering, and proportionality."[11] Briefly, the principles demand that acts of violence in the context of war distinguish between combatants and civilians, are necessary for the achievement of military objectives, avoid the imposition of unnecessary hardship or harm, and are proportionate either to the perceived infraction (if the act is retaliatory) or to the desired objective. Since the middle of the fifteenth century, when the laws of armed conflict began to be codified, there have been flagrant violations of IHL and intense debate across multiple cases of whether one or more of its foundational principles have been violated by a specific military action. That war proves ungovernable at times does not, however, detract from the coherence of its system of governance: just because there are law-breakers does not nullify the existence of the general rule of law. A greater challenge to IHL, in contemporary world politics, is its derivation from an era of interstate armed conflict; as is the case with *jus ad bellum*, IHL is historically founded on the assumption that, in accordance with Charles Tilly's enduring aphorism, "war made the state, and the state made war."[12]

This assumption – that states are the actors that wage war – has implications for IHL in situations of intrastate conflict. Simply put, aspects of IHL may be deemed inapplicable where parties to the conflict are not state actors.

Moreover, there are other assumptions embedded in the IHL framework that inform war's governance in potentially problematic ways. While there are many dimensions of war's governance that might raise concern, I address two here: the extent to which the (always-already gendered) combatant/civilian dichotomy structures IHL and its effects and the extent to which IHL is a continuation of an international legal architecture that is founded on the denial of legitimacy to other governance and regulatory structures – a legacy that is being challenged and critiqued by contemporary postcolonial and decolonial legal scholars. The partiality of IHL and its constitutive effects are well explicated by Helen M. Kinsella in her analysis of the primary principle of distinction. She argues that "in international humanitarian law, the distinction of combatant and civilian determines the difference between impermissible and permissible, legitimate and illegitimate, lawful and unlawful acts of war."[13] Much rests, therefore, on this dichotomy, and through genealogical inquiry Kinsella shows how the distinction is structured and secured through "discourses of gender, innocence, and civilization,"[14] with particular effects. The stabilization of the distinction between combatant and civilian relies on these discourses, such that the categories themselves are gendered and value laden. The associative chains that establish enduring connections between femininity, innocence, and the subject of the civilian act as permissive conditions for acts of violence in the name of protection and in defense of civilization. Through war's governance, therefore, aspects of war's legitimacy are reproduced in ways that perpetuate existing structures of power and mitigate against transformative change.

Postcolonial scholarship on international law makes a series of similar and related interventions, demonstrating that the European heritage of international law shapes the contemporary governance framework in ways that reproduce colonial logics of domination and oppression. International law relies on Westphalian notions of sovereignty and denies legitimacy to the various forms of sovereignty and autonomy that predate colonial encounter and in many cases existed prior to the signature of the two treaties in 1648.[15] The expansion and universalization of international law must be read as part of the ordering of international "society" along racial and geospatial lines; this is not to deny the benefits derived from efforts to govern war but to recognize that law is itself political and frequently partial. As Anthony Anghie elaborates:

> The brutal realities of conquest and dispossession can hardly be ameliorated by asserting that the legal framework legitimizing this dispossession was contradictory and incoherent. But it is perhaps by pointing to these inconsistencies and ambiguities, by interrogating how it was that sovereignty became the exclusive preserve of Europe, and by questioning this framework, even while describing how it came into being, that it might be possible to open the way not only towards a different history of the discipline, but to a different understanding of the workings and effects of colonialism itself.[16]

These interrogations of the productive power of international law draw attention, therefore, to the ways governance more broadly should be understood as implicated in the production of legitimacy, authority, and order in world politics.

The critical engagement with both *jus ad bellum* and *jus in bello* presented draws attention to the ways the governance of war functions to reproduce specific configurations of power in contemporary world politics. These arrangements can create and perpetuate inequalities and exclusions even as they purport to minimize or mitigate harm. Moreover, analyzing war's governance in this way reveals war itself as a technology of governance: war is rendered visible not only as a political process, the governance of which has particular effects, but also as a means of governing communities, populations, even states. The governance effects of war fall differently, and are felt differently, by differently positioned bodies within the war (and peace) system. War's governance mechanisms reward some ways of being in the world and relating to our many others, while disincentivizing other ways of being and relating; war itself has this governance function also. The following section explores some dimensions of war and governance that draw attention to these productive effects.

Dimensions of war and governance

War's governance is complex. Recently, scholars of international organizations, global governance, and regimes have begun to examine different forms of complex governance systems in order to understand what insights can be gleaned from centering and working with complexity in relation to governance.[17] Starting from a position of complexity engenders "three assumptions: that there is no necessary proportionality between 'causes' and 'effects;' that the individual and statistical levels of analysis are not equivalent; and that system effects do not result from the simple addition of individual components."[18] Taken together, these assumptions intersect to constitute an object of analysis that is not reducible to a single, simple set of interactions. Complex systems are dynamic, decentralized, and unpredictable; most crucially, they are always in process. In the context of war's governance, process theory invites an exploration of what kinds of things are produced through the process of its development and application. The focus of this section, therefore, is on two dimensions of war's governance that are frequently understudied or overlooked: the governance of bodies in war, as a manifestation of gendered power, and the "domestic" governance of ongoing colonial violence and its effects.

Bodies are produced through the governance of war. Specifically, fighting bodies are gendered, and gendered bodies are given (or denied) permission to fight, through governance mechanisms relevant to war. Efforts to govern war and war-fighting not only are products of gender norms and expectations but also function to reproduce those norms and expectations. The governance of who can and cannot take up various roles and responsibilities in a military organization – and the training of their bodies and minds once they are accepted into the organization – perpetuates ideas and ideals about war-fighting, strength, and citizenship. A vibrant and important body of research traces the operation of gendered power within the military, as it constructs both cultures and bodies. The explicit and tacit regulation of bodies and behavior within the military as an organization creates and perpetuates particular military cultures, most of which valorize and reward expressions of heteronormative hypermasculinity while also denigrating expressions of femininity.[19] These gender expressions and associative chains need not be affixed to "female" or "male" bodies. During the 1990–1991 Gulf War, for example, "defeat for the Iraqis was portrayed as humiliating anal penetration by the more powerful and manly United States" in crude satirical cartoons showing the penetration of prostrate male bodies by missiles.[20] More recently, "the public discrediting, mocking, and broader feminizing of drone pilots who have claimed that they are engaged in combat" demonstrates how the operation of military machines is interpolated into gendered imaginaries of war.[21]

Beyond the gendered associations that relate bodies to behavior, and the specific ways this plays out in military cultures (including cultures of national militaries, private military and security companies, and paramilitary groups), there are other ways the governance of war maintains structures of gendered power. Combat exclusion is an example of this process, along with the inclusion or exclusion of gendered bodies in training programs designed for "men" (people assigned male at birth) and "women" (people assigned female at birth). In a detailed analysis of the "band of brothers" mythology that permeates and influences US military culture, Megan MacKenzie shows how the ideational dimension governing the behavior of bodies is tied to the regulation of who fights, and who is trained to fight, and how. MacKenzie debunks the myth that bodies assigned female at birth are incapable of performing in accordance with a (presumed objective) set of military standards in training, demonstrating that "physical standards have changed over time, have been developed in relation to men's bodies, and do not reflect one's ability to complete military tasks."[22] Recognizing this complicates combat exclusion, which is at least in part premised on the existence of enduring and biological "sex" differences. Further, the enlistment and experiences of trans women and trans men into military service challenges simplistic readings of "sex" and war(fighting), as trans bodies are also simultaneously governed and constituted within military cultures. Such is the strength of the gender governance regimes that structure war that, despite serving at proportionately higher rates than cisgender individuals, most trans service personnel "remain closeted to their military unit and, among those who are out about their trans status, most indicate experiences with discrimination and harassment while serving."[23] Governing gender in war(fighting) is frequently assumed to be synonymous with categorizing by "sex" (and permitting bodies assigned "M" or "F" to undertake certain roles and responsibilities while precluding others), but this creates and perpetuates exclusions and violence in its own right.[24]

War enacts violence, even when there is no theater of combat operations, battalion or battlefield to bear arms, or witness to brutality. War as metaphor brings such violence to bear on issues that would otherwise be the focus of welfare, health policy, or security strategy: the war on poverty, the war on drugs, and the war on terror. The direct and indirect political consequences of declaring war are well documented. Less frequently explored, however, are the ongoing violence of silenced and forgotten wars: of disenfranchisement, displacement, and colonial domination. These are equally subjects – and products – of governance. Decisions made in the governance of colonial wars, and colonized subjects, continue to structure experience and encounters in a "postcolonial" world. There are many possible avenues of inquiry to pursue. In the remainder of this section, I point toward two: first, the continuum of violence against Indigenous and colonized peoples that connects war to governance explicitly; second, the willful disciplinary ignorance of the ways colonized subjects were put to work in war-fighting and the erasure of these conscriptions as a way of maintaining the Whiteness of the idealized imperial (always-already male) soldier subject.

The disciplinary ignorance of colonial wars is (re)produced in how we conceive of and study war. Colonial wars, for example, have been described as "small wars,"[25] but this nomenclature has a politics: "[W]ars of empire were 'small' because so few Europeans were involved, not because of their consequences for the countries they were fought in."[26] In fact, the violence of colonial encounters continues to resonate through settler colonial societies and across the world. Just as "war made the state," war also makes its subjects, and the governance of Indigenous populations in and through war is part of how Western political imaginaries continue to dominate. Vivienne Jabri conceptualizes a "matrix of war,"[27] composed of direct acts of violence, the power to discipline individuals and communities (supported by state violence), and the exercise of bio-power to manage the lives and well-being of populations. This perspective opens up the study of war and demands its recognition as a complex and multifaceted apparatus that produces governed/governable subjects. The construction of governed/governable subjects as an imperial project includes war as a moment on a broader continuum that connects racist imaginaries of White supremacy and the benevolence of civilizing missions to the designation of Aboriginal Australians as part of the "flora and fauna" of a *terra nullius*, for example. Thus, power operates through governance and war to create the conditions of humanity. The prosecution of war has always been, in some sense, about the delineation between lives for whom war is fought – those whose lives are "grievable"[28] – and lives that are expendable. This delineation operates in ways both mundane and remarkable: what counts as a "casualty of war," for example, is part of the bureaucracy of war and is instructive, vis-à-vis the question of war's "proper" victims. And this is not a matter of history:

> While Foucault identified genocidal state racism and colonial wars as exemplars of racialised war, late modern manifestations of war used as a technology of control, a technological of government, are more indicative of the permeation of war into the everyday experience of the populations rendered its targets. Calculating hierarchies of worth is in turn based on the assumption that certain bodies are disposable.[29]

The governance of war, and the effects of war as governance and governance as war, thus shapes what it means to be fully human in contemporary world politics, which, in turn, permits (and begets) violence. As a technology of governance, war constitutes raced and gendered human subjects, disciplining and regulating human life and experience far beyond the theater of combat operations.

A second avenue of inquiry relates to another dimension of the refusal of political personhood: the erasure of Indigenous and colonized soldiers in stories and memorials of war-fighting.[30] As outlined prior, the masculinity of the soldier-subject is reproduced through war's governance in ways that imbricate war in the operation of gendered power. Racialized power – and the valorization of Whiteness – operates in a similar way in practices and mythologies of war. Such performances of "Aboriginal erasure and heritage dissonance"[31] maintain the myth of the White (settler) soldier as the universal soldier subject, which denies the war experiences (and war trauma) of soldiers who are Black, Indigenous, or people of color. As Michèle Barrett notes,

> Perhaps unsurprisingly, subaltern colonial troops were not commemorated equally, but the history of these decisions has not been fully acknowledged. In this way, a further silencing of the subaltern takes place: not only are these lives not commemorated, the acts of exclusion are themselves erased.[32]

Moreover, through the perpetuation of myth of the White (settler) soldier, Indigenous and colonized fighters were – and continue to be – denied the citizenship benefits that accrue to those associated with the state-making, state-protecting, state-servicing war machine.

The governance of war is not limited to the codified laws of war that notionally afford protections to those engaged in combat. War is also governed by the ways we imagine and mythologize its violence and manifest in the forms of subjectivity that it produces. This section has outlined two dimensions of war's governance and elaborated on some of the ways war is generative. Working at the interstices of war and governance reveals not only the productive power of state-led war-fighting but also the banalities of war's bureaucracy and the governance rationalities embedded (and reproduced through) in its memorial sites and practices. The following section expands on this analysis to consider some of the ways we might engage in war's governance in the future.

Future governance of war

To govern war, it must be apprehended as an object and technology of governance, varying throughout history and by context. This approach envisions war as an object of *governmentality*: the rationalities and technologies of governance that are enacted in specific contexts and have varying effects from battlefield to boardroom and bedroom. Simply put, the governance of war not only "lives" or occurs in the overt expression or application of power and authority – in what we might think of as the "implementation" of governance mechanisms. Its reproduction and the conditions of its legitimacy can also be traced through the discourses and practices that articulate and (at least temporarily) stabilize its various meanings. In many ways, the futures of war's governance will resemble its histories, as many of these meanings remain stubbornly stable: Kinsella's analysis of the subject of the civilian in the laws of armed conflict referenced prior demonstrates the durability of these constructions.[33]

But there will also be shifts; new technologies of war create new sites of violence, for example, and similarly, modern war is dispersed across different temporalities. These new landscapes and horizons of war will require different vocabularies and modes of inquiry. Of particular interest are the ways the governance of war, seen from this perspective as a set of discursive practices that have material effects in the world, produces subjects, objects, and the relationships between them. Alex Edney-Browne's research on the affective dimensions of drone warfare, the mental health effects of "leakage" across body/machine boundaries, and the denial of spatial/temporal anchoring (as drones reach across space to operate simultaneously in multiple time zones and with lasting effects) requires that we think about the governance of war, and war as a technology of governance, in innovative ways. Edney-Browne argues that "constant transitioning between proximity and separation is likely to be a highly emotional experience for drone personnel, as they struggle to situate the 'boundaries' of their bodies in relation to, and culpability within, a technological apparatus of killing."[34] This insight is then developed as a rationale for taking seriously post-human and phenomenological approaches to the study of war, which I would extend to the study of war's governance. As outlined, the governance of war is implicated in the operation of gendered and racialized power. From Edney-Browne's research, we can derive inspiration for the evaluation of the affective and embodied effects of war technologies and the ways the technologies themselves, and their uses, are governed.

Much of war's governance depends on how war is imagined and what possibilities can exist for its ending. The way that governance concepts and mechanisms create "looping effects" has been well explored in, for example, the context of discourse on "fragile states."[35] "Looping effects" describe the phenomenon of governance discourse being reproduced by its subjects, in what might be considered an example of "successful" interpellation into a particular subject-position (in this case, the subject-position of a "fragile state").[36] The words we use and think with construct the parameters of our imaginings. It is imperative to ensure that the concepts of war governance enable its undoing: that, as a discipline, attentive to structures and ordering effects of power, we continue to focus not solely on war and its governance but also on the governance of peace and the peaceful possibilities the exist in the governance of war. The global governance of peace and war prevention has cohered over the last decades in the form of the so-called liberal peace paradigm, "based on a consensus that democracy, the rule of law and market economies would create sustainable peace in post-conflict and transitional state and societies, and in the larger international order that they were a part of."[37] The legitimacy, or otherwise, of the liberal peace has been fiercely contested in scholarly literature, with the emergence of a robust research agenda that interrogates the ways peace interventions "tend to reify state sovereignty, fail to address adequately issues related to justice, reconciliation, welfare, and gendered power, and validate 'top-down institutional neoliberal and neocolonial' practices."[38] Critical literature on peace interventions, post-conflict peacebuilding, and development has examined the ways the techniques and rationalities associated with peace and war governance – those that inform and structure behaviors, practices, and the formulation of "solutions" to the "problems" identified in what Séverine Autersserre calls "peaceland," the space of post-conflict peace interventions by international institutions[39] – are produced by, and produce, specific configurations of power and thus are constitutive of specific forms of subjectivity. We need not be bound by the imaginaries of liberal peace, however; war's governance is open to radical peace also, through the determined pursuit of new alternatives to the absence of peace. As teachers, scholars, activists, and practitioners, "[w]e must have the will to dream alternatives based on issues of social justice and refuse to be limited by the proposals on offer."[40]

Conclusion

This chapter has elaborated the politics of war's governance and explored some of the governmentality effects of efforts to discipline and manage war. War itself is "strangely decentred and fragmented as an object of inquiry, in ways intensified by the institutional diversity of the sites at which war is studied."[41] Understanding war, and its effects, is a multidisciplinary endeavor; I have focused here on war's governance, the effects of its governance, and its governance effects. Part of the normative impetus in writing this chapter is to draw attention to these effects and to articulate the argument that the governance effects of war are inextricably interwoven in the fabric of what is referred to as the present "world order." Systems of war governance are implicated in systems of domination and oppression, and part of responsible scholarship is acknowledging that the effects of war and its governance are visible in our objects of analysis, even those that seem removed.

This responsibility is not restricted to historians, or sociologists, or anthropologists who account for the social ordering of "others." Political scientists and political theorists who "are enamored of liberal principles" must be held to account, so as not to "soft-pedal or efface the violence at the birth of political societies that are now proudly liberal democratic."[42] Governance, present and future, must grapple with such violence and exclusion if we are to be able to mitigate its worst effects and imagine alternative worlds without war.

Suggested readings

Antony Anghie, "The Evolution of International Law: Colonial and Postcolonial Realities," *Third World Quarterly* 27, no. 5 (2006): 739–753.

Tarak Barkawi, "On the Pedagogy of 'Small Wars,'" *International Affairs* 80, no. 1 (2004): 19–37.

Vivienne Jabri, *The Postcolonial Subject: Claiming Politics/Governing Others in Late Modernity* (London: Routledge, 2013).

Vivienne Jabri, *War and the Transformation of Global Politics* (Basingstoke, UK: Palgrave Macmillan, 2007).

Helen M. Kinsella, *The Image Before the Weapon: A Critical History of the Distinction Between Combatant and Civilian* (Ithaca, NY: Cornell University Press, 2011).

Notes

1 Despite recognizing the ecological devastation caused by war and the inadequacies of governance efforts to minimize such harm, this chapter remains apologetically anthropocentric in its analytical focus.
2 Gary D. Solis, *The Law of Armed Conflict: International Humanitarian Law in War* (Cambridge: Cambridge University Press, 2012), 3.
3 Michael Barnett and Raymond Duvall, "Power in Global Governance," in *Power in Global Governance*, ed. Michael Barnett and Raymond Duvall (Cambridge: Cambridge University Press, 2005), 1–32, 7.
4 David Armstrong, Theo Farrell, and Hélène Lambert, *International Law and International Relations* (Cambridge: Cambridge University Press, 2007), 37–38.
5 Solis, *The Law of Armed Conflict*, 4.
6 Armstrong, Farrell, and Lambert, *International Law and International Relations*, 40–41; see also Solis, *The Law of Armed Conflict*, 4–5.
7 Thomas G. Weiss and Ramesh Thakur, *Global Governance and the UN: An Unfinished Journey* (Bloomington, IN: University of Indiana Press, 2010), 56.
8 James Rosenau, "Governance, Order and Change in World Politics," in *Governance Without Government: Order and Change in World Politics*, ed. James Rosenau and Ernst-Otto Czempiel (Cambridge: Cambridge University Press, 1992), 1–29, 4.
9 Mary Kaldor, *New and Old Wars: Organised Violence in a Global Era* (Cambridge: Polity Press, 1999).
10 Amanda Alexander, "A Short History of International Humanitarian Law," *European Journal of International Law* 26, no. 1 (2015): 109–138, 111.
11 Solis, *The Law of Armed Conflict*, 250.
12 Quoted by Ronald Cohen, "Warfare and State Formation: Wars Make States and States Make Wars," in *Warfare, Culture, and Environment*, ed. Brian A. Ferguson (New York, NY: Academic Press, 1984), 329–358.
13 Helen M. Kinsella, "Gendering Grotius: Sex and Sex Difference in the Laws of War," *Political Theory* 34, no. 2 (2006): 161–191, 162.
14 Helen M. Kinsella, *The Image Before the Weapon: A Critical History of the Distinction Between Combatant and Civilian* (Ithaca, NY: Cornell University Press, 2011), 13.
15 Antony Anghie, "The Evolution of International Law: Colonial and Postcolonial Realities," *Third World Quarterly* 27, no. 5 (2006): 739–753, 740; see also: Antony Anghie, "Finding the Peripheries: Sovereignty and Colonialism in Nineteenth-Century International Law," *Harvard International Law Journal* 40, no. 1 (1999): 1–71.
16 Anghie, "Finding the Peripheries," 7.
17 See, among other notable examples: Rebecca M. Hendrick and David Nachmias, "The Policy Sciences: The Challenge of Complexity," *Policy Studies Review* 11, nos. 3–4 (1992): 310–328; Mark Lubell, "The Ecology of Games Framework," *Policy Studies Journal* 41, no. 3 (2013): 537–559; David Chandler, *Resilience: The Governance of Complexity* (London: Routledge, 2014); Christopher Ansell and Robert Geyer, "'Pragmatic Complexity': A New Foundation for Moving Beyond 'Evidence-based Policy Making'?" *Policy Studies* 38, no. 2 (2017): 149–167.
18 John Law and John Urry, "Enacting the Social," *Economy and Society* 33, no. 3 (2004): 390–410, 401.
19 See, for example: Paul Higate, "Drinking Vodka from the 'Butt-Crack': Men, Masculinities and Fratriarchy in the Private Militarized Security Company," *International Feminist Journal of Politics* 14, no. 4 (2012): 450–469; Megan MacKenzie, *Beyond the Band of Brothers: The US Military and the Myth That Women Can't Fight* (Cambridge:

Cambridge University Press, 2015); Marsha Henry, "Problematizing Military Masculinity, Intersectionality and Male Vulnerability in Feminist Critical Military Studies," *Critical Military Studies* 3, no. 2 (2017): 182–199.

20 Carol Cohn, "Wars, Wimps and Women: Talking Gender and Thinking War," in *Gendering War Talk*, ed. Miriam Cooke and Angela Woollacott (Princeton, NJ: University of Princeton Press, 1993), 227–246, 236.

21 Katharine M. Millar and Joanna Tidy, "Combat as a Moving Target: Masculinities, the Heroic Soldier Myth, and Normative Martial Violence," *Critical Military Studies* 3, no. 2 (2017): 142–160, 156; see also: Cara Daggett, "Drone Disorientations: How 'Unmanned' Weapons Queer the Experience of Killing in War," *International Feminist Journal of Politics* 17, no. 3 (2015): 361–379; Lindsay C. Clark, "Grim Reapers: Ghostly Narratives of Masculinity and Killing in Drone Warfare," *International Feminist Journal of Politics* 20, no. 4 (2018): 602–623.

22 MacKenzie, *Beyond the Band of Brothers*, 133.

23 Meredith G. F. Worthen, "Transgender Under Fire: Hetero-cis-normativity and Military Students' Attitudes Toward Trans Issues and Trans Service Members Post DADT," *Sexuality Research and Social Policy* 16, no. 1 (2019): 289–308, 290.

24 See, for example: Laura J. Shepherd and Laura Sjoberg, "Trans-bodies in/of War(s): Cis-privilege and Contemporary Security Strategy," *Feminist Review*, no. 101 (2012): 5–23.

25 C. E. Callwell, quoted in: Tarak Barkawi, "On the Pedagogy of 'Small Wars,'" *International Affairs* 80, no. 1 (2004): 19–37, 21. The more general point about disciplinary categorization is also applicable to "terrorism studies," the study of "civil wars,", and the study of "asymmetrical warfare."

26 Ibid.

27 Vivienne Jabri, *War and the Transformation of Global Politics* (Basingstoke, UK: Palgrave Macmillan, 2007), 55.

28 Judith Butler, *Frames of War: When Is Life Grievable?* (London: Verso, 2009).

29 Vivienne Jabri, *The Postcolonial Subject: Claiming Politics/Governing Others in Late Modernity* (London: Routledge, 2013), 129.

30 There are, of course, similarly devastating effects of war on Indigenous and colonized populations not required to fight. Environmental damage caused by nuclear weapons testing, for example, has profoundly affected the lives of human and non-human communities in Australia and the Pacific, while civilian populations are forcibly displaced as a result of ongoing conflict the world over.

31 Raynald Harvey Lemelin, Kyle Powys Whyte, Kelsey Johansen, Freya Higgins Desbiolles, Christopher Wilson, and Steve Hemming, "Conflicts, Battlefields, Indigenous Peoples and Tourism: Addressing Dissonant Heritage in Warfare Tourism in Australia and North America in the Twenty-first Century," *International Journal of Culture, Tourism and Hospitality Research* 7, no. 3 (2013): 257–271.

32 Michèle Barrett, "Subalterns at War," *Interventions* 9, no. 3 (2007): 451–474, 472.

33 Kinsella, *The Image Before the Weapon*.

34 Alex Edney-Browne, "Embodiment and Affect in a Digital Age: Understanding Mental Illness Among Military Drone Personnel," *Krisis: Journal of Contemporary Philosophy*, no. 1 (2017): 19–33, 29.

35 Iver B. Neumann and Ole Jacob Sending, *Governing the Global Polity: Practice, Mentality, Rationality* (Ann Arbor, MI: University of Michigan Press, 2010), 152.

36 The concept of interpellation was developed by Louis Althusser, as cited in Jutta Weldes, "Constructing National Interests," *European Journal of International Relations* 2, no. 3 (1996): 275–318, 287.

37 Susanna Campbell, David Chandler, and Meera Sabaratnam, "Introduction: The Politics of Liberal Peace," in *A Liberal Peace? The Problems and Practices of Peacebuilding*, ed.

Susanna Campbell, David Chandler, and Meera Sabaratnam (London: Zed Books, 2011), 1–10, 1.

38 Oliver Richmond, "A Genealogy of Peace and Conflict Theory," in *Palgrave Advances in Peacebuilding*, ed. Oliver Richmond (Basingstoke, UK: Palgrave Macmillan, 2010), 14–40, 26. See also: Roland Paris, "Saving Liberal Peacebuilding," *Review of International Studies* 36, no. 2 (2010): 337–367; Jan Selby, "The Myth of Liberal Peace-building," *Conflict, Security and Development* 13, no. 1 (2013): 57–86; Oliver P. Richmond and Roger Mac Ginty, "Where Now for the Critique of the Liberal Peace?" *Cooperation and Conflict* 50, no. 2 (2015): 171–189.

39 Séverine Autesserre, *Peaceland: Conflict Resolution and the Everyday Politics of International Intervention* (Cambridge: Cambridge University Press, 2014), 2 and *passim*.

40 Lee-Anne Broadhead, "Re-Packaging Notions of Security: A Skeptical Feminist Response to Recent Efforts," in *States of Conflict: Gender, Violence and Resistance*, ed. Susie Jacobs, Ruth Jacobson, and Jennifer Marchbank (London: Zed Books, 2000), 27–44, 42.

41 Tarak Barkawi, "War, Armed Forces, and Society in Historical Perspective," in *Postcolonial Theory and International Relations: A Critical Introduction*, ed. Sanjay Seth (London: Routledge, 2013), 87–105, 89.

42 Joan Cocks, *On Sovereignty, and Other Political Delusions* (London: Bloomsbury, 2014), 47.

CONTENTS

Geopolitics

Competition in an age of shared global threats

Thomas Hanson

The post-Cold War interlude has come to an end, and the world has entered an era of disruption. The forces driving this development have long been in the making, but the COVID-19 pandemic has sped up three trends shaping these times: a global sustainability crisis, a Pandora's box of onrushing technologies, and shifts in the balance of power. Will these existential threats force countries to join forces and form new systems of international order? Or will geopolitical competition impede cooperation and lead to entropy in global governance? These are crucial questions, not least because the coming decades will pose challenges requiring a response beyond the capacity of any individual country or fragmentary alliance.

In the West, traditional geopolitics has focused on geography, particularly the Eurasian landmass, and power relations among states. At present it is painfully evident that large-scale issues such as global warming and pandemics are as likely to disrupt the world order as armed conflict between countries. These problems also expose the weaknesses of national governance and a host of related threats – from internal polarization and failed states to non-state actors, global corruption, and cybercriminality. Such global threats evoke the words of French-American historian Jacques Barzun: "The ultimate unifying force of an age is its predicaments."[1]

But in tandem with these challenges, the dramatic rise of China and a shift of the world economic fulcrum to Asia are creating heightened

DOI: 10.4324/9781003139836-5

geopolitical tensions. China's rapid advances in technology and entrenched centralized form of governance have provoked a reaction in the West, particularly in the United States, resulting in greater distrust and fewer opportunities for dialogue. Under the Trump administration, steps were taken toward decoupling – in supply chains, technology, and cultural and academic exchanges. The stabilizing effect of economic interdependence, so absent between the United States and the Union of Soviet Socialist Republics (USSR) during the Cold War, is once again at risk.

What are the contours of geopolitical rivalries today and in the medium term? What steps could create some degree of stability and enable progress in global governance? There are early signs that we are heading in the wrong direction. The most troubling is the nascent emergence of contending blocs, reminiscent less of the Cold War than of the geopolitical competition that culminated in the Great War of 1914.

Navigating away from these dangers will require enlightened leadership, strong national governance, and situational awareness. Global institutions, including the United Nations, will need to be restructured and strengthened to achieve compromise between states of various forms of governance and differing worldviews while also protecting the rights of smaller states and individuals.

This chapter explores these and related issues. It begins with a historical overview of geopolitics, highlighting the importance of Eurasia. It describes ongoing US efforts to prevent the rise of a "peer competitor" in Europe or Asia in the face of China's growing influence. Contrasting the geopolitical worldviews of the United States and China, the chapter then discusses hegemonic stability theory and describes trends toward multipolarity and a greater role for regions. Finally, the chapter explores measures conducive to geopolitical stability and world order. Paramount among these are a commitment to diplomacy, a clear assessment of the threat, and insight into the rise and fall of nations.

Geopolitical paradigms

In contemporary usage, geopolitics is an elusive concept with a shady past. From a focus on the influence of geography on national power, it has come to be so broadly defined as to be nearly synonymous with international relations in general. And more recently, the field of "critical geopolitics" has added many new dimensions to the already expansive definition, from feminist geopolitics to geopolitics "beyond the text."[2]

Historically, world order has involved the rise and fall of empires. The Russian, Ottoman, Habsburg, and Chinese empires fell with World War I, and after World War II, European overseas empires followed suit. Some analysts maintain that the vestiges of these former empires strongly influence geopolitics today.[3] In the twentieth century, the world of states expanded. At the UN's founding in October 1945, its membership totaled 51. Today the number is 193. Despite strides by the UN toward greater cooperation, at a time when global challenges require a unified response, the world is more politically fragmented than ever.

In 1945 the UN adopted principles on state-to-state relations that had originated 300 years earlier in Europe. During the Thirty Years' War from 1618 to 1648, continental Europe had been devastated in a struggle between Catholics and Protestants sparked by the Reformation. The motivation for global governance after World War II was forged in a similarly devastating 30-year period of total war from 1914 to 1945.

The 1648 Treaty of Westphalia attempted to set aside the chiliastic emotions of religion and natural law. It focused more narrowly on the rights and obligations of states as a basis for stability. Adversaries unified around principles of state sovereignty, including the inviolability of borders and non-interference in the domestic affairs of sovereign states. Centuries later, these Westphalian principles were incorporated into the UN Charter. Not without irony, the point of departure for decolonization was Westphalian sovereignty.

Even as European states competed in imperialistic ventures during the ensuing centuries, they attempted to balance their relations in Europe through diplomacy and alliances. Termed the Concert of Europe, this system tended to recognize the territorial status quo among the major powers. During the nineteenth century, congresses and conferences served as vehicles for managing geopolitical tensions, with all-too-frequent accommodations over the heads of smaller states.

In *Democracy in America*, written in 1839, Alexis de Tocqueville predicted that the twentieth century would be dominated by Russia and the United States. He could not have foreseen that two smaller countries on opposite peripheries of Eurasia, Germany and Japan, would vie for world power in the first half of the short twentieth century, nor that their rise and defeat would usher in a new era of geopolitics.

The modern study of geopolitics came into vogue in the early twentieth century in the works of theorists such as Halford Mackinder, Alfred Thayer Mahan, Karl Haushofer, and Nicholas Spykman. The context for their ideas was an era of imperialism and the rise of a new power in Europe – a united Germany. For Mahan, ocean and sea power were the strongest base for power. For Mackinder and Haushofer, technological progress on land, especially railroads, made the "world island" of Eurasia the potentially dominant realm. As Mackinder opined, if any power or combination of powers came to control the "world island," it would be positioned to dominate the world.[4]

Haushofer's theories eventually inspired Nazi Germany in its drive eastward into Eurasia for "Lebensraum." This association with Nazism, along with the advent of the nuclear age, caused traditional geopolitics to fall out of favor in the postwar period. Nevertheless, the Cold War evolved – in large measure – into a strategic competition between the world's leading sea power, the United States, and the USSR, the largest land power straddling eleven time zones across Eurasia.

The Cold War era was a time of walls. Much of Eurasia had, in effect, walled itself off from the Western political and economic order. In this truncated world, the middle classes in the West enjoyed several decades of rising prosperity, relative equality, and economic security. With the opening of China in 1978, the collapse of the Soviet Union in 1991, and the gradual opening of India's economy in the early 1990s, a dramatically new situation evolved. Western capital was increasingly free to seek out the cheapest labor worldwide. This fateful dynamic led to geo-economic shifts, including the rise of China to become the world's second-largest economy. Today these shifts are rapidly translating into a new landscape of geopolitics.

During the years immediately following the collapse of the USSR, theories of "hegemonic stability" seemed to be validated in the United States' hegemonic "unipolar moment."[5] In this concept of world order, for any given era, a hegemon is needed for the provision of international public goods.[6] In the nineteenth and early twentieth centuries, that power was the United Kingdom, whose navy protected the sea routes essential to global trade and imperialism and whose currency – pegged as it was to gold – allowed the UK to serve as a lender of last resort in the global economy.

As a concomitant to hegemonic stability, another concept, power transition theory, arose to help explain how power eventually shifts from a fading hegemon to one that is rising to become the new guarantor of the global commons. Such a transition is potentially fraught with the danger of war, as the former hegemon seeks to preempt the rise of its challenger. Recent popular discussion of the "Thucydides Trap" in the wake of China's rise illustrates this contemporary concern.[7] And there is a strong tone of tragic fatalism, amounting to a self-fulfilling prophecy, among prominent US political scientists regarding the inevitability of eventual conflict.[8]

But another danger arises when one hegemon fades with no successor in view. This situation prevailed in the 1930s, when Great Britain had become too weak to function as a hegemon and its logical successor, the United States, had withdrawn into isolationism. The economist Charles Kindleberger analyzed this gap between hegemons as a cause of the economic instability of the 1930s that led to World War II.[9] Such failed transitions are now commonly referred to as the "Kindleberger Trap."[10]

In 1945 the United States embraced the role of hegemon and shaped the political and economic institutions that have provided the intergovernmental infrastructure for contemporary world order. Two points are worth emphasizing. First, the transition from British to American hegemony occurred within an English-speaking subset of Western civilization. For this reason, it was largely (or at least publicly) non-adversarial, as Britain settled into the role of the proverbial Greeks to the United States' Rome court. If we are again entering a period of hegemonic transition toward China, the transition will not only be political, it will also be civilizational, with fertile ground for misperception. Second, although China has risen with unprecedented swiftness within the existing world order, it lacks the traditional wherewithal, such as a strong navy, a global currency, or even the political will, to take on the burdens of a hegemon.

This situation is one reason that many analysts fear the world is entering a period of instability, variously termed a "nonpolar world,"[11] "nobody's world,"[12] or a "G minus 2"[13] world, in which neither the United States nor China assure primacy of the various machineries of global governance, the global commons, or global public goods. And this concern is leading to new perspectives on geopolitics. As global interdependence slows and economic decoupling gives an impetus to regionalization, a more important role in global governance may emerge at the regional level. There is rising interest in regional institution-building and in the potential role of strong regional states either to disrupt the world order or to act as advocates of global governance and as balancers amid strategic flux between large powers.

The United States and China

The United States continues to enjoy formidable advantages in world affairs: a global reserve currency in the dollar; an economy relatively less dependent on external trade; and, not least, a blessed geographical situation. As a quote attributed to Chancellor Otto von Bismarck avers: "The Americans are a lucky people. They are bordered to the north and south by weak neighbors, and to the east and west by fish." This stands in stark contrast to the position of countries in Europe and Asia, with competing countries close at hand. China has borders with 14 countries, not including nearby Japan, while Russia shares a border with an equal number of neighbors across its Eurasian expanse.

Some analysts believe that geography creates a kind of moral hazard for the United States and a lack of empathy or understanding for the geopolitical concerns and historical suffering of other countries.[14] Be that as it may, US strategy has been framed by its geography. Since World War II, the goal of US security policy has been and is today to prevent the rise of a "peer competitor" in Eurasia. The underlying assumption of this geopolitical worldview is that the United States has been able to project power precisely because it is an unchallenged hegemon in its own region. Should a hegemon arise on either side of Eurasia – in Europe or Asia – that power would become capable of projecting power globally and threatening the United States.

Confronting Germany and Japan simultaneously in World War II drove this point home to US policymakers for generations. Containment of the Soviet Union during the Cold War followed the same logic. The *2017 US National Security Strategy* focuses, once again, on great power competition in Eurasia, with Russia and China singled out as "strategic competitors" that seek to counter the United States and undo the liberal world order. A clear example of this constant in US policy is expressed in an October 2020 report to Congress by the Congressional Research Service (CRS):

> From a U.S. perspective on grand strategy and geopolitics, it can be noted that most of the world's people, resources, and economic activity are located not in the Western Hemisphere, but in the other hemispheres, particularly Eurasia. In response to this basic feature of world geography, U.S. policymakers for the last several decades have chosen to pursue, as a key element of U.S. national strategy, a goal of preventing the emergence of regional hegemons in Eurasia. Although U.S. policymakers do not often state explicitly in public the goal of preventing the emergence of regional hegemons in Eurasia, U.S. military operations in recent decades – both wartime operations and day-to-day operations – appear to have been carried out in no small part in support of this goal.[15]

With the collapse of the Soviet Union in 1991, optimism prevailed in the US establishment. In those halcyon days, it appeared that time was on the side of the West and that China would become a "responsible stakeholder" in the liberal world order. Since then, China's rise and the 2008 economic crisis have eroded this confidence and led to fears that time is, in fact, on China's side.

China's growth continues despite tariffs, sanctions, and the problems festering along its periphery. Even as Xi Jinping tightens the Communist Party's grip at home, steering the country toward technocratic authoritarianism, he has embarked on geo-economic projects such as the Belt and Road Initiative (BRI) for infrastructure across Eurasia. These long-term policies are of mounting concern in Washington, as is the prospect that China could take the lead in key technologies of the future.

China's national narrative is one of past greatness interrupted by a century and more of humiliations that are now being overcome. In China, the period from the First Opium War in 1839 to the founding of the People's Republic of China in 1949 is seen as a time of "eating bitterness" (*guo chi*), marked by imperialist intervention, civil war, and Japanese occupation. Latent fears of fragmentation, encirclement, and foreign domination linger even today[16] and lead China to fully embrace UN Charter principles in Article 2 of state sovereignty and non-interference, at least in theory. China's declared "core interests" include Tibet, Xinjiang, and Taiwan. They reflect determination to restore and maintain China's legitimate boundaries as defined by the People's Republic of China (PRC).

China has long claimed that it seeks to rise peacefully. Beijing maintains that it prefers external stability to focus on development challenges at home. As Foreign Minister Wang Yi stated in a speech in 2020, China seeks to rebalance rather than replace the established order and favors consultations, cooperation, and "managed competition."[17] Akin to leaders before him, Xi Jinping declares that China pursues "harmony" for itself and for the world order. Harmony is an important concept in Chinese philosophy and social theory.[18] But for other countries, the question remains on whose terms when it is applied to international relations.

Compared to their Western counterparts, Chinese geopolitical theorists place a far greater emphasis on leadership, governance, and the nature of legitimate authority. In *Leadership and the Rise of Great Powers* (2019), Yan Xuetong, dean of the Institute of International Relations at Tsinghua University, argues:

> When the rising state's leadership is more capable and efficient than that of the dominant state and that of other contemporary major states, international influence is reestablished in a way that allows the rising state to eclipse the dominant state.[19]

Xi Jinping has made concepts of governance a centerpiece of his rule in China, titling three large volumes of his speeches and writings *The Governance of China*.[20]

Such ideas were once central to the traditional Chinese geopolitical concept of suzerainty. China saw itself as the center of a tributary system in which other countries showed political respect in exchange for trade concessions. The Chinese outlook is imbued with the traditional Confucian principle of leadership though virtue and example. Yan Xuetong notes that in the past, the United States also sought to lead by example, as exemplified in the speeches of John Quincy Adams and other early presidents. "It was not for the United States to impose its own principles of government upon the rest of mankind," Yan writes, "but rather to attract the rest of mankind through the example of the United States."[21]

Given China's human rights abuses in Tibet, Xinjiang, and now Hong Kong, Washington feels perhaps less challenged by any allure of Chinese governance than by China's prowess in the technologies of the future. Members of the United States Congress and a recent report by the National Security Commission on Artificial Intelligence warn that China is pulling ahead of the United States, not only in 5G and future 6G technology, for which China has already announced its team of experts from all sectors, but also in artificial intelligence and quantum computing. A wake-up call was China's launch of the world's first quantum satellite and subsequent successful test of quantum communication between China and Europe.

One concern is that China will begin to set technology standards of international governance that are at variance with US positions in key areas such as 5G and 6G, infrastructure investment, and intrusive facial recognition technologies. Another is that Chinese plans for a sovereign digital currency could eventually undermine the global role of the US dollar. China's capacity for long-term planning in technology is especially unnerving at a time when the United States lacks a national industrial policy worthy of the name. The Trump administration's attempt to throttle Chinese tech giants such as Huawei, ByteDance, and SenseTime should be understood in the context of the military and security implications of new technologies and big data.

China's rapid development in recent decades had geopolitical implications for all of Asia. Beijing's military spending has increased rapidly, although its defense budget is still far lower than the United States. China seeks "strategic depth" along its periphery, particularly within the First Island Chain where Taiwan, Hong Kong, and the disputed areas of the South and East China Seas are located. Here the geopolitical interests of China come into direct conflict with US geopolitical determination to maintain naval superiority and prevent China from becoming a regional hegemon in Asia and a peer competitor globally.

As historian John King Fairbank once noted, China has traditionally held sea power in "disesteem." The country's geopolitical orientation has rather been westward, toward the "strategic primacy of inner Asia" from which threats emerged throughout history.[22] Chinese policy under Xi Jinping looks to the sea, where a buildup of Dongfeng missiles puts both Taiwan and US aircraft carriers at risk. But it also looks to the west, where the massive Belt and Road Initiative seeks to project Chinese economic influence into Eurasia. It is ironic that on the heels of the US "pivot" to Asia, China shows signs of pivoting toward the Eurasian landmass.

China downplays the geopolitical implications of the BRI, but voices from US Democrats and Republicans have begun warning that China has embarked on a two-directional path to global hegemony.[23] In the logic of peer competition, China appears to be well underway toward the first step of becoming a hegemon in Asia but has also expanded its influence into the Eurasian heartland.

Multipolarity and regionalization

The world today finds itself at a tipping point between cooperation and an evolution toward competing geopolitical blocs. On one side, the United States has begun casting about for new strategic groupings, with visions of a reinvigorated trans-Atlantic alliance in closer coordination with India and Japan, as well as a naval-based Indo-Pacific strategy along the southern waters of Eurasia to counter Chinese influence. President Biden echoes the Trump administration in placing these initiatives within the framework of strategic contention between democracy and autocracy while urging allies in Europe and Asia to choose sides.

On the other side, key land powers of Eurasia, particularly China, Russia, and potentially Iran, are strengthening their bilateral relationships, including militarily. Although China continues to rule out a formal military alliance, enhanced cooperation between China and Russia supports the hedging strategies pursued by both countries toward the United States. The close ties between China and Pakistan are pertinent as well, with Turkey a seeming wild card in the Eurasian mosaic. China's BRI and the Shanghai Cooperation Organization (SCO), formed in 2001, are potential vehicles for geopolitical cooperation in Eurasia under Chinese and Russian auspices. The evolving situation is illustrated in contrasting statements by Xi Jinping, who describes the relationship between Beijing and Moscow as the most important in the world today, and Narendra Modi, who claims that title for the United States and India.

In Western Eurasia, institution-building has made significant progress since 1945, with the support and encouragement of the United States to create a bulwark against the Soviet Union. The European Union and NATO (North Atlantic Treaty Organization) provide a thick matrix of economic and security institutions of a sort noticeably lacking in Eastern Eurasia. One factor in this discrepancy between Europe and Asia is the ongoing role of the defeated powers from World War II – Germany and Japan.

Political and symbolic reconciliation between Germany and its former European adversaries, particularly France, helped pave the way for postwar institution-building. In Asia, such symbolic reconciliation between Japan and other important Asian countries, such as South Korea, has been incomplete and has left a residue of distrust and animosity. As the world's number three and four economies, Japan and Germany remain pivotal in future global governance, and their non-nuclear status is a lingering anomaly that may be revisited at some point, with serious implications for global geopolitics.

Europe is increasingly pulled between the trans-Atlantic realm and Eurasia, enticed by markets in Asia. There are signs that the European Union – and Germany, in particular – may already be gravitating toward a more balancing role in geopolitics, pace official declarations of unwavering alliance solidarity. Decades of European institutional cooperation and pooled sovereignty have made EU countries more attuned than Washington to the need for multilateral institutions and global governance.

Many European leaders agree that China risks becoming a hegemon in Asia, but they tend to stop short of joining Washington in the second conceptual leap of assuming that China thereby seeks world domination. They are also less likely to agree on a Manichaean view of existential struggle between democracy and autocracy in China's relationship with the West. The EU has been at loggerheads with the United States on a wide range of geopolitical issues following the Trump administration's withdrawal from the Paris Agreement, the Joint Comprehensive Plan of Action (JCPOA) nuclear deal on Iran, the United Nations Educational, Scientific and Cultural Organization (UNESCO), the Trans-Pacific Partnership, and the World Health Organization. They are also critical of the US decision to cut off funding for the United Nations Relief and Works Agency for Palestinian Refugees in the Near East (UNRWA). Although the Biden administration has begun reversing many of these decisions, deep internal polarization makes US policy appear increasingly unpredictable. In a speech to Congress in April 2021, President Biden noted that what he hears most often from world leaders is: "We see America is back, but for how long? But for how long?"[24]

While some EU officials invoke a more independent role for Europe, the EU now declares China a "systemic rival" and proposes stepped-up coordination among Western allies and other democracies in the face of Chinese trade practices. Despite increased vigilance toward Beijing, many in Germany still adhere to the idea of *Wandel durch Handel*, or "change through trade," an echo of Germany's détente-era policy toward the USSR of *Wandel durch Annaeherung*, or "change through rapprochement." Chancellor Angela Merkel continues to support the Nord Stream 2 gas pipeline project with Russia despite strong opposition from the United States and Eastern European allies. And many European observers question the geopolitical wisdom of US policies that directly or indirectly drive China and Russia together.

For the European Union to emerge as a more independent geopolitical actor, it will have to improve its foreign policy and security infrastructure. It will also need to reconcile the different foreign policy approaches of its 27 members, each of which for now has a veto on foreign policy decisions, as well as work out how it coordinates with the United Kingdom now that it has left the European Union. This task is rendered more complicated because Russia, China, and increasingly the United States tend to approach European states bilaterally, rather than through Brussels. China's bilateral approach on the BRI is a case in point.

Barack Obama once famously labeled Russia a "regional power." It is true that Russia punches above its weight in foreign policy, carefully choosing its involvements in line with a National Security Doctrine announced in 2008 by then president Dmitry Medvedev in the wake of Russia's invasion of Georgia. Russian policy has three overarching goals: prevent any further expansion of NATO, deter radical Islam, and create a sphere of influence in its "near abroad."

Like China, Russia seeks strategic depth on its periphery and is wont to accuse the United States of hypocrisy given its own Monroe Doctrine. Since Vladimir Putin's speech at the Munich Security Conference in 2007,[25] Russia has encouraged China to join forces to counterbalance US hegemony. In the wake of the Obama administration's "pivot" toward China in 2010, and now with rising hostility under the Trump and Biden administrations, China has begun to respond to these Russian overtures and has become the senior partner in deepening economic and security ties.

As they draw closer, China and Russia have also taken the first small steps toward greater security cooperation with Iran. The three countries held their first joint military exercise in early 2020. In addition, China and Iran signed a 25-year economic and security partnership agreement in March 2021. Former US national security adviser Zbigniew Brzezinski once warned against such a grouping on the Eurasian landmass: "Potentially the most dangerous scenario would be a grand coalition of China, Russia, and perhaps Iran, an 'antihegemonic' coalition united not by ideology but by complementary grievances."[26]

Japan has been internally divided in its approach to China, which is as important a market for Tokyo as it is for Berlin. These divisions came to light in 2010 when then prime minister Hatoyama Yukio declared that while Japan's security was linked to the United States, its economic future lay in Asia. Even the more pro–United States Abe Shinzo government and the government of Suga Yoshide have vacillated in the face of US pressure to join an Indo-Pacific strategy to contain China.[27]

While Japan has acted to save Obama's Trans-Pacific Partnership, now without the United States and renamed the Comprehensive and Progressive Agreement for Trans-Pacific Partnership, Tokyo has also joined the Chinese-led Regional Comprehensive Economic Partnership (RCEP), which excludes the United States and opens the door to deeper supply chains within Asia. Similarly, the ten members of the Association of Southeast Asian Nations (ASEAN) have experienced divisions on how to balance relations with Washington and Beijing.

Though lagging behind China economically, and China and Russia militarily, India will be a key factor in global geopolitics. It has recently drawn closer to the United States and away from China under Narendra Modi's Hindu nationalist government, yet it enjoys a long tradition of independent neutrality. India's strategic focus is Pakistan: their nuclear confrontation over Kashmir is one of the gravest flashpoints in global geopolitics. Pakistan's close ties with China, which include the BRI and nuclear cooperation, are of great concern to India. In addition, tensions have flared along the Sino-Indian border in the Himalayas, fueling an upsurge in economic and tech decoupling.

Chinese infrastructure projects in ports along the Indian Ocean – in Sri Lanka, in Pakistan at Gwadar, in Djibouti, and potentially in Myanmar – have caused India to step up cooperation on maritime security with the United States, Japan, and Australia, the other three members of the Quadrennial Security Dialogue (QUAD). And in October 2020, the United States and India announced new agreements to strengthen defense ties. The Biden administration has made the QUAD a centerpiece of its Asia policy with a view toward China.

The Greater Middle East region remains a complex matrix of Semitic, Turkic, and Indo-European civilizations, with vestiges of nearly 500 years of Ottoman Turkish dominance over Arab lands. Today some Arab countries, led by Saudi Arabia and the United Arab Emirates, fear future dominance by the Persians, by Iran, to the point of increasing their cooperation with Israel. Meanwhile, conservative Gulf monarchies feel their legitimacy is undermined by Turkey's support for the Muslim Brotherhood, including the democratically elected and short-lived government of Mohamed Morsi in Egypt. Turkey, Iran, and Saudi Arabia all seek hegemonic influence in a competition that will become far more dangerous if they ever join Israel as nuclear states.

With its rich resource base and surging demographics, Africa will become ever more important in global governance. A major step toward regional institution-building is the African Continental Free Trade Agreement in which 54 of 55 African states, except Eritrea, have signed and went into effect on January 1, 2021. China has long conducted infrastructure projects in Africa, many of which have now been subsumed under the BRI initiative. Africa's future importance can be seen in UN demographic projections to 2100, by which time Africa may account for 39 percent and Asia for 44 percent of humanity, while Europe will represent 6 percent and North America just 4 percent of a world population nearing 11 billion, although some recent studies foresee a somewhat lower global total.

Finally, in a world drifting toward regionalization, the Americas should logically be of greater geopolitical and economic importance to the United States. However, Washington has neglected its relations with Latin America in recent decades as it focused more on Asia and wars in the Middle East. China is now the top trading partner in most of Latin America, as it is in Africa.

Geopolitics and global governance

To slow the momentum toward geopolitical blocs, it will be imperative to focus on confidence-building, reform of global institutions, regional institution-building, and clear analysis of the primary threats facing all nations today. It is likely that a more diverse and variegated set of institutions will evolve to reflect multipolar realities and the growing importance of regional dynamics.[28]

The intergovernmental institutions of global and economic governance dating from 1945 no longer reflect the contemporary international landscape 75 years on. There are three potential paths to reform: rebalance existing institutions, forge a consensus on creating new ones, or evolve toward parallel institutions. The latter trend is already in evidence, with the China-led Asian Infrastructure Investment Bank (AIIB) a case in point. In 2015, the United Kingdom opted to take part in the AIIB despite pressure from the Obama administration to stay away. In justifying the decision, then British finance minister George Osborne said it was a "tragedy" that the US Congress continued to block reforms agreed unanimously in 2010 to increase the weight of China, Russia, India, and Brazil in the International Monetary Fund (IMF) and give emerging markets more influence.[29] Failure to reform existing global institutions in the face of changing geopolitics will only increase the likelihood of parallel, competing institutions.

As a result of globalization, such geo-economic "groups" as the G8 (now G7 without Russia) and G20 assured regular communication and coordination among the world's largest economies. Noticeably absent have been any corresponding institutions for geopolitical consultations among the large powers. This practice was more common in the nineteenth century, but the time may again be ripe for broader initiatives toward more regularized dialogue among large powers, jointly and on a regional basis.[30]

Past examples of such structured dialogue include the original Conference on Security and Cooperation in Europe (CSCE; now Organization, or OSCE), which ushered in a period of détente toward the end of the Cold War; the Iran nuclear deal, which brought together the five members of the UN Security Council, plus Germany in a common approach to the Iran issue; and a major climate accord between the US and China that paved the way for a successful Paris Agreement on climate in 2015. A stillborn case of this geopolitical approach is the bipartisan Iraq Study Group in 2006, headed by Democrat Lee Hamilton and Republican James A. Baker, III. The group concluded that the Iraq crisis could best be solved in a regional context, with Iran joining other regional actors in negotiations.[31] This recommendation was rejected by the George W. Bush administration in favor of a military surge in Iraq.

Persistent disagreements in the UN Security Council point to the difficulty of such geopolitical coordination. Proposals to expand Security Council membership, even to include delaying the veto power of new members, have faced opposition from existing permanent members. Beyond this, regularized great power dialogue could raise concerns about geopolitical agreements reached over the heads of smaller nations, as has occurred so often in history. Such fears were apparent in the early 2000s during a brief period of speculation about a potential "G2" between Washington and Beijing.

Historically, large powers have often agreed on neutral buffer zones to prevent armed conflict. For example, in 1955 the Four Powers signed the Austrian State Treaty and agreed to withdraw from quadripartite occupation in return for Austrian neutrality. A few Western analysts have revived the idea of possible neutral zones in Europe. In 2017, Michael O'Hanlon of the Brookings Institution suggested that a new security architecture for Europe could include "sustained neutrality" for those countries not currently in NATO. By treaty, this group of countries would not join NATO in the future, nor would those currently outside the EU be granted EU security guarantees.[32] Such great power accommodation would, of course, be met with vehement opposition from Ukraine, from the "new Europeans" of Eastern Europe, and perhaps even from Russia, which might see this as too great a concession on its doorstep.

Steps to increase predictability, reassurance, and timely consultation are essential to building trust, which former US Secretary of State George Shultz termed "the coin of the realm" in an article written in his 100th year.[33] During the Cold War, the United States and Soviet Union adopted confidence-building measures (CBMs) in a variety of areas, not least in institutionalizing military-to-military contacts. Military dialogue is lacking in the US-China relationship and should be expanded. In addition, transparency should be increased on defense spending.

There are many examples of how a lack of predictability and consultation can adversely impact great power trust. Chinese inability to inform the world in the early stages of the coronavirus pandemic has increased distrust between Beijing and other countries. And by exceeding the agreed UN mandate on Libya in 2011 to topple Muammar al-Gaddafi, the West undermined Chinese and Russian support for future invocation of the Responsibility to Protect doctrine.

Active communication and confidence-building will also be crucial in technology. Protecting against cyber threats from states and non-state actors will require international agreements comparable to those on arms control. The threat posed by new weapons systems, such as hypersonic missiles and the militarization of space, will also require dialogue and agreement. Recent innovations in nuclear weapon technology, including small "dial a yield" battlefield nukes, can be highly destabilizing not just between the great powers but in regions such as South Asia. India and Pakistan will likely attempt to procure such weapons, which by their very nature will lower the nuclear threshold. Russia and the United States have embarked on massive programs to upgrade their strategic nuclear arsenals, while China is increasing its nuclear arsenal from a far lower base. The Trump administration pulled out of the Intermediate-Range Nuclear Forces (INF) Treaty and other arms control agreements, with the stated aim of including Chinese INF in a three-way negotiation with the United States and Russia. China has refused to consider this proposal. There was also uncertainty on renewal of the New Strategic Arms Reduction Treaty (START) prior to a United States–Russian agreement in February 2021 to extend the treaty until 2026. Distrust among the nuclear powers has led to an erosion of agreements and frameworks that have mitigated the arms race in recent decades. In addition, there is far less media coverage and public's awareness of nuclear dangers than during the Cold War at just the wrong moment.

Conclusion

If global threats such as climate change, pandemics, nuclear weapons, and technological disruption are assigned their proper importance, today's predicaments should be conducive to enhanced global cooperation. But for global cooperation to advance in the coming decades, it will be necessary to manage geopolitical competition proactively, not only between the United States and China but also among regional competitors.

Strengthening diplomacy is a prerequisite. As diplomatic historian Paul Sharp has written, the essence of diplomacy is to seek modes of coexistence in a world of constant separateness and difference.[34] This certainly rings true in the multipolar world that is emerging today. The immediate goal of diplomacy should be to manage contesting issues short of war, not necessarily to "solve" them. In recent decades, the United States has been particularly prone to conceive foreign policy in terms of economic sanctions and military strength, to the detriment of investment in diplomacy.[35]

It will be a wrenching dilemma to find the proper balance between values deemed universal by any side, on the one hand, and stability and predictability in relations among large powers, on the other. A high-water mark of declared policy devoted to universal values came with the "transformational" diplomacy of President George W. Bush, based on the principle that the United States should never favor geopolitical stability over freedom in the world. In a 2005 speech in Latvia on the 60th anniversary of the end of World War II, Bush attacked the Yalta Agreement as akin to the Molotov-Ribbentrop Pact in its "attempt to sacrifice freedom for the sake of stability." In the speech, he held out the ambitious goal of ending tyranny in the world.[36]

In contrast, looking back at the total wars of the twentieth century and amid the ideological confrontation of the Cold War, realist Hans J. Morgenthau lamented that the old European order, from Westphalia to the Concert of Europe, had failed in its quest for stability, giving way to a new reality wherein

> each (state) claims in its way of life to possess the whole truth of morality and politics, which the others may reject only at their own peril. In this the ethics of interstate politics reverts to the politics and morality of tribalism, of the Crusades, and of the religious wars.[37]

Variants of these two worldviews coexist today, with contesting prescriptions for the future of global governance. A balance must indeed be found, mindful of the deep and varying traditions of civilizations. The historian Arnold Toynbee once wrote at the dawn of the Cold War, as the world adjusted to the perpetual threat of nuclear catastrophe: "In the world in which we find ourselves today, to live and let live is the first and last word of wisdom for both the armed camps into which mankind has unhappily allowed itself to be sorted out."[38] In this light, the policy focus should be on institutions, not blocs, and on counterbalancing, not containment or confrontation.

Each country will have to weigh the costs of conflict and of failing to address the growing threats to humanity. The historian Paul Kennedy, in his landmark work *The Rise and Fall of the Great Powers*, concluded that two factors bring about national decline: failing to keep ends and means in balance, resulting in "overstretch" and unsustainable debt and failing to keep pace with the technology and economy of the age.[39]

If geopolitical contention must be, then let it be with cognizance of and peaceful competition in such long-term determinants of national power.

Suggested reading

Alyssa Ayres, *Our Time Has Come: How India Is Making Its Place in the World* (Oxford: Oxford University Press, 2018).

Christopher Clark, *The Sleepwalkers: How Europe Went to War in 1914* (New York: Harper Collins, 2012).

Dina Esfandiary and Ariane Tabatabai, *Triple Axis: Iran's Relations with Russia and China* (London and New York: I.B. Tauris, 2018).

G. John Ikenberry, *A World Safe for Democracy: Liberal Internationalism and the Crisis of Global Order* (New Haven, CT: Yale University Press, 2020).

Henry Kissinger, *World Order* (New York: Penguin Press, 2014).

Sulmaan Wasif Khan, *Haunted by Chaos: Chinese Grand Strategy from Mao Zedong to Xi Jinping* (Cambridge, MA: Harvard University Press, 2018).

Yan Xuetong, *Leadership and the Rise of the Great Powers* (Princeton, NJ and Oxford: Princeton University Press, 2019).

Notes

1 Jacques Barzun, *From Dawn to Decadence* (London: The Folio Society, 2015), 529.
2 Jason Dittmer and Joanne Sharp, *Geopolitics: An Introductory Reader* (New York: Routledge, 2014), 279.
3 Robert D. Kaplan, *The Return of Marco Polo's World* (New York: Random House, 2018), 13.
4 Halford Mackinder, *The Geographical Pivot of History* (London: Royal Geographic Society, 1904).
5 Charles Krauthammer, "The Unipolar Moment," *Foreign Affairs* 70, no. 1 (1991): 22–33.
6 Robert Gilpin, "The Theory of Hegemonic War," *The Journal of Interdisciplinary History* 18, no. 4 (1988): 591–613; and George Modelski, *Long Cycles in World Politics* (Seattle, WA: University of Washington Press, 1987), 102.
7 Graham Allison, *Destined for War: Can America and China Escape Thucydides' Trap?* (Boston and New York: Houghton Mifflin Harcourt, 2017).
8 John J. Mearsheimer, *The Tragedy of Great Power Politics*, updated ed. (New York: W.W. Norton and Company, 2014).
9 Charles P. Kindleberger, *The World in Depression 1929–1939*, 2nd ed. (Berkeley, CA: University of California Press, 1986), chapters 7, 14; *Manias, Panics, and Crashes* (New York: Basic Books, 1989), 201, 214.
10 Joseph S. Nye, Jr., "The Kindleberger Trap," *Project Syndicate*, 9 January 2017, www.project-syndicate.org/commentary/trump-china-kindleberger-trap-by-joseph-s-nye-2017–01.
11 Richard N. Haass, *A World in Disarray: American Foreign Policy and the Crisis of the Old Order* (London: Penguin Press, 2017).
12 Charles A. Kupchan, *No One's World: The West, the Rising Rest, and the Coming Global Turn* (Oxford: Oxford University Press, 2012), 5.
13 Arvind Subramanian and Josh Felman, "The G Minus 2 Threat," *Project Syndicate*, 26 July 2019, www.project-syndicate.org/commentary/america-china-policies-economic-threat-by-arvind-subramanian-and-josh-felman-2019–07?barrier=accesspaylog.
14 Paul R. Pillar, *Why America Misunderstands the World* (New York: Columbia University Press, 2016), 19.
15 *Renewed Great Power Competition: Implications for Defense – Issues for Congress*, 29 October 2020 (Washington, DC: Congressional Research Service, 2020), CRS Report R43838/66, https://crsreports.congress.gov/product/pdf/R/R43838/66; see also Thomas S. Szayna et al., *The Emergence of Peer Competitors: A Framework for Analysis* (Santa Monica, CA: RAND, 2001).
16 Sulmaan Wasif Khan, *Haunted by Chaos: Chinese Grand Strategy from Mao Zedong to Xi Jinping* (Cambridge, MA: Harvard University Press, 2018), 7.
17 Wang Yi, *Stay on the Right Track and Keep Pace with the Times to Ensure the Right Direction for China-US Relations: Remarks by State Councilor and Foreign Minister Wang Yi at the China-US Think Tanks Media Forum 2020/07/09* (Beijing: Ministry of Foreign Affairs of the People's Republic of China), www.fmprc.gov.cn/mfa_eng/zxxx_662805/t1796302.shtml.
18 For Asian and Western views on the interplay between Chinese concepts of harmony and Western concepts of justice, see Michael J. Sandel and Paul J. D'Ambrosio, eds., *Encountering China: Michael Sandel and Chinese Philosophy* (Cambridge, MA: Harvard University Press, 2018).
19 Yan Xuetong, *Leadership and the Rise of Great Powers* (Princeton, NJ: Princeton University Press, 2019), 2.

20 Xi Jinping, *The Governance of China*, 3 vols. (Beijing: Foreign Language Press, 2014, 2018, 2020).

21 Xuetong, *Leadership and the Rise of Great Powers*, 23.

22 John K. Fairbank, "China's Foreign Policy in Historical Perspective," *Foreign Affairs* 47, no. 1 (1969): 2–3.

23 Hal Brands and Jake Sullivan, "China's Two Paths to Global Domination," *Foreign Policy* (Summer 2020): 46–51.

24 "Remarks by President Biden in Address to a Joint Session of Congress," 28 April 2021, www.thewhitehouse.gov/briefing-room/speeches-remarks/2021/04/29/remarks-by-president-biden-to-a-joint-session-of-Comgress/.

25 Vladimir Putin, *Speech and the Following Discussion at the Munich Conference on Security Policy*, 10 February 2007, en.kremlin.ru/events/president/transcripts/24034.

26 Zbigniew Brzezinski, *The Grand Chessboard* (New York: Basic Books, 1997), 55.

27 R. Taggart Murphy, *Japan and the Shackles of the Past* (Oxford: Oxford University Press, 2014), 309.

28 Rebecca Lissner and Mira Rapp-Hooper, *An Open World: How America Can Win the Contest for Twenty-First-Century Order* (New Haven, CT: Yale University Press, 2020), 140.

29 Johnathan Spicer, "U.K. Finance Minister Calls U.S. Congress's China Stance a 'Tragedy,'" *Reuters*, December 2015, www.reuters.com/article/britain-osborne-idINKBN0TQ2BG2015120.

30 Richard N. Haass and Charles Kupchan, "The New Concert of Powers: How to Prevent Catastrophe and Promote Stability in a Multipolar World," in *Anchoring the World: Essays from the Lloyd George Study Group on World Order*, 23 March 2021, www.foreignaffairs.com/articles/world/2021-03-23/new-concert-powers. Haass and Kupchan envisage a "global concert for the twenty-first century" to include China, the European Union, India, Japan, Russia, and the United States.

31 James A. Baker, III, and Lee H. Hamilton, Co-Chairs, *The Iraq Study Group Report*, 5 December 2006, www.bakerinstitute.org/research/the-iraq-study-group-report/.

32 Michael O'Hanlon, *Beyond NATO: A New Security Architecture for Eastern Europe* (Washington, DC: Brooking Institution Press, 2017), 65.

33 George P. Shultz, "Life and Learning After One Hundred Years: Trust Is the Coin of the Realm-Reflections on Trust and Effective Relationships Across a New Hinge of History," 13 December 2020, www.hoover.org/research/trust/coin/realm.

34 Paul Sharp, *Diplomatic Theory of International Relations* (Cambridge: Cambridge University Press, 2009), 294.

35 William J. Burns, *The Back Channel: A Memoir of American Diplomacy and the Case for Its Renewal* (New York: Random House, 2019).

36 George W. Bush, *Speech in Riga Latvia*, 7 May 2005, https://georgewbush-whitehouse.archives.gov/news/releases/2005/05/20050507-8.html.

37 Hans J. Morgenthau, *Politics Among Nations: The Struggle for Power and Peace*, 3rd ed. (New York: Alfred A. Knopf, 1960), 159.

38 Arnold J. Toynbee, "The Siege of the West," *Foreign Affairs* 31, no. 2 (1953): 10.

39 Paul Kennedy, *The Rise and Fall of the Great Powers* (New York: Penguin Random House, 1987), 514.

Civilizations

Fusion or clash?

Kishore Mahbubani

The early twenty-first century should be a moment of great celebration for the West. Even though it represents a minority (just 12 percent) of the world's population, it has injected the positive DNA of Western civilization into every other civilization. No other human civilization has had as great an impact on humanity as the West. Many aspects of the positive DNA of the West have improved the human condition significantly across the globe, as documented in great detail by Steven Pinker in *Enlightenment Now*. As he puts it,

> More than ever, the ideals of reason, science, humanism, and progress need a wholehearted defense. We take its gifts for granted: newborns who will live more than eight decades, markets overflowing with food, clean water that appears with a flick of a finger and waste that disappears with another, pills that erase a painful infection, sons who are not sent off to war, daughters who can walk the streets in safety, critics of the powerful who are not jailed or shot, the world's knowledge and culture available in a shirt pocket. But these are human accomplishments, not cosmic birthrights.[1]

Yet, instead of celebrating this great moment of triumph, most Western populations, especially in the United States and the European Union (EU), are depressed. Various surveys show that they fear for the future.[2]

DOI: 10.4324/9781003139836-6

By contrast, the populations of China and India (two relatively underperforming civilizations in the past 200 years) are optimistic. Why has this happened? How did the West lose the plot?

This chapter argues that for all its apparent success, the West made three key strategic mistakes as it entered the twenty-first century. First, after waking up and rejuvenating other civilizations, the West failed to educate its population on the major strategic adjustments in a world it can no longer dominate as in the recent past. Second, as Western power recedes globally, the West tried unwisely to cling to powerful privileges in such key institutions of global governance as the UN Security Council, the International Monetary Fund (IMF), and World Bank. It would have been wiser to share power. Third, the United States as leading power in the West responded unwisely to the challenge posed by the number one emerging power, China, by becoming more unilateral, responding to China on its own, without consulting allies. It would have been wiser to respond more multilaterally. In short, if the West returned to its fundamental principles of equity and fairness in social and political relationships, it could engineer a better future for its people. In addition, adherence to these fundamental principles would help enhance Western soft power and influence in the twenty-first century.

If the West chose to adopt wiser approaches, as suggested in this chapter, it would also help ensure that the world will continue to see a fusion, rather than clash, of civilizations, as Larry Summers and I argued in a *Foreign Affairs* essay in 2016.[3] It is important to emphasize the genuine possibility of optimistic outcomes since the conventional wisdom, even among some of the leading minds, is that the world is headed only toward troubled times. However, to get there, the West must understand these three strategic mistakes and make significant U-turns from some of its deeply established policies.

Ignoring new realities

Even though most Western policymakers are educated in history and have a good knowledge of recent developments, very few are keenly aware of the biggest historical fact of our time: the past 200 years of Western domination of world history, since the Industrial Revolution, were an aberration. Figure 5.1 depicts why.

For the first 18 centuries of the Common Era, the two largest economies of the world were those of China and India.[5] This was a natural outcome of two key factors. First, the level of competence among the key civilizations in the world (including Western, Chinese, Indian, Islamic, Japanese, and others) was comparable. Second, China and India had larger populations and hence the largest economies. This historical balance between the West and other civilizations was disrupted when it bounded ahead after the Renaissance, the Enlightenment, and the Industrial Revolution. The West leapt far ahead of the rest of the world, with new leaps in science and technology and new forms of social organization, as well as advances in military technology and organization. Future historians will marvel how a small group of people, emanating from one small continent, Europe, managed to conquer and control the world for most of the nineteenth and twentieth centuries.

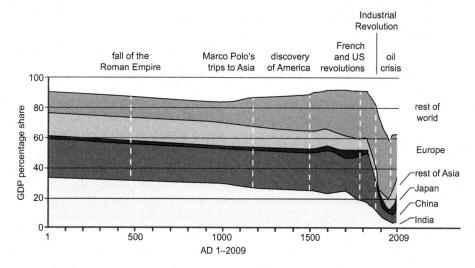

Figure 5.1 Share of total world GDP[4]

This achievement also reflected the relative underperformance of other civilizations. One statistic is worth citing. In 1820, China and India combined accounted for 50 percent of global GNP. By 1950, this figure had fallen to about 5 percent. For almost 50 percent of the world's population to account for such a small share of global GNP was disproportionate and exceptional. Curiously, it ended only because the West generously shared its learning with the world, from its knowledge of hard sciences to modern methods of social organization. For instance, during most of Chinese history, the country remained a deeply feudal society. Only the capabilities of a tiny elite were tapped and used. Through the vehicle of communist ideology, the essentially Western idea of the equal moral worth of every human being entered Chinese society. China's economic dynamism today is in large part a result of educating every citizen, including all its women and its vast population of poor peasants. Samuel Huntington was right when he emphasized, in his essay "The Clash of Civilizations," that communism is also a Western ideology.[6]

Equally importantly, when the West, led by the United States, welcomed China into the World Trade Organization (WTO), it provided a massive boost to the economic productivity of the Chinese population by exposing them to global economic competition. The iron law of comparative advantage worked well for China. Its economy became among the world's most competitive. By contrast, the West ignored another iron law: that new economic competition leads to "creative destruction" – as Joseph Schumpeter predicted.[7] Change was inevitable. When China suddenly injected over 800 million new workers into the global capitalist system in 2001, Western workers would lose their jobs.[8] A widely cited study by Daron Acemoglu and colleagues confirms this point. The study estimates between 2 and 2.4 million job losses in the United States from 1999 to 2011, largely because of competition from Chinese imports.[9] Clearly, Western governments should have helped their own workers adjust to this new competition by launching new training programs and investing in more vocational programs. In short, the West should have been alert to the new challenges.

Instead, Western governments were literally asleep at the wheel. Future historians will notice why. There was a coincidence of two major historical developments. First, the West enjoyed a great victory when the Berlin Wall collapsed in 1989, followed by the implosion of the Soviet Union in 1991. Great victories lead to arrogance and hubris, best captured in Francis Fukuyama's *The End of History*.[10] Even though his message was sophisticated, his Western audience only heard one theme. After the global triumph of Western democracies, the remaining 88 percent of the world's population would have to make painful adjustments to catch up with the West. Western societies could just proceed on autopilot since the West had arrived at "the end of history." The second major historical development was the contemporaneous decision of China and India to open up their economies and join the global economy. As a result, they grew dramatically. In 1980, in purchasing power parity (PPP) terms, China's economy was 10 percent of that of the United States. In 2014, it had become bigger than that of the United States. By 2016, China had overtaken the US economy in PPP terms, and by 2019, World Bank estimates suggested China's economy had eclipsed the US economy by $24 to $21 trillion.[11] Future historians will see what contemporary historians have failed to highlight for Western populations: the West chose to go to sleep at the moment when China and India decided to wake up. In an even crueler historical irony, while the West was enjoying its "end of history," it was blind to the fact that the 1990s actually represented a "return of history." China and India and the rest of Asia were waking up and resuming their normal places in the global hierarchy.

It is not too late for the West to wake up to the resurgence of Asia. Even though the Western share of the global GNP has shrunk as the share of the rest has grown, Western societies still benefit from much higher per-capita incomes than most of their Asian counterparts. They still have the world's best universities, lead the world in research and development (R&D), and enjoy strong institutions. They are still strong societies. Yet, it is also true that they face massive internal challenges. The outbreak of COVID-19 revealed critical weaknesses in leading Western countries, especially in Europe and the United States. In theory, the more advanced Western countries should have performed better in managing the pandemic than East Asian countries. In practice, they performed much worse.[12] In the leading Western countries, the deaths per million from COVID-19 in November 2020 were in the hundreds: United States, 795; United Kingdom, 844; Belgium, 1,400; Spain, 935; Italy, 863. By contrast in East Asia, deaths per million were below 15: Vietnam, 0.4; Japan, 16; China, 3; South Korea, 10; and Singapore, 5.[13] This glaring difference in performance should have stirred a debate in the West about what went wrong. One obvious question its leaders could have and should have asked was: what can the West learn from East Asia? Yet this question was rarely posed. As *Financial Times* columnist Gillian Tett observed, both the United States and the United Kingdom suffered from another virus, "excessive self-confidence."[14]

COVID-19 was sending at least one clear message to the West: the region that had once generously shared its knowledge with East Asia should start considering the possibility that it could now also start learning lessons from East Asia. Instead of a one-way street, history had turned a corner and a two-way street of learning should begin. Similarly, poor US performance also revealed deep structural internal challenges in its society – the effective transformation of US society away from having a government "of the people, by the people, for the people" to a government "of the 1%, by the 1%, for the 1%,"[15] according to such leading observers as Paul Volcker, Joseph Stiglitz, and Martin Wolf.[16] This plutocracy resulted in weakening government institutions. After Ronald Reagan famously said, "Government is not the solution to our problem, government is the problem," there has been a progressive delegitimization, defunding, and demoralization of key US institutions like the Food and Drug Administration (FDA) and the Centers for Disease Control·and Prevention (CDC) – part of the explanation for the poor response of the United States to COVID-19. Trump's ignorance of science aggravated the situation. By contrast, the one thing in common among all East Asian societies, including the communist ones like China and Vietnam and the non-communist ones like Japan and South Korea, is the realization that for societies to progress, they need both the "invisible hand" of free markets and the "visible hand" of good governance. "Governance" is a widely used term. Yet it is little understood. Most of the definitions are academic or abstract. I prefer to use a lay definition of governance. A society enjoys good governance when it improves the well-being of its people, especially the bottom 50 percent. Vice versa, a society enjoys bad governance when the livelihood of its people, especially the bottom 50 percent, deteriorates. Over the past 40 years, the well-being of the bottom half has dramatically improved in China, even as it has drastically deteriorated in the United States. Indeed, the past 40 years have been the best 40 years in 4,000 years of Chinese history for the bottom 50 percent in China.

It is therefore truly striking that even as we enter the third decade of the twenty-first century, as we return to something like a historical balance in the relative performance of Western and non-Western civilizations, it remains inconceivable to many in the West that they could learn lessons from East Asia. Similarly, it would still be politically suicidal for any Western leader to stand up and tell their people that they should visit and learn from East Asia. In general, the West has made precious little effort to learn from the Asian experience. This inability to learn valid lessons confirms the sense of superiority that many in the West feel toward the rest of the world.

Controlling multilateral leadership

This sense of superiority is also a factor in the second strategic mistake made by the West: a refusal to consider relinquishing privileged positions in key organization of global governance, especially in the Security Council, IMF, and World Bank. Such a change is required in order to reflect better the views and economic power of the rest of the world. The inevitable net result is a weakening of legitimacy and credibility of these key institutions. It is therefore unsurprising that other institutions are surfacing to challenge, say, the IMF and World Bank – including the New Development Bank (NDB), set up by the BRICS countries (Brazil, Russia, India, China, and South Africa), and the Asian Infrastructure Investment Bank (AIIB), launched by China with the participation of 102 countries. Coupled with the strategic mistake of clinging to past privileges, the West has also unwisely decided to weaken the family of UN organizations by reducing the portion of mandatory funding available to key UN institutions.[17] In the World Health Organization (WHO), for example, the portion of mandatory funding has gone down from 62 percent in 1970–1971 to less than 20 percent today.[18] By making such key organizations as the WHO and the International Atomic Energy Agency (IAEA) dependent on "voluntary" funding from Western governments and agencies, the West tried to ensure that they would remain pliant to Western pressure. Hence, even though the directions of the WHO should have been decided by the WHO Geneva Assembly on the basis of the "democratic" principle of one country and one vote, they have been effectively decided by the key funders – Western donor countries.

Anyone who doubts that Western countries have influenced the direction of UN agencies by controlling their funding should carefully read Kelley Lee's book on the WHO.[19] Indeed, the practical influence of the West on the WHO has been overwhelming. Nonetheless, the Trump administration announced in May 2020 its intention to withdraw from the WHO because "China has total control over the World Health Organization, despite only paying $40 million per year compared to what the United States has been paying, which is approximately $450 million a year."[20] Trump's claim brought out well the tension between the US and EU member states about Western policies toward the UN, tensions that also arose when the US withdrew from other UN organizations like the United Nations Educational, Scientific and Cultural Organization (UNESCO). On the one hand, the EU member states, despite deferring in general to US political leadership, do not join the US in withdrawing from UN organizations. On the other hand, EU member states, even though they know better, do not stand and oppose even absurd claims like Trump's. Nor did EU members argue categorically that it was irresponsible for Washington to leave and weaken the WHO when 7.7 billion people, especially the poor, were struggling to fight COVID-19. Richard Horton, the editor of the *Lancet*, stated the obvious: "President Trump's decision to harm an agency whose sole purpose is to protect the health and wellbeing of the world's peoples is a crime against humanity. It is a knowing and inhumane attack against the global civilian population."[21] While hardly unique in light of numerous previous US withdrawals from UN bodies, this decision to withdraw and freeze budgetary commitments was nonetheless particularly egregious in the midst of a pandemic.

It is undeniable that the EU member states have been cowardly in not opposing more openly the ill-advised policies of the current US administration toward the UN family of organizations. Such cowardice also goes against the long-term interests of the West, especially EU members, as the wealthiest countries have the most to lose from a breakdown in global governance institutions. The fates of the affluent 12 percent of the population who live in Western societies are now directly intertwined with those of the remaining 88 percent who live in the rest of the world. A simple boat metaphor helps explain how deeply intertwined our fates have become. In the past, when 7.7 billion people lived in 193 separate countries, it was like living in 193 separate boats, with captains and crews to manage each vessel and rules to make sure that the boats did not collide. Today, as a result of the dramatically shrunken world, the 7.7 billion people now live in 193 separate cabins on the same boat. The main structural problem with this global boat is that we still employ captains and crews (or, as we call them, governments) to manage each cabin. There is no overarching authority to steer the global boat.

Anyone who doubts the validity of the boat metaphor should ask a simple question: how did COVID-19 originate from a city in China and travel to every corner of the globe within months? Does this not confirm that we are traveling on the same boat? In fact, before COVID-19, the climate change challenge should have already taught humanity the same lesson. Indeed, if climate change accelerates and we jeopardize our only inhabitable planet, humanity as a whole will suffer. If global policy-making was dominated by rational Western minds, from leading Western universities, they would come up with a clear and logical response. Since humanity as a whole has to come together to address climate change and COVID-19, we should work together to strengthen institutions of global governance, especially of the UN family.

The West has been doing the exact opposite. It has been weakening global institutions by depriving them of predictable and reliable long-term funding from mandatory contributions. The data about the IAEA are perhaps even more shocking. Western governments are very anxious about the dangers of nuclear proliferation. Despite this, they have steadily weakened the IAEA. As an official IAEA communication puts it: "the Agency has been experiencing limited growth in its Regular Budget, and in 2019 the Regular Budget is seeing a decrease in real terms," and there has been "zero real growth" in the 2021 regular budget over the 2020 regular budget.[22]

Even more disturbing than the progressive diminution of mandatory funding is the West's denial that it has been progressively weakening the UN family of institutions. In theory, since the West has the world's freest media and most independent universities, this blatant falsehood should have been exposed. Sadly, this has not happened. Consequently, the most thoughtful and well-informed members of Western elites believe that the West has been the main defender of the UN family. Yet the representatives of the United States, the United Kingdom, and Europe have progressively undermined the financial and normative foundations of these institutions.

In theory, the West has been strongly supporting global governance institutions, like the IMF and World Bank, which are de facto, although not de jure, outside the UN family. The West is happy to do so since it controls them. Since their founding, the West has insisted on the (informal) rule that the head of the IMF should be a European and the head of the World Bank should be an American. Even though Asians make up almost 60 percent of the world's population and now provide the fastest growing economies of the world, no Asian is allowed to run the world's two most powerful economic and financial organizations. To preserve their continued control, Western countries have been fighting hard to reduce any dilution of their voting shares.[23]

Similarly, the West has effectively maintained control of an even more powerful organizations – the UN Security Council – by holding 60 percent of the five permanent seats. To be fair, although in theory all permanent five members of the UN Security Council (P5) favor reforming and expanding the council, in practice they do not. Russia and China are as resistant to reform the Security Council as the Western P3 (Permanent Members of the UNSC: France, United Kingdom, United States).[24] Zalmay Khalilzad also confirmed the US reluctance to reform the council in a cable made public by WikiLeaks:

> We believe expansion of the Council, along the lines of the models currently discussed, will dilute U.S. influence in the body . . . We should base our approach to Council expansion along the following lines in order to prevent significant erosion of our current level of influence: smallest possible expansion . . . no extension of veto . . . maintaining our arithmetic advantage in UNSC voting . . . ensuring predictability in the selection of new members.[25]

The immediate concerns of self-interest are coming at the expense of undermining multilateralism, which, paradoxically, is bad for US national interests in the long run.

The P5 can block Security Council reform by vetoing any proposals to change its composition. Many have called to eliminate the veto, but it entrenches the great powers in the UN system. Indeed, this is the primary reason why the United States has not withdrawn from the world organization, even though it never joined the League of Nations. While the framers of the UN Charter were wise to give the great powers of 1945 the veto, they were not wise in failing to create mechanisms to ensure that the Security Council would have the great powers of today and tomorrow, not of yesterday.

In theory, the "permanent" members of the Security Council could remain "permanently" there. Yet the P5 face a strategic dilemma: should they preserve the council's current composition or credibility? At some point in time, when either a new great power, like India, or a continent, like Africa, feels their views are not adequately represented, they could refuse to abide by the Security Council's decisions. Something like this happened when the Organization of African Unity (now the African Union) refused to suspend flights to Libya in the early 1990s.[26] To preserve its credibility and authority, the Security Council should be expanded with a new 7–7–7 formula: seven permanent members, seven semi-permanent members, and seven elected members. The new seven permanent members would include India, Brazil, and an African state (selected by Africa).[27]

Having said this, such reform is unlikely to happen. Both a deadlock among aspiring member states and a strong agreement by the P5 to prevent change will result in the status quo. Progressively, the Security Council thus will lose its credibility. As Martin Wolf said in 2009, "Within a decade a world in which the UK is on the United Nations Security Council and India is not will seem beyond laughable."[28] A decade later, his observation seems even more prescient.

Increasing unilateralism

In theory, the West, and especially the United States, should not feel threatened if the Security Council and the UN system are weakened. Washington has long believed, probably since the days of President Ronald Reagan, that a weakened UN serves US interests. Indeed, a former director of national intelligence privately told me, "I can understand why small states, like Singapore, prefer stronger multilateral institutions as they enhance the power of small states. However, these multilateral institutions are a constraint on a great power like US." His honesty was commendable. Equally, he revealed a great truth: stronger multilateral institutions constrain great powers.

All this leads to the great strategic mistake by the West. In its response to the challenge posed by the emergence of China as a rival power, the United States has become more and more unilateral, culminating in the Trump administration. It has continued its trend of staying or walking away from major multilateral agreements (like the UN Convention on the Law of the Sea, UNCLOS, and the Anti-Ballistic Missile Treaty, ABM). It has also withdrawn from such UN organizations as UNESCO, the United Nations Relief and Rehabilitation Agency (UNRRA), and the United Nations Population Fund (UNFPA), as well as the Iran Deal and Paris Agreement. When John Bolton was the national security advisor, he openly said that the United States would be better off with a weakened UN. He spoke dismissively of the UN:

> There is no United Nations. There is an international community that occasionally can be led by the only real power left in the world, and that's the United States, when it suits our interests and when we can get others to go along.[29]

Earlier he said mockingly: "The Secretariat building [UN Headquarters] in New York has 38 stories; if you lost 10 stories today, it wouldn't make a bit of difference."[30] While only John Bolton may express such sentiments as baldly and openly, it is undeniable that key personnel in US agencies, including the State Department, the Central Intelligence Agency, the Pentagon, and the National Security Agency, believe that long-term US natural interests are best served by weaker multilateral institutions.

Fortunately, one wiser US leader, former president Bill Clinton, questioned this strong consensus among key government agencies that weaker multilateralism was in long-term American interests when he said that this would be true if the United States could be number one forever. However, in a world where it was "no longer the military, political, economic superpower in the world," he argued that the United States "should be trying to create a world with rules and partnerships and habits of behavior."[31] In short, what Clinton was implying was that the best way for the United States to constrain the next number one power, China, would be to strengthen multilateralism. John Ikenberry has made a similar point:

> Washington is settling in for a protracted struggle for dominance with China, Russia, and other rival powers. This fractured world, the thinking goes, will offer little space for multilateralism and cooperation. Instead, U.S. grand strategy will be defined by what international relations theorists call "the problems of anarchy": hegemonic struggles, power transitions, competition for security, spheres of influence, and reactionary nationalism. But this future is not inevitable, and it is certainly not desirable. The United States may no longer be the world's sole superpower, but its influence has never been premised on power alone. It also depends on an ability to offer others a set of ideas and institutional frameworks for mutual gain. If the United States abandons that role prematurely, it will be smaller and weaker as a result.[32]

Today's strangest reality thus concerns relations between the West and the Rest. In theory, Western states should be building on the great tradition of making policies through objective scientific evidence and sound analytical reasoning. If so, the logical conclusion would be that in a global environment where the West will progressively lose power, their collective interests, including those of the United States, should be to strengthen multilateralism. A logical corollary is that it should be in China's interests to undermine multilateralism so that it will be less constrained when it becomes number one. Ironically, the West, most especially Washington, is weakening multilateralism while China is strengthening it. Here, a distinction is to be made between internal and international behavior. For instance, President Ronald Reagan may have been considered democratic within the United States, but he violated international norms freely. Likewise, we should make a distinction between China's external and internal behavior. If viewed from the prism of human rights, China's way of dealing with the insurgency in Xinjiang, while certainly not to be emulated, is comparatively milder than the actions of the United States and its allies in the Middle East, which have resulted in the deaths of hundreds of thousands.

The West has traditionally been shrewd in assessing where its long-term interests lie. This explains why Western civilization has been exceptionally successful over the past few centuries. Beginning with the Renaissance in the fifteenth and sixteenth centuries, Europe was successful. By the nineteenth century, Europe overtook China and India. Starting especially from the late-nineteenth century onward, the baton was passed to the United States, but the United States and Europe were part of Western civilization. Now the West is losing its ability to look ahead. One example is the alarm that four UN organizations are currently being headed by Chinese nationals – namely the Food and Agriculture Organization (FAO), the International Telecommunication Union (ITU), the United Nations Industrial Development Organization (UNIDO), and the International Civil Aviation Organization (ICAO). Hence, when China put up a candidate to run the World Intellectual Property Organization (WIPO) in 2020, the West put up a fierce campaign, which helped the qualified Singaporean candidate to win.

Was it in the logical self-interest of the West to block China? In theory, the West could answer yes because it was preventing Chinese "Trojan horses" from being smuggled into UN bodies. Yet the correct answer is no because by blocking Chinese nationals from running UN organizations, the West is preventing the smuggling of UN "Trojan horses" into the Chinese body politic. To use WIPO as an example, if a Chinese national had become its head, China would have been under far greater pressure to increase the protection of intellectual property (IP) in China. If the Chinese government protected IP more in China, the biggest beneficiaries would be US corporations that have complained for year about IP theft there. In short, the West could be seen as acting against its own interests in blocking Chinese leadership of UN organizations.

The West is also unaware that China remains committed to strengthening the UN system. This is reflected in the two speeches given by President Xi Jinping in Davos and Geneva in January 2017.[33] Yet, more importantly, it is reflected in Chinese popular culture. Anyone who doubts so should watch two wildly successful movies in China: *Wolf Warrior 2* and *Operation Red Sea*.[34] It would be unimaginable for Hollywood to produce movies where superheroes (like Iron Man and Wonder Woman) are prevented from taking action against evil forces until approval is obtained from the Security Council. Technically, this is the correct position under international law since the use of force is only allowed if it is either in self-defense or authorized by the Security Council. In both movies, the Chinese forces do not act until the Security Council approves. If Hollywood injected this same element into any movies, Western audiences would be baffled at this strange self-restraint on unilateral decision-making and action.

In the military sphere, there is another even more bizarre example of Western, especially US, irrational action. The biggest threat humanity faces is the annihilation of the species through nuclear war. Hence, it is commonsensical to try and reduce the total number of nuclear weapons, as Washington and Moscow wisely tried to do immediately after the Cold War's end. Today, a major geopolitical contest has broken out between two major nuclear powers, the United States and China. The most unwise US tactic is to stoke a nuclear arms race with China. Indeed, it would be absolutely irrational since the United States possesses 6,000 nuclear weapons and China only 300. It would be shrewd and cunning for Washington to preserve this massive advantage. Instead, in an act that future historians will describe as evidence of myopic stupidity, the Trump administration tried to foster a nuclear arms race. Former director of national intelligence Michael Hayden has described these moves as "insane."[35] Global Zero, the nuclear disarmament group, agreed:

> Three years after entering office, the Trump administration lacks a coherent set of goals, a strategy to achieve them, or the personnel or effective policy process to address the most complex set of nuclear risks in US history. . . . Put simply, the current US administration is blundering toward nuclear chaos with potentially disastrous consequences.[36]

Conclusion

This chapter's main takeaways can be summarized in three simple propositions. First, in the twenty-first century, we will undoubtedly see an end to the anomalous preceding two centuries of Western domination of world history. Second, as Western power recedes, it will be in Western interests to strengthen multilateral norms and institutions. Third, it is irrational and unwise for the West to maintain its policies of either dominating or weakening key multilateral institutions.

Is there a wiser route for the West? Yes. The good news is that the West can return to its basic principles. The most fundamental principle of Western political philosophy is that every human being has the same moral worth – in fact, democracy rests on this principle. Hence, a key Western belief is that domestic governance institutions must reflect the values of the entire population, not a select minority. This was the key reason the West abandoned feudalism for democratic governing frameworks. However, in intergovernmental institutions of global governance, the West is essentially insisting on retaining feudal frameworks. In its actual behavior vis-à-vis key institutions, it insists that the voices of only 12 percent of the world's population should be given greater weight than those of almost 90 percent who make up the rest. This is undemocratic, unethical, and, most importantly, a prescription for a troubled twenty-first century.

Would the West suffer, for example, if it allowed a Chinese national (like the former Chinese finance minister, Lou Jiwei), instead of a European, to run the IMF and if it allowed an Indian national (like the former governor of the Indian Central Bank, Raghuram Rajan), instead of a US citizen, to run the World Bank? Neither the Chinese national nor the Indian national would apply Chinese or Indian economics to run these institutions. Instead, they would apply basic Western economics. This is a key point that Larry Summers, the former president of Harvard University, and I emphasized in "The Fusion of Civilizations:"

The march of reason, triggered in the West by the Enlightenment, is spreading globally, leading to the emergence of pragmatic problem-solving cultures in every region and making it possible to envisage the emergence of a stable and sustainable rules-based order. There is every reason to believe, moreover, that the next few decades can be even better for humanity than the last few – so long as the West does not lose confidence in its core values and retreat from global engagement. The greatest danger of the current pessimism, therefore, is that it might become a self- fulfilling prophecy, leading to fear and withdrawal rather than attempts to reinvigorate the existing global system.[37]

The West should therefore build on its triumph of spreading Western reasoning to the world by allowing the views and voices of the Global South, who now share many key principles with the West on how to manage and govern international organization, to be heard and to guide key intergovernmental organizations that provide the foundation for global governance. Curiously, to allow these organization to thrive, the United States should apply a principle it has implemented domestically. One key reason it has created such world-beating institutions as Google and Microsoft is that it has allowed the best talent, no matter where they are born, to run them. Hence, the fact that the heads of both Google (Sunder Pichai) and Microsoft (Nadella Satya) were born in India is not held against them. Similar talent can also be found elsewhere in Asia, Africa, the Middle East, and Latin America. They, too, will apply key Western principles of good governance, including universal representation and meritorious selection of staff.

Similarly, the P5 should switch from picking the least offensive candidate (who will not upset them) to the most effective candidate (like the CEOs of Google and Microsoft) to become the UN secretary-general. Learning from its own history with the world organization, the West should not hesitate to select someone of the caliber and integrity of a Dag Hammarskjold, rather than Kurt Waldheim.

The two most pressing global challenges on the agenda for the UN's 75th anniversary were the COVID-19 pandemic and climate change. Both are sending a clear message. We have to come together as one human species to manage these challenges and save our imperiled planet. The most expeditious path is to work through existing institutions of global governance. The 1945 rules-based order was a generous gift from the West to the Rest. If we began anew today, we could not possibly succeed in building better institutional frameworks. This is the ultimate irony the West faces as it looks pessimistically at the twenty-first century. The best way for the West to reverse course and enjoy a better future is to strengthen, rather than undermine, the Western-inspired family of institutions that it created after World War II. And it would be wise to reverse course now, before the Rest decide to walk away from them.

Having dealt with Western policymakers for almost five decades, I know it will not be easy to persuade them to reverse course. Some policies become deeply entrenched.

Changing them can be as difficult as moving mountains, even though simple common sense would dictate that these deeply entrenched policies should change. A simple example can illustrate this point.

Since the Reagan presidency, the United States has consistently tried to reduce its dues to the United Nations. It has also held back payments. Indeed, the Democratic presidency of Bill Clinton, under the able leadership of Ambassador Richard Holbrooke, launched the fiercest campaign to reduce US dues to the UN from 25 to 22 percent, even though Washington – had it been assessed according to the same formula as other member states – should have been paying 27 or 28 percent. The bargain that Holbrooke offered was that the United States would pay its arrears. Holbrooke succeeded, US dues went down, and US arrears were paid. Sadly, this grand promise not to accumulate arrears was broken by subsequent administrations.

Since I was the Singapore ambassador to the UN, I remember well the massive global effort the US undertook to achieve these goals. And how much did Washington save by reducing its annual dues? It saved an average of US$69.6 million a year.[38] What a pittance this sum represents is illustrated by the following figures: cost of an aircraft carrier, $13 billion (USS *Gerald R. Ford*); cost of an F-35 fighter, $200 million (export price of Lockheed Martin F-35I); and cost of New York City's Fire Department, $2.09 billion (for 2020). The trivial savings potentially undermine a powerful family of UN institutions that are either creating or preserving norms that help create a more stable world order. Indeed, as Bill Clinton hinted in his aforementioned remarks, they could help constrain the next number one power, namely China.

As we move decisively away from the unipolar world that emerged at the end of the Cold War toward a multipolar world, it would serve longer-term US and Western interests to strengthen, not weaken, the UN family. As the editors write in their introduction, "The complexities of the post-Cold War era are concrete expressions of global governance, but formations of global governance have been and will be different in other epochs; they are driven by ideas, interests, and forces that vary and evolve."

The "ideas, interests and forces" of the current decade and beyond dictate that Washington should pay more, rather than less, of UN budgets. Indeed, the single most dramatic step the Biden administration could take is to reimburse the arrears that rose sharply in the Trump administration. How much would it cost? The answer is about $900 million (mostly accrued between 2017 and 2020).[39]

Why would such a payment be important? At the end of the day, we need to have a small litmus test to ascertain whether US and EU policymakers understand that their interests are best served by strengthening, not weakening, the UN-based multilateral system. A simple payment of illegally held-back payments to the UN would send a powerful signal that the West has changed course. To quote the astronaut Neil Armstrong, "That's one small step for man, one giant leap for mankind." A small symbolic step would signify that the West has launched a new global governance era.

Suggested reading

Wang Gungwu, *The Eurasian Core and Its Edges: Dialogues with Wang Gungwu on the History of the World* (Cambridge: Cambridge University Press, 2015).
John Ikenberry, "The Next Liberal Order," *Foreign Affairs* 99, no. 4 (2020): 133–142.
Kelley Lee, *The World Health Organization (WHO)* (London: Routledge, 2008).
Angus Maddison, *Chinese Economic Performance in the Long Run*, 2nd ed. (Paris: OECD Press, 2007).
Kishore Mahbubani, *The Great Convergence: China, Europe and the Making of the Modern World Economy* (New York: Public Affairs, 2013).
Kishore Mahbubani and Lawrence H. Summers, "The Fusion of Civilizations: The Case for Global Optimism," *Foreign Affairs* 95, no. 3 (2016): 126–135.
Steven Pinker, *Enlightenment Now: The Case for Reason, Science, Humanism, and Progress* (London: Penguin, 2018).
Shashi Tharoor, *Inglorious Empire: What the British Did to India* (London: Hurst, 2017).

Notes

1 Steven Pinker, *Enlightenment Now: The Case for Reason, Science, Humanism, and Progress* (London: Penguin, 2018).
2 John Gramlich, "Looking Ahead to 2050, Americans Are Pessimistic About Many Aspects of Life in U.S.," *Pew Research Center*, 21 March 2019, www.pewresearch.org/fact-tank/2019/03/21/looking-ahead-to-2050-americans-are-pessimistic-about-many-aspects-of-life-in-u-s/; Jim Norman, "Americans Becoming More Pessimistic About the Economy," *Gallup*, 22 January 2019, https://news.gallup.com/poll/246179/americans-becoming-pessimistic-economy.aspx; Lisa Lerer and Dave Umhoefer, "On the Future, Americans Can Agree: It Doesn't Look Good," *New York Times*, 12 June 2020; and Ronald Brownstein, "America's Growing Pessimism," *The Atlantic*, 10 October 2015, www.theatlantic.com/politics/archive/2015/10/americans-pessimism-future/409564/
3 Kishore Mahbubani and Lawrence H. Summers, "The Fusion of Civilizations: The Case for Global Optimism," *Foreign Affairs* 95, no. 3 (2016): 126–135.
4 Kishore Mahbubani, *Has the West Lost It? A Provocation* (London: Penguin UK, 2018), 5.
5 Angus Maddison, *The World Economy, Volume 1: A Millennial Perspective, Volume 2: Historical Statistics* (Paris: OECD, Academic Foundation, 2007).
6 Samuel P. Huntington, "The Clash of Civilizations?" *Foreign Affairs* 72, no. 3 (1993): 22–49.
7 Joseph Schumpeter, *Socialism, Capitalism and Democracy* (New York: Harper and Brothers, 1942).
8 Robert E. Scott and Zane Mokhiber, *The China Toll Deepens* (Washington, DC: Economic Policy Institute, 2018), https://epi. org/156645.
9 Daron Acemoglu, David Autor, David Dorn, Gordon H. Hanson, and Brendan Price, "Import Competition and the Great US Employment Saga of the 2000s," *Journal of Labor Economics* 34, no. S1 (2016): S141-S198.
10 Francis Fukuyama, "The End of History?" *The National Interest* 16 (Summer 1989): 3–18.
11 The World Bank, "Databank," https://data.worldbank.org/.
12 Kishore Mahbubani, "Kishore Mahbubani on the Dawn of the Asian Century," *The Economist*, 20 April 2020.

13 Statista, "Coronavirus (COVID-19) Deaths Worldwide Per One Million Population as of November 26, 2020, by Country," www.statista.com/statistics/1104709/
coronavirus-deaths-worldwide-per-million-inhabitants/.

14 Gillian Tett, "The Trouble with Self-confidence," *Financial Times*, 9 July 2011, www.
ft.com/content/2c00b91e-a849-11e0-9f50-00144feabdc0.

15 Joseph Stiglitz, "Of the 1%, by the 1%, for the 1%," *Vanity Fair*, May 2011, https://www.
vanityfair.com/news/2011/05/top-one-percent-201105.

16 The author documents how the United States has become a plutocracy in Kishore Mahbubani, *Has China Won? The Chinese Challenge to American Primacy* (New York: Public
Affairs, 2020), chapter 7.

17 UN Multi-Partner Trust Fund Office and Dag Hammarskjöld Foundation, *Financing the
UN Development System: Time for Hard Choices* (Uppsala, Sweden: DH, 2019).

18 Kishore Mahbubani, *The Great Convergence: China, Europe and the Making of the
Modern World Economy* (New York: Public Affairs, 2013), 97–103.

19 Kelley Lee, *The World Health Organization (WHO)* (London: Routledge, 2014).

20 Donald Trump, "Remarks by President Trump on Actions Against China," 29 May 2020,
www.whitehouse.gov/briefings-statements/remarks-president-trump-actions-china/.

21 Richard Horton, "Offline: Why President Trump Is Wrong About WHO," *The Lancet* 395,
no. 10233 (2020): 1330.

22 IAEA, "The Agency's Programme and Budget 2020–2021," July 2019, www.iaea.org/
sites/default/files/gc/gc63-2.pdf.

23 "US Blocks IMF Voting Rights Distribution," *Bretton Woods Project*, 12 December 2019, www.
brettonwoodsproject.org/2019/12/imf-voting-rights-redistribution-blocked-by-the-us/.

24 See Sebastian von Einsedel, David Malone, and Bruno Stagno, eds., *The United Nations
Security Council: From Cold War to the 21st Century* (Boulder, CO: Lynne Rienner, 2016).

25 See Sebastian von Einsedel, David Malone, and Bruno Stagno, eds., *The United Nations
Security Council: From Cold War to the 21st Century* (Boulder, CO: Lynne Rienner, 2016).

26 Jaleh Dashti-Gibson and Richard W. Conroy, "Taming Terrorism: Sanctions Against Libya,
Sudan, and Afghanistan," in *The Sanctions Decade: Assessing UN Strategies in the 1990s*,
eds. David Cortright and George A. Lopez (Boulder, CO: Lynne Rienner, 2000), 107–108.

27 Mahbubani, *The Great Convergence*, 239–246.

28 Martin Wolf, "What India Must Do If It Is to Be an Affluent Country," *Financial Times*,
8 July 2009.

29 Tim Reid, "There Is No Such Thing as the United Nations," *The Times*, 2 August 2005.

30 Matthew Haag, "3 Examples of John Bolton's Longtime Hard-Line Views," *New York
Times*, 22 March 2018.

31 Mahbubani, *The Great Convergence*, 8.

32 John Ikenberry, "The Next Liberal Order," *Foreign Affairs* 99, no. 4 (2020): 133–142.

33 Xi Jinping, "Jointly Shoulder Responsibility of Our Times, Promote Global Growth,"
17 January 2017, www.china.org.cn/node_7247529/content_40569136.htm; and "Work
Together to Build a Community of Shared Future for Mankind," 18 January 2017, http://
iq.chineseembassy.org/eng/zygx/t1432869.htm.

34 *Wolf Warrior 2* is a story of a Chinese special-ops team that foils the plot of mercenaries
to overthrow the government of an unnamed African state. The film shows the Chinese
team cooperating with UN forces. An article in *Foreign Policy* (1 September 2017, https://
foreignpolicy.com/2017/09/01/china-finally-has-its-own-rambo/) states, "Yet unlike the
gun-toting cowboy tendencies of America, the film's Chinese superpower respects the
United Nations. Its navy abides by international law and will not act until receiving U.N.
Security Council authorization. It's an overt reminder that China simply wants to be your
friendly neighborhood P5 member with nuclear weapons." In the final scenes, rescued
victims are taken to the UN camps for safety. *Operation Red Sea* is a story of Chinese
naval forces foiling the plot of terrorist and rebel groups that threaten to destabilize the
(fictional) nation-state of Yewaire in the Arabian Peninsula.

35 Justin Key Canfil, "Trump's Nuclear Test Would Risk Everything to Gain Nothing," *War on the Rocks*, 8 July 2020, https://warontherocks.com/2020/07/trumps-nuclear-test-would-risk-everything-to-gain-nothing/

36 Jon Wolfsthal, ed., "The Trump Administration After Three Years: Blundering Toward Nuclear Chaos," *Global Zero*, May 2020, www.globalzero.org/wp-content/uploads/2020/05/Blundering-Toward-Nuclear-Chaos-ANPI-Report-May-2020.pdf

37 Mahbubani and Summers, "The Fusion of Civilizations."

38 UN, *Regular Budget and Working Capital Fund: Assessments*, www.un.org/en/ga/contributions/budget.shtml (averaged from 2001 to 2019).

39 Congressional Research Service, "United Nations Issues: U.S. Funding of U.N. Peacekeeping," 2 November 2020, https://fas.org/sgp/crs/row/IF10597.pdf.

CONTENTS

Regions and regionalism

Confronting new forms of connectedness

Rosemary Foot

Regional cooperation, in its various forms, has long been seen as important in the search for the most productive forms of global governance. Regional groupings, for example, have been perceived as one response to the lack of democracy, representation, and political legitimacy that many see as infecting those formal expressions of global governance – largely international organizations – that have been in place since 1945. Regional organizations have also been seen as carriers of ideas that derive from these formal expressions or as active generators of their own ideas and practices that contest or improve those on offer at the global level. As Frederik Söderbaum confidently writes, while many scholars point to the "porous and pluralistic nature of contemporary regionalism," in his view, "it can safely be said that regions are here to stay."[1] Louise Fawcett agrees, pointing to the "enduring relevance of regionalism in world politics" and the vast numbers that are in place working on an ever more extensive range of activities.[2]

Skeptics have long existed, of course, but new voices have joined the initial doubters and question the relevance of regions as governance mechanisms in today's globalized world. For some, the contemporary era is characterized by numerous other, more significant, kinds of connectedness; yet,

DOI: 10.4324/9781003139836-7

for others, global society is marked by various forms of disconnectedness, aided by the broader assault on multilateralism that has become more prevalent in the second decade of the twenty-first century.

The debate between skeptics and supporters of regionalism is explored in this chapter in the context of developments that I identify as posing the most significant challenge to the regional level and its continuing role in global governance. The chapter begins by defining the topic at hand. It then provides a brief assessment of why regional groupings have become so prominent over the last three decades. Thereafter, it looks at four main features of the current world order that threaten the notion of regions remaining a core component of global governance in the short and medium terms.

The future of regionalism, the argument concludes, is insecure but not fatally so. The new forms of connectivity that have developed, some with China at their core, have often sparked the onset of new regional imaginaries. In addition, old regional forms still form a major port of call at times of crisis or uncertainty. Despite potent challenges to governance at the regional level, regional groupings will persist into the future, and regions and regionalism will remain important analytical categories in the study of global governance. This is not to deny, however, that we are in a period of significant transition involving the diffusion of power and ideas, the outcomes of which are indeterminate. New forms of connectivity might strengthen at the expense of regionalism in ways as yet unanticipated. Were this to happen, a contest between governance mechanisms would ensue. Regions will still exist as an organizational form and vision well into the future, but no longer as a core teleological endpoint of a governance process.

Defining the terms and assessing the role

For many years, Joseph Nye's definition of regions and regionalism, emphasizing geographical proximity and mutual interdependence, influenced the way that analysts approached the topic.[3] However, the uncovering of processes associated with these terms moved the analysis beyond Nye's succinct definition, highlighted that there is no precise endpoint implied in a variety of regional approaches, and questioned the emphasis on regional integration – and therefore Eurocentrism – as the underlying rationale for regionalist endeavors. The regional governance project embodies various forms, including *regionalization* – that is, the informal often undirected process of social and economic interaction; *regional awareness* where connection is reliant on mental maps or an "imagined community"; *interstate cooperation* arising from the need to find solutions to problems that occur in a range of issue areas; *state-led integration*, which requires states formally to commit to the reduction or removal of barriers to various forms of exchange; and *regional consolidation*, which likely embraces the pooling of sovereignty in a political arrangement that downgrades the place of the individual nation-state in political decision-making.[4] What this implies is great diversity in the forms of activity that we label regionalism in global politics.

Attentiveness to these different forms of necessity expands the landscape of analytical attention.

Beyond more abstract definitional issues, actually broadening the empirical focus to include consideration of the Global South or the "emerging powers" has also energized scholarship on this topic. It has added significantly to the range of geographical sites that are deemed worthy in the study of regions and regionalism. The global diffusion of power and related reduction in US hegemony, together with the consolidation of former colonized states, have provided space to consider and implement alternative governance ideas in normative, economic, and security areas. Such a change in focus has prompted awareness of the possibility of diverse and distinctive regional experiences and new ways of thinking about the regional level.

In the political realm, for example, what is termed "new regionalism" has pointed to the ways regionalism can be conceptualized as a means of consolidating the state: as a path to enhance individual state sovereignty rather than restraining or pooling it, and even for using a regional grouping as a tool to shield member states against external criticism.[5] Work on the Association of Southeast Asian Nations (ASEAN) and ASEAN-related organizations has been particularly important in this regard.[6] In this instance, the argument has been that building state resilience not only has major benefits for regime security but is also a major contributor to regional resilience. It may eventually lead to the development of a set of norms (the "ASEAN way," for example) that could contribute to the building of a regional identity. What is important here, however, is that the national level is recognized as the major driving force behind any regionalist endeavor.

A focus on economic aspects underpins an argument that the regional level of governance might better facilitate cooperation, as well as solve economic problems associated with the uneven consequences of globalization. Doubts about the effectiveness of the World Trade Organization (WTO) and the difficulties of reforming its practices, for example, have promoted the growth in regional or subregional trading arrangements. Thus, the twenty-first century has witnessed the signature of such agreements as the 15-member-state Regional Comprehensive Economic Partnership (RCEP) in Asia, as well as Africa's Intergovernmental Authority for Development (IGAD) and the Southern Africa Development Community (SADC).

There have also been important developments in the areas of peace and security. The post-Cold War era resulted in increased burdens for security governance being bestowed or foisted on the United Nations. This swiftly generated an appreciation of the contribution that regional organizations might make to UN aims. The UN Charter's Chapter VIII had initially determined this role for regional organizations, and a return to Charter provisions provided welcome validation of this increased emphasis on regional and subregional organizations. The African Union (AU) has played a particularly predominant role in this regard, setting up, for example, hybrid AU-UN peace operations in some of the continent's most intractable conflict zones, as well as adopting an African Peace and Security Architecture, including components relating to the prevention, management, and resolution of conflict.

Yet wider aims have underpinned these developments – the sense that new forms of legitimation involving regions and regionalism needed to be developed to address changes in global governance arrangements that were unambitious in their reactions to the diffusion of power in world politics. The inability to reform representation on the UN Security Council or to conclude the WTO's Doha Development Agenda (the so-called Doha round) – started in 2001 and intended to produce new arrangements for trading in agriculture, services, e-commerce, intellectual property protection, and the like – prompted a regional-level reaction.[7] So too did the delays in giving emerging powers greater influence at the International Monetary Fund and World Bank.[8] These failures encouraged China in its decision to establish the Asian Infrastructure Investment Bank.

Undoubtedly, the post-Cold War era has witnessed a rapid expansion in the numbers of regional organizations associated with regional governance. However, increased attention to different regional forms has come not only from a post-Cold War increase in regionally based groupings, together with the more elaborated definition of what constitutes a region or regionalism, but also from associated conceptual and theoretical developments. The adoption of post-positivist, constructivist, and critical theorizing in international relations (IR) scholarship has encouraged an awareness of different regional experiences across the globe and, in particular, has generated increased sensitivity to the non-European experience of the regionalist project. These developments have reinforced an understanding that regions are not solely functionalist problem-solving entities but instead have emphasized their reactive and social underpinnings.

Constructivist scholarship, for example, has been important in signaling attention to cultural and social factors that are likely to aid the enmeshment of states and peoples that share values and interact at levels denser than those operating at the global level. Such approaches have also advocated greater appreciation of the role of non-state actors in facilitating regionalism. This is especially the case with reference to social movements that encourage new forms of identity at the regional level. Striking in this regard has been work on transnational networking in fields as diverse as human rights and military security. Such networked non-state groupings, for example, made their own powerful contribution across Europe to the peaceful ending of the Cold War on that continent.[9]

In sum, the multiple roles that regional groupings can perform of a functional, social, and legitimating kind suggest that they are unlikely easily to disappear in the coming decades. Developments that suggest the world is at a critical juncture can also aid stasis. At times of crisis or uncertainty, the appeal of turning to extant regional mechanisms can be difficult to resist. The COVID-19 global health pandemic, for instance, eventually prompted the European Union (EU) in 2020 to introduce a 750 billion Euro rescue package for those states most damaged by the crisis. In addition, ASEAN states have thrown their weight behind the establishment of a High-Level Special Commission to aid economic and health recovery from the ravages that the pandemic has left in its wake.[10]

Loyalty to those organizations already in place, at least among participating elites, is not easily diminished, even where organizations are relatively inactive and have undemanding design features. Indeed, there are times when those seemingly unpropitious features can help prolong the life of such organizations and expand their appeal to a wider population. The question then becomes: how do design features, social bonds, and functionalist aims relate to the potential endurance of regional organizations at a time when potentially more powerful alternative forms of connectedness confront them as future purveyors of global governance?

Alternative forms of connectedness in the contemporary era

Four main forms of connectedness with the potential to confront and constrain regions and regionalism as governance mechanisms are discussed in what follows: populism, non-state and transnational politics, new spaces, and geopolitics. The Asia-Pacific and Europe have been selected as the most frequent geographical reference points – the former because it has been emerging as the center of gravity in world politics, and Asia's regional and other groupings have proliferated in tandem; the latter because it has been home to the deepest form of regionalism in the post-1945 era yet has been buffeted by the alternative forms of connectedness discussed in what follows.

The chapter discusses these four themes in discrete analytical categories, but they may overlap, sometimes to reinforce and on other occasions to dilute the impact of the other factors. Populism and transnational identity politics both draw on cultural forces, for instance, but tend to push in opposite directions. Transitions in power that have resulted in new policy directions intended to be global or transcontinental in their desired results have both strengthened geopolitical perspectives that promote division and given rise to the development of new spatial groupings that either challenge or reinforce the notion of connection based on geographical contiguity.

Populism

Populism, in both its leftist and rightist forms, has become a significant political force in most if not all of the world's regions, though its degree of permanence is under debate. Even when defined in minimalist form, populist sentiment shows its potential challenge to regionalism. As Jeffrey Chwieroth and Andrew Walter describe it, "populism is any candidate or party that seeks to mobilize political support based on a rhetorical dualism between the 'people' and 'elites' or other out-groups."[11] In a more elaborate description, embracing both leftist and rightist ideologies, populism is said to contain within it those who are "against elites . . . against the centre . . . against compromise, and . . . against the status quo system," though indeed these are all elements that we might see as pertinent to multilateral organizations of both a regional as well as a global kind. Populists are said to be united in a twin belief that "a country's 'true people' are locked into a moral conflict with 'outsiders' and . . . that nothing should constrain the will of the 'true people.'" The "true people" – a presumed homogenous grouping with a clear set of identified and agreed interests – are viewed as the only legitimate source of political authority. These "authentic" political actors are unwilling to accept constraints on the sovereignty of the state. Moreover, they challenge those socio-economic elites with the power to undermine their predetermined interests and rail against the ability of elites and other "outsiders" to profit from the labor of the "true people."[12]

Where the attractions of this narrative hold fast, it can pose a threat to the future of regionalism. Indeed, this is the case even in an area of the world where regional awareness and cooperation have reached their most dense and demanding forms – Europe. According to one database published in 2020, the numbers of populist leaders and parties in power worldwide has increased almost five-fold since the end of the Cold War and three times more since the end of the twentieth century. Europe has certainly figured in those numbers. Indeed, it may be that as a result of the EU's demanding form of regionalism, populist sentiment has especially affected this regional organization. Conflict in the Middle East has brought thousands of refugees to European shores, the political impact of which has been magnified by free movement after the first point of entry under the Schengen agreement. European Commission rules on fiscal propriety, particularly after the 2008 global financial crisis, were highly damaging to southern European economies, such as Greece. Both these EU rules have deepened populist sentiment. Indeed, one in three of the EU's voters voice support for parties that are critical of or hostile to the EU, with Britain's voters having taken the wounding decision – wounding to both the EU as well as the United Kingdom – to leave the most powerful regional organization in world politics. However, some qualifications are in order since that might not be voters' main reasons for offering their support to these parties. Crucially, the demand this part of the electorate tends to make of their political allies – where they are not rejectionists altogether – is that populist leaders work for an EU that is looser in form and returns more areas of sovereignty to the level of the nation-state.[13]

Moreover, there is little in this populist depiction to suggest that global governance would be any more supported than those mechanisms operating at the regional level. It is a depiction that is essentially backward looking and seeks the return of a less centrally governed world, leaving important decisions to the individual state (and to the "true people" within it). As the populist US president Donald Trump put it in front of the UN General Assembly in 2018, posing a false dichotomy: "We reject the ideology of globalism, and we embrace the doctrine of patriotism."[14] A minimally coexisting pluralist, Westphalian order is the implied future goal for populists of this stripe who appear to abhor both global and regional governance. For them, connectivity means a firmer embrace of a nativist national identity.

A Biden presidency is associated with a strong, internationalist perspective, although it must remain attentive to the sentiments of 74 million Americans who voted for Trump in November 2020. Moreover, for many Europeans as well as others outside that continent, there is still a future role for regionalism, provided it is in a loose or looser form. Indeed, for non-European societies, less demanding forms of regionalism are already the norm and have rendered the EU an outlier in terms of its expansive regional organizational design. Elsewhere, we see far weaker centralized bureaucratic structures and more evidence of "lowest-common-denominator" modes of decision-making.

Non-state forms and transnational identity politics

One challenge to populist rhetoric, with different kinds of geographies attributed to the notion of "insiders" and "outsiders," comes from appreciation of the role of non-state forces determined to forge transnational connection. Yet, a transnationalism that reflects relationships built on other kinds of identities potentially, like populism, contests the idea of regional ties as the future main basis for cooperation and governance. Private actors, such as the Gates Foundation, for example, that are able to mobilize substantial resources in the field of global health could be seen either as complements or competitors to global or regional bodies devoted to the same end goal.

In the economic field, global supply chains link firms and peoples across continents, potentially providing them with a density of connectedness that ranges well beyond those in operation at the regional level. Indeed, students of International Political Economy (IPE) have viewed such globalized forms of exchange not only as sources of interdependence that benefit economic development but also as capable of spilling over into the security field: they can change the calculus of conflict, rendering it less likely that states across a wide geographical space will go to war.[15] The Asia-Pacific region, for example, has relied extensively on export growth and networked trade across the region and on to the global market to facilitate its emergence as the most dynamic and relatively stable region in the global economy. A fragmented production process in areas such as electronics and technology, automobiles, footwear, and toys is not impossible to decouple, but it is difficult to undertake that decoupling without short- to medium-term economic losses and various other forms of disruption.

Not all forms of transnationalism are built on benign intent. After the 11 September 2001 terrorist attacks in the United States, there developed a greater appreciation of the power of loyalties, based on religion or other forms of community beyond the state or region, to dissolve the social and other ties that are purported to come from the geographical contiguity of territorial boundaries and that are said to form the basis for building social identities. At the same time, the 9/11 attack led to a vast expansion in state power in the United States and other parts of the developed world. The COVID-19 pandemic similarly demonstrated the globalized nature of today's world but also resulted in reliance on the state as the main port of call for those in distress. Moreover, the pandemic reinforced the arguments of those distrustful of globalization, strengthened the demand for stronger frontier controls, and magnified the perceived dangers of relying on both global supply chains and single-center supply lines, in this instance for the medical equipment urgently needed in response to this pandemic.

A serious deterioration in US-China relations, afforded both by the longer-term implications of China's resurgence as well as its more proximate role in the initial stages of the pandemic, fed into these kinds of arguments. The pacifying role that networked forms of economic interdependence once played in that relationship has diminished, raising the attractiveness for both protagonists of developing their domestic markets while attempting to decouple from the global production chains from which both have benefitted.

New spatial possibilities

The China example also raises two other issues of note which are relevant to the future of global governance. The first reflects the effects on regions or regionalism of new transregional or interregional policy initiatives deriving from a center or hub. The second reflects the creation of new regional imaginings or groupings as part of a more general reaction to China's resurgence, as well as to some of its policy initiatives.

China's Belt and Road Initiative (BRI), launched officially in 2013 and designed to link China over the coming decades via a maritime silk road and overland economic belt with Asia, the Middle East, Europe, and Africa, is one such example. In its early form, it was projected as a response to the 2011 Obama administration's "Pivot to Asia" and in this regard carried within it the seeds of geopolitical rivalry. But the BRI represents far more than that. For those interested in the BRI as a neo-regionalist project, it has been labeled "a transregional spatial imaginary." It has been built around transregional connections of many kinds, including transport links, goods, investment, cultural exchange, digital networks, and the like.[16] As a Beijing government report describes it, the BRI will overlay regionalism in the coming years. Its goal is to promote "the connectivity of Asian, European and African continents and their adjacent seas," using regional groupings to help realize "all-dimensional, multi-tiered and composite connectivity networks."[17] For those who see it in yet more ambitious terms, it becomes a project for projecting a Chinese world order.

Nadine Godehardt and Paul J. Kohlenberg have argued that regionalism is not at the root of the BRI: the initiative "should not be compared to mechanisms such as the European Union, Mercosur. . . , or the Association of South East Asian Nations." Unlike these regional or subregional groupings, the BRI is not defined by any specific membership qualities, by fixed rules, or even in terms of a fixed space. From these authors' perspective, it "primarily operates with differing notions of geographic or functionalist space – not bound to any fixed understanding of (world) regions."

Moreover, Beijing has elevated the idea of "connectivity" above that of ideas of integration, a shift in terminology that is potentially profound. Godehardt and Kohlenberg argue that the Chinese leadership under Xi Jinping has shown an increased determination to bind other actors to the Chinese Communist Party's ways of seeing the world. This is in contrast to a view of China that is working primarily to enmesh itself in extant (and reformed) regional or global structures.[18] Moreover, through the BRI, China may gain the tools to coerce or persuade states and other political actors to accept the inevitability of that binding, a topic to be taken up in more detail in the next subsection.

Scholars of regionalism, inevitably, have tried to recover from this type of challenge to territorially based understandings of the concept. Critical theorists working on regions and regionalism would be less perturbed by developments such as the BRI, the formation of the BRICS (Brazil, Russia, India, China, and South Africa), or other new forms of community, arguing that the territorial fixation in traditional regional studies needs to break free from such thinking in today's globalized world.[19] This rupture is particularly necessary given the widespread agreement that all regions are social constructs and have varied in terms of membership according to the particular problem political actors perceive to require collective solution or management. Alternatively, such "regional" or new spatial imaginaries could primarily be seen as a reaction to the failure of extant organizations to reflect the redistribution of power in world politics.

However, this acceptance of all forms of connectivity below the global level as regionalism takes matters too far. Without some semblance of geographical contiguity, these groupings simply become a " 'less than global' organization. Without some geographical limits, the term 'regionalism' becomes diffuse and unmanageable."[20] Perhaps we should concede the challenge that globalization has posed and acknowledge the way that global forces have penetrated regions but accept that for the concept of region to be meaningful requires some connection to be made with territory and boundedness.

Thus, from more traditionalist perspectives, the BRI does pose a challenge to concepts and processes that have become associated with regions and regionalism and portends a future decline in regional forms of governance. That prediction is mitigated, however, by the BRI's status as a project that is extraordinarily difficult to enact. Some analyses have pointed to the difficulties for Beijing to ensure the success of such a complex and grandiose scheme, with a result that at best may lead to a patchwork of connectedness.[21] Investment decisions made under the rubric of the BRI often have to contend with complex societies undergoing security breakdowns that may at times be caused or exacerbated by the operations of a regional security complex. This is the case in South Asia, or the Great Lakes region in Africa, for example.[22] The BRI has also generated various forms of resistance that will complicate its passage to successful completion. The high levels of indebtedness among BRI partners, which sometimes has been exacerbated by the terms of BRI contracts, as well as the economic damage wrought by the global health pandemic, is already leading to the renegotiation or rejection of past agreements. Of note for one major additional theme of this chapter, resistance has also been generated by the presumed geopolitical underpinnings of this grand project. The BRI has added weight to the argument for creating new (if still nascent) regional groupings such as the Indo-Pacific, which is an attempt to change the strategic geography of the East Asian or Asia-Pacific region.

Geopolitics returns

As argued already, at one level (and for some analysts) the BRI represents a new spatial grouping akin to a regionalist project. However, the geopolitical turn in world politics means that the project has also been seen as a source of division and the basis for an alternative form of connectedness reflecting great power rivalries. From the geopolitical perspective, the BRI represents important leverage for China as the second-largest economy in the world and the largest trading partner for most of the world's economies. Benedict Kingsbury reminds us that "the technical in technology is not independent of organizational forms, social relations and responses, economic structures and finance."[23] Jonathan E. Hillman spells out more directly how states have historically used infrastructure assistance to advance strategic objectives, taking a close look in particular at "connectivity infrastructure" in sectors such as transportation, energy, and information and communications technology – all sectors that are at the forefront of BRI projects. Hillman's main findings are that financing provides opportunities "to extract diplomatic concessions, reward supporters, shape project plans, access resources, and gain operational control." The design and construction stage can lead to the setting of standards, the transfer of technology, and the collection of intelligence. Moreover, the final stage of ownership and operation provides further opportunities for deeper forms of intelligence collection and the ability to restrain a competitor's access.[24]

This particular interpretation of the BRI takes it well beyond a debate in the IR literature about the degree of "region-ness" that can be associated with it. Hillman is suggesting that we should view the BRI as a way of shaping the future based on forms of connectedness that derive from a central hegemon, with one result being that more familiar regional connections will be overlaid and will inevitably weaken. The BRI already has shown its potential to diminish levels of regional cooperation among EU member states. Some Central and Eastern European states, such as the Czech Republic and Hungary, have accepted BRI financing. The Western European states of Greece and Italy have signed provisional cooperation agreements. This contradicts the European Commission position that the bloc should remain aloof, unless and until the BRI's approach conforms more closely to official EU preferences for transparency, openness, and financial and environmental sustainability. One result of this breach among EU member states is that those European states that have engaged with the BRI find themselves less willing to sign up to EU statements critical of some aspects of Chinese policy, particularly in the area of human rights.

Other countries have chosen the path of competition with the BRI via some degree of emulation. States such as India, Japan, Russia, and the United States have emphasized the alternatives that are on offer and the infrastructure support that they can provide. Russia, for example, in 2015 established the Eurasian Economic Union (EAEU), based on the participation of more geographically contiguous states which happen also to have been part of the former Soviet space.[25] Later, Moscow attempted to link the EAEU with the BRI, in part to retain some kind of control over the potential for the deepening of competitive dynamics with China in that space.

Geostrategic spatial developments in response to China's ambitious policy initiatives have also quickened. The United States government, for example, in 2019 launched its first *Indo-Pacific Strategy Report*, which claims in the first sentence that the Indo-Pacific is the most "consequential region for America's future."[26] That region is defined as embracing a vast area of continental and maritime space from India's west coast to the West Coast of the United States. The Biden administration has maintained that spatial focus, hosting the first ever summit-level meeting of the Quadrilateral Security Dialogue – Australia, India, Japan, and the United States – in March 2021.[27]

The United States is not alone in trying to diminish the significance of the Asia-Pacific as the defining terminology of that part of the world's regions, a course of action that is likely to continue in the years ahead. India, Japan, and ASEAN have all recorded in official policy papers some level of commitment to or acknowledgement of the Indo-Pacific concept. ASEAN's paper noted in its opening paragraph that the regions of the Indian Ocean and Asia-Pacific "continue to experience geopolitical and geostrategic shifts." ASEAN member states accept that their subregional organization will need to work hard to retain an ASEAN-centered regional architecture and that extant regional organizations will have to think of creative ways of embracing the new regional geography in order to retain their future relevance in regional governance.[28]

Why is this redefinition of the boundaries of the region an objective of these governments? In adopting a geostrategic lens, the attractions of this concept for many Asia-Pacific states relate to a twin desire to change the regional distribution of power in ways that favor actors other than China and that help local actors cope with the prospect of gradual US disengagement and relative decline. The assumption is that it is a more significant challenge for China to dominate the maritime and continental aspects of the Indo-Pacific than is the case with respect to the Asia-Pacific or East Asia, where China's "natural" leadership role is sometimes assumed. US naval power remains preeminent for the time being, and the US navy is still capable of roaming both the Pacific and Indian Oceans. But US relative decline suggests the possibility for the emergence of a multipolar Asia in which India, Japan, and the ASEAN states display more agency and play the balancing role once left to the United States. Were the Indo-Pacific to become a meaningful construct for Asian states, it would detach the continent from the idea of Sino-centrism and from the United States as core security provider, resulting in new regional imaginaries that would multiply the security demands made on Beijing.[29]

Undoubtedly, regional resculpting of this kind is familiar from the experience of regionalism during the Cold War, as well as in earlier eras. Labels such as the "Middle East" and "Near East" are constructs from the British imperial era. Few would bet against a continuation of Sino-American rivalry in the coming decades, one implication being that ideas such as the Indo-Pacific are likely to attract the levels of resources and commitment that they require to become meaningful. However, important to note is that even though a desire to balance or contain a resurgent China might have prompted this new regional imaginary, this still underlines the idea that regional cooperation is perceived as a useful way to respond to a rise in geopolitical rivalries – reminiscent, then, of those forces that prompted the establishment of past regional groupings such as ASEAN.

This new regional imaginary may, however, fail to establish a significant presence. In these circumstances, the expectation is that there will be increased pressure on states in the Asia-Pacific – and particularly the less powerful among them – to choose between the two protagonists at the heart of this attempted regional redefinition, China and the United States. An allegiance battle, thus, will form a powerful dimension of the tests that Asia-Pacific regional organizations – and ASEAN states, in particular – will face in the coming decade.

Conclusion

The vitality shown in the study of regions and regionalism, together with the continuing presence of regional organizations in providing governance mechanisms, points to the continuing relevance of such organizations for collective decision-making, at least into the medium term. First, many are deeply rooted and have a kind of "stickiness" that aids their continuation, and new groupings continue to be established – RCEP, for example, is likely to accelerate trade integration among 15 states in Asia. Second, the creation of new non- or interregional spatial imaginaries and the command of new loyalties take time to discuss, establish, and gain the confidence of members. Moreover, complex connectivity projects such as the BRI have no guarantee of successful completion, and developments to date indicate the level of success will be partial at best.

Third, new forms of connectivity have often sparked the creation, rather than the demise, of new regional organizations. Populist sentiment led the Trump administration, for example, to "unsign" the Trans-Pacific Partnership, but the broad idea went ahead without Washington in the form of the Comprehensive and Progressive Agreement for a Trans-Pacific Partnership (CPTPP).

As has been suggested, an additional source of vitality in the regionalist project has come from redefining what is meant by "region," in particular relaxing the condition of geographical contiguity as one response to today's globalized world and elevating the power of other kinds of spatial connection. I have questioned the pertinence of this argument because such definitional flexibility distorts the notion of region and regionalism as a meaningful level between the state and the globe; as such, it dilutes the analytical traction of a grouping built upon a denser set of interactions than those that exist outside the regional collectivity.

Nevertheless, the tests that regional groupings have always faced remain stern in a world where populist sentiment appears likely to remain strong and where geopolitical and geostrategic thinking similarly will continue to be prominent. Populism has revived support for placing the state back at the center of decision-making in world politics amid a more sustained assault on multilateral cooperation. It will continue to pose a particular threat to the unity of EU states, the area with the deepest form of regional cooperation the contemporary world has witnessed. Geopolitics will constrain the regionalist project in Asia in the coming years, particularly deriving from the power transition connected with China's ascendancy and relative US decline. We have already witnessed how China's resurgence, coupled with the severe deterioration in Sino-American relations, has spurred competing spatial formations.

Notably, however, the depth of the challenge posed by the four themes discussed in this essay is manifest not simply for the regional level of governance but also for global governance. Were these trends to intensify, this would portend more variation in future forms of governance among societies and states and increased fragmentation when many of the world's most challenging problems require planetary solutions.

Suggested reading

Amitav Acharya, "Global International Relations (IR) and Regional Worlds: A New Agenda for International Studies," *International Studies Quarterly* 58, no. 4 (2014): 647–659.

Mark Beeson, *Rethinking Global Governance* (London: Palgrave/MacMillan, 2019).

Louise Fawcett, "Regionalism," in *The Sage Handbook of Political Science*, ed. Dirk Berg-Schlosser, Bertrand Badie, and Leonardo Morlino (London: Sage Publications, 2020), 1349–1365.

Nadine Godehardt and Paul J. Kohlenberg, eds., *The Multidimensionality of Regions in World Politics* (Abingdon, UK: Routledge, 2020).

Fredrik Söderbaum, *Rethinking Regionalism* (London: Palgrave/Macmillan, 2016).

Etel Solingen, *Comparative Regionalism: Economics and Security* (Abingdon, UK: Routledge, 2015).

Notes

1 Fredrik Söderbaum, *Rethinking Regionalism* (London: Palgrave/Macmillan, 2016), 172.

2 Louise Fawcett, "Regionalism," in *The Sage Handbook of Political Science*, ed. Dirk Berg-Schlosser, Bertrand Badie, and Leonardo Morlino (London: Sage Publications, 2020), 1349–1365. Fawcett's chapter and conversations with its author have been particularly beneficial to the development of my ideas.

3 Joseph S. Nye, *International Regionalism: Readings* (Boston, MA: Little Brown, 1968).

4 Andrew Hurrell, *On Global Order: Power, Values, and the Constitution of International Society* (Oxford: Oxford University Press, 2007), 242–243.

5 For this latter point see Alexander Cooley and Daniel Nexon, *Exit from Hegemony: The Unraveling of the American Global Order* (New York: Oxford University Press, 2020), 115–117.

6 Amitav Acharya's work has been especially important in this regard. See *Constructing a Security Community in Southeast Asia: ASEAN and the Problem of Regional Order*, 3rd ed. (Abingdon: Routledge, 2014); see also Rosemary Foot, "Pacific Asia: The Development of Regional Dialogue," in *Regionalism in World Politics: Regional Organization and International Order*, ed. Louise Fawcett and Andrew Hurrell (Oxford: Oxford University Press, 1995), 228–249.

7 Rorden Wilkinson, Erin Hannah, and James Scott, "The WTO in Nairobi: The Demise of the Doha Development Agenda and the Future of the Multilateral Trading System," *Global Policy* 7, no. 2 (2016): 247–255.

8 Ali Burak Güven, "Defending Supremacy: How the IMF and the World Bank Navigate the Challenge of Rising Powers," *International Affairs* 93, no. 5 (2017): 1149–1166.

9 Among a number of such publications, see Daniel C. Thomas, *The Helsinki Effect: International Norms, Human Rights, and the Demise of Communism* (Princeton, NJ: Princeton University Press, 2001).

10 "E.U. Adopts Groundbreaking Stimulus to Fight Corona Virus Recession," *New York Times*, 21 July 2020; "ASEAN Focuses on Fighting Pandemic, Economic Recovery," *New Straits Times*, 30 June 2020, www.nst.com.my/opinion/letters/2020/07/604854/asean-focuses-fighting-pandemic-economic-recovery.

11 Jeffrey M. Chwieroth and Andrew Walter, "Pensions, Place, and Populism: Do Post-Crisis Wealth Shocks Matter?" (forthcoming).

12 Jordan Kyle and Brett Meyer, "High Tide? Populism in Power, 1990–2020," *London: Tony Blair Institute for Global Change* (February 2020): 5–7, https://institute.global/sites/default/files/2020-02/High%20Tide%20Populism%20in%20Power%201990-2020.pdf.

13 Ibid., 3; Jon Henley, "Support for Eurosceptic Parties Doubles in Two Decades Across EU," *The Guardian*, 2 March 2020.

14 "Trump Addresses the U.N.: We Reject the Ideology of Globalism, Must Defend Sovereignty," *Real Clear I*, 25 September 2018, www.realclearpolitics.com/video/2018/09/25/trump_addresses_un_we_reject_the_ideology_of_globalism_must_defend_sovereignty.html. Trump has also, on many occasions, applauded the UK's decision to leave the EU.

15 Stephen Brooks, *Producing Security: Multinational Corporations, Globalization, and the Changing Calculus of Combat* (Princeton, NJ: Princeton University Press, 2005).

16 Ngai-Ling Sum, "The Production of a Trans-regional Scale: China's 'One Belt One Road' Imaginary," in *Handbook on the Geographies of Regions and Territories*, ed. Anssi Paasi (Cheltenham, UK: Edward Elgar, 2018), 428–443.

17 "Vision and Actions on Jointly Building Silk Road Economic Belt and 21st Century Maritime Silk Road," 28 March 2015, http://en.ndrc.gov.cn/newsrelease/201503/t20150330.669367.html.

18 Nadine Godehardt and Paul J. Kohlenberg, "China's Global Connectivity Politics: A Meta-Geography in the Making," in *The Multidimensionality of Regions in World Politics*, ed. Paul J. Kohlenberg and Nadine Godehardt (Abingdon: Routledge, 2020), 192–193, 207 and see more generally 202–210.

19 Allan Cochrane, "Relational Thinking and the Region," in *Handbook on the Geographies of Regions and Territories*, ed. Anssi Paasi (Cheltenham, UK: Edward Elgar, 2018), 79–88.

20 Hurrell, *On Global Order*, 241.

21 Chuchu Zhang and Chaowei Xiao, "China's Belt and Road Initiative Faces New Security Challenges in 2018," *The Diplomat*, 21 December 2017, https://thediplomat.com/2017/12/chinas-belt-and-road-initiative-faces-new-security-challenges-in-2018/; Lee Jones and Jinghan Zeng, "Understanding China's 'Belt and Road Initiative': Beyond 'Grand Strategy' to a State Transformation Analysis," *Third World Quarterly* 40, no. 8 (2019): 1415–1439; Luke Patey, *How China Loses: The Pushback Against Chinese Global Ambitions* (New York: Oxford University Press, 2021).

22 The idea of a regional security complex is discussed in Barry Buzan and Ole Wæver, *Regions and Powers: The Structure of International Security* (Cambridge: Cambridge University Press, 2003).

23 Benedict Kingsbury, "Infrastructure and InfraReg: On Rousing the International Law 'Wizards of IS,'" *Cambridge International Law Journal* 8, no. 2 (2019): 173.

24 Jonathan E. Hillman, *Influence and Infrastructure: The Strategic Stakes of Foreign Projects, 22 January 2020* (Washington, DC: CSIS, 2020), at https://reconnectingasia.csis.org/analysis/entries/influence-and-infrastructure/.

25 State members include Armenia, Belarus, Kazakhstan, Kyrgyzstan, and Russia.

26 US Department of Defense, *Indo-Pacific Strategy Report*, 1 June 2019, https://media.defense.gov/2019/Jul/01/2002152311/-1/-1/1/DEPARTMENT-OF-DEFENSE-INDO-PACIFIC-STRATEGY-REPORT-2019.PDF. See also Oliver Turner and Inderjeet Parmar, eds., *The United States in the Indo-Pacific: Obama's Legacy and the Trump Transition* (Manchester: Manchester University Press, 2020).

27 "Quad Leaders' Joint Statement: 'The Spirit of the Quad'", 12 March 2021, https://www.whitehouse.gov/briefing-room/statements-releases/2021/03/12/quad-leaders-joint-statement-the-spirit-of-the-quad/.

28 "ASEAN Outlook on the Indo-Pacific" [no date], https://asean.org/storage/2019/06/ASEAN-Outlook-on-the-Indo-Pacific_FINAL_22062019.pdf.

29 Particularly helpful in thinking this through has been Manjeet S. Pardesi, "The Indo-Pacific: A New Region or the Return of History?" *Australian Journal of International Affairs* 74, no. 2 (2019): 124–146, DOI:10.1080/10357718.2019.1693496.

CONTENTS

Cities

Understanding global urban governance

Daniel Pejic and Michele Acuto

As burgeoning sites of economic agglomeration, construction, institutional change, and population growth, cities present some of the most pressing challenges for contemporary global governance. From mundane neighborhood garbage disposal to grand commitments at the United Nations General Assembly, city governments have become responsible for bridging localized pressures and increasing demands to implement global urban policy agendas. Cities and city leaders now participate in a semi-formalized architecture of "global urban governance," the implications of which are poorly understood in either international relations theory (IR) or urban studies. This realm is far from limited to the international agency of local governments alone. Rather, it involves a vast populace of multilateral, multinational, academic, and non-governmental actors that, over the course of the last three decades, have come to shape a variety of more or less institutionalized structures for governing the trajectory of urban development worldwide. By crosscutting scales of governance, cities now might inhabit a halfway space between competing local, national, and global agendas, progressively raising fundamental tensions with the current international system.

This chapter argues that these tensions can be productive and that quasi-localized policy responses have progressively become one of the most effective methods of addressing global governance challenges. It also

DOI: 10.4324/9781003139836-8

argues that scholars and practitioners in global governance need to come to terms with both the emerging networked nature of urban politics as well as the complexity of global urban governance beyond simplistic assumptions as to the role of cities in international processes. While perhaps more evident to those working on issues like climate, resilience, or culture, the centrality of city leadership to global challenges has been demonstrated time and time again during this century. This centrality has been reiterated through global–local responses to the COVID-19 pandemic and its inextricable link with international urban migration.

This chapter compares the role of city leaders and the new modes of governance generated by these joint issues with those presented by other "global urban" challenges, highlighting sectoral discrepancies, institutional lock-ins, and critical policy siloes. Our contention is that to understand these shifts in global governance, we need to move beyond one-dimensional views of the "urban age," which have advanced cities on the world political stage but have also increasingly overshadowed crucial complexities of the governance of an urbanized planet.

The chapter begins with a brief introduction to the concept of global urban governance and the evolving role of city leaders and other urban agents as both local and global governors. The chapter then moves to a discussion of the thematic way that global urban governance has been analyzed, enriching our understanding of networked governance across distinct policy domains but too often ignoring the critical policy independencies and the formal and informal modes of global urban governance emerging outside of city networks. Thereafter, the chapter discusses the way that COVID-19, to date an overwhelmingly urban crisis, has further exposed the central role that urban leadership is playing in the governance of modern challenges like international migration, as well as the policy dependencies of a global urban world.

Emerging forms of global urban governance

It has become almost a cliché to discuss the "arrival" of cities on the global stage and into our discussions of global governance. The reality is that throughout history, urban settlements have been the central points of organized international activity in forms that well predate the Westphalian system.[1] There is no argument, however, that the international attention paid to cities as both sites of global processes and legitimate global political agents across a range of policy areas has increased dramatically over the previous two decades.[2] With more than half of the global population currently residing in urban settlements – predicted to rise to 70 percent by 2050[3] – we have not only entered into an "urban age," but, as Gleeson argues, we are in a new "urban condition" as a species.[4] Modern global governance challenges, including the majority of those explored in this book, must largely be viewed through an urban lens, problematizing IR-driven notions of how the world is governed.

This presents both conceptual and practical challenges. In terms of the practical dimensions of global governance, states and other organizations working internationally often lack urban expertise and the formal decision-making structures or legal processes to engage directly with cities. In the case of states, there has been some recognition of this knowledge and policy void, catalyzing a move toward the development of national urban plans. However, a joint report by UN-Habitat and the Organisation for Economic Co-operation and Development (OECD) found that, despite most of the 150 countries analyzed having a full, or at least partial, national urban plan, only 13 percent had evaluated or monitored the effectiveness of these policy frameworks.[5] The same report found that 62 percent of states do not have a dedicated urban agency at the national level and only a handful have a minister for cities or equivalent. Other international organizations and groups working on issues as diverse as environment, energy, health, migration, security, culture, and many more are increasing their engagement with collaborative urban initiatives, recognizing the need for urban expertise and governance strategies. Large philanthropic actors such as Bloomberg Philanthropies, the Rockefeller Foundation, and Open Society Foundations have also begun to directly engage with cities and city-led initiatives in order to advance their global goals.

For scholars of global governance and IR more broadly, an urbanized world represents a potential shift in the locus of agency and the way that we understand and address twenty-first-century global challenges. Consideration of this shift has been happening on the sidelines of mainstream IR for over a decade, inserting cities and other urban agents into our conceptions of global governance.[6] We do not argue that the "urban age" will lead to supplanting traditional multilateral processes, as some have suggested.[7] Equally, we do not subscribe to the notion that cities will "save the planet" by catalyzing progressive action in areas where multilateral gridlock has reigned.[8] Rather, the world is observing a rescaling of global political agency, in an non-zero-sum manner, allowing city leaders and other urban agents to act in a way that progressively raises tensions through and between multiple scales of governance. These tensions can be productive and effective at addressing global challenges. Cities have the advantage of proximity to their constituents and everyday experience with globally driven challenges.[9] They also do not have the luxury of ignoring these challenges when they impact urban realities.

An emerging, if underdeveloped, concept to understand the meshing of scales, which often in political science have been thought to operate independently, is "global urban governance." This concept recognizes that co-dependent globalization and urbanization have created an environment where the governance of urban challenges has become infeasible without consideration of their global dimensions. It is an evolution of earlier "global city" thinking which characterized a world system of major cities as nodes of transnational (predominately financial) flows.[10] As students of IR, our understanding of global challenges in an urban world is weakened when we attempt to understand governance processes by separating them into distinct local, national, regional, and international scales. Global governance here comes "to the rescue" as a perspective on IR, as it offers a more holistic reading of how more-than-local challenges take place across scales while still attending to crucial IR questions like sovereignty and power politics.[11] From this point of view, a focus on global *urban* governance considers the way urban political agency and governance operate in a "multiscalar" fashion, interacting with processes and agents at the local, national, regional, and international levels, in formal and informal ways. This does not require passing through nested scales of governance but can act as a "scalar trampoline," intimately linking urban, national, and global politics.[12] Neil Brenner has adopted the metaphor of "a flaky *mille-feuille*" to describe this dynamic process of "scalar structuration."[13] The processes and institutions generated through global urban governance tangibly have an impact on approaches to city leadership and everyday urban life.[14] These involve a range of activities such as transnational city-to-city partnerships, collaborative peer initiatives, community-driven international urban advocacy, the implementation of international agreements within cities, and the formal or informal engagement of cities, both independently and jointly, into traditional multilateral processes.

In line with this book's theme, we specifically focus on the global dimensions of this structuration, both the increasing importance of city leadership to addressing global challenges within cities and the expanding role of city leaders in the formal and informal processes of global governance. As Kristin Ljungkvist attests, IR scholars must understand not only "what the world spins into cities" but also "what cities spin back out to the world."[15]

Networked global urban governance

A significant proportion of research on cities as agents in global governance has concerned the growth of city networking initiatives – formalized partnerships designed to support international engagement between local governments. This has been put on the forefront of several global governance agendas by particularly high-profile transnational networks such as the C40 Cities Climate Leadership Group, a group of 96 of the world's largest cities working collaboratively to mitigate the impacts of climate change; the United Cities and Local Governments (UCLG) network, one of the largest transnational associations blending municipal, regional, and metropolitan governments; and ICLEI Local Governments for Sustainability, a global network of local and regional governments launched in the 1990s to drive a bottom-up environmentalist movement of cities, to name but a few of over 300 such existing institutions. The focus on these forms of networked transnational urban governance has been justified since the 1990s, and there has been a concomitant and exponential increase in the number of networks, their membership, and the policy domains in which they are operating.[16]

Some of these larger networks have also been embedded in traditional multilateral processes, such as UCLG's chairing of the United Nations Advisory Committee of Local Authorities (UNACLA), ICLEI's partnership agreements with UN Environment, UN-Habitat, and the United Nations Office for Disaster Risk Reduction (UNISDR), and the Mayors Migration Council co-steering (with UCLG and the International Organization for Migration) of a dedicated Mayor's Mechanism as one of the pillars of the Global Forum on Migration and Development. They have also demonstrated some effectiveness in influencing multilateral processes, for example through the C40's coordination of large-scale mayoral input into the Paris Agreement negotiations, most famously represented by a photo of hundreds of mayors from around the world standing side by side on the eve of the agreement in December 2015. After advocacy to be included in the development of the United Nations Global Compact for Safe, Orderly, and Regular Migration and Global Compact on Refugees,[17] city leaders also provided direct input into the drafting of these agreements, particularly in ensuring that non-discriminatory access to health and education were retained in the provisions.

While it has been highlighted that the final documents rarely mention the terms "urban," "cities," or "mayors,"[18] they identify local authorities and local actors as key partners in meeting the aims of the agreements. This is in line with evidence we have presented on the increasing recognition of cities as actors in UN frameworks.[19] In the following, we return to a more detailed discussion of international migration as a policy area that demonstrates both the glocalization of urban governance and policy interdependency.

City networks with broad membership have afforded small to medium cities the opportunity to advocate for urban issues in multilateral fora, where they would otherwise be unlikely participants. While the geography of membership in these organizations is shifting, representation remains an issue, and many of these groups are still dominated by larger metropolises of the Global North.[20] It has also been argued that the secretariats of these larger networks may exhibit international agency apart from their member cities, drawing comparisons with conceptualization of international organizations in IR.[21] While this may be the case, it is likely limited to a handful of highly resourced networks with established connections to existing multilateral processes. Survey research has revealed that despite the proliferation of these city networks, many are experiencing financial challenges and are vying for resources in an increasingly crowded "ecosystem."[22]

While the explosion of research on city networks has generated valuable insights into the operation of networked forms of global urban governance, it has also led to a form of academic "lock-in," potentially ignoring other forms of formal and informal city diplomacy and "everyday" global urban governance. The focus on networks has also to some extent created siloes for an appreciation of the range of independent policy areas where forms of global urban governance are emerging. The majority of scholarship on transnational city networking has addressed environmental concerns, particularly strategies to mitigate the impacts of climate change.[23] This is perhaps unsurprising as a 2017 study found that 29 percent of city networking initiatives are focused on environmental issues and the majority of the best resourced and visible networks work on issues of climate and energy.[24] This thematic focus has brought many specialist climate and energy researchers to questions of city diplomacy, producing a range of valuable empirical work. At the same time, their work has perhaps obscured other thematic areas and policy links as well as limited broader theorization of the way cities emerge as foreign policy actors with influence across a range of fields.

Rather than working in isolation, the policy interdependency of city networking is also supported by data from the aforementioned study, which found that the largest area of city networking focus was governance issues, with 71 percent of networks working on more than one policy area.[25] A 2019 global survey of 47 cities found that over 85 percent have official international offices dedicated to managing the foreign affairs of these cities across their policy portfolios.[26] The international activities of city governments are far from limited to the work of these international units, however. Indeed, city officials across local authorities are increasingly working internationally through more "everyday" forms of global urban governance. Moreover, the pluralization of urban governance processes increasingly reflects global neoliberal pressures of the coordination of public, private, and civil society actors.[27] This has meant looking beyond local authorities to understand the ways cities emerge as international agents. Thus far, this need has been often overlooked in the literature on cities and global governance in favor of a reductionist conception of cities as "miniature republics."[28]

A wider view of global urban governance

Far from being isolated islands in a sea of world politics and economics, cities are now embedded deeply into the realities of global governance that operate across a range of interconnected political scales. Yet this progressive international engagement with the dynamics of urban development has also resulted in the emergence of more or less formalized international structures, agendas, and interests that involve a much wider range of actors than just local governments for what we have called "global urban governance." In fact, the rise of city networks and networked forms of city leadership on major platforms and debates throughout this century (and in many cases earlier), like those detailed previously, might have contributed to obscuring this broader realm. The emergence of networks like UCLG, ICLEI, and C40, along with the expansion of the role of mayors on the world stage, has often gone hand in hand with a "states talk, cities act" adversarial narrative against the international system. As such, it pits mayors who "rule the world"[29] and cities that can "save the planet"[30] against the failures of states and other traditional IR actors. Yet, as many advances in the global governance literature have demonstrated, the international realm is neither a zero-sum game nor a context in which actors can be easily disentangled from one another. Rather, the growth of an "urban" presence in the world of diplomacy and international relations needs to be understood in context of the widening of broader – and not exclusively local-government-centric – workings of global urban governance.

In this context, multilateral actors and processes still play an important part in constructing urban issues as matters for international relations and opening up windows for cities to partake in otherwise non-local politics. For example, many UN organizations continue to play an important animator role to facilitate the access of local governments to international fora and the engagement of non-city actors – e.g., non-governmental organizations (NGOs) or companies – into the international dynamics of urban development. Yet multilateral actors often do so tentatively and in very different ways.

The World Health Organization (WHO), for instance, is illustrative. It has stressed the continuing importance of regional politics in urban governance via its European and East Asian programs, but it has also epitomized the hesitation of most multi-lateral institutions to formalize a place for cities at the heart of their infrastructure, not just their agendas and projects. Equally, the WHO's engagement with cities also epitomizes how "city diplomacy" still takes place in a predominantly state-based international system. While in Europe the WHO Healthy Cities Network is closely managed and facilitated by the WHO Regional Office for Europe – where cities and city networks (like Eurocities and the European Forum for Urban Security in sectors other than health) are strongly encouraged, not least through explicit European Union (EU) funding – the same cannot be said of East Asia. There, the WHO keeps at arm's length the Alliance for Healthy Cities because it includes local authorities from Taiwan whose network membership is jarring for the role played by the People's Republic of China in the WHO Regional Office for the Western Pacific.

Similarly, the institutionalization of cities in the workings of multilateral organizations is still quite limited. Only a handful of UN bodies have explicit "urban" units.[31] Usual cross-sectorial suspects emerge once again as important nodes between disparate concerns. The World Bank's role echoes this once again as it steps in both very tangibly as an urban investor but also, as we flag in the following, as an animator of the global urban discussion.

Certainly, the COVID-19 crisis has further propelled local governments and their city leaders to remain (even if just "virtually") present on this international stage. Transnational coalitions of city leaders have fast risen to the occasion even though none of them had infectious disease at the heart of their discourse and agendas. The C40 Cities group fast pivoted into action, as it "temporarily transformed from being a climate leadership organisation to a COVID-19 support group."[32] The crisis has offered a chance for a relaunch of the Rockefeller 100 Resilient Cities Network (now Global Resilient Cities Network) as a much more bottom-up initiative focused on cities sharing experiences and expertise from the "frontlines." Participation by clear and sound academic voices in these debates remains central, as much, in our view, as according to widespread calls for scientists (social ones included) to have a say in the future of cities and of an increasingly "urban" planet.[33] Academic engagement and a clear scholarly voice in global urban governance have been proven, and advocated, to help veer away from either simple policy mobility (of premade "solutions" sold and marketed across cities via city networks) or from reductive readings of the "global city" as but a simplistic model to be replicated across geographies and a hierarchical world system structure driven by global finance alone.[34] This, of course, has again been proven to depend on the role of private philanthropy and national donors, which are all too often forgotten as critical elements of the structure of global urban governance. For example, in the wake of COVID-19, Bloomberg Philanthropies rapidly announced both a nationally focused program for US mayors and the release of $40 million for participation by mayors in a global response initiative aimed at cities in vulnerable low- and middle-income countries.

The role of multilateral and philanthropic institutions in shaping global urban governance takes place while a set of other key actors in the ecosystem, namely the for-profit private sector and the media, shape the dynamics of how we perceive this "urban age" and how practically cities' infrastructures are built from the ground up. This role is often acknowledged, but it is rarely discussed in systematic and in-depth ways, especially from global governance and IR perspectives.[35] The locked-down nature of the COVID-19 crisis may put an even greater premium on the capacity to shape the global urban imagination that mass media have. News brokers and information circulators like the *Financial Times*, with its much-cited contagion trajectory graphs, but also popular urban blogs like CityLab, have been central in casting this not just for the general public but also for other core actors in global governance. At the same time, as well documented already, the multinational private sector has progressively taken a key role in driving the evolution of cities in the Global North and South and has often played an important part in animating the international stage upon which cities act and urban issues are discussed – whether through multilateral or other fora.

Yet we should also not discount that much international action on urban issues also comes from the very "bottom up," propelled by the expansion and institutionalization of non-governmental advocacy, solidarity, and exchange coalitions such as the influential Slum Dwellers International (SDI). Such initiatives are driven from outside, and sometimes in criticism of, local authorities. Even in a context of crisis like COVID-19, and perhaps even more so because of the wide disparities brought to the fore by the resulting economic downturn and the impact on vulnerable urban livelihoods, transnational urban institutions are essential. For example, the Habitat International Coalition and the Asian Coalition for Housing Rights have been playing a critical part in shaping responses, policy mobility, and resource mobilization across countries and complex regional politics like those of Southeast Asia or the Gulf.[36]

Introspection by urban studies or IR scholars involved in major urban-oriented multilateral processes would also underscore how this edifice of global urban governance is tightly knit together by the central role of knowledge circulation.[37] This is not just the realm of internationally partnered urban research or the news cycles of urban-attuned mass media. Many tangible decisions are made by national, regional, and local governments – as much as the private sector – on the basis of the global depiction of the "state" of the pandemic. Major global urban governance actors inherently understand. The World Bank's $12 billion COVID-19 recovery package is, for instance, flanked by a review calling for attention to the "new urban poor" emerging from the crisis in the Global South and by an "urban resilience" exchange with the Global Resilient Cities Network, which has driven significant local action on the basis of international urban knowledge exchanges. This common story emerges in other contexts like climate action by the C40, economic policy via the OECD Champions Mayors program, or migration through the Mayors Migration Council. Overall, our depiction is of legitimate complexity regarding the global governance of urban development (or "global urban governance," for short) that involves multiple types of actors, processes, and institutions. These processes draw parallels to more commonly discussed IR themes such as security, environmental policy, and health; in fact, it intersects all of them.

International urban migration and COVID-19

Alongside these emerging interconnected areas for global urban governance, international urban migration represents an intriguing case study for how new forms of global urban governance emerge and operate in areas previously monopolized by states, multilateral organizations, and private actors. Equally, it reveals the policy dependencies of global urban challenges and the need for hybridized forms of "glocal" governance.[38] These tensions have been further revealed through the evolving COVID-19 crisis, which is inextricably linked with international urban migration. The vast majority of international migrants move to urban areas, and cities rely on migrants for labor, skills, expertise, and international connections.[39] Devolution of social services to municipal authorities has also meant that cities are increasingly responsible for delivering services that support newly arrived migrants, such as welcoming services, language services, employment, and accommodation support. The urban dimensions of international migration have been readily apparent in both the causes and impacts of COVID-19. The pandemic has to date been an overwhelming urban crisis, with over 95 percent of cases presenting in urban areas.[40] The centrality of urban governance and resilience to the mitigation of this crisis have been identified in recent reports from the United Nations and OECD.[41] The virus has also spread globally through people moving internationally between cities. With the advent of major outbreaks in urban areas, city leaders quickly mobilized their resources into response strategies, at times ahead of national government action.

As noted, we have also begun to see some thematic shift in the city network focus as the crisis has revealed the crucial independencies of urban health, labor, migration, and other policy areas. C40 Cities has created a COVID-19 taskforce that is focused not only on their traditional issues of climate but also on health and inclusive crisis response strategies. C40 also hosted a global online meeting of 45 city leaders facilitated by the mayor of Los Angeles just weeks after the WHO declared a pandemic.[42] The Global Resilient Cities Network has included a focus on urban migrants as part of their "Cities on the Frontline" program. Here the network draws on the narratives of urban resilience developed in urban studies and now featured prominently in the recent UN report on cities and the pandemic.[43]

As we have written, international urban migrants are crucial to both the current crisis and the recovery phases from it.[44] Migrants have to date been disproportionately impacted by COVID-19; they are more likely to live in precarious housing and health-care situations, and they are represented in a greater proportion of the essential industries that have kept cities functioning through the crisis, such as health care, maintenance, and logistics.[45] The history of urban economic development also indicates they will be essential to global recovery as cities emerging from economic crisis will need the skills, labor, and expertise of migrants.[46] This recognition has been quickly met by cities advocating transnationally for recovery strategies that are inclusive of migrants and refugees. For example, in July 2020 the Mayors Migration Council launched a global advocacy campaign encouraging leaders to include migrants and refugees in their pandemic and recovery responses.[47] This call was broadly supported by a range of international urban-focused organizations. Part of this campaign was a series of vignette case studies and a resource hub to indicate a range of activities in cities globally seeking to meet these goals. Within this focus is an endorsement of the catalytic potential of city leadership and urban migration governance in achieving these outcomes.

Across Europe we have seen cities jointly advocating to the EU to welcome more refugees from camps in Greece, whose conditions reached a breaking point with the implementation of strict quarantine measures. These efforts have been mostly driven without the support of their national governments.[48] In Germany specifically, a number of cities have advocated directly to their local state (*Bundesland*) and to the EU regarding their capacity to house a greater number of refugees. There is a burgeoning subnational resistance regarding refugee policy in the country, with the national government recently blocking federal state Thuringia and city-state Berlin from implementing unilateral programs to receive additional refugees from camps in Greece. There is also precedent for subnationally driven refugee initiatives in Germany, such as Baden-Wuttemberg's collaboration with the International Migration Organization to accept 1,200 Yazidi refugees in 2012.[49]

The emerging forms of global urban governance we have seen in the area of migration, which have been somewhat galvanized by the COVID-19 crisis, have not only been driven from cities of the Global North. The mayors of Kampala, Amman, Freetown, and São Paulo are members of the Mayors Migration Council Leadership Board; they have emerged as prominent advocates for urban agenda in the global governance of migration and have drawn on their own local experiences to help inform global response strategies. For city leaders, the range of interconnected policy domains requiring international engagement for effective governance is increasing, and their emergence as "global governors"[50] is largely viewed as one of pragmatism, rather than ambition.

Conclusion

In a predominately urban world, cities represent a significant challenge but also a unique opportunity for addressing the majority of twenty-first-century global issues. To understand the "urban age" and emerging forms of global urban governance, we must look beyond simplistic interpretations that pit states against cities in a contest for international attention and legitimacy. Instead, we should seek to recognize the way that city governments and other urban actors are intersecting with governance processes at local, national, regional, and global levels.

This chapter has argued that this phenomenon forms a dynamic structuration that eschews traditional political stratifications. These processes are not well understood in either international relations or urban studies literatures. We contend that for scholars of global governance, understanding the ways the locus of political agency is shifting toward urban settlements is crucial for a holistic appreciation of the way the world is governed. This involves a double recognition: the shift that must occur within the traditional international system to build urban expertise and modes of working that are suitable for formal and informal settlements in the Global North and South and the ways that city governments and their partners are increasingly engaging with international processes, both within and outside the multilateral edifice. While collaborative city networks represent a significant emerging mode of global urban governance, the attention from scholars that these initiatives have received has at times obscured a focus on other everyday forms of global urban governance and the critical policy interdependencies that exist between them.

In particular, COVID-19 and its relationship with international urban migration demonstrates a number of features of global urban governance and city diplomacy that cement the crucial importance of cities in an informed conception of global governance. The speed and flexibility with which city leaders have responded to the crisis and the need to quickly develop and share effective mitigation strategies have demonstrated the pragmatic nature of global urban agency. The crisis has also revealed that cities cannot address global challenges alone and require effective partnerships with national governments and international organizations to maximize their advantages as global governors.

Suggested readings

Helmut Philipp Aust and Janne E. Nijman, *Research Handbook on International Law and Cities* (Cheltenham: Edward Elgar, 2021).
Lorenzo Kihlgren Grandi, *City Diplomacy* (London: Springer, 2020).
Ran Hirschl, *City, State: Constitutionalism and the Megacity* (Oxford: Oxford University Press, 2020).
Simon Curtis, *Global Cities and Global Order* (Oxford: Oxford University Press, 2016).
Stijn Oosterlynck, Luce Beeckmans, David Bassens, Ben Derudder, Barbara Segaert, and Luc Braeckmans, eds., *The City as a Global Political Actor* (New York: Routledge, 2018).

Notes

1 Simon Curtis, ed., *The Power of Cities in International Relations, Cities and Global Governance* (New York: Routledge, 2014).
2 Simon Curtis, *Global Cities and Global Order* (Oxford: Oxford University Press, 2016).
3 United Nations Department of Economic and Social Affairs, "68% of the World Population Projected to Live in Urban Areas by 2050, Says UN," 16 May 2018,

www.un.org/development/desa/en/news/population/2018-revision-of-world-urbaniz-ation-prospects.html.

4 Brendan Gleeson, *The Urban Condition* (New York: Routledge, 2015).

5 OECD and UN-Habitat, *Global State of National Urban Policy* (Paris and Nairobi: OECD Publishing, 2018), https://doi.org/10.1787/9789264290747-en.

6 Curtis, *Global Cities and Global Order*.

7 Benjamin R. Barber, *If Mayors Ruled the World: Dysfunctional Nations, Rising Cities* (New Haven, CT: Yale University Press, 2013).

8 Hillary Angelo and David Wachsmuth, "Why Does Everyone Think Cities Can Save the Planet?" *Urban Studies*, 3 June 2020, https://doi.org/10.1177/0042098020919081.

9 Ian Klaus, *Invited to the Party: International Organizations Evolve in an Urban World* (Chicago: Chicago Council on Global Affairs, 2018).

10 Daniel Pejic, "Cities and International Relations," *Oxford Bibliographies, International Relations*, 2020, https://www.oxfordbibliographies.com/view/document/obo-9780199743292/obo-9780199743292-0283.xml.

11 Thomas G. Weiss and Rorden Wilkinson, "Global Governance to the Rescue: Saving International Relations?" *Global Governance* 20, no. 1 (2014): 19–36.

12 Saskia Sassen, *Sociology of Globalization*, Contemporary Societies Series (New York: W.W. Norton, 2007); and Donald McNeill, "Barcelona as Imagined Community: Pasqual Maragall's Spaces of Engagement," *Transactions of the Institute of British Geographers* 26, no. 3 (2001): 340–352.

13 Neil Brenner, "A Thousand Leaves: Notes on the Geographies of Uneven Spatial Development," in *The New Political Economy of Scale*, ed. Roger Keil and Mahon Rianne (Vancouver: University of British Columbia Press, 2009), 27–49.

14 Michele Acuto, "Engaging with Global Urban Governance in the Midst of a Crisis," *Dialogues in Human Geography* 10, no. 2 (2020): 221–224.

15 Kristin Ljungkvist, "Toward an Urban Security Research Agenda in IR," *Journal of Global Security Studies* (8 June 2020): 2057–3170, https://doi.org/10.1093/jogss/ogaa019.

16 Michele Acuto and Benjamin Leffel, "Understanding the Global Ecosystem of City Networks," *Urban Studies*, 7 July 2020, https://doi.org/10.1177/0042098020929261.

17 "Global Compact for Safe, Regular and Orderly Migration," UN General Assembly Resolution, A/RES/73/195, 19 December 2018, www.un.org/en/ga/search/view_doc.asp?symbol=A/RES/73/195; "Global Compact on Refugees," United Nations High Commissioner for Refugees, A/73/12 (Part II), 13 September 2018, www.unhcr.org/gcr/GCR_English.pdf.

18 Sheila R. Foster and Chrystie F. Swiney, "City Power and Powerlessness on the Global Stage," in *Urban Futures: Alternative Models for Global Cities*, ed. Eva Garcia Chueca and Lorenzo Vidal (Barcelona: CIDOB edicions, 2019).

19 Michele Acuto, Anna Kosovac, Daniel Pejic, and Terry Louise Jones, "The City as Actor in UN Frameworks: Formalizing 'Urban Agency' in the International System?" *Territory, Politics, Governance*, 18 January 2021, https://doi.org/10.1080/21622671.2020.1860810.

20 Acuto and Leffel, "Understanding the Global Ecosystem of City Networks."

21 Emma Lecavalier and David J. Gordon, "Beyond Networking? The Agency of City Network Secretariats in the Realm of City Diplomacy," in *City Diplomacy Current Trends and Future Prospects*, ed. Sohaela Amiri and Efe Sevin (Cham: Palgrave Macmillan, 2020), 13–36.

22 Daniel Pejic, Michele Acuto, and Anna Kosovac, "Tracking the Trends in City Networking: A Passing Phase or Genuine International Reform," Workshop on *Cities, Geopolitics and International Legal Order*, Perry World House, University of Pennsylvania, 2019.

23 David J. Gordon, *Cities on the World Stage: The Politics of Global Urban Climate Governance* (Cambridge: Cambridge University Press, 2020).

24 Acuto and Leffel, "Understanding the Global Ecosystem of City Networks."

25 Ibid.

26 Anna Kosovac, Kris Hartley, Darcy Gunning, and Michele Acuto, *Conducting City Diplomacy: A Survey of International Engagement in 47 Cities* (Chicago: Chicago Council on Global Affairs and University of Melbourne, 2020).

27 Jon Pierre, *The Politics of Urban Governance* (New York: Palgrave Macmillan, 2011); and John Lauermann, "Municipal Statecraft: Revisiting the Geographies of the Entrepreneurial City," *Progress in Human Geography* 42, no. 2 (2018): 205–224.

28 Michele Acuto, *Global Cities, Governance and Diplomacy: The Urban Link*, Routledge New Diplomacy Studies (New York: Routledge, 2013).

29 Barber, *If Mayors Ruled the World*.

30 Angelo and Wachsmuth, "Why Does Everyone Think Cities Can Save the Planet?"

31 Michele Acuto, Shaun Larcom, Roger Keil, Mehrnaz Ghojeh, Tom Lindsay, Chiara Camponeschi, and Susan Parnell, "Seeing COVID-19 Through an Urban Lens," *Nature Sustainability* 3, no. 10 (2020).

32 C40 Cities, "Cities Unite to Tackle COVID-19 as President Trump Attacks the World Health Organization," *C40 Cities Medium Blog*, 16 April 2020, https://medium.com/@c40cities/cities-unite-to-tackle-covid-19-as-president-trump-attacks-the-world-health-organisation-and-bcaa7e65e086.

33 Michele Acuto, Susan Parnell, and Karen C. Seto, "Building a Global Urban Science," *Nature Sustainability* 1, no. 1 (2018): 2–4; and Timon McPhearson, Susan Parnell, David Simon, Owen Gaffney, Thomas Elmqvist, Xuemei Bai, Debra Roberts, and Aromar Revi, "Scientists Must Have a Say in the Future of Cities," *Nature* 538, no. 7624 (2016): 165–166.

34 Saskia Sassen, "The Global City: Strategic Site, New Frontier," in *Moving Cities – Contested Views on Urban Life*, ed. Lígia Ferro, Marta Smagacz-Poziemska, M. Victoria Gómez, Sebastian Kurtenbach, Patrícia Pereira, and Juan José Villalón (Wiesbaden: Springer, 2018), 11–28; and Michele Acuto, "Global Science for City Policy," *Science* 359, no. 6372 (2018): 165–166.

35 Jeremy Youde, "The Role of Philanthropy in International Relations," *Review of International Studies* 45, no. 1 (2019): 39–56.

36 See for instance Peter Herrle and Astrid Ley, eds., *From Local Action to Global Networks: Housing the Urban Poor* (London: Routledge, 2016).

37 Susan Parnell, "Defining a Global Urban Development Agenda," *World Development* 78 (2016): 529–540.

38 Chris Skelcher, Helen Sullivan, and Stephen Jeffares, "Governing Migration," in *Hybrid Governance in European Cities: Neighbourhood, Migration and Democracy*, ed. Chris Skelcher, Helen Sullivan, and Stephen Jeffares (London: Palgrave Macmillan, 2013), 71–93.

39 Peter Scholten, "Migration, History and Urban Life," in *The Routledge Handbook of the Governance of Migration and Diversity in Cities*, ed. Tiziana Caponio, Peter Scholten, and Ricard Zapata-Barrero (London: Routledge, 2019), 9–11.

40 UN-Habitat, "UN-Habitat COVID-19 Response Plan," Nairobi, Kenya, April 2020, https://unhabitat.org/sites/default/files/2020/04/final_un-habitat_covid-19_response_plan.pdf.

41 United Nations, "Policy Brief: COVID-19 in an Urban World," New York, June 2020, www.un.org/sites/un2.un.org/files/sg_policy_brief_covid_urban_world_july_2020.pdf; and OECD, "Policy Responses to Coronavirus (COVID-19): Cities Policy Responses," *OCED*, 23 July 2020, https://read.oecd-ilibrary.org/view/?ref=126_126769-yen45847kf&title=Coronavirus-COVID-19-Cities-Policy-Responses.

42 Anthony F. Pipa and Max Bouchet, "How to Make the Most of City Diplomacy in the COVID-19 Era," *Brookings* (blog), 6 August 2020, www.brookings.edu/blog/up-front/2020/08/06/how-to-make-the-most-of-city-diplomacy-in-the-covid-19-era/.

43 United Nations, "Policy Brief: COVID-19 in an Urban World."

44 Michele Acuto and Daniel Pejic, "Migrants Hold the Key to Urban Resilience and COVID-19 Recovery," *URBANET* (blog), 2 June 2020, www.urbanet.info/migrants-hold-the-key-to-urban-resilience-and-covid-19-recovery/.

45 Creighton Connolly, S Harris Ali, and Roger Keil, "On the Relationships Between COVID-19 and Extended Urbanization," *Dialogues in Human Geography* (15 June 2020), https://doi.org/10.1177/2043820620934209.

46 Saskia Sassen, *Cities in a World Economy*, 5th ed. (Thousand Oaks, CA: SAGE Publications, 2018).

47 Eric Garcetti, Yvonne Aki-Sawyerr, and Bruno Covas, "Migrant and Refugees Are Being Forgotten in the COVID-19 Response: This Has to Change," *World Economic Forum* (blog), 12 August 2020.

48 Jessica Rankin, "Cities Lobby EU to Offer Shelter to Migrant Children from Greece," *The Guardian*, 25 April 2020, www.theguardian.com/world/2020/apr/24/cities-lobby-eu-to-offer-shelter-to-migrant-children-from-greece.

49 Thomas McGee, "Saving the Survivors: Yezidi Women, Islamic State and the German Admissions Programme," *Kurdish Studies* 6, no. 1 (2018): 85–109.

50 Deborah D. Avant, Martha Finnemore, and Susan K. Sell, eds., *Who Governs the Globe?* (Cambridge: Cambridge University Press, 2010).

PART II
DIVIDES

Introduction

The second part of the book probes five "divides" that are likely to endure in the global governance of the future – and in future existential challenges to it. Chapter 8 begins with Stephen Hopgood's provocative assessment of a visible divide in "Human Rights after the West." The passing of an era and the new human rights realities of the twenty-first century are an insightful way to begin this part of the book because Hopgood explores the changing fortunes of ideas about how humanity treats its constituent members and the implications for populations across the planet as we move toward the middle decades of the century. His argument is that we need to rethink the shape of fitter-for-purpose global human rights organizations because, he argues, the existing array of liberal institutions that emerged after World War II are oriented toward the past, not the future. He points to the transformation in the state system, the collapse of the liberal social contract, and the general politicization of human rights as three key forces driving this change. Hopgood also cannot ignore COVID-19, which provides an especially unsettling argument in that restricting freedom of movement and other individual rights initially helped stop the spread of the virus in China and other parts of Asia.

Many of the themes that Hopgood introduces are picked up powerfully by the contributions that comprise the rest of this part. In Chapter 9, Alexander Betts offers an incisive account of the likely system of migration governance at the twenty-first century's mid-point. Betts probes a central division between people on the move – fleeing violence, war, persecution, and climate change as well as pursuing economic betterment – and those living in host countries that receive such migrants and whose lives and life experiences are almost inevitably more affluent. Two disequilibria penetrate his analysis, both linked to the toxic anti-immigrant politics so prevalent worldwide: demographic and economic inequality that will generate more supply of migrant labor but temper demand in host countries, and a mixture of climate change

DOI: 10.4324/9781003139836-9

and state fragility that will exacerbate the disconnect between mobility and the willingness of host countries to open their borders. States, non-states, business, and technology are complicating factors. But Betts is not fatalistic and points to the importance of human agency – the shape of global migration governance will ultimately depend on citizens and voters to determine tomorrow's values, narratives, and priorities.

Chapter 10 confronts squarely another divide that cleaves societies and the planet – namely, "The Global Governance of Poverty and Inequality." David Hulme and Aarti Krishnan trace the arduous ideational and policy journeys from the relative neglect of poverty as an issue in international conversations of the 1950s to the prioritization of extreme poverty alleviation at the start of this century to the subsequent broadening of aspirations to eliminate poverty and set targets to reduce inequalities as integral to the UN's Sustainable Development Goals (SDGs). Their analysis lays the blame for these continuing and often widening divides with the failure of Western capitalism and post–World War II governance institutions. They also explore the "rise" of China and other emerging economies as well as non-Western institutions. An essential part of their story consists of the UN's long-standing and ongoing efforts at goal-setting, from the first four "development decades" to the global conferences of the 1990s, and from the Millennium Development Goals (MDGs) and most recently to the SDGs and the development agenda for 2030.

In Chapter 11, Robbie Shilliam tackles head-on one of the most profound divides that continues to articulate global politics and that is key to understanding the differential experiences of people across the planet and the governance systems that they encounter. He employs a narrative form and an annotated suggested reading instead of endnotes to explore "Race: Apartheid Governance on a Global Scale." Shilliam offers three powerful stories as a means of constructing a view of the intersections among technology, organizational mandate, and health control, and the dangers and possibilities ahead. His is not a prediction of how a new apartheid is going to shape global governance as we move toward mid-century but rather a way to depict and analyze structures, tendencies, and trends of racial ordering that currently exist across cites, states, regions, and the world. Shilliam's purpose is not only to sound an alarm but also to point to the demonstrated capacity and will of human beings to find creative ways to ameliorate, resist, and perhaps take steps toward overcoming inequality and repression.

This part of the book concludes with Laura Sjoberg's "People: Who Governs and Who Is Governed?" Sjoberg mobilizes her own reflections on encountering and colliding with "truths" about representation, equality, democracy, and progress to explore how social hierarchies are continually reconstituted in systems of governance at all levels and the silences and violences embedded in their underlying processes. She highlights the use of discourses of Otherness and inclusion in the United States and elsewhere, which has implications for global governance more generally; and she shows how at the same time that diversities of gender, race, nationality, sexuality, religion, class, and dis/ability have become essential components in determining who governs, how governance works, and what constitutes the very subject of governance itself, it has also been an era of growing violence toward them. Sjoberg's is a sobering account of the violences done to others by systems of governance that self-identify as good, moral, and superior. Moving beyond the necessity of doing harm to others to celebrate one's value is an appropriate place to end this part of the book and a point of departure for the challenges that follow in Part III.

CONTENTS

Human rights after the West

Goodbye to all that

Stephen Hopgood

Let's begin by giving human rights their due. They have become a ubiquitous language for the condemnation of a vast array of maltreatment both by the state and by individuals, groups, and even corporations. They have done this on the basis that all human lives have the same moral value as all others regardless of identity, personality, or behavior. Activists for human rights have labored to create multiple far-reaching international and regional treaties and courts. They have pressed for the passing of countless pieces of domestic rights legislation and established important monitoring bodies. They have run a whole array of global campaigns demanding fair and decent treatment for people persecuted because of their opinions, beliefs, identities, and needs. They have linked together a vast ecosystem of human rights non-governmental organizations (NGOs) and protest movements. Their efforts helped inaugurate an Office of the United Nations High Commissioner for Human Rights (OHCHR), a Human Rights Council, and an International Criminal Court (ICC) that, while not strictly a human rights court, has come to be treated as one. The ten human rights treaty bodies, with their associated experts, and the Universal Periodic Review process in Geneva have proven to be innovative ways to apply peer pressure

DOI: 10.4324/9781003139836-10

to states, as has the precedent of human rights–related cases before various courts. Recently, for example, furious protestors in Poland demanding repeal of a Constitutional Tribunal ruling that bans abortions in the case of fetal abnormalities were marching under the banner of women's rights which brought tens of thousands onto the streets.[1]

Given all this progress and activity, why do I argue here – as I have elsewhere – that the era of human rights has passed?[2] I make this argument for several reasons, organized under three headings: the transformation in the states system, the collapse of the liberal social contract, and the politicization of human rights. My claim is that the liberal institutions with which we are familiar – international and domestic – are past rather than future oriented. Echoing Robert Graves's sardonic lament for what he saw as the demise of England after World War I, the new realities that we face in the early twenty-first century require that we say "goodbye to all that" and think anew about the shape of fit-for-purpose global governance institutions.[3] In world politics, those that survive need to serve the interests of a wider group of powers than are served by existing United Nations institutions and agencies or the major international financial institutions: the World Trade Organization (WTO), the International Monetary Fund (IMF), and World Bank. The hostility of resurgent states like China and Russia to many global norms is well documented, with the human rights system enjoying special enmity as the epitome of interference in sovereign affairs. The number of states openly violating human rights is too long to list here. Several Western states – even core European Union (EU) members like Hungary and Poland – are pushing back against human rights, while for liberal Western states like the United States and the United Kingdom, often guilty, it has to be said, of breath-taking hypocrisy, complaints about their own human rights failings are often treated with disdain. Human rights had utility, in a Western-centered world, as a form of reputational shaming, for a period lasting roughly from the Helsinki Accords of 1975 to the North Atlantic Treaty Organization's (NATO) intervention in Libya in 2011. These dates bookend the era of peak human rights.

What about domestic liberal institutions? The ascendancy of human rights maps almost perfectly on to the period of neoliberalism.[4] The globalization of markets, the freeing up of financial flows, the digital revolution, the erosion of organized labor power, tax cuts, and the privatization of education and health care all have created tremendous wealth for the rich and upper middle classes at the same time as inequality within developed countries has widened dramatically and the costs of unregulated industrial growth on the climate have become increasingly clear. Growing anger on both the left and the right about the perceived injustices of this unbalanced system have put liberal institutions like democracy, the rule of law, and the idea of human rights in the spotlight.

Describing the Trump-Biden presidential debate of 22 October 2020, for instance, Elizabeth Bruenig noted: "Since the right and left no longer agree on what institutions or figures should be seen as authorities on any given issue, there's no *debate* there, just an aggressive presentation of two different worlds."[5]

One thing both sides do agree on, however, is that unaccountable elites are part of the problem, with international human rights advocates a prime example. In other words, for left and right, there is no longer much middle ground; the true liberals, including the traditional supporters of human rights, are out of the picture. In this classic formulation, as I show in the following, human rights are about the rules of the game that *all* political competitors agree to abide by. Without agreement on these rules, human rights become part of what is being contested. This is politicization.

The success of human rights has come from the broad tent they have erected, allowing a diverse array of political and social movements to march under the human rights banner. But this accommodation has come at a price. In what follows, I distinguish between two forms of liberalism – the kind that focuses, as previously, on the rules of the game ("political liberalism") and a more politically active form that is directly involved in the fight for justice, for winning power and passing new laws ("social liberalism"). This second form treats human rights as part of a democratic political platform, seeking majority support for a thicker conception of appropriate social and cultural norms against determined opposition from the right and the hard left. This turns human rights demands into political claims, galvanizing support but sacrificing authority at the same time.

I start by saying something about the history of human rights before differentiating moral and political versions. I then look at the three shifts noted previously, concluding with some reflections on how the coronavirus illustrates these dynamics at work.

A brief history of human rights

Human rights–like ideas predate the modern era. Whether through the ideas of natural rights and natural law, the rights of man, and even bills of rights, the notion that human persons (a status from which many were exempted on the basis of race, gender, class, age, and disability) had certain "inalienable" rights was common, going back several hundred years. But the modern era began in 1948 with the Universal Declaration of Human Rights and soared in the 1970s when Western governments, especially the United States, began to use human rights as a form of soft power to pressure first the Soviet Union (USSR) and then other states who were not solidly in the Western camp. They reached their apogee in the 1990s when the Cold War was over and the West, led by the United States, stood triumphantly alone, its political and ideological message seemingly hegemonic. This sense of potential did not last long. It ignored Western hypocrisy, festering social problems with the liberal-democratic model, and the explosion of pent-up political aspirations and demands that the Cold War's demise released. Then came 9/11. By 2011, and NATO's intervention in Libya, it was clear that China, followed by Russia, was ready to challenge US institutional leadership of the international system in areas like trade, security, and the environment. From that moment, multipolarity, already nascent, has been a fact of global life.

The institutions that the Allied powers built after 1945 were liberal ones. They were about opening up markets, fostering free trade, rebuilding war-torn economies, and, to the extent that market societies could be built elsewhere, pushing democracy. All these institutions were heavily influenced by the power of the United States. Human rights were not, as it turned out, very useful or popular at this point for US leaders; they could always get their way by other means, and they endured much international criticism for their treatment of African Americans and for the war in Vietnam. Washington's adoption in the 1970s of the language of human rights was a sign, therefore, that the Cold War was moving against the Communist bloc. In an act of startling appropriation – what we might today call "gaslighting," something at which imperial powers are adept – the United States and its allies turned the language of human rights against the USSR and the postcolonial states. At the same time, they meddled in the politics of those states to ensure leaders who would not threaten Western commercial interests assumed power. By the 1990s, Western leaders were talking the language of human rights as part of what legitimated Western foreign policies. The US invasion of Iraq in 1991 was justified in part by President George H. W. Bush with reference to an Amnesty International report that turned out to be a fabrication perpetrated against Amnesty.[6] Since then, certainly in the decades from 1991 to 2011, human rights have been used countless times to legitimate Western policy, with their high point perhaps the "illegal but legitimate" bombing of Serbia over Kosovo in 1999 that led, along with the Balkan Wars and the genocide in Rwanda, to the establishment of the International Commission on Intervention and States Sovereignty and the concept of the "Responsibility to Protect."

Until the end of the 1980s, the focus of human rights work had been heavily on the commitments made by states, culminating in several landmark human rights conventions (e.g., on discrimination against women, torture, and children's rights). This gave added leverage to the core human rights strategy of "naming and shaming" governments who failed to meet their obligations. However, human rights work was expanding to take in a much wider variety of issues to do with economic and social rights and identity rights, especially around gender and sexuality. These developments were irresistible for at least three reasons. First, the collapse of the organized left in Europe – a precursor of the much more impactful Soviet implosion to follow – tipped an array of activists into the public sphere who were looking for ways to mediate the excesses of capitalist states. Second, wider social changes wrought by the 1960s brought issues to the fore – like racial and gender discrimination and sexual diversity – that human rights, with their emphasis on individual life choices, seemed well suited to handle. Third, a newly affluent middle class in Western societies, benefiting from lower real tax rates and technological advances, saw in human rights the ideological legitimation of their own rise. Hence, politics in the West moved from redistribution to recognition – from class to identity.[7] This worked until those in the West who considered their identities inviolate – white, mainly working-class people – found themselves surplus to requirements economically and stigmatized culturally. It was to democracy, not rights, that they turned.

Moral and political human rights

We can make a case for human rights in both moral and political terms. If they are moral, then they transcend state-level political demands made via treaty agreements as well as subjective claims about how certain people choose to live. They do so in favor of a set of abstract standards about how each person, understood as a human being, not as a bearer of any specific identity or interest, ought to be treated. This brings us close to the natural law sense of human rights as fundamental moral rules that preexist any human institutions. As powerful as this approach is, it does not resolve any of the difficulties involved in getting people and states to behave well. There is, however, a political variant – close to what some have termed political realism or political liberalism – of these "rules of the game."[8] There are important differences between political realism and political liberalism, but the core idea is similar enough: that we do not need sophisticated moral and philosophical justifications to accept that there are some basic and fundamental rights that almost all of us, thinking about it rationally and reasonably, would recognize as such, and any state that abuses them – for example, by killing its own citizens without due process (at the very least) – cannot claim to be legitimate for that reason. In other words, states, in order to justify their existence, must provide political order for their citizens. Bernard Williams called this the "basic legitimation demand."[9] Put simply: to have authority, a state must persuade most of its citizens most of the time that its actions are legitimate.

The basic requirements of this legitimacy are a version of, don't kill us, torture us, disappear us, deprive us of our liberty, silence us, without due process and cause. To be legitimate, a state must be the solution to the problem of fear and violence, not the cause. Much international law works in this way – states working out rules that they will agree to accept as self-binding. The results are often dismal and rarely stray into areas that threaten to limit any strong state's room to maneuver. The weakness of this conception is that it can only condemn what the objects of its condemnation agree to regard as worthy of condemnation. Such agreements are easy for powerful states to resist and are unenforceable without them. This should not surprise us given that sovereign power in the system as a whole is held by states. Following Rawls, we will call this conception "political liberalism."[10]

In addition to moralism and political liberalism, there is a third way to understand the human rights movement, and one that better approximates what we see today. There are many labels here, each capturing a little of what is going on: progressivism, cultural liberalism, the Green New Deal, Black Lives Matter, the #MeToo movement, and trans rights movements. This broadly "left" series of activist campaigns combines a variety of causes, both cultural and political, and thus, for want of a better phrase, I call it "social liberalism" to link its commitment to cultural liberalism with its rejection of contemporary capitalism. Where moralism stands outside the democratic struggle, and political liberalism seeks to create rules to limit that struggle, social liberalism is determined to overhaul the system as a whole by winning the struggle itself. Here, demands for a change in economic policy, even a transformation of the economy itself, align with demands about sexual orientation and gender identity, including trans rights, the protection of the climate, and the recognition that Black Lives Matter, to create a movement of people for whom "human rights" are about the subjective recognition of a fundamental entitlement to have one's interests met. They are about substantive justice. To realize human rights understood this way, social liberals know that they must win the battle of democracy, something they believe existing liberal institutions have made more, not less, difficult.

Transformation in the state system

Historically, the relative decline of a great power has meant warfare between the previously dominant state or empire and its challenger. Little in our nuclear-armed era suggests that will be the result of China's coming to be the equal of the United States. Both governments face significant internal problems: in the United States, how to maintain its promises to its people when its comparative advantages have evaporated; and in China, how to move from middle- to high-income status without democratizing. There is little prospect of the Western alliance – if Europe, the United Kingdom, and the United States remain allies – ceasing to be the equal of China or any other grouping of states in terms of military and economic power. But the era in which Western states designed and dominated global institutions is over, with little apparent appetite from any other grouping to remake those Western-fashioned treaties and treaty bodies as effective constraints on the policy-making autonomy of twenty-first-century states.

That is the problem: human rights were at their most potent in the 1970s, when they could be used to attack an already teetering Soviet Union and its allies, and in the 1990s, when, as the Cold War ended, the United States stood unrivaled as a global power. Human rights thrived, in other words, in a hierarchical system where they were used by dominant powers to augment other forms of leverage with a dose of moral condemnation (for domestic more than international consumption). In a system that is no longer as hierarchical, the penalties for human rights abuses are significantly reduced. Indeed, with China and Russia openly authoritarian states, other state leaders feel increasingly confident in suppressing dissent using state power.

The rules and institutions that survive this shift must function in some way to meet the needs and interests of newly prominent states. International humanitarian law, for example, has a variety of elements around reciprocity on the battlefield from which all states benefit. The wider field of humanitarian action – for example, the Office of the United Nations High Commissioner for Refugees (UNHCR) – provides an alibi and clean-up operation for major crises that result from state policies. Human rights, by contrast, are about remaking state practice, not about smoothing the path of interstate relations. Now that Western states are taking as much flack as others, in particular the United States, they will be even more willing to disregard these varied normative and legal demands. Exhibit One is the Trump administration's sanctions against ICC prosecutors for investigating alleged US war crimes. Failure to see this kind of eventuality, when playing hardball with the United States during the Rome Statute negotiations, is what turned the ICC into a vast monument to the hubris of the human rights era. No great power is going to join. Indeed, not joining is evidence of being a great power in 2021. Who will stand up for human rights at the global level? The EU, minus the UK? But what influence will it have with the United States and China – a United States that withdrew in 2020 from the Human Rights Council and a China that is running a vast concentration camp system for the Uyghurs? Their first step will be choking off the money that funds the global human rights system, something that is already happening.[11] Strategic competition to win allies in a multipolar system, not more elaborate human rights treaties, will be the story of the next two decades, even with a Democratic president, Joe Biden, in the White House.

Collapse of the liberal social contract

There were always skeptics about human rights, but they enjoyed goodwill from citizens with the resources to support them: the better-educated, more cosmopolitan wealth creators and professionals who contributed to the tax system and were invested in political stability and good governance. Countless studies find that this middle class sustains liberal institutions to protect themselves from redistributive demands from below and ruling class power from above.[12] For them, the classic civil and political rights – the right to vote, freedom of assembly, freedom of expression, protection of mental and bodily integrity (the rule of law) – protect their interests and those of their children. Their approach to economic and social rights has been less avid, leading to skepticism on the left about rights as an effective way to advance radical economic change. But the middle class has been the mainstay of the political liberalism conception of human rights and therefore of the liberal social contract as a whole. The Western model of development is legitimated domestically by education-driven social mobility and rising living standards for all. At the national level, the coveted move from middle- to high-income status is strongly correlated with the formation of a middle class and its push for political liberalism, a trend the Chinese government is hoping to buck.

Since the 1970s, however, the growth in inequality has meant that for more and more people in the lower and middle of the middle class, social mobility is an illusion – their debts, particularly in the United States, a millstone more than the passport to a lucrative profession. The middle class is under pressure, in other words.[13] The wealthy top end is detaching itself from the lower and middle, the life chances of children now increasingly reliant on birth and inheritance. This is compounded by major structural changes in the workplace to do with computerization and artificial intelligence. Many careers and professions are going to cease to exist.[14] New jobs we cannot yet imagine will emerge, of course. But with historically low growth and no sense yet of the next technological leap on the horizon, people have started to consider the idea of basic minimum incomes as a way to sustain demand.[15] Evidence suggests that increasing inequality erodes social trust and capital, even among the middle classes.[16] When this class feels insecure, their incentives change. They become concerned about protecting themselves and their wealth. And without this class pushing for human rights, there is no prospect of any politician making human rights part of an election pitch.

With mobilized skeptics on the right and left, and an increasingly ambivalent middle class, populist politicians have gained ground. In some cases, like that of Hungarian prime minister Viktor Orbán, "illiberal democracy" has been openly advocated as a political platform. This means democracy – the power of the majority – over rights. Liberal and democratic are severed. Political contest now means getting one's own supporters into office and using the power they acquire there to erode the possibility of one's opponents winning power in the future. In Orban's case, this involves embedding norms about Western Christendom, as it does for Poland's Jaroslaw Kaczynski, the politician behind the almost total banning of abortion. Donald Trump, meanwhile, called for his domestic political opponents to be locked up, while Republican politicians in many parts of the United States seek to gut voting rights. These are just the most obvious of those Western politicians seeking to rewrite the West's attachment to the cause of human rights. Outside the West, there are too many cases to cite. In India, for example, the coexistence of democracy with illiberalism is all too apparent, with Amnesty International having been hounded out of the country recently because it pointed out the government's blatantly discriminatory treatment of Muslims.

Human rights politicization

The deep malaise in the liberal model within Western societies accelerated after the financial crisis of 2008. Even if Western powers wanted to put their full weight behind human rights in the post-West era, which they do not, they would find their own societies too fractured to do so. The populist right has always been skeptical of human rights, arguing that they devalue the interests of national citizens. International human rights activists represent in pure form those Samuel Huntington once called "dead souls," the cosmopolitan, highly educated elite whom the supporters of Trump, Brexit, Marine Le Pen, Jair Bolsonaro, Viktor Orbán, and others see as their enemy.[17] Kaczynski called on Poles to wage war on the current abortion protests, arguing that they were an attack on the nation fostered by foreign influences. On the other side, the left alleges decades of failure to address inequality, climate change, immigration, police brutality, and identity crimes and is skeptical about the ability of an arch liberal mechanism like human rights to facilitate radical change.

Which brings us to the core of my claim. We can see that human rights have grim prospects internationally. Additionally, members of the middle class who have sustained liberal political institutions are also suffering from insecurity and anxiety about their place in the world. But there is a more radical understanding of human rights, which I have labeled, with some misgivings, as "social liberalism." Human rights are not, in this case, about moral condemnation or about reasserting the rules of the liberal game; they are part of a set of political demands for social transformation. These movements are the natural inheritors of the successes of earlier rights activism in areas like women's rights and gay rights. The calls for a "Green New Deal" are not framed other than rhetorically in the language of human rights but in demands for a total overhaul of the economy. Liberal institutions give too many veto points to politically connected opponents. The shocking history of desegregation efforts in the US South is ample evidence. The way to overturn such injustice is not, principally or even mainly, through human rights, which protect privilege and focus on the state, but by gaining political power with a mandate for far-reaching changes to society and its institutions.

In the 1970s, Amnesty International was faced with the beginnings of this growth in "issue-driven" members. Its global leaders were concerned. They saw in members advocating that Amnesty campaign on new issues – especially around sexuality and gender – a danger to the legitimacy of the whole idea of a human rights movement. In 1978, a key group of Amnesty professionals made the decision that being imprisoned for "sexual offences alone" was not an Amnesty (and not, therefore, a human rights) matter. It took more than a decade to change this position.[18] For Amnesty at the time, human rights were powerful, and their advocates effective, precisely because members were committed on principle to everyone's rights regardless of whether or not they stood to gain from the rights in question. They were skeptical, as a result, of the "gay rights lobby" seeking to join Amnesty and move the organization away from a narrow focus on political liberalism.

This stance seems almost quaint now. As a stark example, Amnesty famously considered sending a man to the first major global women's rights conference precisely because the identity of the messenger was irrelevant.[19] Amnesty in the 1970s would definitely have been in the All Lives Matter camp, arguing that Black Lives Matter precisely because all lives matter. Today, we would find this response tone deaf. In building a global movement, the umbrella must be large, the causes many, the voices diverse and empowered. If human rights have retained relevance for social liberals, it is because they are so inclusionary. They name a movement with a place for everyone. The Amnesty leadership was trying to protect a mandate focused on political liberalism by holding states to account on the basis of the very laws they had signed (positive law) or the moral laws to which they were assumed to be responsive (natural law). In the human rights movement, by the 1990s, holding out for a narrow and perhaps even arcane understanding of human rights would have been bad business – other organizations had grown up to compete for supporters – but also impossible because Amnesty was a membership organization, and these were its new members. This is part of the success story of human rights.

The growth in "the human rights movement" brought many new issues onto the agenda in the 1980s and 1990s. This took human rights away from their focus on liberal institutions toward a more direct engagement with issues of how we should live, how our economies should be run, how we should deal with the climate and the arms trade and pandemics and poverty and gender recognition and race. This social liberalism was about fighting and winning the democratic struggle itself. It was not about "constitutional principles" and did not take the basic rules of the game as a given at all. The lesson that social liberals learned from the culture wars of the 1960s and 1970s was that the rules were stacked in favor of the status quo. Over the intervening decades, political liberalism has given way to a more direct confrontation between left and right, reaching a high point in current US Supreme Court politics, for example, where social liberals fear that an embedded majority independent of political influence will frustrate democratic choices, possibly for decades.

For more conservative critics of the social liberal approach, questions about gender and sexuality, as much as those about social welfare and tax, are decisions that a society takes together. The point about politics – the debate within the sovereign body through which we decide how to live together – is that outcomes become collective decisions enshrined in law. Protection of the human person in terms of physical and mental integrity – the thing the classic understanding of human rights was intended to advance – does not extend to choices those persons might make about aspects of their identity. Limits to acceptable lifestyles are to be resolved in the political sphere. For those of us committed to a thicker version of liberal protections, seeing race, sexuality, and gender brought into this conversation is essential. But unlike the core basic rights – limits to how the state can treat the human body – these identity-based questions are seen by many people as things we must agree on together *because we are a society*. These social and cultural norms require collective recognition. Critics say: "The human rights you claim are not attached to our national and historical culture and therefore lack saliency in this environment." The national sovereign public sphere trumps cosmopolitanism. British and US efforts to come up with their own charters of natural or universal rights are examples of attempts to square this circle. The same might be said for questions about social policy and economic redistribution. These are political questions, and the way to fight for them is through collective mobilization in the political process via coalitions of people whose interests, as well as identities and ideologies, are at stake. This will incite rage from those whose historical and contemporary claims to be treated as full members of society have been, and still are, often violently rejected. It will seem like the worst kind of hypocrisy. But is this not a brute fact about shifting majorities in favor of more equal treatment? It is where liberals have tried to get purchase over democracy, whether through political liberals trying to preserve life or social liberals trying to expand the sphere of applicable cultural norms to encompass the life choices of those who are discriminated against because of their race, gender, sexuality, disability, or religion.

All of which explains why more is expected of human rights than they can sustain. Given the upheaval in global governance structures, it might be time to focus on the narrower politically liberal conception of human rights.[20] That is, the concentration should be on the obligations that states have with respect to the human rights of all subjects and citizens: freedom of conscience; freedom of expression; fair trials; the right not to be tortured, extrajudicially executed, or disappeared; the right not to suffer the death penalty. These rules are basic and largely focus on the state's treatment of the physical bodies of its citizens. Once human rights are yoked to the fight for power, they become one set of claims against others and thus lose their privileged status. Their contribution is lessened in the direct business of political contestation because what they have to offer – the detached claim that they are independent of politics – has been abandoned. Moreover, we find human rights clashing with each other in this contest, a sure sign that they have lost their transcendent moorings and become part of the democratic struggle. Free speech claims come up against the right not to suffer harm from speech that is considered hateful. Climate change pits property rights against economic rights. Feminist and trans rights activists disagree virulently about the question of who counts as a "woman," an ontological burden that human rights are simply incapable of bearing. We are a long way from early struggles that were precisely about mapping the category of "human" onto all people, overturning centuries of racism, sexism, homophobia, and religious zealotry. Human rights become lost in political struggles, and that is where the struggle must be fought – that is, the battle for democracy.

Conclusion

It seems hard to imagine human rights making this withdrawal back into the world of political liberalism. Their achievements – for those of us committed to a more left-liberal social vision – were magnificently on display in the Polish marches against banning most types of abortion. Such a retreat would also privilege those who are members of states rather than the tens of millions of refugees, displaced persons, and immigrants whose plight is at the heart of social liberalism's cosmopolitan approach to questions of justice and so at odds with the nationalist core of the populist right and, frankly, the hard left. But this says more about me, and the world I would want to live in, than about how the society of which I am part will choose, collectively, to live. Mine is but one voice. What we decide to do, we must decide together. And social liberal human rights are one among many voices in that process. Their hubris is often grating; their approach suffers from a presentist bias, that is, their sense that we are breaking new ground, traversing uncharted territory, discovering truths uniquely our own. It is probably a psychological necessity, with all the sacrifices that must be made, to comfort ourselves with the thought that, unlike Ozymandias, people will look back and praise our accomplishments. But our certainties are gone. As Antonio Gramsci put it, speaking of the 1920s and 1930s: "The crisis consists precisely in the fact that the old is dying and the new cannot be born; in this interregnum a great variety of morbid symptoms appear."[21]

Our era is marked by these morbid symptoms, none more so than the wildly inconsistent response to the coronavirus – by turns cruel, permissive, contradictory, authoritarian, laissez faire, irrational, and counterproductive. The cooperation of medical researchers has been a highlight, but despite the need to pull together in the face of a common enemy, polarization has only increased. Vaccine politics have become inevitable.

The COVID-19 response has put human rights on the defensive. Michelle Bachelet, the UN High Commissioner for Human Rights, has said: "The pandemic clearly demonstrates that respect for human rights is beneficial to everyone."[22] The pandemic demonstrates no such thing. Severely restricting freedom of movement has helped stop the spread of the virus in China and other parts of Asia. Control over information has prevented panic. To protect the lives of some vulnerable, and mostly elderly, people, significant economic and psychological damage has been done to generations of young people shut away at home without proper schooling, without jobs, and without the physical presence of friends; the deaths of loved ones alone in medical facilities; and the suspension of the social bonds that most of us rely on to feel healthy and whole. To refuse to confront such trade-offs is a typical move in human rights. Otherwise, too much emotional and cognitive dissonance results.

Bachelet's difficulty illustrates the classic liberal response: protecting human rights in the face of governments greedy to take a chunk out of citizens' rights must run alongside claims about "well-being" that are core human rights concerns only on the social liberal reading. I suggested that to survive into the future, human rights advocates focus on the core and on reinvigorating political liberalism and leave questions about well-being to the democratic process as a whole. This seems to me smart but also infeasible and undesirable. We are fully engaged in the democratic struggle now and need to reestablish the rules of the game only once the substantive harms of a world of inequality, climate change, and discrimination have been fought and won. The fight now is for democracy, however imperfect a process it might be. And this is a domestic fight. The function that human rights can perform, in as deeply inhospitable an environment as one could imagine, is to ensure that the process remains as fair and free as possible. Which might not, sadly, be very fair and free at all.

Suggested reading

Nigel Biggar, *What's Wrong with Rights?* (Oxford: Oxford University Press, 2020).

Stephen Hopgood, Jack Snyder, and Leslie Vinjamuri, eds., *Human Rights Futures* (Cambridge: Cambridge University Press, 2017).

Samuel Moyn, *The Last Utopia: Human Rights in History* (Cambridge, MA: Harvard University Press, 2012).

Kathryn Sikkink, *Evidence for Hope: Making Human Rights Work in the 21st Century* (Princeton, NJ: Princeton University Press, 2017).

Beth A. Simmons, *Mobilizing for Human Rights: International Law in Domestic Politics* (Cambridge: Cambridge University Press, 2009).

Notes

1 Monika Pronczuk, "How Poland's New Abortion Law Became Such a Flash Point," *New York Times*, 27 October 2020.

2 Stephen Hopgood, *The Endtimes of Human Rights* (Ithaca, NY: Cornell University Press, 2013); "Human Rights on the Road to Nowhere," in *Human Rights Futures*, ed. Stephen Hopgood, Jack Snyder, and Leslie Vinjamuri (Cambridge: Cambridge University Press, 2017), 283–310.

3 Robert Graves, *Goodbye to All That* (London: Penguin Classics, 2000 [1929]).

4 See Samuel Moyn, "Powerless Companion: Human Rights in the Age of Neoliberalism," *Law and Contemporary Problems* 77, no. 4 (2015): 147–169.

5 Elizabeth Bruenig, "Biden and Trump's Final Debate: Who Won?" *New York Times*, 23 October 2020.

6 Stephen Hopgood, *Keepers of the Flame: Understanding Amnesty International* (Ithaca, NY: Cornell University Press, 2006), 120.

7 Nancy Fraser, "From Redistribution to Recognition? Dilemmas of Justice in a 'Post-socialist' Age," *New Left Review*, no. 212 (July–August 1995): 68–93.

8 See Bernard Williams, *In the Beginning Was the Deed: Realism and Moralism in Political Argument*, ed. Geoffrey Hawthorn (Princeton, NJ: Princeton University Press, 2005); and John Rawls, *Political Liberalism* (New York: Columbia University Press, 1993).

9 Williams, *In the Beginning Was the Deed*.

10 Rawls, *Political Liberalism*.

11 International Justice Resource Center, "UN Human Rights Bodies May Curtail Work Amid Funding Crisis," 23 May 2019, ijrcenter.org/2019/05/23/un-human-rights-bodies-may-curtail-work-amid-funding-shortage/.

12 Daron Acemoglu and James Robinson, *Economic Origins of Dictatorship and Democracy* (Cambridge: Cambridge University Press, 2006).

13 OECD, *Under Pressure: The Squeezed Middle Class* (Paris: OECD Publishing, 2019).

14 Carl Benedikt Frey and Michael A. Osborne, "The Future of Employment: How Susceptible Are Jobs to Computerisation," *Oxford Martin Program Working Paper*, September 2017, www.oxfordmartin.ox.ac.uk/downloads/academic/future-of-employment.pdf.

15 Robert J. Gordon, *The Rise and Fall of American Growth: The U.S. Standard of Living Since the Civil War* (Princeton, NJ: Princeton University Press, 2016); and Philippe van Parijs and Yannick Vanderborght, *Basic Income: A Radical Proposal for a Free Society and a Sane Economy* (Cambridge, MA: Harvard University Press, 2017).

16 Guglielmo Barone and Sauro Mocetti, "Inequality and Trust: New Evidence from Panel Data," *Economic Inquiry* 45, no. 2 (April 2016): 794–809; Eric D. Gould and Alexander Hijzen, "Growing Apart, Losing Trust? The Impact of Inequality on Social Capital," *IMF Working Paper*, August 2016.

17 Samuel P. Huntington, "Dead Souls: The Denationalization of the American Elite," *The National Interest*, 1 March 2004, 5–18.

18 Hopgood, *Keepers of the Flame*, 116–121.

19 Ibid., 150.

20 See Hurst Hannum, *Rescuing Human Rights: A Radically Moderate Approach* (Cambridge: Cambridge University Press, 2019).

21 Antonio Gramsci, *Selections from the Prison Notebooks* (London: Lawrence and Wishart, 2005).

22 Michelle Bachelet, "Video Statement on 'Good Trouble: A Virtual Panel on the Right to Protest,'" *OHCHR*, 29 September 2020, www.ohchr.org/EN/NewsEvents/Pages/DisplayNews.aspx?NewsID=26313&LangID=E.

Contents

Migration governance 2050

Utopia, dystopia, or heterotopia?

Alexander Betts

The start of the twenty-first century was described as "an age of migration."[1] Amid accelerating globalization, international migration increased four-fold in half a century to a stock of over a quarter of a billion people by 2020, and international travel was estimated at well over a billion people a year. However, amid rising populist nationalism, initially peaking in 2016 with the European "refugee crisis," Brexit, the election of Donald Trump, and the rise of far-right parties across Western Europe, states' openness to immigration began to wane. By 2020, COVID-19 had brought international mobility to an abrupt halt, leading some commentators to question whether we had reached an end to "the age of migration."[2]

The health, lockdown, and economic impacts of COVID-19 all had immediate cyclical implications for migration – changing the demand for labor in advanced industrialized countries, exacerbating a range of outward migration pressures from low- and middle-income countries, and politically legitimating a raft of securitized immigration control measures ostensibly intended to reduce the spread of the virus. But beyond the short-term, COVID-19 brought into sharp relief some of the longer-term structural changes shaping global migration. Indeed, it has served as an accelerator of many preexisting trends.

The demand, supply, and governance of migration are shaped by a variety of structural influences that transcend policy fields. Although

DOI: 10.4324/9781003139836-11

amplified by COVID-19, they have not been caused by it. The structural trans-formation of the global economy, including the implications of automation and offshoring on the future of work and the prospects for full employment in the West, are radically altering the economics and politics of migration. The rise of China, the end of US hegemony, and their consequences for multilateralism are contributing to an unstable world in which state fragility and semi-authoritar-ian governance are increasingly prevalent. Climate change and environmental degradation are leading increasing numbers of people to use migration as an adaptation strategy. Demographic change is reconfiguring the demand and supply of labor unequally around the world, with inevitable implications for migration. Meanwhile, digital transformation is strengthening transnational social connec-tions and shaping migration aspirations.

The challenge is to make sense of what these wide-ranging trends mean for migra-tion and its governance. While forecasting – and even scenario-building – future migration is challenging, existing social science can at least offer some insights into current trends and how they may play out in the future. This chapter considers where migration and migration governance are going and what they may look like at the century's mid-point. It is divided into two main parts. The first part considers future trends relating to migration, exploring the overlapping categories of labor migration, refugee migration, and irregular migration. The second part unpacks a number of scenarios and considers how the international politics and global governance of migration are likely to evolve.

Migration trends

In order to consider how migration governance is likely to evolve, we need first to reflect on what will happen to migration trends during the decades ahead. Scen-ario-building relating to migration is challenging because there are so many inter-connected variables, and migration is shaped by social, cultural, economic, political, environmental, and technological factors. Nevertheless, the combination of social science theory and empirical trends can offer some insights into the current direction of travel. Here I reflect on three interrelated aspects of migration: the labor-market paradox, the age of displacement, and irregular migration.

The labor-market paradox

Labor migrants – defined as people moving primarily for the purposes of work – make up more than 60 percent of the world's international migrants.[3] There is relatively little binding global governance relating to labor migration, and states' willingness to admit labor migrants into their territory is generally regarded as dis-cretionary, being based on the principle of reciprocal benefit to receiving countries and the migrants themselves.

From an economic perspective, migration is a consequence of geographical dif-ferences between labor supply and labor demands. Disequilibria between demand and supply lead to disparities in wage rates across countries, and this – according to neoclassical economics – causes migration, notably from labor-rich but capital-poor countries to capital-rich and labor-poor countries. The so-called new economics of migration has nuanced this to understand migration decision-making at the household level.

One of the main factors underlying the demand and supply of labor is demography. On a global scale, declining fertility and mortality rates are causing unprecedented changes in population size and age structures. However, these changes have unequal implications around the world.[4] In the rich world, populations are aging rapidly, with growing dependency ratios between age groups not typically in the labor force and those typically in the labor force.[5] For example, Japan's "super-aging" population has led to an inverted population pyramid, illustrating the direction of travel for many advanced industrialized economies. In emerging and low-income economies, on the other hand, population pyramids show a significant "youth bulge." For example, 20 percent of Africa's population and 40 percent of its workforce are estimated to be 15–24 years old. It is widely debated whether Africa's youth bulge will represent a boon or a curse for the continent.[6]

As economic and demographic disparities grow, the demand for and supply of labor migration – particularly by young adults – is likely to increase, mainly from relatively poorer to relatively richer countries. Moreover – and contrary to popular belief – rising GDP per capita in emerging and low-income countries will not reduce the supply of migrant labor. The so-called "migration hump" relationship shows that as incomes rise to an average of around $8,000 GDP per capita, the preference and ability to emigrate actually increase.[7]

That said, there are also complicating factors. In particular, the future of work is being rapidly reconfigured. Automation, artificial intelligence (AI), and machine learning will displace jobs in sectors traditionally filled by migrant workers, especially in advanced, industrialized economies. McKinsey estimates that around 15 percent of the global workforce could be displaced by automation by 2030 and that the effect will be greatest in advanced economies with high wage levels.[8] There will be increases in labor demand in some sectors, such as health care and technology development and deployment. In other areas, partial automation may create new jobs that complement AI. Jobs with repetitive tasks, for example, could shift toward a model of managing and troubleshooting automated systems.

The net implication for the demand for labor migration is unclear, but it seems likely that some of the demand we might expect to see for low-skilled immigration as a result of demographic transition may be offset by technological change and automation. A further complication is politics.[9] As has long been recognized, migration is nearly always beneficial from an economic perspective.[10] Michael Clemens, for example, estimates that open borders would make the world $78 trillion richer. Labor migration has the potential to benefit receiving countries by providing workers, taxpayers, and disproportionately high levels of entrepreneurship. It has the potential to benefit sending countries through remittances and skills development. And it benefits migrants and their families by increasing their own incomes. However, in contrast to other factors of production with the potential to cross borders, labor forms human relationships and is highly political.

Over recent years, immigration has increased dramatically in political salience, rising from generally not featuring in the top 10 most important issues for voters to regularly featuring in the top 5 most important issues for voters within advanced industrialized democracies. This is partly because labor migration has distributive consequences. While it may generally make receiving societies better off, these benefits are not equally shared. Low-skilled immigration, for example, can exert downward pressure on wages, put upward pressure on housing costs, and increase competition for access to public services such as health and education, especially among the poorest members of a receiving society.[11]

The political science literature on attitudes to immigration generally suggests that anti-immigration sentiments are not just shaped by economic factors but also by perceptions of cultural difference. In most of the empirical literature, these cultural factors are linked more to perception and the rhetoric of political elites than the material impact of immigration per se.[12] But there is a complicated relationship between economic and cultural factors. In many Western liberal democracies, the geographical regions with the highest levels of anti-immigration sentiment have been those with the relatively lowest stock of immigrants but that have experienced the collapse of labor-intensive manufacturing jobs. These patterns can be seen from the US presidential elections of 2016 and 2020 to Brexit and the rise of Alternative für Deutschland (AfD) in Germany. Put simply, anti-immigration attitudes are often shaped by politics and people's fears about wider structural economic change, rather than by migration per se.

In this sense, labor migration is characterized by a paradox: the economic case for more open labor migration is strong, but political trends – especially in rich countries – tend to go in the opposite direction. There is no long-term inevitability to this. Indeed, societal attitudes to immigration are often segmented by age and generation, creating the possibility for increasing tolerance toward immigration among the young but also increasing intolerance among aging populations in advanced industrialized societies. Redistributive public policies that enable marginalized communities to share in the benefits of immigration may also contribute to greater tolerance. There is also the possibility for political leaders to make the economic case for immigration more strongly and for narratives of inclusion to emerge.

Politics is not inevitable. Indeed, restrictive immigration policies in rich countries have historically been cyclical. History tells us that major recessions often lead to a backlash against immigration. In the United States, a spate of restrictive legislation began with the Emergency Quota Act in 1921, in the context of the 1920–1921 depression. In the UK, openness to immigration in the aftermath of World War II came to a halt with the Commonwealth Immigration Act of 1962, as GDP growth declined from 6 percent to less than 2 percent in the preceding two years. Germany suspended its *Gastarbeiter* scheme in 1973 amid the onset of the 1973–1975 oil shock–induced recession. In the aftermath of the 2008 financial crisis, countries adopted a range of policies to restrict immigration, with Spain, the Czech Republic, and Japan paying migrants to go home amid fast-rising domestic unemployment.[13] Joachim Vogt Isaksen provides evidence from time series data across 25 European countries that public attitudes become less positive toward immigration during economic crises.[14] Related work describes a variety of potential mechanisms, including drawing upon "scapegoat theory" and effects on competition for scarce resources, including jobs, housing, and public services.[15]

However, several factors imply that the trends underlying anti-immigration politics are also structural and hence likely to endure. Transformation in the global economy, the end of full employment, automation and offshoring of labor-intensive manufacturing, the rise of China and the change in the global distribution of economic and political influence, long-term public underinvestment in education and retraining, and technological opportunities for extremist politics to mobilize and polarize societies, for example, all contribute to the structural conditions within which restrictive immigration politics is likely to thrive.

All this means that the long-term trend will be a significant increase in the supply of migrant workers – linked to demographic and economic change – and a demand for migrant workers that will be tempered by automation and politics. How will this mismatch between supply and demand be reconciled? One possibility is through significant innovation in public policy to redistribute the benefits of migration, change public narratives to remove political barriers to mobility, and address popular concerns with migration through societal transformation. The other – currently more likely scenario – is that it will be reconciled through three interrelated mechanisms: state control, the rise of informal labor markets, and human smuggling networks.

The age of displacement

This picture will be further complicated by increasing numbers of forcibly displaced people. Human displacement is one of the defining issues of the twenty-first century. Already, the 80 million displaced people, including over 25 million refugees, are the highest on record.[16] The main cause is fragile and failed states. From Syria to Venezuela and South Sudan, governments are either unable or unwilling to ensure the basic conditions for life. In the absence of effective governance, the interaction of oppression, violence, and economic collapse has forced people to leave their villages, cities, and even countries.

And the challenge is likely to worsen as climate change makes whole areas uninhabitable and exacerbates other drivers of displacement. Already, we are seeing the effects on forced displacement. In the Northern Triangle of Central America, the surge in forced movement of people from rural communities in Honduras and Nicaragua to the United States has been partly attributed to the effects of climate change on food security and its interaction with weak governance.[17] Across the Sahel, resource competition attributable to climate change is exacerbating existing conflicts in ways that have led to displacement in Niger and the Central African Republic.[18] The World Bank estimates that by 2050, some 140 million people may be displaced by climate change, and global economic recession threatens to amplify other drivers of displacement such as conflict and weak governance.

The ideal solution to the migration crisis would be to address the underlying causes. Ending wars, creating human rights–respecting governments, and mitigating climate change would dramatically reduce displacement numbers. Yet the world has struggled to find solutions to these root causes, and the international community of states has proved especially ill-suited to repairing chronically fragile states.

Consequently, we are left with second-best solutions: finding ways to temporarily accommodate or permanently integrate displaced people in other communities and enabling them to live with dignity and purpose.

Further complicating matters, while it is likely that displacement numbers will rise, there are signs of a declining willingness of states around the world to admit refugees and other forcibly displaced people onto their territory. The so-called European refugee crisis of 2015–2016 was opportunistically mobilized by populist politicians in a way that polarized societies and ushered in electoral success for the Far Right.[19] In the absence of the crisis, and the way it was presented politically, it is questionable whether Brexit in the United Kingdom and AfD in Germany would have taken place.[20]

The overwhelming majority of the world's refugees – some 85 percent – are hosted in such low- and middle-income countries as Jordan, Lebanon, Iran, Pakistan, Uganda, and Ethiopia. This is not because they are disproportionately generous but because they neighbor conflict and crisis. But even in these countries, the willingness to provide refuge has been increasingly challenged. Major host countries such as Bangladesh, Kenya, Jordan, and Tanzania, disillusioned with a lack of international "responsibility-sharing" (also referred to as "burden-sharing") and facing domestic political backlash, have all threatened to deport refugees since the 2015–2016 European refugee. In 2016, for example, observing how Europe paid off Turkey to curtail the movement of Syrians across the Aegean Sea, Kenya threatened to immediately close the Dadaab refugee camps and expel all Somali refugees as a thinly veiled means to induce greater international support.[21]

We live in an age of displacement insofar as we see rising numbers of refugees and declining political will from governments around the world. The global economic recession created by COVID-19 is likely to exacerbate this trend, increasing levels of displacement while also accentuating the conditions in which xenophobia thrives.

Figure 9.1 summarizes the way the pandemic-induced global recession is likely to affect the causes, consequences, and responses to forced displacement. It highlights the relationship between economic recession, on the one hand, and the three main drivers of displacement (conflict, authoritarianism, and state fragility), the three main sources of support for displaced people (employment, assistance, and remittances), and three of the main behaviors that shape governments' responses to refugees (public attitudes, travel, and human rights). In each case, the figure highlights examples of social science research that shed light on the relationship between these variables and global recession.

But there are also grounds to suggest that these trends of rising numbers, increasing needs, and declining wills are more than simply cyclical. Although the long-term global trend suggests declining armed conflict and lower levels of authoritarianism over time, fragile states are proliferating, new forms of semi-authoritarianism have started to emerge, and climate change will have transformative effects on displacement, not least amid the rise of multipolarity contributing to paralysis within the UN system's ability to respond effectively to fragility, authoritarianism, and climate change.

Causes	Consequences	Responses
Conflict	**Employment**	**Public attitudes**
e.g. Miguel et al 2004: a 5% negative economic shock leads to a 0.5% increase in likelihood of conflict in Africa	e.g. Dempster et al 2020: 60% of forced migrants work in sectors highly impacted by COVID-19, compared to 41% of hosts	e.g. Isaksen 2019: attitudes to immigration in Europe are positively correlated with GDP growth and employment levels
Authoritarianism	**Assistance**	**Travel**
e.g. Svolik 2008: a $1,200 USD increase in GDP/capita increases the likelihood of democratic consolidation from 20% to 80%	e.g. Dabla-Norris et al. 2010: aid flows contract sharply during donor economic downturns	e.g. Fix et al 2009: the 2008 global recession led to a proliferation in government restrictions on immigration
Fragile states	**Remittances**	**Human rights**
e.g. Carment et al 2008: GDP/capital statistically significant and negatively correlated with indicators of state fragility	e.g. World Bank 2020: remittances to low- and middle-income countries predicted to fall 14% due to COVID-19	e.g. the Council of Europe 2013: austerity measures reduce governments' willingness and ability to uphold human rights
⬇	⬇	⬇
Rising numbers	**Increasing needs**	**Declining will**

Figure 9.1 The impact of global recession on the causes, consequences, and responses to forced displacement[22]

Irregular migration, the state, and non-state actors

There will therefore be two long-term disequilibria relating to international migration: a mismatch of the demand for and supply of migrant labor and a gap between rising displacement numbers and a diminishing willingness to provide asylum. How will these mismatches be reconciled? The answer is: through irregular migration.

In the absence of legal pathways for migration, people will resort to irregular migration options. In particular, they will rely upon paying human smuggling organizations and networks to facilitate their entry into another state. As state restrictions grow and the demand for irregular migration increases, so the price of smuggling may increase, but existing patterns suggest it is likely to endure and expand as the gap between demand and supply widens.

It is difficult to estimate even current numbers of irregular migrants because they are, by definition, moving outside formal legal routes. However, there were an estimated 12 million undocumented migrants in the United States in 2016; there were 850,000 apprehensions at the US-Mexico border in fiscal year 2019; and around 200,000 people a year were estimated to have crossed the Mediterranean through irregular channels in 2019. The best available global estimates suggest there are at least 50 million irregular migrants living around the world.[23]

Meanwhile, the human smuggling industry is booming. The United Nations Office on Drugs and Crime (UNODC) estimates that smuggling of people from Africa to Europe and from Central America to the United States is worth about $6.75 billion a year for criminals operating in these regions.[24] It has also shown that many smuggling networks are highly organized, often with links to a range of other criminal activities, including illicit drugs and the illegal trade in firearms. Thousands of people each year lose their lives while attempting dangerous journeys with human smuggling networks and organizations.

The cause of the smuggling industry is the mismatch between migrants' preferences and the willingness of prospective destination states to admit those migrants into their territory. In recent years, states have adopted a range of ever more complex immigration control mechanisms. In response to the growing politicization of migration and concerns relating to the impact of immigration on security, the economy, and culture, states have deployed a growing range of "non-entrée" policies.

Many of these border-control measures have had two key features. First, they have become increasingly extraterritorial in scope.[25] In other words, they have attempted to manage migration upstream, focusing on transit countries or even countries of origin. These measures include visa regimes, carrier sanctions, the extraterritorial processing of asylum claims, the deployment of border officials on the territory of other countries, and the use of militarized control measures within territorial waters.[26] Such approaches have frequently been part of bilateral agreements between destination and transit countries. Extraterritorial responses have become widely used in the context of so-called mixed migration flows, in which refugees and would-be labor migrants travel along the same routes.[27]

Faced with the operational challenge of how to distinguish refugees within mixed migration flows, states have resorted to extraterritorial measures to avoid incurring responsibility to assess asylum claims.

Second, border controls have become increasingly technological in orientation. Biometrics, surveillance technology, the use of transnational databases and big data in predicting migration movements, and automated immigration decision-making are all being deployed by states to control migration. An increasing proportion are provided by businesses and private contractors who innovate and sell technologies to states through a range of international forums and exhibitions spaces. From companies like Palantir Technologies to business lobby groups like the Security Identities Alliance (SIA), the private sector is not only a key provider of migration control products; it is also actively engaged in lobbying, rulemaking, and shaping the governance of migration control.

In this context, extraterritoriality, technology, and industrial development are rapidly shaping border-control practices relating to the management of irregular migration. They are likely to provide the primary means through which states engage in a strategic arms race with human-smuggling networks and organizations. It seems likely that this will continue and accelerate, given the dynamics described prior. The cost will be borne by those who lose their lives attempting dangerous journeys, and the greatest benefits may lie with private sector organizations whose technology is deployed as part of the $100 billion migration control industry.[28]

COVID-19 has provided a window into some of these dynamics relating to irregular migration. Within the first months of the pandemic, more than 200 countries imposed unprecedented restrictions on immigration. Entire immigration systems were suspended, including refugee resettlement and asylum. In the European Union (EU), for example, nearly all governments suspended processing new asylum applications. Elsewhere, the United States, Mexico, and Canada suspended access to asylum and imposed blanket deportation on new arrivals. Meanwhile, pushbacks of asylum seekers took place in Greece, Malta, and Italy. The practice of refoulement (returning people to a country in which they face a well-founded fear of persecution) became normalized virtually overnight. Other countries have imposed greater internal mobility and encampment restrictions on refugees. These limitations were justified on the grounds of preventing transmission of the virus.

One important litmus test will be the extent to which these control measures remain in place once the pandemic abates. Many commentators suggested that the pandemic represents a thinly veiled pretext for some leaders to implement long-held preferences for restrictive migration policies. Meghan Benton of the Migration Policy Institute argues that the sequencing to reliberalize mobility after COVID-19 will see states prioritize particular forms of migration, based on short-term economic interests.[29] And forms of migration – such as asylum – that lack public support may be subject to prohibitively high barriers, such as "immunity passports" and participation in contract tracing apps, which are not always available to people who arrive through irregular channels. Benton suggests that in this new world, a key fault line of global inequality will be between "movers" and "non-movers," which is similar to Zygmunt Bauman's famous distinction between "tourists" and "vagabonds," with the rich and privileged able to resume travel and the poorest and most marginalized excluded.[30]

Governance scenarios

The changing nature of the "problem" of migration is one important factor that will shape the preferences of powerful states and the trajectory of governance. Its impact will also be mediated by power, ideas, and interests.[31] In this section, I consider the factors that will shape how global governance is likely to evolve.

Power asymmetries and the multilateral impasse

Migration lacks formal multilateral governance. Until recently, when the International Organization for Migration (IOM) joined the UN system, there was – other than refugee governance – no UN migration agency and few globally ratified migration treaties, making migration "the missing regime."[32] The governance that has emerged has been fragmented, consisting of a tapestry of formal and informal institutions coexisting at different levels of governance, without a clear hierarchical ordering principle.[33] In the absence of a single referent institution or coherent regime, migration governance has had some of the features of a "regime complex," encompassing a range of overlapping and parallel institutions in different policy fields and at different levels of governance.[34]

During the second half of the twentieth century, migration governance was largely composed of two multilateral organizations: the UNHCR covering refugees and the IOM covering other aspects of migration. However, the IOM remained outside the UN system until 2016, mainly providing migration-related services to states. Gradually, a debate emerged about the prospects for more coherent global migration governance, notably shaped by the increasing politicization of migration. In 2006, the UN convened its First High-Level Dialogue on Migration. At this event, however, there was significant opposition – predominantly from migrant-receiving countries – to bringing migration formally into the UN system. As a result, a new Global Forum for Migration and Development was created, which has run annually ever since, but which was conceived to operate outside of the UN system. The 2015–2016 European refugee crisis brought a renewed multilateral engagement with migration. The 2016 New York Declaration led to a commitment by states to develop two global compacts, one on migration and the other on refugees, which were launched in 2018. These wide-ranging compacts were explicitly non-binding; they reflect, on the one hand, an increased willingness to discuss migration within a multilateral context, and, on the other hand, an ongoing reluctance by predominantly migrant-receiving states to renounce sovereign autonomy relating to migration.

In the absence of strong, binding multilateralism, most migration governance – other than refugees – is bilateral, regional, or interregional. A vast range of bilateral agreements represent the core of migration governance, with states engaging in (mostly) mutually beneficial, reciprocal agreements on issues such as visas, border patrols, readmissions, extradition, circular migration, capacity-building, and technical standard-setting. One of the dominant vehicles for migration governance has been Regional Consultative Processes (RCPs), informal governance structures that exist within or across regions. Beginning with the Intergovernmental Consultations on Asylum, Refugees, and Migration (IGC) in 1985, these have proliferated to every region of the world, including with IOM facilitation. They have often focused on offering technical support to states, enabling them to engage in behind-closed-doors dialogue among like-minded governments.

Why has migration governance remained so fragmented? Will it remain that way? The simple explanation for fragmentation is power. Migration governance has been shaped by power asymmetries between predominantly migrant-sending and predominantly migrant-receiving states.[35] Of course, the claim that the world is empirically divided among "sending," "receiving," and "transit" states is false: states like Turkey, Mexico, and Malaysia exemplify this fact. But the distinction offers a heuristic starting point for understanding power within migration politics. In any given migration relationship (bilateral, regional, or multilateral), sending states tend to have limited influence over emigration decisions while receiving states with border-control capacity exercise discretion over whom to let in. Other things being equal, this effectively makes sending states "takers" of migration governance and receiving states "makers" of migration governance. In game theoretical terms, this could be illustrated by what has been variously called a "Rambo game" or a "Suasion game" (a standard-game theoretical model for illustrating strategic interaction given a power asymmetry between two actors).

Indeed, this power asymmetry between so-called sending and receiving states on migration, and between "donor" and "asylum" states on refugees, has underpinned collective action failure within global migration governance. It is frequently reinforced by more general power asymmetries relating to states' structural positions within the global economy. This asymmetry is also central to migration diplomacy, shaping the type of agreements that emerge within migration governance. For example, several authors have shown how bilateral agreements on migration and refugees are often shaped by issue linkage, with North-South cooperation on migration based on horse-trading across policy fields, including trade and development.[36] Bilateral agreements between Italy and Libya, the EU and Turkey, the United Kingdom and Tanzania, Spain and Morocco, or Denmark and Kenya, for example, have often emerged because of a quid pro quo between northern immigration control agendas and the desire of southern elites to attract development aid or trade concessions, sometimes to underpin patronage or rent-seeking behavior.

In this context, the role of multilateralism has generally been as a forum for dialogue or a source of political legitimation. The Global Compact on Safe, Orderly, and Regular Migration, for example, lacks anything binding but offers states a "menu" of ideas that they can draw upon. The hope for those who advocate for multilateralism is that such documents will lead to gradual change in the norms and practices of international migration diplomacy, leading to increased opportunities for multilateralism to emerge over time. However, in practice, it would take a major shift in the values and preferences of powerful states to make multilateralism more than a sideshow within labor migration governance, as states that hold the power continue to jealously safeguard their sovereign authority.

Protection in the region

Contrary to popular belief, most refugees are not in Europe or North America. Most refugees do not have the means, aspirations, or freedom to travel beyond the camps or cities in the region from which they come. And this may offer some advantages: sometimes a common language, a similar economy, and the ability to easily retain contact with the homeland. For example, Somalis fleeing to the so-called Somali Region of southern Ethiopia are able to speak Somali with the host community, engage in similar income-generating activities as back home, and sometimes go back and forth to south-central Somalia to maintain farms or property.

However, refugees in such countries, and the low- and middle-income countries that host them, usually face significant challenges. Refugees are often required to reside in camps, with restrictions on their right to work and their mobility. Their access to basic services such as education and health care may be inadequate. And, even close to home, they may face discrimination. It is unsurprising that a small but probably growing number choose to move onward in search of a better life. For the countries that host them, the inequitable distribution of refugees around the world means that it is the countries with the fewest resources that bear the greatest responsibility. For decades, Tanzania, for example, has repeatedly argued that despite hosting hundreds of thousands of refugees, it has lacked adequate support from the international community, sometimes scaling back on refugee rights in protest.[37]

There is a growing consensus among policymakers that the best way to achieve sustainability is to focus on providing refuge in the countries that neighbor conflict and crisis, and to do so based on shifting from humanitarian aid for refugees toward development aid for both refugees and proximate host communities. If refugees can be supported close to home, this framework can benefit refugees and create economic opportunities for the host society. It can also reduce the need for irregular migration by refugees from poor countries to rich countries. In other words, the dominant idea, buttressed by concepts such as "self-reliance," "refugee livelihoods," and "the humanitarian-development nexus," has become that supporting refugees close to home can be mutually beneficial and a basis for international cooperation.[38]

This idea is not new: indeed, it has been *the* enduring idea in refugee assistance for the past two decades. Since the beginning of this century, a core group of European states – notably Denmark, the Netherlands, and the United Kingdom – have pushed for an approach called "protection in the region of origin," which is premised upon strengthening assistance close to home as a means to reduce the need for "irregular secondary movement." The idea endures partly because it is grounded in simultaneously meeting the key interests of all the main relevant actors. For example, in 2015 the EU created a nearly 5 billion Euro fund relating to migration from Africa (the EU Trust Fund for stability and addressing root causes of irregular migration and displacement in Africa); it focuses explicitly on both refugee self-reliance *and* reducing onward refugee migration from Africa to Europe.

The protection-in-the-region approach has been critiqued because it has been conceived, variously, as containment, a neoliberal machinery, and an adjunct of modern imperialism.[39] Yet few critics have managed to identify politically viable alternatives that reflect the geographical reality that most refugees and displaced people are in the poorest regions of the world and that rich countries largely exercise discretion in the contributions, financial or through resettlement, that they make to support refugees.

Given current power relations as well as government and public preferences, it seems likely that the protection-in-the-region approach will remain the basis of the refugee system. These interests are likely to ossify further as displacement numbers increase and states search for solutions that can operate at scale and endure over time. However, what could change dramatically is the conception of what refuge and sanctuary mean in such countries. Given growing numbers of people displaced by climate change, how might camps, settlements, and urban integration for refugees be reimagined over time? It seems likely that digital technology and the private sector will play an increasing role, connecting even remote, arid border locations to the global economy. The normative challenge will be to ensure that such "solutions" lead to meaningful and dignified lives. Cloud technology, Blockchain, and remote work are among the current ideas being discussed as a means to transnationally connect even remote refugee settlements. Alongside this, however, there may also be scope to reimagine what refugee resettlement can look like – for example, using technology to match resettlement places to refugees' own preferences, skills, and talents.

In addition to the challenge of "how to protect" will be the issue of "whom to protect." It is clear that the focus of the 1951 Convention on the Status of Refugees on "persecution" is poorly adapted to the main drivers of displacement in this century. Climate change, and its interaction with state fragility, for example, will force tens of millions of people from their homes and across borders. And this will inevitably require new international agreements on who is deserving of "international protection" or the right to migrate on human rights grounds. At the moment, states and international organizations are avoiding this debate, metaphorically burying their heads in the sand. But a decisive moment of renegotiation of "who is a refugee" is inevitably on the horizon.

Norms and international organizations

Beyond the interests of powerful states, where will sources of influence come from in migration governance? Traditionally, within global governance thinking, international regimes have been considered to influence and shape behavior through norms and international organizations.

In the realm of migration, international law plays an important role in the institutional landscape, albeit that much of international migration law is not labeled as such. International human rights law and international refugee law, for example, set out a series of norms that, in theory, establish limitations on states' conduct toward refugees. The 1951 Convention on the Status of Refugees, for example, is the most important legal instrument in the refugee system, defining who is a refugee and the rights to which such people are entitled. Meanwhile, human rights treaties set out a range of obligations toward migrant, not only as migrants but as human beings, including the right of people not to be forcibly returned to countries in which they may face serious harms. These norms are highly institutionalized and have been domesticated within many countries' municipal law and policies. They provide an embedded liberal bulwark against the egregious violation of the human rights of people who cross borders.

One particular challenge, however, has been the gradual erosion of the legitimacy and influence of international law, not only within this policy field but more generally. Many destination states, from Europe to Australia, have openly questioned the ongoing relevance of the 1951 Refugee Convention, publicly criticized lawyers, and openly violated international legal obligations. While international law still matters – judiciaries can and do regularly block majoritarian legislation and policy – migration and refugee protection are now more often shaped by politics than law. This is even more the case in emerging and low-income countries where governments may not have signed and ratified relevant conventions or, where they have, recourse to courts and the judiciary may be limited. For example, in the case of the 1951 Refugee Convention, many states in South Asia, Southeast Asia, and the Middle East are not even signatories.

Yet many international organizations and advocates continue to focus on law as the most important source of influence in migration and refugee politics. While it remains an element of influence, it is unlikely to remain the factor the predominantly shapes governmental decision-making relating to migration and refugees. Furthermore, there are many structural reasons to suggest that the influence of international law is likely to decline. The emergence of multipolarity, and the rise of China and the BRICS (Brazil, Russia, India, China, and South Africa), for example, challenge the authority of multilateral governance and the legitimacy of norms agreed in a bygone era of liberal internationalism. Instead, political pragmatism and interest convergence are more likely to be the basis for influencing the behavior of powerful states.

The challenge for international organizations is to recognize and adapt to this changed world. Many, like the UNHCR, have mandates that were a product of US-backed liberal internationalism. They therefore have mandates closely tied to the legal and normative framework of the allied victors of World War II. As power shifts toward China and India, and US hegemony wanes, international organizations, including in the realm of refugees and migration, will be required to reconsider the tools that lead to effective international cooperation. Facilities will rely less on knowledge of law and more on high-quality political analysis and brokering interest convergence. In many ways, the IOM is a reflection of this changing world: it has no normative mandate and provides services to the most powerful states. Meanwhile, UNHCR is a product of liberal internationalism. Both will be compelled to adapt and reconsider how they exert influence on state behavior over time and what it means to facilitate effective, and normatively desirable, international cooperation.

Conclusion: Utopia, dystopia, or heterotopia?

Building scenarios, let alone forecasting the future, is especially challenging in relation to migration. As the chapter shows, migration and its governance are shaped by a wide range of variables and the politics of several policy fields, including security, development, trade, human rights, and humanitarianism.

The preceding analysis is based on the assumption of holding constant current power relations, interests, and dominant ideas. Yet there is no inevitability that these cannot and will not be subject to change or radical alteration. New narratives are possible, and visionary leadership could emerge in a policy field in which it has been historically absent. There is nothing inevitable to the migration futures described prior; they are mediated by politics, which, in turn, reflects our own collective choices – as citizens, voters, consumers, and activists.

In many ways, one might think of four schools of thought for politically engaged scholarship on migration futures: realists, idealists, activists, and innovators. The *realists* hold power, interests, and ideas (or at least their current trajectory) constant; they try to identify the opportunities for interest convergence to achieve ethically desirable goals. The *idealists* assume that power, interests, and ideas can be changed; they engage in critiquing power while building an alternative and better normative vision. The *activists* seek to identify mechanisms for how power, interests, and ideas can be changed in order to reshape the boundaries of the possible. The *innovators* seek to identify the practical solutions that can reconfigure power, interests, and ideas; they seek to reimagine the "good society." None of these positions is mutually exclusive; many exist in all of us and almost certainly coexist to different degrees in everyone engaged in thinking critically about migration and migration governance. All four archetypes are needed to build better futures for migrants and receiving communities that can be politically sustainable over time.

What migration governance will mean for people's lives and welfare will depend on standpoint. Reflecting wider trends, migration governance risks being open to elites and closed to the already marginalized. For some it will be utopian, offering a source of economic opportunity, security, and human rights. For others it may be dystopian, pitting them against the full force of sovereign states competing in a challenged and multipolar world, denying rights, thwarting dreams, and undermining human dignity. The normative challenge will be to ensure that the benefits of migration are shared equitably.

Overall, though, global migration governance is likely to be "heterotopian." It will be diverse and remain contested. Migration governance has never been settled for long and will continue to be highly political and politicized. Reflecting the complexity of migration, its governance will likely remain multilevel, operating at the bilateral, regional, and global levels. It will include a disparate range of public and private actors. It will increasingly be shaped by technology, business, and such "new actors" as mayors, diaspora organizations, and migrant-led networks, who sit at the vanguard of the reconfiguration of political geography. The trajectory of migration governance, and how it reconciles the competing normative agendas of security, economy, and human rights, will offer a litmus test for the overall political health of our global society.

Suggested reading

Lamis Abdelaaty, *Discrimination and Delegation: Explaining State Responses to Refugees* (Oxford: Oxford University Press, 2021).
Alexander Betts, *The Wealth of Refugees: How Displaced People Can Build Economies* (Oxford: Oxford University Press, 2021).
Alan Gamlen, *Human Geopolitics: States, Emigrants, and the Rise of Diaspora Institutions* (Oxford: Oxford University Press, 2019).
Andrew Geddes, *Governing Migration Beyond the State: Europe, North America, South America, and Southeast Asia in a Global Context* (Oxford: Oxford University Press, 2021).
Gerasimos Tsourapas, *The Politics of Migration in Modern Egypt: Strategies for Regime Survival in Autocracies* (Cambridge: Cambridge University Press, 2018).

Notes

1 Mark Miller and Stephen Castles, *The Age of Migration: International Population Movements in the Modern World* (Basingstoke, UK: Palgrave Macmillan, 2009).
2 Alan Gamlen, "Migration and Mobility After the 2020 Pandemic: The End of an Age," *COMPAS Coronavirus and Mobility Forum*, 3 June 2020, www.compas.ox.ac.uk/2020/migration-and-mobility-after-the-2020-pandemic-the-end-of-an-age-2/.
3 ILO, *Fact Sheet: Labor Migration Highlights* (Geneva: ILO, 2015), www.ilo.org/global/topics/labour-migration/publications/WCMS_384858/lang--en/index.htm.
4 Ronald Skeldon, *Global Migration: Demographic Aspects and Its Relevance for Development* (New York: United Nations, 2013).
5 Rainer Münz, "Demography and Migration: An Outlook for the 21st Century," *Migration Policy Institute Policy Brief*, no. 4 (September 2013): 1–14.
6 Jackie Cilliers, *Africa First! Igniting a Growth Revolution* (Cape Town, South Africa: Jonathan Ball, 2020).
7 Michael Clemens, "Does Development Reduce Migration?" in *International Handbook on Migration and Economic Development*, ed. Robert E. B. Lucas (Northampton, MA: Edward Elgar Publishing, 2014), 152–185; Hein De Haas, "Turning the Tide? Why Development Will Not Stop Migration," *Development and Change* 38, no. 5 (2007): 819–841.
8 McKinsey, *Skill Shift: Automation and the Future of the Workforce* (McKinsey and Company, 2018).
9 Gary Freeman, "Migration Policy and Politics in the Receiving States," *International Migration Review* 26, no. 4 (1992): 1144–1167.
10 Jonathan Portes, "The Economics of Migration," *Contexts* 18, no. 2 (2019): 12–17.
11 George Borjas, *Immigration Economics* (Cambridge, MA: Harvard University Press, 2014).
12 Jens Hainmueller and Daniel Hopkins, "Public Attitudes Toward Immigration," *Annual Review of Political Science* 17 (May 2014): 225–249.

13 Michael Fix, *Migration and the Global Recession* (Washington, DC: Migration Policy Institute, 2019).

14 Joachim Vogt Isaksen, "The Impact of the Financial Crisis on European Attitudes Toward Immigration," *Comparative Migration Studies* 7, no. 1 (2019): 24.

15 Michael Savelkoul et al., "Explaining Relationships Between Ethnic Diversity and Informal Social Capital Across European Countries and Regions: Tests of Constrict, Conflict and Contact Theory," *Social Science Research* 40, no. 4 (2011): 1091–1107.

16 UNHCR, *Global Trends in 2018* (Geneva: UNHCR, 2019).

17 Dan Restrepo et al., *Getting Migration in the Americas Right: A National Interest-Driven Approach* (Washington, DC: Center for American Progress, 2019).

18 World Bank, *Sahel Refugees: The Human Face of a Regional Crisis* (Washington, DC: World Bank, 2017).

19 Edgar Grande et al., "Politicizing Immigration in Western Europe," *Journal of European Public Policy* 26, no. 10 (2019): 1444–1463.

20 Matthew Goodwin and Caitlin Milazzo, "Taking Back Control? Investigating the Role of Immigration in the 2016 Vote for Brexit," *The British Journal of Politics and International Relations* 19, no. 3 (2017): 450–464.

21 Karen Hargrave et al., *Closing Borders: The Ripple Effects of Australian and European Refugee Policy: Case Studies from Indonesia, Kenya, and Jordan* (London: ODI, 2016).

22 Edward Miguel et al., "Economic Shocks and Civil Conflict: An Instrumental Variables Approach," *Journal of Political Economy* 112, no. 4 (2004): 725–753; Helen Dempster et al., "Locked Down and Left Behind: The Impact of COVID-19 on Refugees' Economic Inclusion," Center for Global Development, 2020, www.cgdev.org/publication/locked-down-and-left-behind-impact-covid-19-refugees-economic-inclusion; Milan Svolik, "Authoritarian Reversals and Democratic Consolidation," *American Political Science Review* 102, no. 2 (2008): 153–168; Era Dabla-Norris et al., "Budget Institutions and Fiscal Performance in Low-Income Countries," *IMF Working Papers*, Washington, DC, 2010, 1–56; Fix, *Migration and the Global Recession*; Council of Europe, "Austerity Measures Across Europe Have Undermined Human Rights," 2013, www.coe.int/en/web/commissioner/-/austerity-measures-across-europe-have-undermined-human-rights; David Carment et al., "State Fragility and Implications for Aid Allocation: An Empirical Analysis," *Conflict Management and Peace Science* 25, no. 4 (2008): 349–373.

23 See "IOM's Irregular Migration Database," https://migrationdataportal.org/themes/irregular-migration

24 UNODC, *Smuggling of Migrants for a Better Life*, 2020, www.unodc.org/toc/en/crimes/migrant-smuggling.html

25 Ralph Wilde, "Legal Black Hole-Extraterritorial State Action and International Treaty Law on Civil and Political Rights," *Michigan Journal of International Law* 26, no. 3 (2005): 739.

26 Thomas Gammeltoft-Hansen, "International Refugee Law and Refugee Policy: The Case of Deterrence Policies," *Journal of Refugee Studies* 27, no. 4 (2014): 574–595.

27 Roger Zetter, "More Labels, Fewer Refugees: Remaking the Refugee Label in an Era of Globalization," *Journal of Refugee Studies* 20, no. 2 (2007): 172–192.

28 Thomas Gammeltoft-Hansen and Ninna Nyberg Sorensen, eds., *The Migration Industry and the Commercialization of International Migration* (London: Routledge, 2013).

29 Meghan Benton, *The Rocky Road to a Mobile World After COVID-19* (Washington, DC: Migration Policy Institute, 2020), www.migrationpolicy.org/news/rocky-road-mobile-world-after-covid-19

30 Zygmunt Bauman, *Globalization: The Human Consequences* (New York: Columbia University Press, 1998).

31 Amitav Acharya, ed., *Why Govern? Rethinking Demand and Progress in Global Governance* (Cambridge: Cambridge University Press, 2016).

32 Bimal Ghosh, ed., *Managing Migration: Time for a New International Regime?* (Oxford: Oxford University Press, 2000).

33 Alexander Betts, *Global Migration Governance* (Oxford: Oxford University Press, 2011); Alan Gamlen and Katherine Marsh, *Migration and Global Governance* (Northampton, MA: Edward Elgar Publishing, 2011); Khalid Koser, "Introduction: International Migration and Global Governance," *Global Governance: A Review of Multilateralism and International Organizations* 16, no. 3 (2010): 301–315; Rey Koslowski, "Global Mobility Regimes: A Conceptual Framework," in *Global Mobility Regimes* (New York: Palgrave Macmillan, 2011); Susan Martin, *International Migration: Evolving Trends from the Early Twentieth Century to the Present* (Cambridge: Cambridge University Press, 2014); Kathleen Newland, "The Governance of International Migration: Mechanisms, Processes, and Institutions," *Global Governance: A Review of Multilateralism and International Organizations* 16, no. 3 (2010): 331–343.

34 Karen Alter and Sophie Meunier, "The Politics of International Regime Complexity," *Perspectives on Politics* 7, no. 1 (2009): 13–24.

35 Lena Kainz and Alexander Betts, "Power and Proliferation: Explaining the Fragmentation of Global Migration Governance," *Migration Studies* 9, no. 1 (2021): 65–89.

36 Alexander Betts, *Protection by Persuasion: International Cooperation in the Refugee Regime* (Ithaca, NY: Cornell University Press, 2009); Emanuela Paoletti, *The Migration of Power and North-South Inequalities: The Case of Italy and Libya* (Basingstoke, UK: Palgrave MacMillan, 2011); Gerasimos Tsourapas, "The Syrian Refugee Crisis and Foreign Policy Decision-Making in Jordan, Lebanon, and Turkey," *Journal of Global Security Studies* 4, no. 4 (2019): 464–481.

37 Sreeram Sundar Chaulia, "The Politics of Refugee Hosting in Tanzania: From Open Door to Unsustainability, Insecurity and Receding Receptivity," *Journal of Refugee Studies* 16, no. 2 (2003): 147–166; James Milner, "Can Global Refugee Policy Leverage Durable Solutions? Lessons from Tanzania's Naturalization of Burundian Refugees," *Journal of Refugee Studies* 27, no. 4 (2014): 553–573.

38 Alexander Betts and Paul Collier, *Refuge: Transforming a Broken Refugee System* (London: Penguin, 2017).

39 See, for example, Claudena Skran and Evan Easton-Calabria, "Old Concepts Making New History: Refugee Self-reliance, Livelihoods and the 'Refugee Entrepreneur'," *Journal of Refugee Studies* 33, no. 1 (2020): 1–21; Katharina Lenner and Lewis Turner, "Making Refugees Work? The Politics of Integrating Syrian Refugees into the Labor Market in Jordan," *Middle East Critique* 28, no. 1 (2019): 65–95; Julia Morris, "Extractive Landscapes: The Case of the Jordan Refugee Compact," *Refuge* 36, no. 1 (2020): 87–96; Lewis Turner " '#Refugees Can Be Entrepreneurs Too!' Humanitarianism, Race, and the Marketing of Syrian Refugees," *Review of International Studies* 46, no. 1 (2020): 137–155.

The global governance of poverty and inequality

David Hulme and Aarti Krishnan

Poverty and inequality are among the most pressing issues of our time, as well as one of the most stubborn divides. In 2019, almost half of humanity lived below $5.50 per day, and the world's richest 1 percent have more than twice the wealth of 6.9 billion people.[1] How did we get here? This chapter examines the evolution of the global governance of poverty and inequality and explores implications for the future. A particular focus is the shift from the relative neglect of poverty as a formal international issue in the 1950s to a high-income country–led prioritization of extreme poverty reduction in the 1990s and the subsequent broadening of the Sustainable Development Goals (SDGs), including the setting of an inequality goal in 2015. The chapter contends with the evolution, priorities, and failure of so-called western-dominated global governance institutions in mitigating poverty and inequality, shedding light on the rise of governance institutions from the Global South (e.g., China, India, and Latin America) and the role they play in the contemporary and future governance of poverty and inequality.

The conceptual framework draws on Robert Cox's thinking, especially the importance of material capabilities and of changes in such productive/destructive potentials and the role of ideas in challenging

DOI: 10.4324/9781003139836-12

orthodoxy, reshaping normative debates, and impacting policy and action.[2] These forces interact to shape each other in varying directions and strengths in any particular case.[3] The next section explores the global governance of poverty while the third examines the recent recognition of the need to reduce global inequality. The final section analyzes the future of global governance and the way changes in the material capabilities of countries have interacted with the ongoing "war of ideas" about the specification and pursuit of global goals. Understanding the forces that have shaped the evolution of ideas, policies, and action on poverty and inequality reduction provides a base for examining the future of the global governance of poverty and inequality.

Global governance and poverty

The first three UN development decades (1960s, 1970s, and 1980s) neglected poverty reduction in the belief that economic growth would lead to socio-economic convergence among peoples and countries. However, this changed after the Cold War ended, when the Organisation for Economic Co-operation and Development (OECD), the Bretton Woods institutions (BWIs), and donor agencies fostered the 2001 Millennium Development Goals (MDGs). These prioritized the halving of extreme poverty by 2015 through BWI-approved poverty reduction strategy papers (PRSPs). Poverty did reduce greatly over 2000–2015, but this was achieved through the rise of emerging economies more than the prescriptive agendas of developed nations. This section sets out the historical political economy of the global governance of poverty and the implications on achievement of the MDGs, highlighting the varied yet related approaches taken by western and southern countries in tackling absolute poverty.

Global governance of poverty: 1950s–1990s

In the post–World War II architecture for global governance, poverty reduction was merely a sub-element of the broader pursuit of "international development." The institutions leading on this task were the BWIs – the World Bank (originally the International Bank for Reconstruction and Development) and the International Monetary Fund (IMF) – the UN General Assembly, various UN specialized agencies, and bilateral foreign aid agencies (especially the United States, the United Kingdom, and France). The goal of development was not tightly specified but was seen intuitively as poorer countries "catching up" with industrialized countries through economic growth that would improve the lives of their peoples.[4]

Alongside industrial growth, agricultural modernization would be needed to reduce hunger and provide the peasantry with more productive livelihoods. In most countries, industrialization strategies achieved relatively little (with state-owned enterprises inefficiently pursuing heavy-industry and import-substitution strategies), but agricultural modernization was achieved through the "green revolution" (high rates of investment in crop research, infrastructure/market development, and institutional support), increased crop productivity, and over 30 percent increase in land area cultivated. These results were seen in Asia and Latin America but not in sub-Saharan Africa.[5]

The green revolution was spearheaded by the Consultative Group on International Agricultural Research (CGIAR) network and the Rockefeller Foundation. The results were varied. There is evidence to suggest that in Asia, a 1 percent increase in crop productivity reduced poverty by 0.48 percent.[6] Food prices were also reduced, and food security and diet diversity improved. However, others contend that agro-intensification widened intergenerational disparities and increased the incidence of poverty for small farmers, as technology access and support were only provided to targeted farmers in agro-favorable areas and to those with land rights.[7]

The voices of two international thought leaders and Nobel laureates – Gunnar Myrdal and John Kenneth Galbraith – calling for an end to world poverty had little influence.[8] For a few years in the 1970s, the UN and the BWIs seemed to be moving toward an anti-poverty ideational and policy convergence. The World Bank focused lending on multi-sectoral Integrated Rural Development (IRD), and UN organizations pursued "basic human needs" (BHN). However, by the late 1970s, the World Bank had returned to its market-based growth approach and the UN had limited finance to promote BHN.

These international agencies focused more on the "how" of development while "who" (the global poor) were only vaguely specified. Almost from its inception, the UN Secretariat, various of its specialized agencies, and the BWIs diverged dramatically on this "how" question. The UN system focused on direct, state-led approaches to improving the quality of life – access to food, potable water, health services, housing – while priority for the BWIs was private sector–led economic growth: trickle down from growth would improve the lives of the poor as higher average incomes meant that people could buy more food and pay for services.[9]

In the late 1970s, the BWIs moved to structural adjustment programs (SAPs). This economic agenda reflected the ascendancy of neoliberal thinking in the West, which sought to improve livelihoods through market-led growth. Throughout the 1980s, the BWIs dominated development policy with the mantra of "privatize, liberalize, and deregulate" and minimize state intervention. The UN was bypassed as it did not provide large-scale loans for development and could not stop the BWIs from imposing market-opening policy conditionalities on indebted borrower countries.

However, by the 1990s, a series of events and ideas challenged BWI conditionality and rekindled UN influence. First, the collapse of the Soviet Union led to calls for global strategic rethinking, and around the world, civil society began to rapidly mobilize.[10] Second, there was widespread recognition that in many countries, BWI SAPs had fostered a "lost decade" in which tens of millions of people, and especially women and the urban poor, had become worse off, rather than better.[11] This coincided with the publication of the 1990 *World Development Report* focusing on "poverty."[12] The World Bank developed a global yardstick for measuring extreme (consumption-based) poverty, the "dollar-a-day" (or $370 per annum upper poverty line) measure. The 1990 report calculated that in 1985, approximately 30 percent (1.116 billion) of the population of the developing world population were living in poverty. This policy failure encouraged social activists and some politicians to demand concerted action to tackle global poverty.

Third, in 1990, the United Nations Development Programme (UNDP) published the first *Human Development Report*, including the Human Development Index (HDI). Building on the ideas of Nobel Prize winner Amartya Sen, it argued that poverty should be measured in terms of capabilities (health, education, and income), rather than purely in monetary terms.[13] As a result, the case for increased public spending on basic services provision by national governments was strengthened.

Finally, in September 1990, the United Nations Children's Fund (UNICEF) convened the Child Summit in New York. This attracted world leaders who committed their governments to increasing spending on education and mother and child health and encouraged the start of a series of large-scale UN summits that fueled the rise of civil society and social activism.[14] The 1992 Rio Earth Summit and the 1995 Fourth World Conference on Women in Beijing had civil society events bigger than the official summits and attracted significant international media attention. In turn, these events were skillfully used by civil society norm entrepreneurs[15] to negotiate formal non-governmental organization (NGO) representation at UN meetings and plan for the launching of the World Social Forum in January 2000 as a means of offering an inclusive, counter-hegemonic challenge to the western-dominated institutions governing globalization.

However, this mid-1990s push for international development was not matched by action by rich countries. The OECD's Development Assistance Committee (DAC) was desperate to staunch reductions in foreign aid. The collapse of the Soviet Union meant that geopolitical considerations – bribing poorer countries not to support the Soviet Union – had evaporated. The DAC cast around for something to rekindle public support for aid. Unexpectedly, a short list of UN conference declarations selected by interns – the International Development Goals (IDGs) – took on a life of their own. An informal group of female ministers of international development, the Uttstein Group, championed the IDGs. In June 2000, as the UN prepared for the Millennium Summit, the leaders of four big institutions – the OECD, World Bank, the IMF, and the UN – publicly committed their agencies to IDGs achievement.

The MDGs and the role of the G77 in global governance

In September 2000, the UN General Assembly's Summit produced the Millennium Declaration, a much longer and messier endeavor than the IDGs. After heated private conversations, because of different ideologies, it appeared there would be two different sets of global goals: a UN set and an OECD/BWI set. Ultimately, however, a common final agreement on the UN Millennium Development Goals was reached in March 2001 after extensive negotiations. Many of the MDGs were very similar to the IDGs: eradicating poverty (specifically halving – between 1990 and 2015 – the proportion of people whose income is less than $1 a day) and hunger, achieving universal primary education, promoting gender equality and empowering women, reducing child mortality, improving maternal health, combating diseases, and ensuring environmental sustainability. However, at the insistence of some rising powers such as India, goal 8 was added to the MDGs. This called for a "global partnership for development" and identified changes that should occur in OECD countries so that the MDGs were not purely about what developing countries should do.[16] The Group of 77 (G77 – the 135 UN member states that call themselves "developing countries") was not going to accept a set of goals that had no targets for high-income UN members.

Another important deal was agreed in March 2001 between the big four institutions.[17] The UN could take the lead on the new goals (the MDGs), but the BWIs would lead on the negotiation of macroeconomic policy for countries seeking loans for development or stabilization. Borrowing countries would prepare PRSPs that would need joint IMF/World Bank approval. The PRSPs were aimed at creating poverty-focused government policies which included civil society participation. The primary goal of the MDGs was halving poverty, but access to finance for this objective would need BWI approval and the continued acceptance of BWI macroeconomic conditionalities. For example, this involved complications with monitoring processes conditionalities on the participatory nature of PRSPs and role of civil society participation; PRSPs did not account for domestic political processes.[18]

The MDGs soon began to filter into broader global governance processes, but the 11 September 2001 (9/11) attacks on the United States stalled their progress. Washington and its allies focused on the global war on terrorism, moving troops to Afghanistan and Iraq. The inevitable result was that the MDGs and poverty reduction became side issues at Group of 7 and 8 (G7/8) and OECD meetings.

Elsewhere, the economies of China, India, and other large developing countries were growing at historically unprecedented rates, and extreme poverty (then $1.08/day, moved to $1.25/day in 2005) began falling across much of Asia, Latin America, and Africa (see Figure 10.1). The "global financial crisis" of 2007–2008 did little to slow poverty reduction in developing countries. In Figure 10.1, the x-axis depicts the headcount ratio, or percentage of people living below the poverty line each year, and the y-axis the region/country. The data show that there have been considerable declines across all countries and regions. But overall, the headcount ratio for low-income countries has not fallen much. Most of the reduction in world poverty headcount has been because of the staggering fall of poverty in China, which fell at a compounded rate of 25 percent between 1990 and 2015. The compounded rate of decrease in India was 8 percent while that of low-income countries was only at 2.2 percent (results for the poverty gap measure show similar trends).

While there was a reduction in absolute consumption poverty, many voices (led by the UNDP) argued for a broader idea of poverty reduction as "human development." This spearheaded the creation of a human development measure of poverty, which captured the acute deprivations in health, education, and living standards that a person faces simultaneously and would be expressed in the global Multidimensional Poverty Index (MPI). This measure suggested that by 2015, approximately 1.6 billion people in the world, 54 percent in South Asia and 31 percent in sub-Saharan Africa

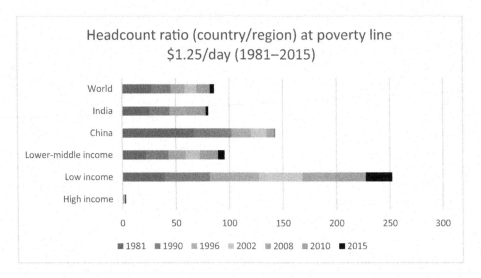

Figure 10.1 Share of poverty headcount by country/region, 1981–2015
Source: Author's construction from Povcal calculated at 2011 purchasing power parity (PPP) (India: nearest year inclusion when data not available)

(SSA), were living in multidimensional poverty.[19] There were stark differences in the results of the MPI versus the $1.25/day poverty measure. For example, in Chad and Ethiopia, the incidence of MPI was about 87 percent, whereas for $1.25/day poverty, it was only 37 percent. For China in 2015, the results showed that 5.5 percent of the Chinese population were MPI poor,[20] compared to the World Bank's poverty headcount, which was under 1 percent. The idea of human development helped challenge policies based on "growth-is-enough" thinking and supported a greater focus on social policy – basic education and health, gender equality, and social protection.

As the MDG era ended in 2015, the "halve poverty" global goal was achieved, but this was primarily attributed to China's progress because poverty fell there from 689 million in 1990 to 205 million in 2011.[21] India and Brazil also did well – both reduced their poverty headcount between 15 and 25 percent between 1990 and 2011.[22] Economic growth was an important driver of poverty reduction in all three cases, but policies differed. For example, while China focused mainly on growth, Brazil pursued social policies (e.g., social protection, minimum wages) alongside growth.[23]

The SDGs and poverty eradication

The initial global governance processes to create the post-MDG goals pursued "business as usual," with the UN, its specialized agencies, and major bilateral aid donors, such as the UK, heavily involved. The UN system produced a technical report identifying their priorities, and a UN high-level panel looked to update the MDGs into a "post-2015 development agenda." But, after the 2012 Rio+20 Earth Summit, an alternative governance process emerged with Brazil, Colombia, and other G77 members joining the leadership. This new process promoted the identification of a sustainable development agenda through a UN Open Working Group (OWG) including all UN members. This radical and inclusive shift in global governance processes weakened OECD and BWI influence over the development agenda.

Effectively, the SDGs had "southern origins."[24] They were launched in September 2015 and continued with an extreme poverty reduction goal for 2030, but the goal was upgraded from halving to "eradicating." Academics[25] and NGOs have challenged the "dollar-a-day" poverty lines (presently $1.90) as being based on bare survival. A concept of extreme poverty as being survival plus basic services and resilience capacity (security of not falling back into poverty) leads to a call for a higher line, such as the $3.20 line. This $3.20/day line suggests that in 2017, about 30 percent of the world's population needed to be lifted out of poverty: a much higher number than the $1.90 measures estimate of some 10 percent.[26] This gap strengthened the case for the SDGs to help people above the $1.90 line and encouraged the demand for the SDGs to set a goal for reduced inequality.

The Global South, and particularly China and India, are now playing a much greater role in shaping and financing development strategies in other countries.[27] China has encouraged infrastructure-led economic growth approaches to poverty reduction made possible through its vast Belt and Road Initiative (BRI). However, researchers estimate that only modest and spatial-concentrated reductions in poverty are possible.[28] India is also extending lines of credit to countries such as Uganda and Rwanda to promote industrialization and support employment creation opportunities, thereby seeking to reduce poverty.

In addition, new institutions from the Global South are emerging as players in development finance, such as the Asian Infrastructure Investment Bank (AIIB) and the New Development Bank (NDB), which are willing to invest in riskier infrastructure projects (energy, transport, and water) and have rapid turnarounds in terms of loan disbursements.[29] The policy influence of the BWIs has weakened as countries with significant numbers of poor people now have more choices about whose finance and advice to accept. In case of the BRI and the AIIB, "no poverty" is seen as cutting across key SDG goals 6, 7, 9, and 11. Thus, rather than investing in poverty as a stand-alone, the overarching understanding is that market-led models (infrastructure and investment) are key to poverty reduction through improved livelihoods, as evidenced in the AIIB's latest investments, depicted in Figure 10.2. While national leaders in G77 countries welcome Chinese loans, Western critics see them as a geopolitical strategy to make countries indebted to China.[30] These critics, however, remain strangely quiet about the growing indebtedness of African countries to Western private sector lenders.

In sum, the global governance of poverty has transformed since 1990. What was a vague goal for international development has become a defined UN global goal. Market-led models dominate both western and southern ideas of attaining poverty reduction. The global poverty agenda no longer belongs exclusively to the OECD and BWIs; emerging powers and the G77 have asserted themselves at the UN and bilaterally since 2000. However, the strategies that mean extreme poverty reduction 2000–2015 can be presented as a global success have had quite different impacts on economic and social inequality. Contemporary economic growth has fueled increased inequality and economic polarization.

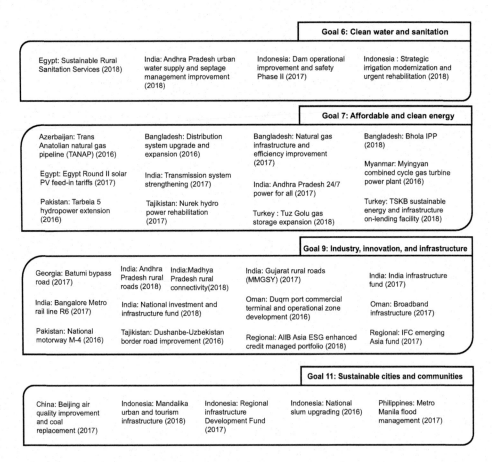

Figure 10.2 AIIB investments in relation to poverty reduction, 2015–2019
Source: Drawn from Mapping Infrastructure Investments Against the SDGs of the Asian Infrastructure Investment Bank (2019)

Global governance and inequality

While processes of global governance have prioritized poverty reduction, the goal of reducing inequality has only recently become a formal policy focus for the UN, the BWIs, and related agencies. Emerging data has shown that inequality is a major contemporary social issue, which is illustrated by Oxfam's analysis that in 2019, the world had 2,153 billionaires, who had more wealth than the "bottom" 4.6 billion people (60 percent of the planet's population).[31]

As with poverty, inequality can be conceptualized and measured across different dimensions. Commonly, it is examined in relatively narrow, money-metric terms as income (usually illustrated via a Gini coefficient) or wealth inequality. But such broader conceptualizations as human development (health or educational inequalities) or intersecting inequalities can also be useful indicators.[32] Inequality can also be examined in terms of inequality of opportunities or outcomes.[33]

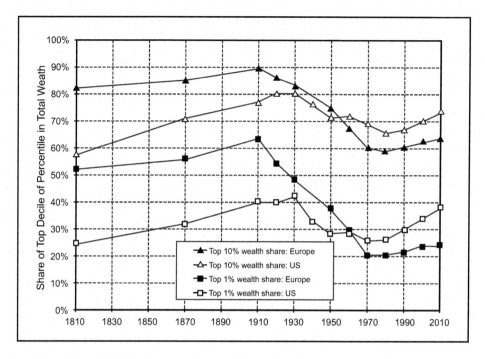

Figure 10.3 Top wealth shares, Europe vs. United States, 1810–2010
Source: T. Piketty and G. Zucman, "Wealth and Inheritance in the Long Run," in *Handbook of Income Distribution*, Vol. 2. (Amsterdam: Elsevier, 2015), 1303–1368.

Inequality expressed in the form of wealth differentials is defined as the current market value of all the assets owned by households, net of all debts, which is seen as a more robust measure than household income measures.[34] Patterns of inequality vary greatly over time. For instance, Thomas Piketty and Gabriel Zucman show that, in the nineteenth century, the United States was to some extent equal, at least for white men.[35] Wealth concentration was much less extreme than in Europe, but Figure 10.3 shows that over the course of the twentieth century, this pattern reversed, and wealth concentration is now significantly higher in the United States. In recent decades, there is evidence that while inequality between countries has reduced (as China, India, and other countries have "caught up" with OECD countries), inequality within most countries has been rising. Why has inequality reduction been so relatively neglected by global governance, and what does this mean for the future of global governance?

The tussle between poverty versus inequality across global institutions

The global governance of inequality has been relatively opaque, especially when compared to the structured approaches to poverty reduction taken by global institutions in the last three-quarters of a century. Unlike poverty, there is no straightforward and widely accepted measure of inequality. The lack of a prescriptive measure has hampered the evolution of formalized policy and planning processes for

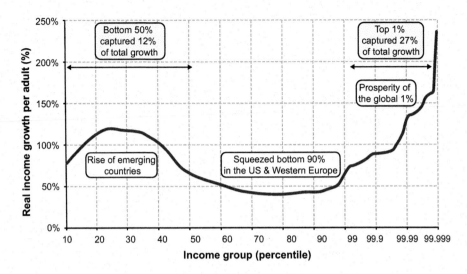

Figure 10.4 The elephant curve of global inequality and growth, 1980–2016
Source: F. Alvaredo, *The World Inequality Report* (Cambridge, MA: Harvard University Press, 2018).

inequality reduction. Indeed, with the notable exception of gender inequality (which has received considerable analytical and policy attention in most countries), discussions about reducing wealth and other inequalities within and between countries only became part of formal global governance activities after 2012.

Western-dominated global governance institutions prioritized goals for poverty but not inequality reduction. For instance, the OECD members who pushed for MDG 1 to be reducing extreme poverty were not keen on the idea of an MDG for inequality reduction. For them, its active pursuit might require the slowing down of the growth of their national income and wealth or, more threatening still, redistribution of income and wealth. Tackling inequality was seen as potentially fostering unwelcome discussions about "leveling down" rich-country incomes, consumption, or use of resources.

Not surprisingly, in an era still favoring neoliberal economic ideas and experiencing technological disruption, the period since the 1990s has witnessed growing within-country inequality and, commonly, polarization – including a massive increase in the wealth of the top 1 percent or even 0.1 percent of national populations. The results are often depicted through the elephant curve on global inequality.[36] The horizontal axis in Figure 10.4 divides the world population into centiles, according to gross income level; the vertical axis shows total income growth of an average individual in each group between 1980 and 2016. The top 1 percent captured 27 percent of total income growth from 1980 to 2016, while the bottom 50 percent captured only 12 percent.

While the UN summits of the 1990s often called for reduced inequality, the OECD's IDGs and the UN's MDGs did not. The one exception was the pursuit of gender equality in both the IDGs and the MDGs. The influence of the international women's movement in the twentieth century was allied to the diffusion of an international social norm of gender equality; this supported the progress of "reducing

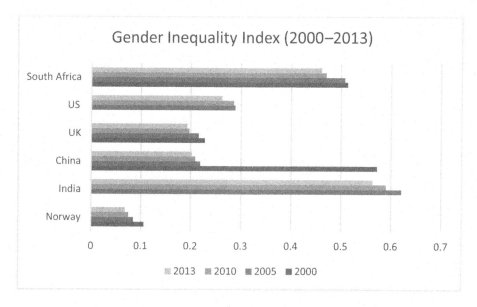

Figure 10.5 Gender Inequality Index
Source: UNDP, Human Development Report 2013. *The Rise of the South: Human Progress in a Diverse World*, New York, 2013, http://hdr.undp.org/en/content/human-development-report-2013

gender inequality at national level" as a global goal. Although a small number of religiously conservative countries such as Iran and Sudan opposed this goal, it eventually entered the MDGs. Since 2000 progress has been made in most countries in terms of gender equality, as illustrated by UNDP's Gender Inequality Index (consisting of indicators around maternal mortality ratios, adolescent birth dates, share of seats in parliament, labor force participation, and secondary education levels). Figure 10.5 shows that South Africa and India have relatively high gender inequality when compared to high-income countries and China.

The growing role of southern actors and inequality

As the 2000s proceeded, it became clear that the rise of the Global South would challenge rich-country reluctance to discuss inequality as a social concern. By 2012, when the UN launched the debate about the post-2015 development agenda, it was clear that geopolitical power relations had changed and a multipolar world was advancing. The UN's OWG that emerged from the Rio+20 Summit of 2012 took control of the process of global goal specification from international development agencies, and all UN member states were invited to participate. The OWG discussions broke new ground, such as permitting serious discussion about reducing inequality becoming a global goal.

The inclusion of inequality in the SDG framework is widely attributed to the insistence of developing countries and the persistent advocacy of international civil society networks. During the final stage of OWG negotiations in April–July 2014, the stand-alone inequality goal was one of the most difficult on which to reach agreement.[37] Many opposed the stand-alone goal of poverty, arguing that the definition of inequality was fluid; they questioned whether it would address poverty or was focused on redistribution (within countries) and curbing inequality between countries. The UN's High-Level Panel of Eminent Persons (HLP) of 2012 had representatives from the Global North and South; they pursued a poverty-focused agenda, suggesting that inequality should cut across other SDG goals but not be a goal in itself. The HLP focused on a "leave no one behind" agenda (i.e., the marginalized and excluded, keeping out issues of concentration of income and power at the top and inequality among countries).

Much of the support for SDG 10 emerged from civil society, and international policy networks had strong representation of NGOs and think tanks from the Global South, including Oxfam, Third World Network, and the South Centre. They pushed for broader understandings of inequality (and the inclusion of specific measures) around gender; social and cultural rights, within countries; structural causes; and macroeconomic and taxation policies. Eventually, many developing countries and ultimately the G77 and China also got on board with this vision.

The entry of inequality reduction into discussions about global goals pushed the World Bank to modify its mission. Alongside its eradication of extreme poverty goal, in 2013 the World Bank added a second goal of promoting shared prosperity.[38] This goal is understood as "income growth of the bottom 40 percent of the population in each country."[39] Ideationally, this addition can be seen as both a major change (moving beyond the low bar of only tackling extreme poverty) and a minor change (ignoring between-country inequalities and not tackling wealth polarization within countries).

Civil society has been one of the main forces that promoted inequality onto the global agenda. For instance, the *Oxfam Inequality Report* 2014 attracted global media attention and became a major topic at the World Economic Forum that year. This was a significant advance as the WEF had only recently included inequality on its agenda. In 2011, wealth inequality was highlighted as "most serious challenge for the world," according to Min Zhu, former deputy governor of the Bank of the People's Republic of China.[40] However, ideationally, poverty reduction was key, and it was acknowledged that economic growth must include the poor.[41] The WEF has been reluctant to explore inequality with subjects like taxation. It has a skewed set of participants – for instance, the 2019 summit included 1,500 elite business delegates but only 37 NGOs and 10 from labor. While NGOs like Oxfam tabled the issues of tax havens and increasing wage gaps (within and between countries), the Davos debates were focused on technological change and its links to inequality. By 2019, the Davos report – *Public Good or Private Wealth?* – returned to a focus on "millions of people living in poverty" rather than inequality.

Furthermore, private businesses have strong lobbying groups who actively push for lower personal and corporate tax regimes. Many countries facilitate such avoidance through international agreements that create offshore tax havens. According to the European Parliament, seven European Union (EU) countries (Belgium,

Cyprus, Hungary, Ireland, Luxembourg, Malta, and the Netherlands) display traits of tax havens. Furthermore, lax global governance has increased illicit finance flows. According to Global Financial Integrity, the top quintile of countries, ranked by dollar value of illicit outflows, included several developing countries (e.g., Mexico, Brazil, and Malaysia) but also European ones (e.g., Poland).[42] To mitigate private sector tax avoidance and profit shifting, the OECD developed the base erosion and profit shifting (BEPS) protocol in 2013 in cooperation with the G20. This involves policing corporate tax planning strategies used by multinationals to shift profits from higher-tax to lower-tax jurisdictions, thus eroding the tax base of the higher-tax juris-dictions. However, these attempted reforms have not been successful, as such key issues as transfer pricing and profit accounting for foreign branches remain unclear.[43]

In sum, while the SDGs made progress on creating a global goal on inequality reduction, this has met with mixed reactions from different actors. While many voices from the Global South and civil society strongly advocated for understandings of inequality that encompassed multidimensional aspects of society and redistribution and the need for a stand-alone goal, international business forums, many western governments, and private sector institutions continue to promote a poverty-focused inequality agenda. They seek to avoid issues such as redistribution and taxation.

The rise of southern institutions in the global inequality agenda

The rise of new institutions in the Global South such as BRI and the AIIB have had mixed implications for inequality. Inequality is not framed as a stand-alone goal but rather endogenized within market-led models of growth in much the same way that early approaches to development assumed that poverty would be reduced as a natural outcome of industrialization in poor countries. Some research has shown that BRI may narrow inequalities by increasing potential for job creation while other research indicates that this heightens spatial and wage inequalities because of the concentrated and risky nature in which investment is injected.[44] For instance, the increased pro-pensity of low-income countries to default on repayments (e.g., Uruguay Puntas De Sayago port, dams in Uganda, the Standard Gauge Railway in Kenya, Hambantota Port in Sri Lanka) has cyclical implications on wage and job-related inequalities. Thus, in many ways, the new actors are creating an alternate, yet similar, narrative to the neoliberal solutions of the West.

Beyond transnational issues, there are great divergences of income inequality within countries. For instance, in India, China, and Brazil, the share of national income earned by the top 10 percent of the population has increased from 29 percent in 1978 to 46 percent in 2015, while the share earned by the bottom 50 percent has dropped from 24 to 12 percent.[45] These have been attributed to the rural-urban divide as well as to burgeoning divides within towns and cities. However, how much can we expect global governance to influence or support national-level policies to reduce inequality? The answer is, probably, not much. For instance, much of the SDG 10 plan for China is to continue and extend existing labor, industrial, and social policies that have not reduced inequality. Similarly, India is extending its social protection schemes rather than adopting public "Yojana" strategies to enhance social protection coverage, create new social insurance schemes, or create special funds for lagging regions. Modest initiatives to "level up" inequalities rather than adopt reversing strategies to share wealth more fairly – land reform, progressive income, and corporate taxation have increased public investment in the quality of education and health services – seem to be as good as it gets. More radical strategies are obstructed by those with wealth and power as promoting "leveling down." In sum, even those countries in the Global South that have pushed the OWG to have an inequality-reduction goal have been reluctant to actively pursue that goal.

Conclusion: Looking to the future global governance of poverty and inequality

To date, the goals of tackling poverty and inequality have often fronted policy statements on international development made by the UN, BWIs, the G7, the OECD, BRICS (Brazil, Russia, India, China, and South Africa), and other institutions. But systematic action and tangible achievements have been mixed. On the positive side, great progress has been made in reducing extreme poverty (although the poverty line adopted is very low so that small increases in the consumption of poor people register as big gains). On the negative side, reforms that would dramatically reduce inequality – progressive national and global taxation, universal basic income, land reform, reparations for colonialism, salary maxima – have been kept off national and global agendas. In terms of processes, the case can be made that things have improved as G77 members and China now engage actively in shaping global goal selection and monitoring progress.

Global changes in the material capabilities of organizations, countries, and regions (especially the rise of China and Asia) facilitated new thinking on the specification of global problems at key institutions. These changing ideas on poverty and inequality have had an impact on both narratives and access to resources of institutions. Most importantly, these material capabilities and ideas set the stage for better understanding of the future of global governance of poverty and inequality. The future will be shaped by the tensions arising from the two related but different challenges that the UN identified in 2015: eradicating the extreme poverty of the "last 10 percent" and reducing inequality within and across countries.

Global governance of poverty: Where do we go from here?

Pursuing the poverty reduction goal will continue to be built around the existing global governance architecture, including the UN-BWIs ideational tussle, and new entrants such as China and other institutions and associations from the Global South. The years since 1990 have witnessed the restructuring of the global economy with phenomenal growth in developing regions of Asia, Latin America, and Africa (an increase in material capabilities).

This has had a knock-on effect for global institutions but also reshaped the behavior of developing countries in international negotiations. In particular, at UN meetings the emerging and middle powers have been more assertive.[46] While the selection of the MDGs and their implementation (a focus on extreme poverty and planning by the BWIs) was driven by OECD interests, the negotiation of the SDGs (poverty eradication, human development, social justice, and sustainability) was significantly shaped by other "voices" – for instance, Colombia, Indonesia, and African countries enthusiastic for growth and job creation.

As a result, the global governance of international development has shifted its focus from a narrow conceptualization of reducing absolute poverty to a broader idea of promoting human development and, more recently, reducing inequality. What explains this ideational shift in the balance of power between Therien's "two competing tales of world poverty"[47] and the contrasting UN and BWI paradigms? In the 1970s, the UN and BWIs seemed to be moving toward ideational convergence on who to help and how to help,[48] but by the late 1980s, the World Bank's specification of poverty as an income below a "dollar a day" in terms of purchasing power parity (PPP) meant that rather than being an unidentified "mass" of disadvantaged people, the geography of extreme poverty could be mapped and the poor identified and potentially targeted for public action. This dollar-a-day measure gradually mobilized international action against extreme poverty; it still permitted a BWI focus on economic growth and trickle-down as the priorities.

The specificity of the measure, along with the changing architecture of global governance with increasing voices of the Global South, has facilitated a form of "global buy-in" to eradicate extreme poverty. The chapter has thus far shown the importance of national governments (e.g., China and India) and new institutions (e.g., the AIIB), but the growth of multilateral, bilateral, and plurilateral trade arrangements (e.g., African Continental Free Trade Area, or AfCFTA, and Regional Comprehensive Economic Partnership, or RCEP) as well as the rise of regional associations (e.g., the African Union) can play a critical role in poverty reduction. A recent report by the Economic Commission for Africa showed that implementing the AfCFTA effectively by 2035 would lift 100 million Africans out of poverty, with 30 million of these being the extreme poor.[49] Thus, there is a need to effectively incorporate poverty into multilateral and bilateral trade deals, as well as in vision statements of regional associations.

The final "push" to eradicate extreme poverty will not be easy because the geography of much remaining poverty is so closely overlaid by weak national governance, state failure, and violent conflict. Reducing poverty in such contexts as the Democratic Republic of the Congo, Somalia, Afghanistan, Papua New Guinea, and Haiti has proven elusive in the post-Cold War era. Future progress toward the achievement of SDG 1 will also be dependent on progress on SDG 16 (promote peaceful and inclusive societies). Thus, with the UN reporting that the number of people displaced by violence, persecution, and conflict is at its highest level since the UN was founded, poverty reduction is proving more and not less difficult to address.

Global governance of inequality: Where do we go from here?

The idea of international development as directly tackling inequality advanced much more slowly than for attenuating poverty. Why was this the case? Material capabilities and associated institutional dynamics are the key to understanding. From a material capabilities perspective, the pursuit of income- or wealth-inequality reduction is likely to involve a direct challenge to wealthy countries, organizations, groups, and individuals. Almost always, such actors have considerable political and economic power and can dominate, and sometimes obstruct, public debate.

Ideationally, there are also potential obstructions to inequality reduction as an international norm. Neoliberalism valorizes inequality as a positive because it fosters entrepreneurship, competition, and innovation; those who achieve economic success deserve high incomes for hard work and risk-taking. Efforts by state or society to curb inequality will create disincentives for enterprise and slow down economic growth. For income and wealth, if one ignores inheritance and monopsony, there may appear to be some validity to this argument, but for other dimensions, it is morally dubious. For instance, how is enterprise fostered by the odds of a Malian woman dying during pregnancy being 150 times greater than a British woman?

The tensions that will shape the future global governance of reducing inequality derive from directly confronting the material interests of countries, groups, organizations, and individuals with economic power and wealth. These powerful players will seek to ensure that reducing inequality remains purely a topic for debate but not for action. Both the US government and citizens have directly opposed economic convergence with both China and Mexico. The world's wealthy may have deigned to talk about the inequality problem at Davos, but that is as far as most will go.

The historical grand narratives of reducing inequality through socialism have faded since 1990. Less ambitious ideas such as encouraging Scandinavian "varieties of capitalism" have even eroded in their European homelands. Whether national and global civil society can take a lead in converting reducing inequality from policy talk to policy action remains to be seen. When pushed, the wealthy prefer World Bank–type, minimalist conceptualizations of the problem. It is no accident that the agreed target for SDG 10.1 is to "achieve and sustain income growth of the bottom 40 per cent of the population at a rate higher than the national average," which comes straight from the World Bank. The wealthy keep clear of the ideas of wealth redistribution or global tax reforms. Civil society could challenge this approach if they could advance the "war of ideas." But it is the solution to reinvent socialism or identify a third way of forming a coalition of pro-equality social movements?

Nevertheless, perhaps some progress is possible. There has been a recent push toward taxation and redistribution by governments (e.g., the EU, the United States, and China through invoking competition policy) and limitations on the economic power of key corporations and individuals (Amazon and Jeff Bezos, Facebook and Marc Zuckerberg, Alibaba and Jack Ma). Optimists could interpret these as limiting the capacity of corporations and individuals to control excessive wealth and material capabilities, with the potential for redistribution of taxes earned into equality-promoting programs.

The global governance of extreme poverty has seen major advances over the last 25 years; its future governance seems likely to build on the UN-led structures that have evolved (and to benefit from the side effects of growth). But, increasingly, the achievement of reducing poverty will depend on conflict reduction; delivery will become more difficult and complicated. By contrast, the future global governance of reducing inequality is unclear as this goal directly confronts those with existing wealth (high levels of material capabilities). Whether global governance focuses on rhetoric and platitudes or can mobilize civil society worldwide and foster action (on global taxation, wealth redistribution, and even alternatives to neoliberal capitalism) will be shaped by the contemporary war of ideas about inequality. Don't hold your breath!

Suggested reading

Angus Deaton, *The Great Escape: Health, Wealth and the Origins of Inequality* (Princeton, NJ: Princeton University Press, 2013).

David Hulme, *Global Poverty: Global Governance and Poor People in the Post-2015 Era* (London: Routledge, 2015).

David Hulme and Rorden Wilkinson, eds., *The Millennium Development Goals and Beyond: Global Development After 2015* (London: Routledge, 2012).

Paul Shaffer, Ravi Kanbur, and Richard Sandbrook, *Immiserising Growth: When Growth Fails the Poor* (Oxford: Oxford University Press, 2019).

Joseph Stiglitz, "Inequality and Economic Growth," in *Rethinking Capitalism*, ed. Mariana Mazzucato and Michael Jacobs (Oxford: Blackwell, 2016), 134–155.

Thomas G. Weiss and Rorden Wilkinson, *Rethinking Global Governance* (Cambridge: Polity Press, 2019).

Notes

1 Oxfam International, "5 Shocking Facts About Extreme Global Inequality and How to Even It Up," 2019, www.oxfam.org/en/5-shocking-facts-about-extreme-global-inequality-and-how-even-it#:~:text=The%20world%27s%20richest%201%25%20have,1.&text=Billionaires%20have%20now%20more%20wealth,percent%20of%20the%20planet%27s%20population.

2 Robert Cox, *Approaches to World Order* (Cambridge: Cambridge University Press, 1996).

3 David Hulme, *Global Poverty: Global Governance and Poor People in the Post-2015 Era* (London: Routledge, 2015).

4 Sakiko Fukuda-Parr and David Hulme, "International Norm Dynamics and 'The End of Poverty': Understanding the Millennium Development Goals," *Global Governance* 17, no. 1 (2011): 17–36.

5 Parbhu Pingali, "Green Revolution: Impacts, Limits, and the Path Ahead," *Proceedings of the National Academy of Sciences* 31, no. 109 (2012): 12,302–12,308.

6 Peter Hazell et al., "The Future of Small Farms: Trajectories and Policy Priorities," *World Development* 38, no. 10 (2010): 1,349–1,361.

7 Shenngen Fan, Peter Hazell, and Sukhadeo Thorat, "Government Spending, Growth and Poverty in Rural India," *American Journal of Agricultural Economics* 82, no. 4 (2000): 1,038–1,051.

8 Gunnar Myrdal, *The Challenge of World Poverty: A World Anti-Poverty Program in Outline* (London: Penguin, 1970), and John Kenneth Galbraith, *The Nature of Mass Poverty* (Cambridge, MA and London: Harvard University Press, 1979).

9 Hulme, *Global Poverty*, 45–60.

10 Michael Edwards and David Hulme, eds., *Making a Difference: NGOs and Development in a Changing World* (London: Earthscan, 1992).

11 UNICEF, *Adjustment with a Human Face* (New York: UNICEF, 1987), https://digitallibrary.un.org/record/46296?ln=en

12 World Bank, *World Development Report 2000/2001: Attacking Poverty* (Washington, DC: The World Bank, 2001).

13 UNDP, *Human Development Report 1990* (New York: UNDP, 1990).

14 Hulme, *Global Poverty*, 35–36.

15 Martha Chen, "Engendering World Conferences: The International Women's Movement and the UN," *Third World Quarterly* 16, no. 3 (1995): 477–494.

16 Hulme, *Global Poverty*, 39–40.

17 Ibid., 159–164.

18 Geske Dijkstra, "The PRSP Approach and the Illusion of Improved Aid Effectiveness: Lessons from Bolivia, Honduras and Nicaragua," *Development Policy Review* 29, no. 1 (2011): 110–133.

19 Oxford Poverty and Human Development Initiative, *Global MPI 2015: Key Findings*, 2015, https://ophi.org.uk/multidimensional-poverty-index/mpi-2015/

20 Sabina Alkire and Yangyang Shen, "Exploring Multidimensional Poverty in China," *Policy Briefings, Oxford Poverty & Human Development Initiative (OPHI)*, 2015, www.ophi.org.uk/wp-content/uploads/OPHIBrief_34_2015-Exploring-MD-pov-in-China.pdf.

21 China, *Report on China's Implementation of the Millennium Development Goals (2000–2015)*, July 2015, www.fmprc.gov.cn/mfa_eng/zxxx_662805/W020150730508595306242.pdf; and UNDP, "Eight Goals for 2015," www.in.undp.org/content/india/en/home/post-2015/mdgoverview.html

22 Besides MDG 1.A, only MDG 3A was achieved (eliminate gender disparity in education), while none of the others mentioned were actualized.

23 Martin Ravallion, "A Comparative Perspective on Poverty Reduction in Brazil, China, and India," *The World Bank Research Observer* 26, no. 1 (2011): 71–104.

24 Sakiko Fukuda-Parr and Bhumika Mucchala, "The Southern Origins of Sustainable Development Goals: Ideas, Actors, Aspirations," *World Development* 126 (2020): 104706.

25 Thomas Pogge and Sanjay Reddy, "How Not to Count the Poor," 29 October 2005, https://papers.ssrn.com/sol3/papers.cfm?abstract_id=893159.

26 The World Bank, *Povcal*, 2020, http://iresearch.worldbank.org/PovcalNet/povOnDemand.aspx. All values measured at 2011 PPP, as calculated by the authors.

27 Emma Mawdsley, "South – South Cooperation 3.0? Managing the Consequences of Success in the Decade Ahead," *Oxford Development Studies* 47, no. 3 (2019): 259–274.

28 John Hurley, Scott Morris, and Gailyn Portelance, "Examining the Debt Implications of the Belt and Road Initiative from a Policy Perspective," *Journal of Infrastructure, Policy and Development* 3, no. 1 (2019): 139–175.

29 David Dollar, "China's Rise as a Regional and Global Power," *Horizons*, no. 4 (Summer 2015): 162–172.

30 Deborah Brautigam, "China, Africa and the International Aid Architecture," *African Development Bank Group Working Paper* 107, 2010, www.afdb.org/fr/documents/document/working-paper-107-china-africa-and-the-international-aid-architecture-20268.

31 Clare Coffey, Patricia Espinoza Revollo, Rowan Harvey, Max Lawson, Anam Parvez Butt, Kim Piaget, Diana Sarosi, and Julie Thekkudan, "Time to Care: Unpaid and Underpaid Care Work and the Global Inequality Crisis," *Oxfam Policy and Practice*, 2020, https://policy-practice.oxfam.org/resources/time-to-care-unpaid-and-underpaid-care-work-and-the-global-inequality-crisis-620928/.

32 Naila Kabeer and Ricardo Santos, "Intersecting Inequalities and the Sustainable Development Goals: Insights from Brazil," *London School of Economics, Working Paper* 14, 2017, www.lse.ac.uk/International-Inequalities/Assets/Documents/Working-Papers/III-Working-Paper-14-Intersecting-inequalities-and-the-Sustainable-Development-Goals-insights-from-Brazil-Naila-Kabeer-and-Ricardo-Santos.pdf.

33 Francois Bourguignon, Francisco Ferreira, and Michael Walton, "Equity, Efficiency and Inequality Traps: A Research Agenda," *The Journal of Economic Inequality* 5, no. 2 (2007): 235–256.

34 Emmanuel Saez and Gabriel Zucman, "Wealth Inequality in the United States Since 1913: Evidence from Capitalized Income Tax Data," *The Quarterly Journal of Economics* 131, no. 2 (2016): 519–578.

35 Thomas Piketty and Gabriel Zucman, "Wealth and Inheritance in the Long Run," in *Handbook of Income Distribution* (Amsterdam: Elsevier, 2015), vol. 2, 1,303–1,368.

36 Facundo Alvaredo, Lucas Chancel, Thomas Piketty, Emmanuel Saez, and Gabriel Zucman, eds., *World Inequality Report 2018* (Cambridge, MA: Belknap Press, 2018); and Sakiko Fukuda-Parr, "Keeping Out Extreme Inequality from the SDG Agenda – The Politics of Indicators," *Global Policy* 10, no. 1 (2019): 61–69.

37 Fukuda-Parr and Mucchala, "The Southern Origins."

38 World Bank, *Shared Prosperity: A New Global Goal for a Changing World*, 2013, www.worldbank.org/en/news/feature/2013/05/08/shared-prosperity-goal-for-changing-world

39 World Bank, *Trading for Development in the Age of Global Value Chains, World Development Report* (Washington, DC: World Bank, 2020).

40 World Economic Forum 2011, *Annual Report 2011–12*, WEF_AnnualReport_2011-12.pdf; weforum.org.

41 World Economic Forum 2012, *Annual Report 2012–13*, www.weforum.org/reports/annual-report-2012-2013

42 Global Financial Integrity, *Illicit Financial Flows to and from 148 Developing Countries: 2006–2015* (Washington, DC: Global Financial Integrity, 2019).

43 Yariv Brauner, "Treaties in the Aftermath of BEPS," *Brooklyn Journal of International Law* 41, no. 3 (2015): 973.

44 S. V. Lall and M. Lebrand, "Who Wins, Who Loses? Understanding the Spatiality Differentiated Effects of the Belt and Road Initiative," *Journal of Development Economics* 146 (2020): 102496.

45 Thomas Piketty, Li Yang, and Gabriel Zucman, "Capital Accumulation, Private Property, and Rising Inequality in China, 1978–2015," *American Economic Review* 109, no. 7 (2019): 2,469–2,496.

46 Matthias Vom Hau, James Scott, and David Hulme, "Beyond the BRICs: Alternative Strategies of Influence in the Global Politics of Development," *European Journal of Development Research* 24, no. 2 (2012): 187–204.

47 Jean-Philippe Therien, "Beyond the North-South Divide: The Two Tales of World Poverty," *Third World Quarterly* 20, no. 4 (1999): 723–742.

48 In the 1970s, the World Bank focused its loans on multi-sectoral Integrated Rural Development programs and UN organizations pursued basic human needs, especially for rural people.

49 Economic Commission for Africa, *AfCFTA Strategy to Chart a Path for Lifting Millions out of Poverty in DRC*, 2019, www.uneca.org/storys/afcfta-strategy-chart-path-lifting-millions-out-poverty-drc.

CONTENTS

Race

The new apartheid on a global scale

Robbie Shilliam

Futurology is the study of future probabilities. Scientists involved in futurology analyze patterns and trends in order to come up with a set of different scenarios, each of which has a different probability of occurring. Out of these studies, the hope is that policymakers might be able to make decisions that encourage positive future scenarios and discourage negative ones. This chapter is not futurology, but it shares many of its ambitions.

The chapter is a fictional story set about a decade into the future. It is not a prediction of how a new apartheid is going to shape global governance by mid-century. Rather, it is a story that rests upon the structures, tendencies, and trends of racial ordering that exist now across a set of different scales – city, state, and global. The story gives these tendencies and trends ten years' worth of play – that is, it accelerates their movements. So, readers should not interpret it as a prediction but a story about the here and now, about how some futures might be birthed in today's apartheid structures. These structures are to be found in geographies of segregation, new information technology, neoliberal economics, public health, and global development and the way these structures articulate – that is, fold into each other. Yet this story is also not dystopian. There are worrisome and alarming details, but there also exists the capacity and will of human beings to find creative ways to ameliorate, avoid, resist, and perhaps overcome inequality and repression.

DOI: 10.4324/9781003139836-13

Part I, Michelle Delany

Imagine your whole life as just one straight line. You would only be able to stick to one groove. Your wheels would jar and shudder if you tried to change course. Life would be unsurprising: you would know where you had ended up because you would know where you had started. Your senses would be attuned to one direction. You would develop a certain tunnel vision. The sides of your life would be a constant motion, a kind of static streak.

All that Michelle Delany knew of the elite college in Baltimore was a static streak. For years her mother had driven up Charles Street, passing Johns Hopkins' Home-wood campus to turn right at 39th Street toward Ednor Gardens, a median-income, owner-occupied, and Black northeast neighborhood. Michelle's parents were socially aspirational. Or, at least, they hoped to preserve and pass on their lower-middle-class status to their children. That's why they were committed to a college education for their eldest daughter – and a prestigious college, at that.

The best laid plans. It's funny how Michelle never imagined that there could be a campus behind Charles that had green and idyllic depth. All she knew was the sign by the east gate streaking past. Her mother's micro-directed timetable, full of purpose and contoured to the grid of the city, had paradoxically begun to unravel the family's painfully crafted Master Plan. If you can't even imagine the site of your future, how could you ever inhabit it?

Straight lines come from somewhere. Maleficent or careless designs of colonial rule that last an age. Strict concerns for heredity and inheritance: only my children/race shall inherit the earth. Concretized boundaries that demarcate communities and separate the good and normal folk from bad and abnormal populations. (The harder to reach the latter, the better.) Straight lines are fundamental to racial constellations.

Consider the origins of the term *la raza*. Fourteenth-century meanings include: a coarseness in fine cloth; a defect in poetic speech. Come late fifteenth century, with the reconquest of Iberia from the Muslim Moors and then the conquest of the Americas, *la raza* predominantly referred to the branding of purebred horses and the various religious lineages that made humans human. Jews, Muslims, and heathens had degraded or sinful lineages compared to the Catholic who had been born into a Catholic family – no conversion or diversion.

Limpieza de sangre – purity of blood – established the straight line as the basic cosmological feature of global order, 500 years long and counting. You had one irremovable root and you extended out from there. For the few whose root was virtuous and close to god, all for the better; for the rest, undoubtedly for the worst. The expectation of straight lines disciplined a motley humanity the world over. Michelle's mother sought to graft her daughter's life course onto a different branch of destiny. Education, she gambled, could bend straight lines, shift constellations.

Fate came knocking one day in the form of a charity devoted to the "public good," Michelle could never figure out what that term meant. Was it like a Sunday service, she once asked her mother, who assured her that at one time government had indeed administered to the public. Her father suggested she imagine praying to god for water and then asking the congregation to all pitch in with the utility bill. That was what government did when it was serving the "public." Still, try as she might, Michelle couldn't comprehend doing any of those things without using Transactional.

And Transactional was the app she was on right now, as she slouched in the living room, trying to complete her college admission forms, with a small air-conditioning unit humming desperately through the window in the quiet outside heat. A year ago, Michelle's high school had received a visit from a charity that connected neighborhood schools to elite colleges. She had put her name into a lottery and was selected for a "campus tour" of Hopkins – just a couple of miles west and south.

Michelle had jumped out of the charity's minibus, dizziness instantly hitting her because Charles Street should have been moving, but she was standing still. At the checkpoint on the east entrance, endless scans and affidavits micro-targeted her profile (costs paid for by the charity). Finally processed, Michelle stepped past the side streak into green depth. And blue air. And a differently dizzying sense of unguided, haphazard strolling alongside students only a year or two older than her but a lifetime distant.

Between Michelle and a future of expanded space and 360-degree motion lay that app. Transactional was the most prominent of a suite of apps belonging to data management companies that, in a short time span, had been effectively delegated governance functions by most administrations in the Group of 18 (G18). (Brazil and South Africa were ejected from the Group of 20 (G20) following their disastrous response to COVID-19. Despite their own terrible record of pandemic response, the United Kingdom and the United States remained in the grouping of the world's richest economies because of "the irreplaceable heritage of these countries within the fabric of the international community," as the Australian representative pontificated at the time.)

Of course, the whole relational database industry had begun long before COVID-19, and digital risk management was common among medium and large companies of all kinds. But it was between 19 and 23 that apps such as Transactional had really come into their own as platforms for administering the risk that came with the provision of public goods. Now, in the era of COVID-30, public and private risk had effectively morphed into one. Some academics labeled this a shift from "public administration/digital risk management" to "digital risk administration." Michelle's father tried to keep up with the more cerebral current affairs podcasts and seemed to be aware of the terminology, occasionally pronouncing the phrase as if it explained his whole world.

Actually, it had begun at Johns Hopkins itself, and its COVID Dashboard. An electrical engineer called Ajeet Kumar used the freely available data from Hopkins to create a virus checker app called Symptomatic. Modeled on apps that reported crime levels in neighborhoods, Symptomatic initially assessed COVID cases at the street level, giving red or green indicators. One evening at dinner, Michelle's father pushed a YouTube video in front of her featuring an academic at Morgan State University who proceeded to wax lyrical on "digital redlining," declaring Symptomatic to be an "apartheid app." Michelle had heard of Apartheid in high school. But that was something very peculiar and particular to a country called South Africa, right?

Baltimore's Roland Park Company was one of the first urban developers in the United States to exclude Black people from owning property in their planned communities, a practice that came to be known as "redlining." As the twentieth century progressed, redlining took on different modalities. For instance, those who lived in predominantly Black neighborhoods were often denied civic and financial services on account of their zip code or made to pay over the odds. It was an open secret that the "redlining" of neighborhoods was homologous to Apartheid rule in South Africa. Indeed, racialized segregation in South Africa shared with the Americas a root in slavery, especially around Cape Colony. The "separateness" that the Afrikaans word "Apartheid" invoked referred to the racialization of people into White, Black, Indian, and Colored races. Apartheid rule formalized redlining. The Population Registration Act of 1950 introduced identity cards for all adults, professing their assigned plot in the constellation of race. Meanwhile, the Group Areas Act of the same year segregated settlements along the lines of race by forced removal.

Around the time that Kumar was developing Symptomatic, Apple and Samsung updated their operating systems to include a non-optional COVID tracker that recorded the Assisted Global Positioning System (AGPS) movements of the handset. (Huawei did the same in the separate Sino-network). This data was Bluetoothed to official government agencies on the assumption that movements would be anonymized and used only to build large-scale predictive models. However, beginning in those G18 states whose populist leaders had not only mishandled COVID-19 but had simultaneously gutted any capacity for public health initiatives, phone AGPS data was progressively franchised to private interests and de-anonymized, so long as a "public health" case could be made.

Symptomatic was one of those companies that made the shift from Hopkins to government data and in doing so converted a public good into a function of assessing risk for predominantly private interests. Put another way, Symptomatic turned medical diagnosis into racialized risk management. The pharmaceutical industry had, for some time, used race as a category to determine biological differences in the testing of drugs. Many historians, sociologists, and biologists repeatedly pointed out that racial categories were created way before genes were discovered and that these categories could never provide a meaningful measure of biological or genetic differences between humans. Regardless, the bio-industry launched genes in a straight line of racial inheritance that cut right through the humans it sought to improve. Still, by treating race as if it had a shared fate, the descriptive reality that the bio-industry presented had some fidelity; it was just that the determinants of that fate were cumulatively historical, social, economic, political, psychical, and spiritual rather than biological purely and simply. In a way, then, Symptomatic was just coding medical convention.

Across the G18 – and no doubt beyond, too – indigenous, Black, Latino, Muslim, and other ostensibly non-white communities were variously but disproportionately affected by COVID-19 all the way up to the latest, COVID-30. Genes were nothing much to do with it. Not only had environmental and social factors contributed to a greater prevalence of some diseases among non-white communities. But the kind of jobs that, for example, Black peoples predominantly held, when combined with the tasks their bosses tended to give them, meant they spent much of their day undertaking dysgenic and contaminative labor even during pandemics.

"Essential workers" might have been the front line. However, there was a darker front line within the front line. The financial cost of illness and unemployment fell disproportionately on the front-of-the-front-line peoples, which, in turn, depressed house prices in their areas and thus neighborhood desirability, ultimately intensifying the segregating tendencies that were already evident at the local and municipal level. When Michelle was 10, she remembered occasionally playing with a couple of white children down the road. But it was a long time now since even she, still in her youth, had seen anybody who wasn't Black in Ednor Gardens.

Symptomatic intuitively short-circuited biology with race and space. Its algorithm scaled up street-level data so as to reference a vast array of zip codes, each becoming associated with one race, perhaps two non-white races, but never a mix of white and non-white races. Theoretically speaking, the app parsed the consequences of race segregation as the cause of racial difference and the numerator of risk. Practically speaking, Symptomatic used AGPS data to determine where individuals spent most of their time, and that location provided a risk score for disease. Numbers ranged from 1–5, with 1 being no risk at all and 5 being the highest risk. In all her days so far, Michelle had never seen a green number ping up on a phone belonging to her family or friends. The red numbers started at 4.

But Symptomatic also talked to other apps and, in so doing, laid the groundwork for digital risk administration. While Symptomatic provided the score, the Transactional app provided the indemnity to undertake a range of public (such as still existed) and (mostly) private actions. Almost all contracts of association, whether to do with work, business, civics, culture, municipality, or religion, ran through Transactional. Associative activities took place in a locale, and Transactional used Symptomatic to parse the difference between the COVID score of that locale and the COVID score of the locale the contracting individual predominantly spent time in. If the latter was larger than the former, then an indemnity was required to cover the cost of insuring against litigation for introducing disease into an area. The larger the difference between the two scores, the heftier the indemnity required to contract.

Transactional was the brainchild of Rex Coetzee. A South African–born white man naturalized as a Canadian citizen in his late teens, Coetzee had at college sculpted a utopic vision of a tech-full future for humanity. He ardently held to the claim that technological innovation solved political conundrums and so the means of advance were ethically unimportant – only the ends mattered. Coetzee's big innovation, he liked to believe, was the concept of a "life drive." The "social," Coetzee argued, was constituted through creatively aggressive actions. While the means of these actions might be violent or unsavory, the actions themselves cut through existing practical and ethical barriers to greatly extend systems of accumulation and production, thus prolonging human life. Transactional, Coetzee claimed, sought to extend lives by opening them up to any opportunity that might be said to mark an associational "life moment," whether that be voting, employment, charity, church, health care, property acquisition, credit, or education.

Now, it was entirely possible to register for a COVID-19–30 blood test to determine genetically and accurately whether you were infected. Yet the cost of that test was purposefully not covered by medical insurance, had to be paid up front, in full, and was simply prohibitive even to those aspirational families living in Ednor Gardens. The only practical alternative was to pay the monthly insurance to indemnify against private litigation for spreading coronavirus outside your zip code.

And that was the sticking point. Frequenting a 1 or 2COVID zip code – for work, study, or any other organized activity – placed the indemnity option way beyond the means of Michelle's family and pretty much every other family she knew. True, Ednor Gardens was not 5 territory, which came in about a mile south. And a 4COVID, the score for her neighborhood, could be doable for contracting to a 1 or 2COVID zip code so long as the activity or membership being applied for and contracted to was a one-off or extremely short term. But the four-year stint that came with an elite college degree in a 1COVID zip code made 4COVID indemnity costs entirely unaffordable to Michelle's family.

Activists and intellectuals regularly challenged Coetzee with a tranche of questions: which lives were counted as sufficiently human so that they might be prolonged? If some peoples' lives were shortened in the course of "extension" did it mean that they were insufficiently human? And wasn't this life energy driven by the pursuit of racialized genocide? Coetzee never provided a counter-argument. But he did react unfailingly to the South African connection his critics often made. "I am a Canadian citizen," Coetzee would bluster (some people could, it seemed, convert their inheritance), "is there anything less Canadian than racism and genocide?" Symptomatic PR provided a far-blander response to such challenges: the app was not racist but merely described reality, all the better to deal with it.

Nonetheless, it was an open secret. Everyone who felt the effect knew that Symptomatic and Transactional worked to render digital risk administration as an apartheid mode of governance. Everyday slang drew together the connections among wealth, location, and race. In hair salons and barber shops, 1COVID was known as "1white-1wealth," 4COVID – "4black4sure" – 5COVID – "blackasred," attenuated before long to "blackass."

If you listen carefully enough, you'll catch the wisdom in the creative-conventional. Take, for instance, the standard mode of categorizing race by way of phenotypes. The root of "pheno-" is "to show" or "to present." But *la raza*'s global constellations have always plotted both physical features *and* behaviors into straight lines. Who one associates with and how, how one talks, what one wears or eats, where one travels and resides, and so on are as much "presentation" as skin color or hair texture. Hence: 1white1wealth and blackass.

What those who felt it knew was that in the post-public era of digital risk administration, wealth equated to location equated to race, all of which equated to almost free access to capital, opportunity, and influence. If you were 1white1wealth then you made and remade your own heredity: you could circle, zigzag, idle, and roam with pure freedom. Even if you decided to slum it in a 5COVID neighborhood for a protracted period of time, and even if you thrilled at the Symptomatic color shift from green to red on your phone, you could simply pay the Transactional indemnities and proceed as normal until the algorithm eventually returned you to your 1COVID zip code.

That kind of freedom was a world away from Michelle. But the campus idyll still called her, just two miles southwest. She had hatched a plan. It was the kind of plan that her father could not directly agree to because to do so would be to acknowledge his digital incarceration and subservience to the apartheid app. It was the kind of plan that her mother had sanctioned, albeit through a recitation of Psalms 121: "I will lift up mine eyes unto the hills, from where cometh my help."

Part II, Joyce Moyo

Joyce Moyo was one of an increasingly diminishing group of foreign students who came to Johns Hopkins on scholarship, in her case from Zimbabwe. Like Michelle, Joyce belonged to one of the few remaining aspirational families, with parents who still believed that an education could set you apart and launch you into a future of low-density suburb living. Joyce had studied her way into the University of Zimbabwe, navigated around the boys, the strikes, the military incursions into campus, the ET (emergency taxi) drivers, and diminished library materials to win a place on Hopkins' English literature graduate program. (By strategic acts of omission, Joyce's parents had on more than one occasion created the impression to their friends and extended family that their daughter was studying to become a medical doctor).

First, though, Joyce had to travel to Pretoria, South Africa, to conjure the magic visa from one of three US embassies left on the continent. There, she undertook a procedure that Symptomatic had made virtually obsolete (and unaffordable) in the United States: actual blood tests – one, two, three draws of blood covering all the "Black diseases" that the United States Alien Control Services (USACS) had listed on their protocols. Surprisingly, Joyce's blood confessed to no sin. On arrival at Dulles airport, Virginia, Joyce was made to take the tests again in a side room to passport control; 36 hours of lying uncomfortably on the plastic chairs and she was finally admitted to the country. Fellow non-American graduate students had already advised her to stay in the US, once admitted, until the degree was finished. And now she understood why.

Joyce had met Michelle on her campus visit, one year ago. Joyce had been asked to speak about "international diversity" and had provided a stream of consciousness that was all at once a harder indictment of the US system than even Malcolm X would have given *and* a diatribe about how American Blacks don't seize the incredible opportunities the country offers them. Michelle had not really recognized herself in any of Joyce's speech, but she was enamored by the speaker's confidence.

They had kept in casual touch via messaging. One day, the conversation torqued. Joyce had had to send most of her stipend back to her folks in Kadoma, a farming town two hours' drive from Harare, the capital of Zimbabwe. A 30 outbreak had combined with a local resurgence of anthrax poisoning. The poison had been laid long ago by the Rhodesian army in rural farming areas. Remaining dormant beneath the soils, it pushed itself up every now and then as a colonial after-death. 30 + anthrax had devastated both the local farms and the local markets. Joyce's parents and sisters and brothers were suffering. There was no choice. But that left her in deep financial trouble stateside.

Michelle had always joked that neither security nor staff could really tell her and Joyce apart if it came down to it. All they needed to do was to harmonize their hairstyles. Michelle had a point. Most of the security personnel who manned the Hopkins checkpoints were white and from the counties that surrounded the city. Not too long ago, cleaners, cooks, groundkeepers, and security staff were all Black Baltimoreans, with perhaps a pinch of Latinx. But then Symptomatic and Transactional came along. To be employed in a 1COVID location like the Hopkins' Homewood campus required a 3COVID score at least, else the indemnity required made the wage worthless. Black security now secured only Black property in Black areas.

And so, three months prior to submitting her application, Michelle began to meet Joyce at the bus stop outside the Hopkins east entrance. Joyce would give Michelle her pass and she would slide through the checkpoint onto campus. See, it wasn't sufficient to give Joyce her phone to keep overnight. Symptomatic was a little cleverer than that. The app also recorded phone use and personal mobility over a period of 24 hours and aggregated that data into a pattern. Any unusual usage or movement would send a red flag with an automatic penalty that downgraded your COVID score by 1 point. It was simply not possible to identify each and every one of your digital and somatic habits when many of them were hidden within repetition and muscle memory. This was why Michelle had to physically occupy the space that Joyce did, on campus, while her co-conspirator shared with a graduate friend just across the road, off campus.

But the whole plan rested on a gambit. The insurrectionary information came from WhatsApp. It came from high school friends and their elder siblings who had read this and that, and most of all, it came from a few people around the neighborhood – and other such neighborhoods – who had somehow managed to land a job, a deal, a scholarship that would definitely have required the out-of-reach 3COVID.

It went like this. Symptomatic averaged out a user's residency in weekly slots, for efficiency's sake. Flags would be raised if the majority of your time was spent in a different metric neighborhood, and a grinding set of documents would have to be produced to prove that you had indeed moved up to a higher location. If these documents were not forthcoming, then a red flag and a point deduction came your way instead. However, the system would not flag if you spent a minority of each week in a different metric and racial neighborhood. And that time spent elsewhere *could* factor positively into your COVID score.

Symptomatic could only be so clever. After all, app algorithms extended the straight line of race constellations. And that was the flaw in the system – namely, the extreme rigidness of theory and application that made race thinkable and effective. Digital risk administration could not imagine that you might split time across different neighborhoods. Multiplicity of abode, just like circling, zigzagging, errantry, was not a mode of existence that poor neighborhood people were supposed to be able to access. The algorithm said "null."

Five hundred bucks would be enough to live on, Joyce calculated, before the next stipend was due. Meanwhile, Michelle calculated that moonlighting in a 1white-1wealth zip code three times a week – just under half of the weekdays – might bump her score into 3, opening the prospect for a just-about-affordable indemnity and possible entrance into the world she currently only inhabited under camouflage. At least, that was the gambit. In her quiet moments, Michelle conceded to herself that no one really knew.

Just then Symptomatic flashed green. 3. Michelle's body shifted in the chair. She tapped the "report," button and the screen morphed back into Transactional. Her eyes didn't really want to catch the whole vista at once. She saw a blur in the corner, which approximated a Hopkins logo.

Part III, Tedros Makonnen

Tedros Makonnen stepped onto the speedboat at Port Andraxt. Once, the meeting would have taken place at the Raddison Blu in Addis Ababa; it had then moved to the United Nations Development Programme (UNDP) office in New York after non-Africans refused to fly to the continent; and now it was to occur on board a superyacht. This final shift in location was less to do with entry into the United States for the likes of Tedros and much more to do with the shift in global governance toward international administration.

Palma, the capital city of Majorca, had a world-standard marina. But Tedros's location was 45 minutes' car ride to the southwest tip of the Spanish island. And now, he realized, as he scanned the horizon of Port Andraxt, it was naive of him to have thought that the yacht would be moored directly in the port's bay. Instead, the chartered speedboat took him around three headlands, eventually depositing him just off the coast of Sa Dragonera – an island off an island, and uninhabited at that. This is how these people like to conduct their business, Tedros reflected. Not only away from their stakeholders but away from humanity at large.

Tedros worked for the UNDP's Regional Service Centre for Africa, specifically in the area of disaster risk management. Work was chaotic. No surprise: parts of the African continent were experiencing a triple crisis of climate, COVID, and crops. Many African states were desperate for funding to build capacity in COVID public health as well as nationally and regionally coordinated food redistribution networks. But that money was no longer forthcoming.

In some ways, Tedros and his fellow travelers had won the hardest battle yet lost the war. All of them, apparatchiks of medium-growth states of the Global South that had become regional hubs, were now firmly in command of the offices and the orientation of the UNDP. But just as they had won such a victory, G18 states had effectively recused themselves of any meaningful involvement in the formal institutions of global governance. As they empty-chaired, the funding dissipated. Currently, the UNDP was reduced to a bureaucratic statistics machine; there were no resources to redress problems, only to record them.

The easiest way to explain the loss of this leverage was to compare two indicators that had over the last years contended for influence in the halls of the UNDP: the Human Development Index (HDI) and Overview. HDI was designed to counter the reduction of development to economic growth by flexing education and living standards into the equation as well as paying attention to various inequalities on a national level. Overview was a very different indicator. But it was the one the vicarious elites of the G18 countries used to determine the states in which they should bilaterally invest.

Overview was like an international version of Symptomatic and Transactional all bundled into one. It had been developed by a nameless consortium of investment companies, drawing from the calculus of political risk that had long directed their investment strategies across a rocky geopolitical terrain. Overview took the historical rates and numbers of infection in each country from UNDP data and scaled it according to GDP. The premise was that the richer the economy, the better it could deal with COVIDs. To arrive at its 1–5 score, Overview did not parse quality of growth or the distribution of wealth (or illness) as HDI did.

All this resulted in Overview providing a paradoxical set of evaluations: the societies that had been most destabilized by COVIDs – for example, the United States, the United Kingdom, and the like – scored well in theory because of their GDP while in practice they had consistently performed appallingly when it came to the human cost of pandemics; those that had succeeded in their public health measures despite their poverty – for example, Senegal and Botswana – had been burdened with an impossible-to-shake "shithole." (A shithole was established slang among the development industry for a 5 COVID score). The higher the score, the higher the interest rates on any bilateral loans. And if one suffered a shithole, to receive any loan at all one would have to put up a portfolio of natural resources as indemnity.

The initial country scores that Overview generated after COVID-19 had remained the same all the way through to COVID-30. Some developmentalists Tedros knew had complained about the utility of Overview because those scores never changed even as the world did. But that sounded like a weak complaint to him. It would be to misstate Overview's purpose, which was to act as a credentializing instrument by which financial capital and associated insurance industries could leverage what was left of the development project.

In fact, Overview leveraged development at both the state level and the individual level. You could download the Overview app and set up a "citizen" account so long as you resided in any country outside the G18. Overview used the same UNDP database as HDI to parse the worthiness of individuals seeking microcredits. (No irony was lost on the likes of Tedros that the UNDP fed the instrument of its own destruction.) This database aggregated COVID rates by reference to every country's equivalent measure of a "zip code." Then the Overview app deployed the Symptomatic algorithm to parse the data. Depending on the country, data could be regionally patchy and quite coarse. But this coarseness was no less so than Overview's evaluation of states.

The speedboat lapped up to the stern of the superyacht. Tedros looked up. Go where you want in unrivaled luxury by tacking into whatever wind or current your whims decide (there are no tracks laid down on the ocean); anchor where you want and run your own quarantine and border guard from your deck; pay no tax to anyone; live as if you are the only human left on earth. (Servants didn't count.) Then Tedros thought of the majority of citizens from non-G18 states. When it came to Overview, they were the state, and the state was them – and these states had heavy adjectives: "African," "Asian," and "Pacific." Their emplotment in the constellations of race were so cardinal that no trade wind could shift them.

Fortifying himself for the meeting, Tedros recalled all his career achievements, his mind tracing its way back to his MBA in international administration at the London School of Economics. Just a year before he began the professional degree, the last master's in global governance had closed. The shift from a graduate degree in social sciences to a professional qualification reflected the evolution of digital risk administration in G8 countries. Academics had finally admitted that it was no longer possible to speak of the art of governing at a global level – an art that involved ideas of trust, mutuality, public good, and judgment. "Administration" seemed to fit better the sense of transaction, instrumentalism, and private interest that now effectively shaped conduct at the highest level. A few radicals pointed out that the new name of the field invoked its early twentieth-century origins in imperial administration, although even empire mooted some sense of trust, good, and judgment, albeit fickle, paternalistic and hierarchical.

Actually, the domestic shifts within G18 countries toward digital risk administration were even more jarring when scaled up to the global level, where the idea of "publics" was already problematic. Public management, a quaint idea of the late twentieth century, promoted the running of the state apparatus as if it were a business. Now, in most domestic jurisdictions, a billionaire class firmly occupied the seats of government. There was no longer an "as if" qualification to the commandment. Billionaires ran state apparatuses as direct extensions of their financial interests. The individuals might come, go, and return, but the family interests remained, and the effect was clear. Government figures who interacted with international organizations did so purely to find the most lucrative investment opportunities for their portfolios. The United States Agency for International Development (USAID), for instance, had become a giant fund manager for the family cabals that rotated through government offices, with the help of Overview at both the state and individual level.

Yes, thought Tedros, the old institutional setup was racist, hierarchical; but at least it had to justify itself according to institutionalized rules and regulations that referenced a global good life. Now racism was unmediated – a direct function of private interests that were naturalized as biological inheritance: those who had the capacity to play the market were destined to inherit the earth. Yet here he was. A rare meeting, to try and sell the idea of a global fund that would not be administered via apps and racialized disease vectors. A fund that equitably addressed basic need. The justification: even markets require external stabilizing measures from time to time. An old argument. It smelled old. But it was all he had.

Tedros climbed the short ladder onto the latest superyacht built by the Chinese high-end luxury company Bucolic. The *Effulgence* – that was the name painted in silver on the gunwale – was the property of Carson Colin, current US secretary of state and a member of the most prominent Black billionaire family on the planet. (Interestingly, each generation was becoming lighter than the previous one.) Colin had loaned out the yacht to a lower functionary of USAID who thrilled at the prospect and sent the bill to the UNDP, of course. At the top of the boarding ladder, Tedros could see the red shawls of the testing station clapping in the breeze. He began the short climb and hesitated as his hand glanced over an intricate yet gaudy gold figurine of a woman riding a dolphin. The point of the detail, Tedros decided, was purposeful cruelty: to make you feel sick enough to evacuate your conscience before you stood on deck. For humanity's sake, he said to himself.

Part IV, Sisi and Bhudhi Vangu

From Harare, the Bulawayo road starts out fat, then past Norton it slims. Through one, two small towns: a burst of activity punctuating the quiet fields and occasional road-side maize or fruit seller. Come Kadoma, you can carry on, passing through the bus transit area, or you can side off into the other side of town – the commercial sector. As soon as you turn, the asphalt gorges and riverines. Local politicians have for decades siphoned off any tax money. Ironically, their imported cars are too delicate and sophisticated to handle the local roads.

A ways to go yet. After the commercial part of town, you turn right again. The Rimuka road starts fat too but slims down quickly. Past small houses that serve as a kaleidoscope of businesses: you name it, it can be repaired. Left past the police station, and a quick right to arrive at the back of the township's shopping mall. Rimuka township suffered greatly from the combined anthrax and COVID outbreak a little while ago. That fact might be surprising, given the hum of low-grade activity. But look closer and the skein of the social fabric has stretched further than anyone thought it could – almost transparent. Still, with every tightening comes opportunity for someone.

She has a name, but it's not for you. She has been waiting patiently for the entire afternoon, just outside Mr. Mandara's store. He comes out with the last phone for the day; a woman called Joyce Moyo has just deposited it. This one has been coming every day for the past week. But there has been no eye contact, just straight into the car and gone. It doesn't really matter: recognition is hardly necessary or expected.

Mr. Mandara holds the money and will not release her share until the next morning, come safe return. So, she leaves in a slow pace with her bag of five phones. It's a long walk down roads with ever dwindling densities of houses until they finally morph into patchwork fields. Soon, partial brick walls litter the sides of her path, overgrown but reclaimed as homes by tarpaulin or, sometimes, nothing at all – just naked chairs and a small gas stove with smoke marking habitation. A rusted sign says "New Ngezi . . ." but the following words – she has always thought they originally said "growth point," although she can't be sure – have been written over with "liberated territory." She is pretty sure she knows who the author of that palimpsest is.

Now she starts to errantly navigate the partially formed maze of stunted walls. There is a whole menu of activity, if you know how to put the small offerings together. Over there, behind the bushes, where a few flags are flying, veiled figures sit in a circle, a murmuring rising just like the ubiquitous smoke haze. Vaposteries: indigenizing the Christian gospel since its first arrival. The cars and small buses nearby tell you that the congregation do not stay out here – they are day maroons.

That is to her left. To her right, she hears from somewhere the chunk-chunk-chunk of mining equipment. The sound lets her know that someone has bought into a rumor and brought a machine. Perhaps there is gold under the once arable topsoil. Should greed get rewarded so relentlessly? She doesn't know. She does know that there is humanity everywhere here, the closer you look. With that thought she veers off track, down a long, winding dust path, over a bank, and through a small piece of bush. Arriving at her destination within three hours. Dusk is falling.

The small clearing has its own kind of order. Sisi Vangu is tending to the imperfect rows of dark blue-black and green. Is that her real name? Probably not. But it's fitting. Sisi – sister – Vangu – my: she is a sister to everyone. The first night that she spent at Sisi Vangu's, she had asked why Sisi had planted the small black maize. Sisi Vangu explained that this variant was more drought resistant than the ubiquitous white maize yet also yielded a higher calorific intake. The larger white variety had been grown on white farms during Rhodesian times, and many of these farms could afford irrigation systems while small-scale farmers could not. Why, Sisi Vangu had asked, is white mielie meal a sign of good living when poor people would survive far better if they planted the black?

Bhudhi Vangu is sitting in his favorite shaded spot. He is reading a battered copy of a book – they are always battered. This one is red with a purple stroke and a title top left: *A Dying Colonialism*. She remembers another book from her last visit, a thicker one. Ah yes, it's still there, top of the pile, entitled *Black Reconstruction*. It looks like it is written by a French man, she guesses.

She knows without any doubt that this erudite brother-to-everyone is the author of the New Ngezi palimpsest. Because on more than one occasion, over a meal of sadza and murewo, he has explained the concept to her. "When we fought Rhodes and his boys, we carved out liberated territories so that we could live the right way, without any shenanigans from the colonizing forces. We did so again, when we fought our own Apartheid under Smith, then when we fought ZANU. We still do it now" – and he would glint at her bag of phones – "when we fight Overview." Bhudhi Vangu loves the flourish of a rhetorical argument well made. He tells it as if he has no idea that he has told it a hundred times already. This, she knows, is the right moment to offer to them the bond notes before they have to ask for their fee.

Bhudhi is right: it is a digitally liberated territory. Or at least, there are no phone masts anywhere nearby. If you bothered to think that the area needed surveillance, you might task a satellite. You'd never bother. So, instead, the AGPS on all phones in the area reports a "null." You stay for eight or more hours out here and you don't get categorized – the algorithm waits. Now, just spend a few hours a day in a 3COVID spot, in a car, on the street under a tree, with some roasted maize, and yes, there are those areas around even in Kadoma, and your score picks right up. You might even be able to afford some cash from Overview. And on such slim margins, local empires have been born.

Do spirits move in a straight line, shadowing the living? Or do they freewheel above and around constricted souls? She is one of many phone runners, colloquially known as ma-mobile-mumweya – the mobile spirits. They dwell in the nighttime places that the phone owners abject. Null is not nothing, it is an incalculable valuation.

Soon, Sisi Vangu takes her by the hand, and she knows it is time to sleep. As they retreat into the low, warm light of the rondaval, Bhudhi Vangu starts to arrange his tarpaulin for the night, just at the circumference where the light falls on the ground outside. She prepares for bed. Silence and the monotony of routine strays her mind. Do they have children, away in Harare, or South, or London, or America, she asks? Sis Vangu pauses. Yes, they do, and they work for murungu. But she doesn't say where, and the word does not reveal. Murungu means white man, but it also means boss. The term fuses race, position, and power. A Black Zimbabwean could be a murungu just as much as a white American. To be a boss is to become white, and to be white is to be boss.

Maybe, she offers, after they have saved the phone fees for a few months, they could join their children? "And what, then?" Sisi Vangu returns the offer, value added. "Work for murungu too? Will that be your path? Or maybe you are saving to become a murungu yourself." The words fall to the ground. "Ah no, I don't know, Sisi. I haven't thought about it that much." The lie hangs in the air. Starting afresh with eyes trained on her own routine, Sisi Vangu explains: "There are the Black workers, there are the white workers, and then there are the murungu. But for our part, we want to see the Coming of the Lord."

Suggested reading

Technology and race

Ruha Benjamin, *Race After Technology: Abolitionist Tools for the New Jim Code* (Cambridge: Polity Press, 2019) argues that algorithms are not immune from the flaws of the engineers who write them. If the code incorporates the implicit and explicit prejudices and biases of the programmer, the algorithm will provide racist outcomes.

Moira Weigel, "Palantir Goes to the Frankfurt School," *B20 – The Online Community of the Boundary 2 Editorial Collective*, www.boundary2.org/2020/07/moira-weigel-palantir-goes-to-the-frankfurt-school/, examines the connection between new digital technologies and new right-wing ideologies. Silicon Valley is not necessarily "liberal."

Space and race

Lawrence T. Brown, *The Black Butterfly: The Harmful Politics of Race and Space in America* (Baltimore, MD: Johns Hopkins University Press, 2021) demonstrates how city politics and policies can provide accumulated structured advantages for some populations and disadvantages for others. The consequences of racism are not individual but are inherited and propagated based on which neighborhoods families are able to live in.

Adam Elliott-Cooper, "The Struggle That Cannot Be Named: Violence, Space and the Re-Articulation of Anti-Racism in Post-Duggan Britain," *Ethnic and Racial Studies* 41, no. 14 (2018): 2445–2463, shows how racist state violence is deployed, experienced, and resisted through zip codes rather than directly through racial categories.

Jason T. Harris, *Redlines: Baltimore 2028: An Anthology of Speculative Fiction* (Baltimore, MD: Redlines Publishing, 2012) is a collection of speculative fiction that fast-forwards the racist structures of Baltimore to the future and imagines what forms of oppression and resistance might develop out of our current conditions.

Biosciences and race

Troy Duster, *Backdoor to Eugenics* (New York: Routledge, 1990) takes issue with the way in which "race" is smuggled into the sociological and political use of new genetic technologies. There is no such thing as a "race gene" or even set of genes.

Sibille Merz and Ros Williams, "'We All Have a Responsibility to Each Other': Valuing Racialised Bodies in the Neoliberal Bioeconomy," *New Political Economy* 23, no. 5 (2018): 560–573, makes the case that even though new advances in bio-medicine seek to ameliorate racial inequalities, the broader inequalities entrenched by neoliberal capitalism subvert the aim of health equality.

Histories and theories of race

Ruth Wilson Gilmore, *Golden Gulag: Prisons, Surplus, Crisis, and Opposition in Globalizing California* (Berkeley, CA: University of California Press, 2007) is a study of racism and the carceral system. Gilmore has been very influential among those who call for "abolishing" the police.

C.L.R. James, *American Civilization* (Cambridge, MA: Blackwell, 1993) is by one of the most famous Black Marxists of the twentieth century. In this book, he tries to translate Marxist principles into the vernacular language of the American creed: life, liberty, happiness, etc. He is especially concerned with associational life and the way in which racism denies freedom of association.

Alana Lentin, *Why Race Still Matters* (Cambridge: Polity Press, 2020) argues that societies are in need of racial literacy, especially the ability to recognize race in ways other than simply individual prejudice. One might "not be a racist" yet still be complicit in reproducing racist structures.

María Elena Martínez, *Genealogical Fictions: Limpieza de Sangre, Religion, and Gender in Colonial Mexico* (Palo Alto, CA: Stanford University Press, 2013) looks at the ways in which race was imbued in the colonization of the Americas through the religious (Catholic) ascription of "purity of blood."

Earl McKenzie, *Against Linearity* (Kingston: Peepal Tree Press, 1993) intonates that those who have survived slavery do so through cultures that resist the imposition of a "straight line."

Sylvia Wynter, "Unsettling the Coloniality of Being/Power/Truth/Freedom: Towards the Human, After Man, Its Overrepresentation – An Argument," *CR: The New Centennial Review* 3, no. 3 (2003): 257–337, argues that our conceptions of humanity since 1492 are fundamentally based upon racist distinctions between who is human and who is not properly human.

Development and race

Stanley L. Engerman, "Slavery, Freedom and Sen," in *Amartya Sen's Work and Ideas: A Gender Perspective*, ed. B. Agarwal, J. Humphries, and I. Robeyns (London: Routledge, 2005), 187–213, provides a critical appraisal of famous development economist Amartya Sen, and his "capability approach," which came to underpin the UNDP's Human Development Index.

Sam Moyo, "Three Decades of Agrarian Reform in Zimbabwe," *The Journal of Peasant Studies* 38, no. 3 (2011): 493–531, provides a critical balance sheet of the land redistribution movements, especially under President Robert Mugabe.

"Zimbabwe: Lessons from Land Reform," *Al Jazeera*, 13 November 2013, www.aljazeera.com/programmes/south2north/2013/06/2013621124213836626.html discusses land redistribution with Sam Moyo and a commercial farmer in the Kadoma region, Charlene Mathonsi, who is involved in innovative and equitable agricultural initiatives.

Books that appear in this story

William Edward Burghardt Du Bois, *Black Reconstruction in America* (New York: Simon & Schuster, 1995) is the book Bhudhi Vangu has been reading. Written by an African American scholar, it is one of the most influential books on the American Civil War and the fate of the subsequent "reconstruction" effort. The first chapters are titled "The Black Worker," "The White Worker," "The Planter," and "The General Strike." The chapter that recounts the moment of emancipation is titled "The Coming of the Lord."

Frantz Fanon, *A Dying Colonialism* (New York: Grove Press, 1967) is another book that Bhudhi Vangu has been reading; it was written by the Martiniquan anti-colonial psychiatrist Frantz Fanon, who writes about "liberated territories."

CONTENTS

People

Who governs and who is governed?

Laura Sjoberg

I learned "the answer" to the question "who governs and who is governed" in primary school. I was a US citizen, and the United States had a government. I would grow up to be that government, either as an elected official or as a voter. I was told that all US citizens are the same – they are equal and will all be a part of governing. Sometimes, new people might come to the United States; after they worked hard, immigrants would take an oath to become citizens, and then they would govern as well. A primary school teacher took my class to a naturalization ceremony and showed us everyone's equality.

Slowly, over many years and in many different forums, I discovered there was no truth to this story. My teachers were not intentionally lying to me. They were telling me what they believed to be true. Their beliefs were reinforced by the standard-issue textbooks they had been provided. Nonetheless, they provided a picture so inaccurate that, in hindsight, I can only think of it as a fairy tale. I learned nothing about the world where I actually live – one with hierarchies upon hierarchies on the basis of races, classes, genders, dis/abilities, and sexualities, to name a few.

These issues were not ignored in my schooling; rather, they were presented as solved. I learned that the United States had a race problem in the past, but now "we" are legally equal. I was not told that one of the

DOI: 10.4324/9781003139836-14

reasons I might be treated as a full citizen was my white privilege. I was told I would grow up, meet a husband, get married, and have children but learned nothing about the violence of the gender norms that set those things as desirable. I learned about religious freedom but not about the unwritten code of mores intimately linked with American nationalism, including but not limited to compulsory heterosexuality, reproductive futurism, militarism, and American exceptionalism. I lived them, but I lived them so "naturally" that I failed to see them. I learned about the "American dream" of economic prosperity. I was not told of the disparities between wealthy and poor, both within the United States and outside, or their structural nature. I learned about free speech but would not discover for a long time that money counts as speech, so some have more free speech than others. I remember singing "We are the World" with Michael Jackson thinking that it was really fixing the lives of "starving people in Africa" and that the only thing separating those hungry people from "us" was the bad luck that the famine struck there. I did not, at the time, understand the structural racisms, sexisms, and classisms that went into constituting my privilege as a white American, in part because everything I was taught emphatically denied the existence of that privilege and was shrouded in stories about the inclusiveness and equality of democracy.

The story of the success of liberal democracy (particularly American liberal democracy) is woven so tightly, repeated so frequently, and told so emotionally that it often seems and feels "true" even in the face of overwhelming evidence to the contrary. As a result, many people in liberal democracies blindly but passionately repeat and pass on its stories of participation and pride, ambition and possibility, rights and equality, superiority with kindness. The repetition is needed to reaffirm "collective" consciousness of these successes. In every need for repetition, in every need for affirmation, the hollowness of this story can be seen. With the advent of easier global travel and internet communication combined with the ever-growing ridiculousness of these claims, the fallacies in these stories may be easier to see now, at least for someone who is looking.

At the time of writing, the United States is in the middle of the COVID-19 pandemic. During the crisis, the then – sitting president, Donald Trump, commented that injecting disinfectants might protect people from the virus.[1] The following day, poison control centers around the United States and even outside received a spike in reports of poisoning from household chemicals.[2] At the same time, Trump experienced record-high job approval ratings.[3] Trump's claims about "leading" the world generally and in its war on COVID were loud.[4] Many Americans know Trump's claims were misrepresentations and ridiculed his "leadership."[5] But the overwhelming majority of those Americans saw the problem as *Trump*, rather than the institutions of the presidency, the United States government, and/or liberal democracy.[6] To these critics, the end of the Trump presidency "solved" the problem – without him, the US government, for all its flaws, is a net positive rather than a net negative.[7] This chapter argues that seeing Trump's false claims as an isolated problem may well be as short-sighted as suggesting that injecting disinfectants cures coronavirus. Instead, the appearance that "people" govern themselves in Western liberal democracy is itself a lie, as is the idea that they do so without harm to either people "inside" or "outside" the democracy. These assertions may be more obviously false at certain times than at others, but they are nonetheless continuously false. Further, this is not new information: many *have* noticed this, and their work is often ignored.[8]

The chapter starts by highlighting the increasing use of language of equality and inclusion in the United States and across the broad swathe of global governance institutions, with the attendant increasing recognition that gender, race, nationality, sexuality, religion, class, dis/ability, and a host of other factors matter in who governs, how governance works, and what constitutes the subject of governance.[9] The second section engages others' work to show that, like its predecessors, contemporary instantiations of Western, liberal, democratic ("domestic" and "international") governance rely as heavily on the violent othering of those "outside" as on rehearsed and repeated narratives of its superiority inside. The third section examines the seeming contradiction between the first two sections: how is an era of increasing recognition of the "rights" of "diverse" people in government also an era of increasing violence toward them? The concluding section reflects on what rethinking democracy, government, and its subjects along this line means for the question of who is governed and who does the governing in global politics, including the impossibility of global governance futures.

The inclusive twenty-first century and its "new" stories

The stories I was told of contemporary equality in the United States embraced rather than denied "past" discrimination. Those stories had three constant and recognizable features. First, discrimination was always described as over – the United States (particularly the South) had a deep and shameful problem with race, but it had disappeared, at last, in the late 1960s and early 1970s. Though our parents attended segregated schools, any traces were gone, and any racial disparity in the schools "we" attended was either relic or coincidence, as were any economic disparities among people of different races.

Second, stories of the American history of slavery and racial discrimination painted the United States as a pathbreaker, "solving" these problems. It was the strength of American democracy that had conquered lingering inequalities among its citizens. Abraham Lincoln's Emancipation Proclamation freeing American slaves was the natural result of the 1776 Declaration of Independence, even if that document was crafted and signed by slave owners. During "Black History Month," we learned about the first black person to do this and that, framed as an accomplishment of the United States, which had "developed" its black people, rather than a mark of shame for the attainment gap, which showed the United States as a center of white supremacy. "Our" racisms were reframed as victories because of how they were overcome.

Third, the stories had an evangelical tone. Now that "we" have "solved" our problems, it is incumbent on "us" to instruct the people (and nations and states) that have not yet realized our level of enlightenment how to "give" their people rights and privileges. In brief, the US victory over racial discrimination was an internal victory that needed to be spread externally.

Stories about gender were less straightforward in my youth but have come to conform to a similar mold. As a child, I was taught traditional gender roles, with the exception that women might work before they had children, in the event of a divorce, or in "women's work" like teaching or nursing. While women were "equal before the law," they lived different lives than men. Sexual orientation discrimination was still largely condoned, even more so in the face of the AIDS (Acquired Immunodeficiency Syndrome) pandemic of the late 1980s and early 1990s.[10] While some people characterized "being gay" as acceptable, far more warned of its moral hazards and physical dangers, and very few people addressed lesbian, gay, bisexual, transgender, and queer (LGBTQ+) rights, though those discussions were going on in more progressive enclaves.[11] Thirty years later, however, past-centered, exceptionalist, evangelical narratives abound in discussions about gender, sexuality, and other axes where discrimination was "once common" in Western, liberal democracies and "remains common" elsewhere in the world. These narratives come from the American government, as well as intergovernmental organizations (IGOs) and transnational advocacy networks (TANs). Counternarratives exist, but these stories are strong.[12]

Regarding gender, we hear that women's rights are human rights across liberal democratic governments and international organizations.[13] We hear that the protection of women is vital to state security – in fact, states that treat "their women" poorly are likely to suffer consequences, including domestic unrest, economic devastation, terrorism, anti-democratic governance, and interstate wars.[14] In response, we see research to "improve" women's lives, for "women" themselves and instrumentalizing them to get the benefits states might get from "liberating" their women. We see the celebration of women's increasing representation in parliaments, their "advances" in workplaces, and resources directed toward a worldwide "fight" to decrease sexual violence(s) against women in armed conflict(s).[15] States condemn other states for the "situation" of women in/of those states.[16] We see charts ranking Western, liberal democracies as the "best" on women's rights, and we see their "National Action Plans" on "women, peace, and security" largely or even wholly externally faced. Because "their women" are secure, they look to spread that evangelically, with little regard for how people's lives will actually be affected.

In discourses about sexuality, "good" states are those that recognize their homosexuals as full citizens.[17] Western democracies increasingly lift the legal barriers to the participation of "the homosexual" in their societies, often not coincidentally starting with "allowing" homosexual participation in institutions of state security like militaries and marriages.[18] With the ink on those proclamations not yet dry, those democracies turn to condemn the treatment of homosexuals in countries that have not "yet" arrived at the "enlightened" and "inclusive" policies that these "democracies" tout. As Sarah Lamble describes, "these trends reconfigure the neoliberal carceral state as the guardian of sexual citizenship rather than the perpetrator of violence," moving the state "from being a key *target* of queer protest to instead become a celebrated *guardian* of a narrowly defined sexual citizenship."[19] Jasbir Puar describes this as "homonationalism" – where the previously excluded queer subject is (seemingly) included in the narrative of the "good" polity, insomuch as that subject meets the "other" requirements of good citizenship.[20] Claims about "advancement" of queer rights can be incorporated into "pink-washing," where states use their apparently inclusive policies to mark superiority.[21]

Discourses about gender and sexuality are not the only place that the "diversity" of member states is considered as an important factor in examining and measuring government and governance. Governments and international organizations have recently paid significant attention to the rights of children, religious minorities, ethnic minorities, the disabled, and the list goes on.[22] I list these quickly not because they are less important than the categories discussed prior but because we can quickly find progressivist narratives about rights, inclusion, and future equality juxtaposed against a background that makes those narratives look suspicious. I am not claiming that the existence or substance of progressivist narratives about "protected" categories like race, gender, sexuality, or religion are universal across Western democracies and their representatives in IGOs and TANs. Indeed, the content of these progressivist narratives varies, and they are sometimes contradicted by the media or people active in government and governance. I am also not arguing that these progressive discourses are either accurate or morally unproblematic – in fact, the rest of this chapter suggests the opposite.

I am suggesting three things. First, in official documents and presentations within Western democracies, progressivist narratives are so dominant that they often drown out their naysayers; even those with anti-progressive agendas frame them in progressive terms. Second, were these discourses to be believed, the governments of Western democracies are not only in tune with the needs of their (newly constitutive) minorities but consistently working to serve those needs in a way that makes "improvement" in those minorities' situations an upward trajectory. Third, whether or not the discourses are accurate, they carry and inspire an evangelical tone evocative of the histories of (among other things) US race relations – now that "we" are "good" at minority "rights," "we" have not only the license but the responsibility to spread that "goodness" to those who are "bad" at it and, therefore, if not "bad" generally, are "underdeveloped."[23] The claimed "leaders" in bestowing minority-group rights demand praise and emulation and practice evangelism, regardless of the status of minorities, women, and/or LGBTQ+ people within their own borders.

The violent production of democracy's "outside" both "at home" and "abroad"

Even as Western, liberal democracy touts the rights of the "Other" and claims bestowing these rights as constitutive of its superiority, alongside and within these claims are terrible violences. The examples are too numerous for this chapter, but an "easy" example permits structuring a more theoretical discussion.

I was eleven when the "First Gulf War" erupted, but it was called "the Gulf War," as if the Persian Gulf was the only gulf in the world and this was its first war. I remember its framing as a rescue mission – "we" would rescue Kuwaitis from Iraqis and, maybe, Iraqis from their own government. It was potentially risky and prolonged – Iraq had a formidable standing military.[24] People wore and displayed yellow ribbons for "our" troops and their bravery. "We" did not "save" the Iraqis from their government because "we" respected international law and could not overthrow a sovereign state. Instead, "we" would sanction the evil Iraqi government until "they" stopped threatening "us" and "our allies" as well as "their" people. The sanctions regime continued, often framed as a "non-violent" alternative to war, despite reports of mass deaths coming from malnutrition, starvation, and crackdowns.[25] Later, the taboo against invading sovereign states seemed to have disappeared, and the United States invaded Iraq. Minority-rights claims were heavily emphasized in discourses justifying that invasion:

> Moral truth is the same in every culture, in every time, and in every place. . . . Brutality against women is always and everywhere wrong. There can be no neutrality between justice and cruelty, between the innocent and the guilty (George W. Bush).[26]

"We" invaded Iraq in part because "we" cared about the rights of Iraqis, particularly women. In this framing, it would have been immoral not to. At "home," patriotic pride saw this as an extension of the "War on Terror," in which the United States was going to "make the world safe" for us and, in the process, for everyone.

Behind that discourse of superiority was horror. Across military actions and the "peaceful sanctions regime" (during which the United States used more tonnage of aerial bombs on Iraq than it had during all of World War II),[27] US actions either directly caused or were heavily complicit in economic devastation, shortages of medical care and supplies, food and nutrition shortages, and infrastructural destruction and decline – some estimates suggest more than a million Iraqi deaths can be blamed directly on the US-led sanctions regime alone.[28] "We" refused to count civilian dead in the "Second Gulf War," and most estimates suggest that more than 100,000 Iraqis fall in that category.[29] Attached to these discourses of human rights, universal morality, and liberal values was a killing machine that inflicted death and suffering on the "Other" putatively to save him (or, often, her). The Iraq wars juxtapose a discourse of the exceptionally humane and inclusive nature of Western democracy with terrible (some might say genocidal[30]) violence. The humanity and inclusiveness are a lie by and built into liberal democracy as an institution that disguises the endemic violence in its structures.

Achille Mbembe discusses this as a general trend fundamental to the question of who governs and who is governed, providing evidence of the way that, among narratives of individual freedom and collective rights, "the brutality of democracies has simply been swept under the carpet."[31] Often, "citizens" who "govern" democracies either do not see their violences or obscure them in narratives about destinies and superiorities. In the context of the juxtaposed existence and frequent invisibility of democracies' violences, Mbembe suggests that modern democracy has two faces, solar and nocturnal.[32] The solar side is the one that I encountered in school, which foreshadows the nocturnal side – one constituted by fear and destruction of the constitutive Other, the "threat" from "outside." The nocturnal side includes colonial empires, pro-slavery states, and abuse of "external" and "internal" outsiders.[33]

The nocturnal face of democracy "in effect hides a primordial and founding void – the law that originates in nonlaw and that is instituted as law outside the law. Added to this founding void is a second void – one of preservation."[34] In other words, for "me" to be "equal before the law" with every other American, an unlawful thing had to happen – the American Revolution. The "lawfulness" of American democracy required the "outlaw" action of revolt. After the Revolution, democracy was so hallowed that it had to be "preserved" by any means necessary and against any enemy. This "fact" justifies democracies' extralegal violence. Those who did not (yet) see the paramount importance of protecting democracy extralegally needed either to be stopped or "developed" into agreement. As such, "civil peace in the West thus depends in large part on inflicting violence far away," "institutionalizing a regime of inequality at the planetary scale" including but not limited to colonial and slave systems.[35]

This makes democracy, plantation, and colonial empire "part of the same historical matrix."[36] Democracies' violences are not incidental but structural; not short-term but long-term; not problems to be fixed *within* democracy but problems *of* democracy. Fundamentally, democracies have always been societies of separation, depending on leaving some outside, without rights.[37] As such, liberal democracy turns "against itself by repatriating to the inside what one strives to discharge to the outside."[38] This system produces large-scale death on a purely instrumental calculation of the political.[39]

This approach reveals a very different landscape of inclusiveness and exclusiveness of contemporary democratic governance than the discourses of many current governments and intergovernmental organizations. Mbembe argues that democracies are becoming more exclusive rather than more inclusive and explains that "today, manifestly little interest is shown in making the circle more inclusive" and that there is more vigilance about keeping out "all those who are not one of us."[40] In other words, the reliance of democracies on the existence of an "outside" Other/enemy (and the need to "destroy" him) is getting stronger, not weaker, and the (apparent) trend of "including" more people often has contradictory effects. To Mbembe, this othering is not random, it is about race: "although markedly distinct," colonialism, fascism, and Nazism "shared the same myth about the absolute superiority of so-called Western culture, understood as a culture of race – the white race."[41]

How can current political orders be manifestly and violently *exclusive* when there are so many claims to inclusivity and "improved" inclusivity is announced frequently and with fanfare? Both the claims about inclusivity and the actual exclusivity are, as Mbembe notes, part of the logic and function of Western, liberal democracy. The "new" inclusion of various minorities in the state's benefits and the state's "new" identity as a protector of minorities is not new at all. Instead, the state disciplines by inclusion, punishes continued deviation, and uses its "inclusiveness" to critique its "enemies" defined by their "exclusiveness" while excluding them. States' discourses about their progressive inclusiveness are not outside the violences of Western, liberal democracy; they are integral, they are likely to endure, and they are endemic to systems of global governance.

Being governed

It is in recognition of this violence that Mbembe describes the contemporary global political arena as one of "paranoid dispositions, hysterical violence, and procedures to annihilate all those that democracy will have constituted as enemies of the state."[42] In this context, having an enemy is a key part of constituting "self."[43] When there are not enemies "out there," liberal democracies begin "taking the internal other as the target."[44] If governance in Western, liberal democracies is violent, being governed within them requires and reifies simultaneous commission of violence and experience of violence.

The example of democracies' "domestic" policy changes "reacting"" to "terrorism" in instructive. Mbembe explains that, in this context, the "government" "of the people" suspends the people's rights, "presented as the condition of survival of these same rights."[45] Your democracy has become anti-democratic to protect its democratic values and your freedom. In search of your freedom, you have become unfree. In Thobani's words, "the empire of terror offers a stark choice to its objects of power: incorporation or extermination."[46] This is the case whether you are among the minority within or outside the "democratic" state or organization.

This targeting of the "internal other" takes a wide variety of forms. It can be found in the internalities of "foreign" othering – the association of those "in" the state with those "outside" who are imagined as "our" enemies. This can be seen, for example, in the post-Brexit surfacing of racist discourses and behaviors about immigrants in the United Kingdom, where recorded hate crimes have increased and racist discourses have become mainstream. Britain was never free of racism, but the redoubled anti-immigration politics of Brexit have emboldened those who would target Britain's "internal Others" with hatred and violence.

Unfreedom is not limited to "foreign" othering, or othering of internal and/or internalized Others. There is also, as many scholars have catalogued, unfreedom in being "included" in the "democratic" operations and government of states and international organizations. Wendy Brown argued that liberal democracy "aims to count every difference as no difference" but also to count every possible "subversive rejection of culturally enforced norms as themselves normal, as normalizable, as normalizable through law."[47] In other words, when people's behaviors fall outside a given norm, that norm is reexamined, recodified, relegislated, and renormalized, so that it can be controlled, owned, and "included" regardless of the desire of the person exhibiting the behavior for "inclusion" or "normalization." In this way, "persons are reduced to observable social attributes and practices defined empirically" and the "language of recognition becomes the language of unfreedom."[48]

Jin Haritaworn, Adi Kuntsman, and Silvia Posocco have called this phenomenon "murderous inclusions" – violences committed by "normalizing" those who do not "fit" into the particular mold of the democratic citizen.[49] In discourses of queer politics, the (accepted, included) ideal homosexual constituted in the patriotic, homonormative queer is contrasted with the (rejected, Other) "non-conforming," "unreadable," "undevelopable" queer.[50] As Elijah Edelman explains, "necronationalism, built on necropolitics, focuses on the ways the erasure and death of the bad (queer) citizen-worker carves out the ideological and physical space for the good (queer) citizen-worker body to emerge."[51] It is thus important to "read queer livability alongside killability, rescue alongside jeopardy, protection alongside abandonment, and celebration alongside violent erasure."[52]

The discussion of the "rights" of "the homosexual" or "the trans* person" carries at least two important, related, substantive violences.[53] The first is the assumption that people's identities are all so clear that they can be easily summarized, so strong that people are defined by one identity and not others, and immutable – "a fixed, timeless, and universally homogenous identity."[54] This not only privileges those who fall into particular, legitimized categories but pressures others to fit and punishes those who either do not or cannot. Shakharsi examines in this in the experiences of Iranian trans* people in Turkey seeking formal recognition as refugees.[55] Shakharsi suggests that there are often discussions and tests of "normative notions of authentic gender and sexuality" in order to categorize "legitimate" refugees, those left liminal, and those returned.[56] The second problem is linking fixed identities to rights discourses – homosexual rights, gay rights, lesbian rights, queer rights, even women's rights or black rights. As Brown explains, rights discourses "emerged as a vehicle for emancipation – protestation against arbitrary use of sovereign power – but rights discourses tend to depoliticize that to which they aspire."[57] The term "rights" and the laws that accompany the "achievement" of those "rights" are assumed to be, labeled as, and reified as imbued with normative good, such that "giving" rights cannot be objectionable.[58] The politics of inclusion can be as insidious as the politics of exclusion. The politics of state othering means that some queers are "protected" by the state while others are attacked by the state in the name of "protection" of citizens. This is the ugly underside of the victorious and evangelical narratives of equality discussed at the beginning of this chapter – where the oppression of those declared equal is made invisible.

Conclusion

The politics of inclusion in Western, liberal democracies does not result in the successful "integration" of those who had previously been "outside." Alongside and within discourses recognizing identity, (previous) exclusion, and the need for (future and increased) inclusion, there is disciplining and violence. Liberal claims to non-violence are false in different ways for different people but remain false nonetheless. This is the case even in social movements seeking rights and emancipation, which can "problematically mirror the mechanisms and configurations of power of which they are an effect and which they purport to oppose."[59]

What does this mean for the question of who governs and who is governed? To explore this, let us return briefly to the discussion of the wars in Iraq from earlier in this chapter. The United States' policies had (domestic) opponents. There were more opponents of the First Gulf War than of the sanctions regime and more opponents of the sanctions regime than of the Second Gulf War.[60] The First Gulf War's opponents largely protested the possible harms to American soldiers and American businesses.[61] While these issues did not disappear in objections to the sanctions regime and the Second Gulf War, they were slowly eclipsed by concerns about what happened to Iraqis.[62] Why were "we" starving Iraqis or killing them? Stopping mothers from getting milk to sustain pregnancies and feed babies? Were "we" letting people die in the name of ("our" or "their") democracy?[63]

Most of these protests boiled down to this: the democratic United States was behaving undemocratically, and a return to "real" democracy would end these policies and their violences. Democracy's violence, then, was both only outside and cast as an anomaly even as it was being protested. Democracies' internal discontents often use both these distinctions to criticize their governments without criticizing their form of government. Mbembe and others have argued that both these "lines" – inside/outside and problem with a democracy/problem of democracy – are incorrect. The violences in Iraq, even if they are more visible (especially in hindsight) than other violences, are not anomalous, or chinks in an otherwise undented armor of democracy – they are required for its function.

The answer that I got in primary school about who governs conceals democratic governance's inherent violences. What I *should* have been told is that I would need to be willing to do substantial violence both to myself and to (internal and external) others as a price of being "included." I *should* have been told that the violence that I and others do "for" equality and democracy would be more horrible than what history books acknowledged as "relics."

To be among those who govern, directly or indirectly, is to do terrible violence to those who are governed, directly or indirectly. As it is, I live many of the privileges associated with my (presumed) axes of inclusion, including, chiefly, being a white American. These privileges constitute my ability to write this chapter and the views that build its content. My positionality is not a vestige of the inequalities that democracy is routing out; it is a constitutive feature of "democratic" governance. Rather than lifting all up, "democratic" global governance selects winners and losers as well as who lives and who dies, all masked by the humanitarian rhetoric of progressivist equality.

Accordingly, asking the question of who governs and who is governed itself cleans up and depoliticizes the process of government and the harm that Western democracies do in their borders, with their borders, and in the world. Accordingly, I "should" tell readers that asking who governs and who is governed is not the question.

Instead, Shakharsi asks a more reasonable version of the question: "how does the government of the life of one population connect to the techniques of the killing of another population?"[64]

Any "future" of global (liberal democratic) governance, then, is the politics of choosing who dies as a function of choosing who lives, all the while both buying and selling the lie of "rising tides" and progressive inclusion. So long as liberal democracy is sold as legally equal, morally superior, and by nature non-violent, at both the state and international levels of global governance, it will continue to both do and hide substantial violence. This creates an equivalency between the question "who governs and who is governed?" and the question "who lives at whose expense?" that is constitutive of, rather than an anomaly in, futures of global governance.

Suggested reading

Wendy Brown, *States of Injury: Power and Freedom in Late Modernity* (Princeton, NJ: Princeton University Press, 1995).

Adi Kuntsman, Jin Haritaworn, and Silvia Posocco, eds., *Queer Necropolitics* (London: Routledge, 2015).

Achille Mbembe, *Necropolitics* (Durham, NC: Duke University Press, 2019).

Laura J. Shepherd, *Gender, Violence, and Security: Discourse as Practice* (London: Zed Books, 2008).

Cynthia Weber, *Queer International Relations: Sovereignty and the Will to Knowledge* (New York: Oxford University Press, 2016).

Notes

1 Dartunorro Clark, "Trump Suggests 'Injection' of Disinfectant to Beat Coronavirus and 'Clean' the Lungs," *NBC News*, 24 April 2020, www.nbcnews.com/politics/donald-trump/trump-suggests-injection-disinfectant-beat-coronavirus-clean-lungs-n1191216.

2 Gino Spocchia, "'Under No Circumstances Administer into the Human Body': Dettol Tells People Not to Follow Trump's 'Dangerous' Recommendation," *The Independent*, 25 April 2020.

3 Gallup, "Presidential Approval Ratings – Donald Trump," *Gallup*, 2020, https://news.gallup.com/poll/203198/presidential-approval-ratings-donald-trump.aspx.

4 Steven Erlanger, "Embattled at Home, Trump Finds Himself Isolated Abroad, Too," *New York Times*, 2 June 2020.

5 See the 105 pages about Trump on factcheck.org.

6 Chris Kahn, "Exclusive: Democrats, Furious with Trump, Much More Keen to Vote Now than Four Years Ago," *Reuters*, 15 April 2020, www.reuters.com/article/us-usa-election-enthusiasm-exclusive/exclusive-democrats-furious-with-trump-much-more-keen-to-vote-now-than-four-years-ago-reuters-ipsos-idUSKCN21X1AQ.

7 Evan Osnos, "Why Democracy Is on the Decline in the United States," *The New Yorker*, March 2020, www.newyorker.com/news/daily-comment/why-democracy-is-on-the-decline-in-the-united-states?source=search_google_dsa_paid&gclid=Cj0KCQjw_ez2BRCyARIsAJfg-ks4gUHCJffmeX9evIBesYlBuTFlorUNYvZLLW5DTfdYVyR6w-mp9igoaAitlEALw_wcB.

8 See Achille Mbembe, "Necropolitics," trans. Libby Meintjes, *Public Culture* 15, no. 1 (2003): 11–40; Judith Butler and Athena Anthansiou, *Dispossession: The Performative in the Political* (London: John Wiley and Sons, 2013); and Michael Mann, *The Dark Side of Democracy: Explaining Ethnic Cleansing* (Cambridge: Cambridge University Press, 2005).

9 Ronald Inglehart and Pippa Norris, *Rising Tide: Gender Equality and Cultural Change Around the World* (Cambridge: Cambridge University Press, 2003).

10 Paula A. Treichler, "AIDS, Homopohobia, and Biomedical Discourse: An Epidemic of Signification," *Cultural Studies* 1, no. 3 (1987): 263–305.

11 Wendy Brown, *States of Injury: Power and Freedom in Late Modernity* (Princeton, NJ: Princeton University Press, 1995).

12 Laura J. Shepherd, *Gender, Violence, and Security: Discourse as Practice* (London: Zed Books, 2008); Cynthia Weber, *Queer International Relations: Sovereignty, Sexuality, and the Will to Power* (New York: Oxford University Press, 2016); and Manuela Lavinas Picq and Markus Thiel, eds., *Sexualities in World Politics: How LGBTQ Claims Shape International Relations* (London: Routledge, 2015).

13 Hillary Rodham Clinton, "Remarks for the United Nations Fourth World Conference on Women," *United Nations*, 5 September 1995, www.un.org/esa/gopher-data/conf/fwcw/conf/gov/950905175653.txt; Janina Pescinski, "Women's Rights Are Human Rights," *Our World*, United Nations University Curriculum, 10 December 2015, https://ourworld.unu.edu/en/womens-rights-are-human-rights.

14 Valerie M. Hudson, Donna Lee Bowen, and Perpetua Lynne Nielson, *The First Political Order: How Sex Shapes Governance and National Security Worldwide* (New York: Columbia University Press, 2020); and Bradley A. Thayer and Valerie M. Hudson, "Sex and the *Shaheed*: Insights from the Life Sciences on Islamic Suicide Terrorism," *International Security* 34, no. 4 (2010): 37–62.

15 Inglehart and Norris, *Rising Tide*; and Pamela Paxton, Melanie M. Hughes, and Tiffany D. Barnes, *Women, Politics, and Power: A Global Perspective* (Lanham, MD: Rowman and Littlefield, 2021).

16 April W. Palmerlee, "The Situation of Women in Afghanistan," *Remarks by the Department of State Senior Coordinator for International Women's Issues at Western Illinois University*, 28 March 2002, https://2001-2009.state.gov/g/wi/9118.htm; and US Department of State, *Guyana: Country Report*, 2019, www.state.gov/report/custom/3fcac07925/.

17 Graeme Reid, "Canada Sets International Example in LGBT Rights," *The Globe and Mail*, 5 September 2017; and Picq and Thiel, eds., *Sexualities in World Politics*.

18 Picq and Thiel, eds., *Sexualities in World Politics*; Brett Remkus Britt, "Pinkwashed: Gay Rights, Colonial Cartographies and Racial Categories in the Pornographic Film *Men of Israel*," *International Feminist Journal of Politics* 17, no. 3 (2014): 398–415; Weber, *Queer International Relations*; Jasbir Puar, "Rethinking Homonationalism," *International Journal of Middle East Studies* 45, no. 2 (2013): 336–339.

19 Sarah Lamble, "Queer Investments in Punitiveness and Sexual Citizenship, Social Movements, and Expanding the Carceral State," in *Queer Necropolitics*, ed. Adi Kuntsman, Jin Haritaworn, and Silvia Posocco (London: Routledge, 2015), 163, 157.

20 Jasbir Puar, *Terrorist Assemblages: Homonationalism in Queer Times* (Durham, NC: Duke University Press, 2007).

21 Picq and Thiel, eds., *Sexualities in World Politics*.

22 See United Nations General Assembly, *Convention on the Rights of the Child* (General Assembly document A/44/25/1989); Voice of America, "U.S. Advocates for Religious Minorities," 13 March 2018, https://editorials.voa.gov/a/u-advocates-religious-minorities/4297058.

html; Janet Lord, "Here's Why Disability Rights Must Be on the Forefront of the Human Rights Movement," *Amnesty International*, 2016, www.amnestyusa.org/heres-why-disability-rights-must-be-on-the-forefront-of-the-human-rights-movement/.

23 See Weber, *Queer International Relations*, about the developed, the developable, and the undevelopable in significations of Western, liberal democracies.

24 See Shannon Collins, "Desert Storm: A Look Back," *United States Department of Defense*, 11 January 2019, www.defense.gov/Explore/Features/story/Article/1728715/desert-storm-a-look-back/#:~:text=On%20Aug.,the%20world%20at%20that%20time.

25 David Cortright and George A. Lopez, "Are Sanctions Just? The Problematic Case of Iraq," *Journal of International Affairs* 52, no. 2 (1999): 735–755.

26 George W. Bush, "President Bush Delivers Graduation Speech at West Point," *The White House*, 1 June 2002, https://georgewbush-whitehouse.archives.gov/news/releases/2002/06/20020601-3.html.

27 Anthony Cordesman, *Iraq and the War of Sanctions* (New York: Praeger, 1999).

28 John Mueller and Karl Mueller, "Sanctions of Mass Destruction," *Foreign Affairs* 78, no. 3 (1999): 43–53.

29 See discussions at iraqbodycount.org for example.

30 Joy Gordon, "When Intent Makes All the Difference in the World: Economic Sanctions on Iraq and the Accusation of Genocide," *Yale Human Rights and Development Law Journal* 5, no. 1 (2002): 57–84.

31 Achille Mbembe, *Necropolitics* (Durham, NC: Duke University Press, 2019), 16.

32 Ibid., 22.

33 Ibid.

34 Ibid., 27.

35 Ibid., 19.

36 Ibid., 23.

37 Ibid., 42.

38 Ibid., 117.

39 Ibid., 34.

40 Ibid., 3.

41 Ibid., 121.

42 Ibid., 41.

43 Ibid., 48.

44 Ibid., 121.

45 Ibid., 33.

46 Sunera Thobani, "Prologue," in *Queer Necropolitics*, ed. Kuntsman, Haritaworn, and Posocco, x.

47 Ibid., 66.

48 Ibid.

49 Haritaworn, Kuntsman, and Posocco, eds., *Queer Necropolitics*.

50 Weber, *Queer International Relations*; and Puar, *Terrorist Assemblages*.

51 Elijah Adiv Edelman, "Walking While Transgender: Necropolitical Regulations of Trans Feminine Bodies of Clour in the Nation's Capital," in *Queer Necropolitics*, ed. Kuntsman, Haritaworn, and Posocco, 174.

52 Kuntsman, Haritaworn, and Posocco, eds., *Queer Necropolitics*, 5 citing Elizabeth A. Povenelli, *Economies of Abandonment: Social Belonging and Endurance in Late Liberalism* (Durham, NC: Duke University Press, 2011).

53 https://time.com/5211799/what-does-trans-asterisk-star-mean-dictionary/#:~:text=-trans*%3A%20originally%20used%20to%20include,.%2C%20alongside%20transsexual%20and%20transgender.

54 Kuntsman, Haritaworn, and Posocco, eds., *Queer Necropolitics*, 5.
55 Sima Shakharsi, "Killing Me Softly with Your Rights," in *Queer Necropolitics*, ed. Kuntsman, Haritaworn, and Posocco, 100.
56 Ibid.
57 Brown, *States of Injury*, 99.
58 Not a coincidence but "symptomatic of a feature of politicized identity's *desire* within liberal bureaucratic regimes, its foreclosure of its own freedom, its impulse to inscribe in the law . . . its historical and present pain rather than conjure an imagined future with the power to make itself." Ibid., 66.
59 Ibid., 3.
60 See Adam Clymer, "War in the Gulf: Public Opinion Poll Finds Deep Backing While Optimism Fades," *New York Times*, 22 January 1991; Lydia Saad, "Top Ten Findings About Public Opinion and Iraq," *Gallup*, 8 October 2002, https://news.gallup.com/poll/6964/top-ten-findings-about-public-opinion-iraq.aspx.
61 Bernard E. Trainor, "Gulf War I," *Foreign Policy Research Institute*, 3 May 2009, www.fpri.org/article/2009/05/gulf-war-i/.
62 Gordon, "When Intent Makes All the Difference," 57–84; and Cortright and Lopez, "Are Sanctions Just?," 735–755.
63 That said, "our" protests made Iraqis' suffering a spectacle without knowing them and often included racisms, Orientalisms, classisms, and heteronationalisms.
64 Shakharsi, "Killing Me Softly with Your Rights," 95.

PART III
CHALLENGES

Introduction

The third part of the book is composed of seven chapters that focus on some of the most pressing and profound challenges facing humanity and the planet as we journey toward the century's mid-point. In Chapter 13, Jennifer Clapp explores the challenge of feeding the planet, now and into the future. Her exploration of "Food: Governance Challenges for a Hot and Hungry Planet" begins with the depressing reality that, despite numerous food crises, the planet still lacks adequate global governance institutions and frameworks to improve, let alone guarantee, food security for many of the globe's denizens. The latest in a series of UN target-setting efforts consists of the SDGs, which were adopted in 2015 and laid out the framework for the sought-after improvements in the 2030 development agenda. As was the case for other challenges, Clapp argues that the COVID-19 pandemic has exacerbated trends that prior to 2020 had already clearly been pointing toward increased food insecurity. Most prominent were climate change, inequalities (within and between countries), corporate concentration, shifting trade, and heightened financial pressures. Her possible silver lining is that the fragmented institutional and governance landscape may also open opportunities for transformative change over the next quarter century.

Chapter 14 explores what the future of global health governance holds in the medium- to long-term. Here, Anne Roemer-Mahler offers insights into a tattered fabric that was strained before COVID-19 and has only become even more problematic since. She takes as her point of departure the slogan "build back better" – used by the United Nations for its 75th anniversary and by the successful presidential campaign of Joe Biden – to question the assumption that what is necessary is to improve the existing system. Roemer-Mahler argues that we need to reflect on the fundamental ideas underpinning the existing system of global health governance: the very notion of "globality," the focus

DOI: 10.4324/9781003139836-15

on health as the driving force of this system, and the Western-driven approach to governance. Based on her reflections, the chapter suggests that the future of global health governance is likely – captured in the subtitle – to be "Less Global, Less Health, Less Governance."

Chapter 15 deals with the existential challenge of climate change that has been on the minds of many during the first two decades of the twenty-first century – which registered 19 of the hottest years on record – but which has not, so far, elicited the kind of concerted action required. In Adriana Erthal Abdenur's "Climate Action: Beyond the Paris Agreement," the pace of catastrophic environmental damage provides a slow-motion – at least in contrast to the rapidity of the COVID-19 calamity – illustration of the limitations of a planet with no overarching authority. Ironically, it is not for a lack of efforts because the last half century has yielded a series of agreements about collective action for preventive efforts as well as a range of possible remedial measures. Abdenur documents the significant intergovernmental conventions and agreements that have been negotiated since the 1972 Stockholm Conference on the Human Environment. However, this uneven and incomplete regime has been shaped not only by the environmental and climate movements but also by internal politics and the changing world order. Despite key advances through numerous negotiations leading to the 2015 Paris Agreement, global climate governance remains subject to the whims of major powers in a world order without compliance mechanisms or a strong centralizing agency to oversee multiple agreements. While noting the dedication of a younger generation of activists, she concludes with the disconcerting observation that time is short.

In Chapter 16, Maria Ivanova and Natalia Escobar-Pemberthy explore the complex issue of biodiversity and nascent attempts to protect the complex life systems on our planet. Their contribution begins with the fact that, among other things, COVID-19 highlighted the close link between the health of the natural environment and the health of people. They examine the evolution of international efforts to foster global biodiversity governance for ecosystems, species, and land resources. More particularly, they analyze the path that led to the definition of SDG 15, which integrates a variety of mechanisms designed to implement this "life on land" goal in the UN's 2030 Agenda for Sustainable Development. Lessons from the successes and challenges of past governance efforts are examined to explore future paths that promote planetary and human health. They conclude with recommendations about the prerequisites for improved global governance that will be critical to guarantee that the powerful impacts of human activities on the environment do not backfire but are addressed in ways that promote both planetary and human health.

Chapter 17 examines the traditionally crucial input for many struggling countries – official development assistance (ODA) – and its governance architecture as essential helping assets for improving life in many low-income countries. Catherine Weaver and Rachel Rosenberg consider the future of aid beyond COVID-19. They argue that even before the pandemic, the aid system was reeling from a dearth of relevance, legitimacy, and effectiveness. This situation has only been made worse with the catastrophic drop in global GDP and the huge demands for assistance to address the pandemic and its economic consequences. While the system limps along, Weaver and Rosenberg make a compelling case for more fundamental reforms to the rules and norms than the efforts currently being discussed by the international donor community. They see that the aid landscape and the principal actors – public and private, governmental and non-governmental – are changing faster than the institutions involved in supposedly governing them. When thinking about future global aid governance for both development and humanitarian purposes, Weaver and Rosenberg offer two proposals: to "Go Global" (move away from an international to planetary framework) and to "Go Global Local" (decentralize ownership and decision-making).

In Chapter 18, Madeline Carr and Jose Tomas Llanos examine the critically important issue of data governance in the unfolding of what they call the "Fourth Industrial Revolution." The "Internet of Things" follows the preceding revolutions driven by steam, electricity, and digitalization. Their account explores the tensions in, and competing approaches to, the global governance of data and the enormity of the challenges that lie therein. Carr and Llanos do not stop with merely identifying the challenge; they also explore the potential for an appropriate governance framework to enable big data to improve the human condition. As they point out, such an outcome will require global cooperation to maximize the full benefits of this transformative period while mitigating common and differentiated threats. Given the nature of profits and the feeble structures underpinning international cooperation, the contribution of big data to ameliorating all human lives is not a foregone conclusion.

The final essay in the book, but by no means the last of the challenges confronting world order's future, offers a compelling examination of global attempts to control the trade in and consumption of illicit drugs. Mónica Serrano's chapter provides two key and related insights for future problem-solving in this and other arenas. First, it documents the path dependency that binds global drug governance into a dated way of thinking. Second, it illustrates how institutional processes can lock in bad ideas and their consequences, thereby ensuring that they reverberate long into the future, with harrowing consequences. As she points out, the economics and violence related to the supply and demand of illegal substances are global problems, yet efforts by the League of Nations and the United Nations have proved ineffectual. An additional problem is the necessity to address this blight while respecting key international human rights and democratic standards. Thus, the future solutions will require rethinking and restructuring the international drug-control regime and, more particularly, the punitive logic that has customarily characterized policies to control illegal substances. Harkening back to the alcohol-prohibition efforts of the 1920s, Serrano sees similarities insofar as prohibition of substances of any kind creates formidable incentives for criminal organizations to exploit. Global drug governance over the next quarter century must strike a difficult balance and not help foster thriving illicit drug markets that reward criminality.

While the specifics of the global governance of the future are not yet known, what the essays in this part and the rest of the book more generally illustrate is that we know some of its likely dynamics. As we move beyond the global governance of COVID-19, the challenges of human domination of the planet are unlikely to subside. War or its threat will remain a force shaping big and small decisions. The nascent geopolitics of the 2020s will evolve into different and equally complex entanglements in the 2050s, in which civilizations, regions, and cities will all play a part. We are likely to continue to be divided by ideas about human rights; the bare existence experiences of migrants and relative comforts afforded populations that are not forced to move; who has what and how much, and who does not; enduring ideas about race; and how we treat Others, of all social groups. And we will face numerous challenges in relation to food systems, health, biodiversity and the natural environment, international assistance, data and its governance, and misfiring regimes such as in the realm of illicit drugs and many others. We will also no doubt see the emergence of new governance actors and the potential of a change in the global system of governance if not just alterations to the current one's arrangement. Without foresight and thinking, the various ways these factors might combine is catastrophic. With engagement and understanding, a better future, for humanity and the planet, is possible. Ours is a small contribution.

Food

Governance challenges
for a hot and hungry planet

Jennifer Clapp

The global governance of food matters profoundly for the future of humanity and the planet. Yet, more than ten years on from a major global food crisis in 2007–2008 that saw soaring food prices and rising levels of hunger, global governance frameworks to address food insecurity are fragmented and lack strong government support. Goal 2 of the United Nations Sustainable Development Goals (SDGs), adopted in 2015, calls on governments to implement policies to end hunger and malnutrition, support sustainable food systems, and ensure that small-scale agricultural producers have decent livelihoods. However, five years after the UN's adoption of the SDGs, governments are not on track to meet SDG 2. In fact, the indicators appear to be moving in the opposite direction, which is problematic given that food systems intersect with many of the other SDGs. Whether humanity can achieve SDG 2 by 2030 – and improve on it beyond that date – will depend on how current trends and dynamics play out with respect to major forces shaping food systems and their governance.

Food systems will have to grapple with the fallout from major changes that are emerging at the global level that will have important implications for food security and sustainability in the future. How institutions and practices of global governance respond to these challenges will influence

DOI: 10.4324/9781003139836-16

the capacity of food systems to provide safe and nutritious food for the world's population over the coming decades. The effects of climate change have already begun to affect food-production systems, and these impacts are set to intensify. Recent decades have also witnessed growing economic inequities across and within food systems because of growing corporate concentration, uneven and shifting trade dynamics, and growing financialization in the agri-food sector. And a fragmented international institutional and governance landscape for food security creates further challenges but may also open some opportunities. The eruption of the COVID-19 pandemic in early 2020 marked a sharp disruption to food systems around the world, shining a light on problems associated with the broader trends already shaping food systems and leading to a rise in food insecurity.

These converging dynamics of long-term trends with the abrupt disruption because of the COVID-19 pandemic give new urgency to charting a path forward for global food security governance. Yet, while there is a broad consensus that a major transformation of food systems is needed, there remain debates about what exactly such a transformation should entail and the appropriate role for global governance in shaping it. This chapter examines the challenges that these trends present to global food security and sustainability going forward, and it outlines key debates over the types of governance responses that will be required in the next quarter century.

Hunger, malnutrition, and food systems in crisis

There is growing awareness that food systems urgently require transformation if humanity is to achieve the Sustainable Development Goal 2, zero hunger, by 2030. The sub-targets of SDG 2 include ending malnutrition in all its forms, promoting sustainable agriculture, and improving the productivity and incomes of small-scale food producers.[1]

At present, the world is far from achieving the targets set out in SDG2. Nearly one in three people faces at least one form of malnutrition. The latest estimates indicate that around 720–811 million people are chronically undernourished as measured by the prevalence of undernourishment (SDG 2 indicator 2.1), a number that has increased by as many as 161 million people from 2019 to 2020, largely due to the COVID-19 pandemic (discussed in the following). Other measures of food insecurity indicate an equally troubling situation. As measured by the Food Insecurity Experience Scale (FIES, another of the SDG 2 indicators), some 2.37 billion people – nearly one-third of the world's population – face either moderate or severe food insecurity.[2] Levels of hunger and food insecurity are especially high in sub-Saharan Africa, Latin America and the Caribbean, and South Asia.

At the same time that the number of people experiencing hunger and food insecurity has been rising worldwide, there has also been an expansion of other forms of malnutrition. Levels of overweight and obesity have been on the rise in recent decades. The latest figures show that around 2 billion adults – worldwide, constituting around 40 percent of individuals over the age of 18 – are overweight, including some 650 million people who are obese. Even among children, over-weight and obesity levels are rising. Around 1.5 billion people are deficient in micronutrients due to poor-quality diets lacking important vitamins and minerals that are vital for good health. Deficiency in micronutrients can affect both those people who are undernourished as well as those who are overnourished.[3]

Problems facing food systems extend beyond hunger and malnutrition. It is increasingly recognized that food systems as they currently operate are not environmentally sustainable and as such pose a risk to the ecological foundations on which they depend. The food and agriculture sector, for example, generates around 20–25 percent of greenhouse gas emissions that cause climate change. The current organization of agricultural production systems, especially those based on large-scale industrial production that relies on machinery and agrochemicals, contributes to biodiversity loss, water scarcity, deforestation, soil fertility loss, and pollution.[4] Several studies document the ways these types of food systems have exceeded several of the "planetary boundaries" that establish a safe operating space for humanity to live sustainably over the long term.[5]

Food system livelihoods have also become more precarious in recent decades. Agriculture and food systems provide around one-quarter of employment around the world; in some low-income countries in Africa and Asia, the sector provides as much as 60 percent of employment.[6] Yet it has become increasingly difficult for agricultural producers, especially small-scale ones, to earn a decent livelihood. Small-scale farms make up most of the farms worldwide, constituting 84 percent of all farms. But small farms of under two hectares in size only account for around 24 percent of farmland while producing around a third of food production globally.[7] Small-scale producers often lack access to resources, including not just land but also farm inputs, and they often lack access to markets to sell their crops. In many cases, small-scale producers rely on just a handful of suppliers of inputs and an equally small number of buyers for their products, putting them in positions of weakened agency that affect their earning capacity.

Major food system trends that will shape future governance needs

The aforementioned food system outcomes have many drivers that generate complex dynamics, making it difficult to identify clear causal mechanisms and universal solutions.[8] Nonetheless, it is possible to sketch in broad terms the contours of some of the main drivers at the global level that are contributing to outcomes in food systems that are stalling progress on SDG 2. Three sets of trends are important to emphasize: climate change and environmental degradation, uneven power dynamics in the world food economy, and the fragmented international food security governance landscape. Each of these trends has important implications for food security and the global capacity to achieve SDG 2.

Climate change and environmental degradation

A major global trend affecting food systems is the acceleration of climate change and environmental degradation. While food systems contribute to these problems, as noted, they are also deeply affected by them to the extent that food system outcomes are altered as a result. Because agriculture and food production are so reliant on weather conditions and ecosystem services, they are especially vulnerable to climate change and biodiversity loss, even as they contribute to these problems.

The changing climate has brought growing weather variability and an increased incidence of natural disasters, for example, which have the capacity to negatively affect yields and overall agricultural productivity. There is already evidence that wheat and maize yields are declining as a result of elevated temperatures. Scientists predict that with a warmer climate, sea levels will rise, which will have huge implications for the availability of farmland. Rising temperatures also increase stresses on plants and animals, contributing to the loss of crop genetic diversity as well as shrinking the availability of drinking water for livestock. There is also a growing understanding that warmer temperatures are also associated with a higher presence of weeds and insect pests. The broader impacts of climate change, including flooding and more violent storms, also have the capacity to affect food storage, processing, transportation, and marketing.[9]

Although a changing climate can have divergent impacts in different parts of the world, most studies indicate that the harshest impacts will be felt in the world's poorest countries. Low-income tropical regions in Asia, Africa, Latin America, and the Caribbean are likely to have the most decline in crop yields, which will have profound implications for food-production patterns. Countries in sub-Saharan Africa, for example, one of the regions currently experiencing high rates of hunger, have been particularly hard hit by drought, floods, and diminishing crop yields due to climate change.[10] Climate change can also reduce the nutritional makeup of certain food crops, which can exacerbate existing problems with malnutrition.[11] The Food and Agriculture Organization (FAO) of the United Nations has warned of "cascading effects" from climate change that can undermine various dimensions of food security, including causing drops in production, rising food prices, compromised nutritional makeup of crops, and instability in production levels leading to more volatile food markets.[12]

Environmental resource degradation in the form of biodiversity loss also threatens the resilience of food and agricultural systems, which, in turn, affects food security and livelihoods.[13] This environmental degradation often results from the spread of industrial agricultural practices. The growing use of modern seed varieties in monoculture systems, for example, has contributed to crop diversity loss, making agricultural ecosystems more vulnerable to pests and diseases and triggering increased use of agrochemicals. Mechanical tilling and heightened agrochemical use contribute to the loss of soil biodiversity, diminishing the capacity of soil to perform vial ecosystem services, such as fixing carbon and water filtration.

Uneven distribution of power in the world food economy

Food system outcomes have been deeply affected by uneven power dynamics in the global economy. Over the past 50 years, agri-food supply chains have become increasingly concentrated in the hands of a small number of large transnational corporations (TNCs). Recent mergers in the agricultural seed and chemical industry are just the latest in a long progression of consolidation in the sector.[14] Similar concentration has occurred in the agricultural commodity trading sector, in the processed and packaged food industry, and in the food retail sector.[15] Growing concentration of agri-food corporations increases the market and lobby power of these firms, enabling them to affect prices, consumer food choices, innovation, and regulations.[16]

Global food trade has expanded enormously in recent decades, following the inclusion of agriculture in global trade rules under the World Trade Organization (WTO). Currently around 20 to 25 percent of world food production is traded on world markets.[17] This expansion in food trade has been uneven, however, as many low-income countries that were once largely self-sufficient, including many in sub-Saharan Africa, have become net importers of food. Growing reliance on imported foods has made low-income countries especially vulnerable to shifts in international food availability and prices.[18] Many analysts have pointed to international trade rules under the WTO's Agreement on Agriculture as a key factor in the growing imbalance in agricultural trade between rich and poor countries. These rules, agreed in 1994, have allowed rich industrialized countries to continue to subsidize food production and food export, while forcing developing countries to open their markets to food imports. Although the Doha round of the WTO, launched in 2001, sought to rectify imbalances that were embodied in the agricultural trade rules, these talks have been fraught and have not led to significant rebalancing.[19]

Financial actors have taken a greater role in the global food system all along food supply chains from production to consumption in ways that have also contributed to uneven power dynamics. Financial investors, seeking financial returns from the food and agriculture sector, have driven up demand for complex financial instruments linked to the agri-food sector, including commodity futures trading, farmland investment funds, and investment in funds indexed to agri-food companies.[20] This heightened role for financial investors in the food system has been highly controversial as many critiqued it for contributing to the food price spikes in 2007–2008 that sparked a major global food crisis, while others have rejected that link. There is growing consensus, however, that speculative financial investment in the sector has the potential to contribute to higher food prices and food price instability, which has negative impacts for poor people who spend a significant share of their income on food.[21]

A fragmented global food governance landscape

A third major trend at the international level affecting food systems is the fragmented global food governance landscape. The UN Committee on World Food Security (CFS), first established in 1974 in the face of a world food crisis, saw significant reforms in 2009 that increased the role of non-state actors in its work. The CFS now incorporates a Civil Society Mechanism (CSM) as well as a Private Sector Mechanism (PSM) to bring these actors into deliberations on world food security matters, albeit as non-voting participants.[22] The CFS takes an explicit rights-based approach to food security and nutrition, emphasizing to members the importance of the progressive realization of the right to food, as enshrined in the in the 1948 Universal Declaration of Human Rights as well as subsequent agreements, including the 1966 International Covenant on Economic, Social, and Cultural Rights and the 2004 Voluntary Guidelines to Support the Progressive Realization of the Right to Adequate Food in the Context of National Food Security (the Right to Food Guidelines). In the decade since its reform, the CFS has taken a more prominent role in global food security governance by overseeing the negotiation of a number of guidance documents and recommendations, including publications from the High-Level Panel of Experts on Food Security and Nutrition (HLPE) that reports to the CFS membership. However, as is the case for other global challenges, there is no specific enforcement mechanism for the implementation of these policy recommendations and guidelines. Moreover, state's support for the activities and recommendations of the CFS is highly uneven.[23]

Beyond formal state-based global food security governance bodies, states have generally scaled back their role in global food governance while civil society and the private sector have assumed more prominent roles through the proliferation of multi-stakeholder governance initiatives. These initiatives include certification schemes for major food commodities that seek to ensure sustainability and fair labor practices for food system workers.[24] A wide range of market-based initiatives have emerged since the 1990s, such as the Global Good Agricultural Practices (Global GAP), the Roundtable on Sustainable Palm Oil (RSPO), the Round Table on Responsible Soy (RTRS), and other commodity schemes that seek to certify suppliers for sustainability criteria. These initiatives, however, especially those that give strong roles to the transnational firms engaged in agri-food commodity trade, incorporate little by way of monitoring and enforcement, making them especially weak. Moreover, they may have unintended consequences that disadvantage small-scale and marginalized producers, with implications for food security.[25]

Governance mechanisms and institutions in other global arenas – such as the WTO and a variety of international environmental agreements and institutions that govern environmental problems such as climate change and biodiversity loss – have enormous bearing on food system outcomes. Like in the arena of food governance, states in recent years have stepped back somewhat from the pursuit of international cooperative governance arrangements. The withdrawal of the United States from the Paris Agreement under the Trump administration (reversed by President Biden) and the failure to reform the Agreement on Agriculture at the WTO, for example, have signaled a weakening of international cooperation in ways that matter for food system outcomes.[26]

COVID-19 and the shock to food systems

The COVID-19 pandemic has major implications for food systems globally, and its effects are likely to be felt for years to come. The lockdowns that sought to stop the spread of the virus triggered a major crisis in food systems worldwide. They also resulted in increased hunger and shone a light on inequities and the weaknesses of governance in the food system.[27] Unlike food crises in the mid-1970s and in 2007–2008 that were sparked by supply concerns, the crisis unleashed by COVID-19 was different. Indeed, food supply at a global scale was at a near record high when the pandemic hit. Rather, the crisis unfolded via several interlocking dynamics unleashed by the pandemic.

Initially, there were major disruptions to the movement of food through supply chains, especially those involving the international food trade. Some of the disruptions were the due to lockdown measures that saw local restaurants and other food services close abruptly in many countries, as well as the closure of international borders, leading to declining demand and cancelled orders, as well as disruptions to the movement of seasonal migrant farm workers. These disruptions resulted in large amounts of perishable foods being wasted in many countries, including dairy and fresh fruits and vegetables.[28] Some large, food-producing countries also imposed restrictions on exports of staple foods, fearful that prices would rise because of the disruptions. This led to higher price pressure on crops such as rice and wheat at the same time as restricting the availability of those crops in countries that had become dependent on food imports. While most restrictions eased by the last quarter of 2020, there was continued risk that exporting states could reinstate export restrictions depending on the dynamics experienced because of the pandemic.[29]

The lockdowns also gave rise to a major global recession, which caused significant loss of income and livelihoods around the world and affected people's access to food. The equivalent of 255 million full-time jobs were lost in 2020 as global growth contracted.[30] Many of these job losses were in the agri-food sector, including vulnerable food system workers such as seasonal laborers and food-processing workers.[31] The IMF estimates that around 95 million additional people fell into extreme poverty over the course of 2020, while an additional 111 million people experienced acute food insecurity from April 2020 to April 2021.[32] Hunger has increased in the countries hardest hit by this recession, with Africa and Asia being the most affected.

These dynamics of disruption and income collapse have affected food prices in different countries in complex ways, which has further undermined food access for many people. Although global cereal stocks were near record levels at the start of 2020 and world commodity prices initially declined when the pandemic took hold, global food prices have risen by over 30 percent on average from April 2020 to April 2021, albeit in highly uneven patterns across countries.[33] As of mid-2020, food prices had risen by under 5 percent in Canada and the United Kingdom, for example, but by nearly 50 percent in Guyana and Venezuela.[34] And prices for different food commodities have also been affected differently. At the start of the pandemic, world prices for meat, dairy, and perishable foods fell sharply with declining demand while global cereal prices were registering modest price increases. Then, as workers in meat-processing plants experienced rising rates of illness and some facilities closed, meat prices also increased.

These multifaceted dynamics unleashed by the pandemic have had profound impacts on both food systems and food security, and the effects are likely to continue, at least until the spread of the COVID-19 virus is brought under control and vaccines are widely available. As noted prior, food insecurity rose sharply around the world as the pandemic unfolded. This COVID-19-induced food security crisis has drawn closer scrutiny to the ways food systems are organized, including its inequities and environmental impacts more broadly.

Competing visions for the future of global food governance

To date, global food governance has been more reactive than proactive in addressing the problems in the food system. The establishment of the CFS, for example, came in the aftermath of the 1974 food crisis. And the reform of the CFS in 2009 came following a major food crisis in 2007–2008. This reactive approach is in large part because of the fragmented nature of global food governance – as outlined prior. It also partly reflects sharp disagreements about the most appropriate way to achieve global food security and sustainability, which has held back strong governance responses. The current moment – which highlights the ongoing failure to meet SDG 2 and COVID-19's devastating impact on food security – has seen a growing consensus across different governance arenas on the need for a *fundamental transformation* of food systems to make them more resilient to shocks and capable of delivering on SDG 2 goals.

The emerging consensus about a wholescale transformation implies a more proactive approach to addressing food security problems. However, it is unclear whether old divides over the future vision for food systems can be overcome. Thus, while the current moment provides a potential opening for a fundamentally different path for food systems governance, the clash of approaches – between rights-based and commodity-based visions of resilience – that has long plagued food security governance and politics may continue to hold back progress toward global food security governance. How this debate plays out in the coming years is likely to be deeply influenced by the outcome of the 2021 UN Food System Summit, which has an explicit aim of providing a bold new road map for food system transformation to deliver on the SDGs.[35] What follows is a brief overview of the latest iteration of this divide, which is likely to shape political struggles over the future of food security governance in the coming decades.

Rights-based resilience: Agroecology and regional markets

Civil society actors that are actively engaged in the CFS have advanced a strong vision for food systems going forward, one that is grounded in the right-to-food framework embraced by the CFS and promoted by the UN Special Rapporteur on the Right to Food. This vision draws on the ideal of "food sovereignty," promoted by civil society groups since the early 1990s, which prioritizes the rights of peasants and small-scale producers to determine the shape of their own food systems. From this perspective, a rights-based approach that is centered on enhancing the agency and productivity of small-scale producers supports more environmentally sound and equitable food systems that are required to meet food security and sustainability goals going forward.

This rights-based vision of resilience calls for food-production systems to be organized along the principles of agroecology, which is based on farming systems that promote regenerative, diverse, and resource-efficient production practices and do not rely on such external inputs as modified seeds and agrochemicals. This approach addresses the ecological problems associated with large-scale industrial agriculture by capitalizing on ecological interactions within diverse production systems that include intercropping and other techniques to naturally build resistance to pests and to absorb rather than release climate-warming carbon.[36] Agroecological farming systems foster resilience in food systems by building soil and animal health and diversity, generating resource efficiencies, and building social equity through its promotion of participatory engagement and low costs to adopt its methods. Agroecological food-production systems also offer more diverse and nutritional foods, which are essential for food security and good health.[37]

In addition to more diverse food-production systems, this vision also calls for more diversity in food-processing and food-distribution systems. The CSM, for example, has advocated for "territorial" markets that operate at the local and regional scale as a means by which to push back against concentrated agri-food markets dominated by large transnational corporations.[38] Markets organized along more local and regional lines can improve food system resilience because they are more nimble and responsive to the kinds of disruptions that occurred when COVID-19 wrought havoc in global supply chains.[39] Territorial market arrangements also work to strengthen the livelihoods of smaller-scale and local food producers, processers, and marketers while reducing reliance on large transnational corporations in concentrated global markets. Because markets at this scale often lack the kind of infrastructural support that is often more available to large-scale corporate actors, proponents of this vision call for a stronger role for the state to support more local and regional processing and market infrastructure.[40]

Commodity-based resilience: Digital precision and globally integrated supply chains

A very different vision is being put forward by large corporations and powerful governance actors that is more grounded in advancing new technologies to address unsustainable dimensions of food systems and improvements in trade-driven markets to transform food systems. This approach builds on earlier "productionist" and liberalized global economic approaches to food security, which focused on producing more food through the adoption of new technologies such as modified seeds, associated agrochemicals, and international food trade. Rather than framing food as a right, this approach sees food very much as a commodity, and it seeks to ensure that food is widely available and accessible through market mechanisms of supply and demand. Yet, while earlier versions of this method called for increased production at all costs, its most recent iteration is more sensitive to the need for environmental sustainability of production systems.

This commodity-based approach to resilience calls for the employment of data-driven technologies in agricultural production systems, specifically digital agriculture and genome editing, to intensify production sustainably. These technologies employ digital sensors, drones, and global positioning systems to improve the efficiency of farm inputs, including technologies designed to minimize agrochemical use.[41] These types of digital technologies are also being employed to respond to labor shortages; for instance, robotic milkers and harvesting machinery now complete tasks previously done by humans. Computer-assisted genome mapping has enabled the rise of gene-editing technologies, such as CRISPR-Cas9, which allow for much more precise genetic edits to plants to give them certain traits such as drought and heat resistance. Blockchain technologies are also envisioned to be useful in establishing more efficient and traceable global supply chains.[42] These data-driven technologies aim to foster environmental sustainability through efficiency gains while simultaneously increasing food production.

This approach also promotes a continuation and extension of globalized food-trading systems to maximize the purported benefits from trade, including the role of trade as an adaptation strategy to climate change. It also requires the continued liberalization of agricultural trade policies, including rules to prevent trade restrictions, as occurred during the early days of the COVID-19 pandemic, combined with continued use of market-based governance schemes to ensure the sustainability of global supply chains.[43]

Destined to clash?

These two visions are currently in full view, with each dominant in different circles. Both are, nonetheless, jockeying for position in global discussions about the future of global food security governance. While those promoting the commodity-based resilience approach see agroecology and localized markets as likely to be inefficient and drive market stagnation, the promoters of the rights-based vision of resilience fear that high-tech farming that feeds into global supply chains dominated by TNCs will undermine sustainable livelihoods with its push for farming without farmers that is bound to extend, not scale back, the environmental costs of food systems. Tussles over these different approaches have been evident in the deliberations leading up to the 2021 Food System Summit (FSS). The CSM has criticized the Summit process for its lack of transparency, including in its process for selecting the leadership teams that will ultimately shape its recommendations for future food system governance. In the view of the CSM, the FSS is being dominated by corporate interests that are pushing the commodity-based technology and trade-heavy approach.[44]

How the COVID-19 food security crisis affects this debate is as yet unclear. While the pandemic's impact on food security has galvanized critiques from advocates of both visions on the dangers of overly complex, global food supply chains, there is less agreement about how best to resolve those problems. While both perspectives come to the issue with a different understanding of the nature of the problem and different proposals for its resolution, there may be some prospects for convergence on the margins for some issues. For example, digital technologies may in some cases be useful for advancing agroecological farming. It is feasible that agroecological principles can be woven into production models that rely on big data and technology, although clear and enforceable global rules will need to be negotiated to ensure that those principles are not watered down and that small-scale producers have equal access to data and technologies and that the benefits go beyond only TNCs. Similarly, it is unlikely that the global trade in food will either be all localized or purely delivered via globalized supply chains. This reality has the potential to open up space for setting rules in global governance arenas for trade in food and agricultural goods that allow for a prioritization of local and regional markets where benefits are clear – such as for locally appropriate staple grains – while still leaving space for global trade in foods that cannot be easily produced in all regions. Such an approach on both the production and distribution fronts could arrive at an appropriate balance and reduce inequities while promoting sustainability in ways that make sense in local contexts. Strong governance institutions at the global level are necessary to arrive at and enforce rules and norms that ensure those outcomes.

Conclusion

The global governance of food matters, and not just now in the midst of a major food crisis. It matters well into the future, as planetary sustainability and human well-being depend on a fundamental transformation of food systems that are more equitable and resilient. Yet, in the absence of significant governance reforms, major trends like climate change, market concentration, and fragmented mechanisms for food security governance are likely to pose major challenges to food system transformation. The COVID-19 pandemic has drawn attention to these food system challenges and galvanized broad support for measures to begin the transformative change that will be required in the coming decades.

There is widespread support for the idea of food system transformation, although disagreements remain about the central operating principle for improving food security: should food systems be centered on the right to food or on food as a commodity? This division with respect to the goal also sows division over how to achieve it: should the planet rely on agroecology and territorial markets or digital technology and further globalization of agri-food supply chains? These vastly different approaches are likely to remain at odds, weakening attempts to reshape global food governance in ways that enable humanity to achieve SDG 2. There are, however, some areas on the margins where convergence may be possible, which could provide room for maneuver, including bringing together digital farming technologies with agroecological approaches and finding appropriate rules-based governance mechanisms to better balance local food production with global trade. These kinds of steps will require strong food security governance frameworks with strong government support, rather than the fragmented landscape that dominates today.

Suggested readings

Jennifer Clapp, *Food*, 3rd ed. (Cambridge: Polity Press, 2020).
High Level Panel of Experts on Food Security and Nutrition, *Food Security and Nutrition: Building a Global Narrative Toward 2020* (Rome: HLPE, 2020).
Nora McKeon, *Food Security Governance: Empowering Communities, Regulating Corporations* (London: Routledge, 2014).
Boyd Swinburn et al., "The Global Syndemic of Obesity, Undernutrition, and Climate Change: The Lancet Commission Report," *The Lancet* 393, no. 10173 (2019): 1–56.
Jan Douwe van der Ploeg, "From Biomedical to Politico-economic Crisis: The Food System in Times of Covid-19," *The Journal of Peasant Studies* 47, no. 5 (2020): 944–972.

Notes

1 UN, "Transforming Our World: The 2030 Agenda for Sustainable Development," Draft Resolution Referred to the United Nations Summit for the Adoption of the Post-2015 Development Agenda by the General Assembly at its Sixty-ninth Session, UN document A/70/L.1, 18 September 2015.
2 FAO, IFAD, UNICEF, WFP, and WHO, *The State of Food Security and Nutrition in the World 2021: Transforming Food Systems for Resilient Food Security, Nutrition and Access to Healthy Diets for All* (Rome: FAO, 2021).
3 FAO, International Fund for Agricultural Development (IFAD), UNICEF, WFP, and WHO, *The State of Food Security and Nutrition in the World 2018: Building Climate Resilience for Food Security and Nutrition* (Rome: FAO, 2018).
4 FAO, *The State of Food and Agriculture 2016: Climate Change, Agriculture and Food Security* (Rome: FAO, 2016); Intergovernmental Science-Policy Platform on Biodiversity and Ecosystem Services (IPBES), *Summary for Policymakers of the Global Assessment Report on Biodiversity and Ecosystem Services of the Intergovernmental Science-Policy Platform on Biodiversity and Ecosystem Services* (Bonn, Germany: IPBES Secretariat, 2019).
5 See, for example, Johan Rockström et al., "A Safe Operating Space for Humanity," *Nature* 461 (September 2009): 472–475; Walter Willett et al., "Food in the Anthropocene: The EAT – Lancet Commission on Healthy Diets from Sustainable Food Systems," *The Lancet* 393, no. 10170 (2019): 447–492; Marco Springmann et al., "Options for Keeping the Food System Within Environmental Limits," *Nature* 562, no. 7728 (October 2018): 519–525.
6 International Labour Organization (ILO), "COVID-19 and the World of Work, 7th ed.," *ILO Monitor*, 30 June 2020, http://www.ilo.org/wcmsp5/groups/public/---dgreports/---dcomm/documents/briefingnote/wcms_767028.pdf.
7 See, for example, Vincent Ricciardi et al., "How Much of the World's Food Do Smallholders Produce?" *Global Food Security* 17 (June 2018): 64–72; Benjamin Graeub et al., "The State of Family Farms in the World," *World Development* 87 (November 2016): 1–15.
8 See High Level Panel of Experts on Food Security and Nutrition, *Food Security and Nutrition: Building a Global Narrative Toward 2020* (Rome: HLPE, 2020).
9 Intergovernmental Panel on Climate Change (IPCC), "Summary for Policymakers," in *Climate Change and Land: An IPCC Special Report on Climate Change, Desertification, Land Degradation, Sustainable Land Management, Food Security, and Greenhouse Gas Fluxes in Terrestrial Ecosystems* (Geneva: IPCC, 2020), www.ipcc.ch/srccl/chapter/

summary-for-policymakers; Meredith Niles and Jonathan Salerno, "A Cross-Country Analysis of Climate Shocks and Smallholder Food Insecurity," *PLoS ONE* 13, no. 2 (February 2018): 1–14; Ana Maria Loboguerrero et al., "Food and Earth Systems: Priorities for Climate Change Adaptation and Mitigation for Agriculture and Food Systems," *Sustainability* 11, no. 5 (2019): 1372.

10 FAO, *The State of Food and Agriculture 2016*.

11 Boyd Swinburn et al., "The Global Syndemic of Obesity, Undernutrition, and Climate Change: The Lancet Commission Report," *The Lancet* 393, no. 10173 (2019): 1–56; Matthew Smith and Samuel Myers, "Impact of Anthropogenic CO_2 Emissions on Global Human Nutrition," *Nature Climate Change* 8 (September 2018): 834–839.

12 FAO, *Climate Change and Food Security: Risks and Responses* (Rome: FAO, 2016).

13 IPES-Food, *From Uniformity to Diversity: A Paradigm Shift from Industrial Agriculture to Diversified Agroecological Systems* (International Panel of Experts on Sustainable Food Systems, 2016), www.ipes-food.org/_img/upload/files/UniformityToDiversity_FULL.pdf

14 Jennifer Clapp, *Food*, 3rd ed. (Cambridge: Polity Press, 2020); and Philip Howard, *Concentration and Power in the Food System* (London: Bloomsbury, 2016).

15 IPES-Food, *Too Big to Feed: Exploring the Impacts of Mega-mergers, Consolidation and Concentration of Power in the Agri-food Sector* (International Panel of Experts on Sustainable Food Systems, 2017), www.ipes-food.org/_img/upload/files/Concentration_Full-Report.pdf.

16 Jennifer Clapp and Gyorgy Scrinis, "Big Food, Nutritionism, and Corporate Power," *Globalizations* 14, no. 4 (2017): 578–595.

17 Paolo D'Odorico et al., "Feeding Humanity Through Global Food Trade," *Earth's Future* 2, no. 9 (2014): 458–469.

18 Manitra Rakotoarisoa, Massimo Iafrate, and Marianna Paschali, *Why Has Africa Become a Net Food Importer? Explaining Africa Agricultural and Food Trade Deficits* (Rome: FAO, 2011); and Jennifer Clapp, "Food Self-sufficiency: Making Sense of It, and When It Makes Sense," *Food Policy* 66 (January 2017): 88–96.

19 On agricultural trade and the WTO, see Matias Margulis, "Negotiating from the Margins: How the UN Shapes the Rules of the WTO," *Review of International Political Economy* 25, no. 3 (2018): 364–391; James Scott, "The Future of Agricultural Trade Governance in the World Trade Organization," *International Affairs* 93, no. 5 (2017): 1167–1184.

20 Jennifer Clapp and S. Ryan Isakson, *Speculative Harvests: Financialization, Food and Agriculture* (Halifax, Canada: Fernwood, 2018).

21 Getaw Tadesse et al., "Drivers and Triggers of International Food Price Spikes and Volatility," *Food Policy* 47 (August 2014): 117–128.

22 Nora McKeon, *Food Security Governance: Empowering Communities, Regulating Corporations* (London: Routledge, 2014); and Jessica Duncan, *Global Food Security Governance: Civil Society Engagement in the Reformed Committee on World Food Security* (London: Routledge, 2015).

23 See High Level Panel of Experts on Food Security and Nutrition, *Food Security and Nutrition*; McKeon, *Food Security Governance*.

24 Doris Fuchs and Agni Kalfagianni, "The Causes and Consequences of Private Food Governance," *Business and Politics* 12, no. 3 (2010): 145–181.

25 Peter Dauvergne, "The Global Politics of the Business of 'Sustainable' Palm Oil," *Global Environmental Politics* 18, no. 2 (2018): 34–52; Peter Oosterveer et al., "Global Sustainability Standards and Food Security: Exploring Unintended Effects of Voluntary Certification in Palm Oil," *Global Food Security* 3, nos. 3–4 (2014): 220–226.

26 High Level Panel of Experts on Food Security and Nutrition, *Food Security and Nutrition*.

27 See Jennifer Clapp and William G. Moseley, "This Food Crisis Is Different: COVID-19 and the Fragility of the Neoliberal Food Security Order," *The Journal of Peasant Studies* 47, no. 7 (2020): 1393–1417; and Susanna Klassen and Sophia Murphy, "Equity as Both a Means and an End: Lessons for Resilient Food Systems from COVID-19," *World Development* 136 (December 2020): 1–4.

28 Christopher Barrett, "Actions Now Can Curb Food Systems Fallout from COVID-19," *Nature Food* 1 (May 2020): 319–320; High Level Panel of Experts on Food Security and Nutrition, *Impacts of COVID-19 on Food Security and Nutrition: Developing Effective Policy Responses to Address the Hunger and Malnutrition Pandemic* (Rome: HLPE, 2020).

29 David Laborde et al., "COVID-19 Risks to Global Food Security," *Science* 369, no. 6503 (2020): 500–502.

30 ILO, "COVID-19 and the World of Work."

31 Maximo Torero, *Prepare Food Systems for a Long-haul Fight Against COVID-19* (Washington, DC: International Food Policy Research Institute, August 2020); and UN, "The Impact of COVID-19 on Food Security and Nutrition," June 2020, https://reliefweb.int/sites/reliefweb.int/files/resources/sg_policy_brief_on_covid_impact_on_food_security.pdf

32 IMF, *World Economic Outlook* (Washington, DC: IMF, 2021); World Bank, "Food Security and COVID-19," 21 May 2021, https://www.worldbank.org/en/topic/agriculture/brief/food-security-and-covid-19.

33 FAO, "Food Price Index," 6 May 2021, http://www.fao.org/worldfoodsituation/foodpricesindex/en/.

34 Clapp and Moseley, "This Food Crisis Is Different."

35 See UN Food System Summit webpage, www.un.org/en/food-systems-summit.

36 See, for example, Miguel Altieri et al., "Agroecology and the Design of Climate Change-Resilient Farming Systems," *Agronomy for Sustainable Development* 35, no. 3 (2015): 869–890. Miguel Altieri and Clara I. Nicholls, "Agroecology and the Reconstruction of a Post-COVID-19 Agriculture," *The Journal of Peasant Studies* 47, no. 5 (2020): 881–898; Ian Bailey and Louise Buck, "Managing for Resilience: A Landscape Framework for Food and Livelihood Security and Ecosystem Services," *Food Security* 8, no. 3 (2016): 477–490.

37 Alexander Wezel et al., "Agroecological Principles and Elements and Their Implications for Transitioning to Sustainable Food Systems: A Review," *Agronomy for Sustainable Development* 40, no. 6 (2020): 1–13; Rachel Bezner Kerr et al., "Farming for Change: Developing a Participatory Curriculum on Agroecology, Nutrition, Climate Change and Social Equity in Malawi and Tanzania," *Agriculture and Human Values* 36, no. 3 (2019): 549–566.

38 Civil Society Mechanism (CSM) of the Committee on World Food Security (CFS), *Connecting Smallholders to Markets: Analytical Guide* (Rome: CSM, 2014), www.csm4cfs.org/wp-content/uploads/2016/10/ENG-ConnectingSmallholdersToMarkets_web.pdf.

39 Jan Douwe van der Ploeg, "From Biomedical to Politico-economic Crisis: The Food System in Times of Covid-19," *The Journal of Peasant Studies* 47, no. 5 (2020): 944–972.

40 See, for example, Claire Lamine et al., "Agri-food Systems and Territorial Development: Innovations, New Dynamics and Changing Governance Mechanisms," in *Farming Systems Research into the 21st Century: The New Dynamic*, ed. Ika Darnhofer, David Gibbon, and Benoit Dedieu (Dordrecht, The Netherlands: Springer, 2012), 229–256; Alison Blay-Palmer et al., "Validating the City Region Food System Approach: Enacting Inclusive, Transformational City Region Food Systems," *Sustainability* 10, no. 5 (2018): 1–23.

41 See, for example, Alfons Weersink et al., "Opportunities and Challenges for Big Data in Agricultural and Environmental Analysis," *Annual Review of Resource Economics* 10 (October 2018): 19–37; Athanasios Balafoutis et al., "Precision Agriculture Technologies Positively Contributing to GHG Emissions Mitigation, Farm Productivity and Economics," *Sustainability* 9, no. 8 (2017): 1–28.

42 Daniel Bumblauskas et al., "A Blockchain Use Case in Food Distribution: Do You Know Where Your Food Has Been?" *International Journal of Information Management* 52 (June 2020): 102008.

43 See, for example, Uris Lantz C. Baldos and Thomas W. Hertel, "The Role of International Trade in Managing Food Security Risks from Climate Change," *Food Security* 7, no. 2 (2015): 275–290; Charlotte Janssens et al., "Global Hunger and Climate Change Adaptation Through International Trade," *Nature Climate Change* 10, no. 9 (2020): 829–835.

44 See CSM, "Open Call for Civil Society and Indigenous Peoples' Engagement to Respond to the UN Food Systems Summit," www.csm4cfs.org/open-call-civil-society-indigenous-peoples-engagement-respond-un-food-systems-summit/; and Matthew Canfield, Molly Anderson, and Philip McMichael, "UN Food Systems Summit 2021: Dismantling Democracy and Resetting Corporate Control of Food Systems," *Frontiers in Sustainable Food Systems* 5 (2021): 1–15.

CONTENTS

The future of global health governance

Less global, less health, less governance

Anne Roemer-Mahler

"Building back better" has become the mantra for post-COVID-19 recovery. With its roots in disaster response,[1] this sounds like an appropriate slogan not only for socio-economic revival but also for improving the governance of global health. The coronavirus pandemic has made the limitations of global health governance abundantly clear. Yet it has also created political space for concerted action because infectious disease control is now high on the agenda of many governments and other organizations. This should make health collaboration, especially around infectious disease control, one of the most promising areas for advancing global governance at a time when geopolitical tensions and rising nationalism make prospects for global governance look altogether more dire.

Yet we should take the call to "build back better" with some caution. "Building *back better*" implies that we just need to create a better version of the system we already have or had. However, to build successful health collaboration in the future, I suggest that we need to reflect on the existing system in some quite fundamental ways as well as on our way of understanding it. This difficult task means reflecting not only on the institutions we have come to refer to as "global health governance" but also on the ideas that have shaped these institutions and the lenses through which we understand them.

DOI: 10.4324/9781003139836-17

Reflections on the global governance for infectious disease control have already started.[2] This chapter focuses particularly on some of the ideas on which this governance system rests. Reflecting on the underlying ideas is important because they tie "global health governance" to a historical period dominated by Western and, especially, US perspectives on world order and associated understandings of globality and governance. With the rise of other powers, especially China, the dominance of these perspectives is being challenged. New institutions and forms of collaboration are being created that we do not usually include in analyses of global health governance. Yet these ideas and institutions are likely to shape the parameters within which health collaboration unfolds in the future.

In order to understand both the constraints and opportunities for building better health collaborations, this chapter explores three broad ideas underlying the existing system of global health governance: the notion of "globality," the focus on health as the driving force of this system, and the idea of "governance" as it has been institutionalized in global health governance. Based on these reflections, I suggest that the future of global health governance is likely to be less global and less about health, and it will contain less "governance" of the type that has characterized the health collaborations of the 1990s and early 2000s. While this prospect may mean that health collaborations become more difficult, it is important to reflect on the ideational claims and foundations of the current system when we seek new opportunities for health collaboration in a rapidly changing environment.

The challenge of "globality"

The term "global health" emerged in the 1990s and began to replace the older term "international health," which had been used since the nineteenth century. The new terminology indicated a shift in emphasis away from a focus on interstate collaboration and a limited number of diseases, such as cholera and yellow fever, toward a more comprehensive perspective on the link between globalization and health.[3] Key to this perspective was the emerging perception that globalization had increased the interdependence of states and populations in terms of their health security. Increasing commercial links, population mobility, and urbanization meant that pathogens could spread more rapidly from remote areas to urban centers and around the globe. The idea of new global health threats was fueled by the spread of HIV (human immunodeficiency virus)/AIDS (acquired immunodeficiency syndrome) in the 1980s and 1990s, the increasing fear of bioterrorism, and several epidemics in the 2000s, including severe acute respiratory syndrome (SARS), pandemic influenza, and Ebola.

To address these new global health threats, many argued that new governance approaches were needed because states, on their own, are incapable of addressing health threats that transcended borders.[4] The revision of a key international treaty on infectious disease control, the International Health Regulations (IHR), in 2005 has been considered a milestone for strengthening interstate collaboration on health.[5] In the revised IHR, states agreed to notify each other about any health issues that can present a public health risk to other states. Furthermore, the revision of the IHR strengthened the role of the private sector by enabling the World Health Organization (WHO) to act on the basis of information about outbreaks provided by non-state actors, rather than having to rely exclusively on the collaboration of states.[6]

Perhaps the most characteristic feature of *global* health governance, which sets it apart most visibly from the earlier *international* variant, is the proliferation of a new type of institution: public-private partnerships. Since the late 1990s, a myriad of public-private partnerships have emerged in global health governance. They take different shapes and forms, and they focus on different issues. Some of the largest and most well-known partnerships work on the financing, development, and distribution of medicines and vaccines in low- and middle-income countries (LMICs); three such organizations are the Global Fund to fight HIV/AIDS, Tuberculosis and Malaria (GFATM), and Gavi, the Vaccine Alliance (formerly the GAVI Alliance, and before that the Global Alliance for Vaccines and Immunization). In addition, there are numerous so-called product development partnerships, which develop new diagnostics, medicines, and vaccines for a range of health threats, ranging from antimicrobial resistance and neglected diseases that occur predominantly among poor populations to pandemic preparedness. In addition, public-private partnerships have proliferated as a vehicle to mobilize funding and organize the implementation of global health programs. Increasingly, the public-private partnership model is being integrated into the work of intergovernmental organizations – for instance, in form of the Global Health Security Agenda Private Sector Roundtable and, most recently, the WHO Foundation.

Global health governance, therefore, has brought about new levels and types of collaboration to address global health threats. Yet questions were soon raised about the extent to which these collaborations were indeed "global." Several analyses have highlighted the dominance of organizations from a small number of countries, notably the United States and the United Kingdom.[7] The US government has long been the single most important funder of global health, providing roughly 30 percent of overall global health spending in 2019, followed by the US-based Bill and Melinda Gates Foundation, with approximately 9 percent, and the UK government, with approximately 8.5 percent.[8] Another study found that the 98.5 percent of global health organizations had their headquarters in high-income countries, with 66.5 percent headquartered in the United States, 11 percent in Switzerland, and 6 percent in the United Kingdom.[9]

Also, the intellectual foundations for the idea of "global health" and, in particular, the notion of "global health security" were strongly shaped by interests and perspectives from US public health, foreign policy, and security communities.[10] After all, US businesses were initially the key drivers of and participants in economic globalization, and US troops were present in many countries worldwide. The United States was, as a result, much more exposed to globalization and the new global health threats than many other countries. It is not surprising, therefore, that many of the health threats identified as "global" were, in fact, a priority for the United States and some Western European governments, rather than for the governments of countries where most "global health" interventions have taken place: notably Africa and Southeast Asia.[11] Here, dominant concerns are infectious diseases that pose little or no threat to the rest of the world, such as malaria, measles, and diarrheal diseases, as well as, increasingly, non-communicable diseases, such as cancers and cardiovascular diseases.

Limitations of the claim to "globality" are evident also at the institutional level, notably with regards to the new public-private partnerships for global health. As discussed in more detail in the following, both the intellectual foundations and the main financial and political support for this governance arrangement have come from organizations in the Unites States and Western Europe. Particularly notable is the limited engagement of China in these public-private partnerships for global health. This is noteworthy for a number of reasons. First, many global health partnerships work on expanding access to diagnostics, medicines, and vaccines and therefore work closely with biopharmaceutical companies. China's biopharmaceutical industry has been rising fast, but this has not yet led to significant engagement with these initiatives. This contrasts somewhat with India – another emerging pharma power – where both the government and pharmaceutical companies have engaged more with global health partnerships.[12]

The lack of China's engagement is also noteworthy because it has rapidly increased and diversified global health collaborations in the past ten years, in particular in LMICs.[13] These initiatives have taken place largely outside the institutional system we usually refer to as "global health governance." Rather, China's health collaborations have been embedded in a wider scheme of economic investment in and assistance to LMICs, and they have been organized within the institutional structures that China has built to support its new global role, such as the Forum on China-Africa Co-operation (FOCAC) and the Belt and Road Initiative (BRI), which now includes plans for a "health silk road."[14]

Chinese sources sometimes place these institutions in the context and language of global governance but also around alternative visions of international relations and the notion of a "community of shared destiny," including "a global community of health for all."[15] While the precise content of these ideas is not always clear, what is clear is that Chinese policymakers believe their country's development experience and trajectory has lessons for other countries, including on improving health.[16]

The idea of an alternative "China model" for improving public health and achieving development more widely is contested,[17] not least because it misses the huge variety of development and policy trajectories that have been observed within China.[18] Yet, perhaps it is precisely in this observation that the greatest significance of debate about the China model lies. As Shaun Breslin argues, "The ultimate significance of the China model may be as a general exemplar of what can be achieved by addressing specific national conditions rather than universal templates."[19] Indeed, Lewis Husain and Gerry Bloom highlight the importance of local policy experimentation as a key feature of China's domestic health reform, which allowed for "experimentation and learning about what might work in its distinct institutional, political and economic environment."[20] Moreover, they argue that China is taking a similar approach to its engagement in global health.[21] Such an approach may well present a challenge to the existing system of global health governance as it expresses different ways of understanding and institutionalizing globality and universality.

The limits of "health"

The goal of global health governance is to improve the health of populations in the face of transborder health threats. This normative agenda is shared not only by many practitioners and scholars of global health governance, it is also engrained in its ideational foundations – "(global) public health" and "(global) governance." While a variety of definitions exist, most agree that "public health" is about improving the health of populations.[22] At least as manifold are definitions of "governance," but they too have certain commonalities, including that they suggest an element of intentionality and purposiveness to address an issue or problem.[23] The public health problem to be addressed by global health governance is the increase in transborder health issues. As a consequence, much of the policy and scholarly debate about global health governance has focused on how global health governance can better fulfil this purpose.[24] Yet, as some have pointed out, it is not only health considerations that have shaped global health governance but also trade and security interests.[25]

The importance of trade interests was manifest already in some of the earliest examples of international health collaboration, such as the International Sanitary Conferences in the nineteenth century. At that time, European countries struggled to cope with successive waves of cholera, which caused not only devastating suffering and death but also considerable trade problems as merchants had to deal with a fragmented system of quarantines and other regulations in each country. During the International Sanitary Conferences, European states agreed on a system of international infectious disease control that is, in essence, still in place in today.[26] The IHR (2005) stipulate that states have to notify each other about outbreaks and limit disease-prevention measures that restrict international trade and travel to those based on scientific evidence.[27] In other words, one of the key global health governance institutions on cross-border disease control is about the protection of both – health *and* trade.

In addition, a set of industrial interests has increasingly shaped international health collaboration in the last three decades: those related to the commercial application of technologies. Technological solutions have become an important feature in public health and global health, initially pharmaceutical technologies – i.e., medicines and vaccines – and, more recently, digital technologies for health surveillance, e-health, and also pharmaceutical development.[28] Those technologies are, to a significant extent, developed by commercial companies who are keen to protect the underlying know-how as commercial assets in the form of intellectual property.

As a result, the development of global health governance has long been shaped by a tension between promoting technological solutions to address global health problems and protecting their commercial value. This tension has become manifest in various global health governance institutions, such as the "Doha Declaration on the TRIPS Agreement and Public Health," negotiated by the World Trade Organization (WTO), the expansion of WHO's work in the area of pharmaceutical innovation and intellectual property, and the emergence of public-private partnerships to facilitate access to pharmaceutical and other technologies for global health. By involving companies as partners in the governance of global health, public-private partnerships and, in particular, product development partnerships mobilize critical know-how while leaving intellectual property protection and, therefore, the commercial value of this know-how intact.

Increasing economic interconnectedness and the rise of technologies have catapulted health not only into the realm of trade and industrial policy but also into the realm of security policies.[29] This development started in the early 1990s predominantly in the United States, where the foreign policy and security communities became concerned about the potential effects of new infectious diseases, such as HIV/AIDS, on the increasingly global presence of US businesses and military troops. Furthermore, there were increasing concerns about the proliferation of biological weapons after the end of the Cold War and the increase in terrorist threats.[30]

Against this background, the concept of "global health security" emerged, which captures the idea that certain health issues, notably pandemics and bioterrorism, can form a threat to national and international security. Since the early 2000s, the concept of global health security has become a constant in global health governance.[31] Institutional manifestations of this are manifold, including, for instance, the increasing involvement of national agencies of foreign affairs and defense in global health governance; the Global Health Security Agenda, which works with WHO on the implementation of the IHR; and the Coalition for Epidemic Preparedness Innovations (CEPI), which was inspired by the US Public Health Emergency Medical Countermeasures Enterprise.

Neither the influence of trade nor that of security interests in shaping global health governance have been uncontested. Criticism has come, for instance, from governments who are concerned about the link between global health security and the national security interests of Western states, especially the United States.[32] And powerful states, including China, have refused to accept external evaluations of their outbreak-preparedness capacities. Contestation and resistance have been evident also at the level of industrial policy. For instance, non-governmental organizations (NGOs) as well as governments and businesses from middle-income countries have contested the strong intellectual property regime embedded in the current global health governance architecture.[33] At the same time, rising powers, most notably China, are pursuing health collaboration in the context of their own industrial and geo-economic agendas through so-called South-South collaborations.

Contestation is likely to be particularly fierce when industrial and security concerns overlap. An area where such overlap has been visible for some time is in the development of so-called medical countermeasures. This terminology was developed in the United States to classify medicines and vaccines that are needed in the case of a bioterrorist attack or pandemic.[34] The knowledge and technologies involved in the development of medical countermeasures, therefore, are of relevance to all three areas: health, commerce, and security. Areas where health, commercial, and security interests overlap have been expanding fast, notably around the control of health data, including the establishment of surveillance systems, laboratory networks, and databases.[35]

The COVID-19 response has highlighted the extent to which industrial, geopolitical, and, indeed, security interests can shape global health collaboration. The issue of how "vaccine nationalism" can hinder access to vaccines in LMICs, harming not only the health but also worsening the economic effects of the pandemic on poor populations, has received much attention.[36] Others have pointed to the distribution of protective equipment, diagnostics, and vaccines by China and Russia in LMICs and have discussed the geopolitical dimension of these efforts.[37] Less publicized but probably more significant are conflicts about the control over supply chains for key industries and technologies. The role of certain industries and technologies, such as biopharmaceutical, next-generation information and communication technologies, and artificial intelligence, for instance, are of critical importance from both an economic and a security perspective.[38] These industries and technologies, therefore, are a point of increasingly fierce competition and contestation between powerful states, first and foremost China and the United States.[39] Yet these industries and technologies are also of critical importance for global health. It is, therefore, likely that industrial and security interests will play an even greater role in shaping health collaboration in the future than they have in the past.

The "governance" of global health

Why would we need to reflect on "governance" in search of better health collaborations? After all, is governance not what this is all about – that is, purposive collective action to help prevent a crisis like COVID-19 (or worse) from happening again? The answer is yes and no. Building better collaboration to improve the health of populations is undoubtedly an important goal. What we need to reflect on is what *kind* of collaboration we mean when we use the term "governance." The idea of governance is not neutral but carries with it a particular set of ideas about state-society relations and effective resource allocation. These ideas are manifest in the "new norms of collaboration"[40] that permeate the system we refer to as "global health governance."

Definitions of governance vary, but they tend to coalesce around activities or processes of steering, managing, and regulating.[41] In the governance terminology, these activities are not understood to be necessarily the prerogative of the state. Indeed, when discussions about governance took off in the 1980s and 1990s, the role of the state in governance was being hotly debated, not only with regards to the global level but also with regards to the domestic level, including in the context of economic development, especially in East Asia.[42] Yet the rise of a neo-liberal political rationality and New Public Management thinking helped spread a particular idea of "(good) governance," namely one that emphasized a limited role for the state and the importance of the private sector for effective regulation.

This notion of governance spread around the world in an era of US primacy. It was further strengthened and propelled into the realm of "global governance" by the argument that globalization was undermining the capacity of states to govern effectively.[43] As Mark Beeson points out,

> One of the most consequential ideational trends and theoretical assumptions . . . is the possibility that effective governance in a global era actually *necessitates* new types of relationships between states and other . . . actors.[44]

Consequently, "new norms of collaboration"[45] between states and private actors were promoted in order to address global health threats. David Fidler famously distinguished between a "Westphalian" and a "post-Westphalian" public health order.[46] In the Westphalian system of *international* health governance, only states were considered legitimate governors; however, the post-Westphalian *global* health governance system involves private actors "making policy on an equal footing with governments."[47]

One of the most significant indicators for this shift in governance approach was the revision of the IHR. In stark contrast to the earlier version, the revised IHR (2005) authorize the WHO to act on the basis of information about outbreaks that are provided not only by governments but also by non-state actors. This change was driven partly by new ideas about effective governance in the era of globalization, which were accentuated by the delayed reporting of an outbreak of SARS by the Chinese government in 2003. In turn, this delay contributed to the spread of the disease across the world. In addition, the push for including information from non-state sources in the IHR (2005) was triggered by the availability of new technologies. New information technologies, notably the internet, broadened the options for WHO and others to receive disease intelligence.[48]

This series of developments leads to another factor that has contributed to an increased role of the private sector in global health governance: the growing import-ance of technologies for (global) public health. The use of pharmaceuticals and other technologies has a long history in public health, but it increased greatly in the 1990s when advances in the biomedical and information technologies fueled optimism about the potential of technological interventions to address global health problems.[49] Yet, to harness this promise, new forms of collaboration were needed because states lacked the capacities and know-how for developing and applying these technologies in global health. Such resources reside largely in the private, commercial sector; in the era of neoliberalism, this has been considered not only necessary but also desir-able. In order to access the finance, know-how, and materials required to use these technologies in global health, commercial companies have been invited as partners in governing global health.

Public-private partnerships thus emerged as "the dominant policy paradigm in global health governance in the 2000s."[50] As detailed previously, this governance arrangement takes different forms and plays out in different ways in different organizations, but it has normalized private sector involvement and, indeed, private sector authority in global health governance. The key drivers and supporters of this governance approach have been US-based and, more recently, UK-based philanthropic organizations; commercial companies, predominantly from North America and Western Europe; the World Bank; European and North American official development assistance agencies; and a few NGOs, such as Médecins Sans Frontières. A study of funding sources for product development partnerships from 2010 found that the Gates Foundation provided nearly half their combined income (49 percent), with another 28 percent coming from US, UK, Dutch, and Irish aid agencies.[51]

The contribution of US and UK philanthropic organizations to establishing this governance model in global health is particularly noteworthy because of their role as relationship brokers.[52] Organizations like the Rockefeller Foundation, the Bill and Melinda Gates Foundation, and, more recently, the Wellcome Trust, have been able to broker collaborations in three main ways. The first is their financial assets, which helped them mobilize financial support from other private actors, including by providing risk capital and seed funding. The second is their position at the intersection of business, NGOs, and government, which enabled them to create dialogue across a variety of organizations. And the third is their highly networked employees, who have facilitated the uptake of policy solutions in governments and international organizations.[53] US and UK philanthropic organizations, therefore, have acted as important transmission belts for new ideas about the roles of public and private actors in global health governance.

How is all this relevant for thinking about the future of global health governance? It highlights that the system we refer to as "global health governance" represents, in fact, a very specific approach to addressing health problems in a collaborative, purposive manner. This approach is linked to ideas about state-society relations that emerged in the particular historical context of Western Europe and are rooted in wider conceptions of separate public and private spheres within which states and markets operate.[54] In the 1980s and 1990s, these ideas took a particular shape and form in neoliberal and New Public Management–inspired notions of (good) governance.

In global health governance, these ideas have become manifest in particular institutions, notably public-private partnerships, which have been supported largely by Western states and organizations and by their dominance in the world during the period when global health governance emerged. This limitation is important to ponder in a context in which alternative understandings and institutional arrangements to health collaboration are on the rise, which are based on different notions of state-society relations and different conceptualizations of the roles, responsibilities, and authorities of the state and other actors, and that are backed by different, and increasingly powerful actors.

As mentioned earlier, the support of rising powers for public-private partnerships in global health has been lukewarm. China, in particular, has stayed mostly clear of these arrangements. For scholars of China's role in international relations, this would not come as a surprise. As Beeson puts it, "The idea that political space within which governance occurs should be expanded and that nonstate actors should play a larger role in policy-making is generally an anathema to most of the rising states."[55] This may, in part, be attributed to the authoritarian nature of the regimes in place in many rising powers. However, it may also, in part, be linked to different conceptions of the role of the state in society, development, and governance.

Alternative ideas of the role of the state in governing economic development have been around for a while and came to prominence in the 1980s and 1990s in the context of the rapid development of the East Asian states. The important role of the state in the East Asian "miracle" was eventually acknowledged by proponents of neoliberal economic theories.[56] However, lessons from this experience did not occupy a prominent position in the development and governance discourses of the 1990s and 2000s. But they have seen a revival recently in a context of a wider geopolitical shift toward Asia. The most visible proponent of this revival is China, where the state has played a pivotal role in domestic economic development. More importantly, the state and the Chinese Communist Party *still* play an important role in the economy despite Beijing's integration into the global economy.[57]

China's global economic engagement and, indeed, its global health engagement have not been driven entirely by the state. Its global health engagement involves a range of different organizations that are not part of the Chinese state apparatus,[58] including companies, universities, and, more recently, philanthropic organizations like the Jack Ma Foundation, created by the founder of Alibaba. Yet this does not mean that their relationships and their respective roles and responsibilities are conceived of in the same ways as in the current system of global health governance. As China and other powerful states increase their engagement in health collaboration, it will become increasingly important to reflect on established notions of (global health) governance in order not to (dis) miss forms of – and opportunities for – health collaboration that do not match the "norms of collaboration" established in a different era.

Conclusion

The parameters for health collaboration are shifting. Some of the key ideas on which the existing system of global health governance is based are being challenged, including claims to globality and approaches to governance. None of these challenges are new, but they are now supported by powerful states, notably China. The parameters for health collaboration are shifting, as well, with the increasing strategic importance of industries and technologies on which global health relies. Separating health collaboration from ideological, industrial, and security conflicts will, therefore, likely become more difficult, especially in the context of rivalry among big powers.

Yet the shifting parameters also offer opportunities for health collaboration. First and foremost, the impetus to collaborate, especially on infectious disease control, is greater than ever before and high up on the political agenda of big powers, old and new. We can expect that existing public-private partnerships, especially around the development of biopharmaceutical technologies, will remain a strong pillar of future health collaborations. All major states and organizations that have supported them in the past have thrown their weight behind them during the COVID-19 response. Moreover, we can expect renewed support for these institutions from the US government under the Biden administration. Collaboration on infectious disease control is also likely to be a priority for China and other rising powers. Yet much of this collaboration will probably take place outside the established global health governance system. China's diplomatic engagement during the pandemic has stressed the continuous importance of collaboration via the BRI and FOCAC.

A second opportunity for more health collaboration may arise in the field of science and technology. At first glance, this may sound counterintuitive given the increasing strategic importance of new technologies and the resulting potential for political conflict. Yet all countries rely on these technologies for transborder health protection. Moreover, for these technologies to be able to support *global* surveillance systems and *global* systems for communication of disease data, there has to be some degree of collaboration between governments and non-state actors, including between rival (state and non-state) powers. It is, therefore, not unlikely that we will see an important role for science diplomacy in health collaboration, which can unfold somewhat under the radar of big-power rivalry.[59]

A potentially interesting area to watch is the role philanthropic foundations could play. As mentioned, US philanthropic foundations have been important relationship brokers for cross-border and cross-sectoral collaboration on the development of new medicines and vaccines in the past. Recently, as noted prior, the Jack Ma Foundation has been playing a prominent role in China's health and tech diplomacy, not only in the context of the COVID-19 response but also in the area of cooperation on digital technologies.[60] Whether philanthropic organizations, including those from rising powers, expand their role as relationship brokers in the new geopolitical environment is unknown but essential.

Finally, one of the oldest pillars of the existing system of global health governance is likely to remain an important pillar for future health collaborations: the WHO. Despite criticism,[61] it has been pivotal for the global COVID-19 response, especially through its ability to collect, analyze, and distribute scientific information and public health guidance. This capability reflects a combination of powers that place the WHO in a unique position for global health collaboration: its power to convene experts from a wide variety of health-related fields, its institutionally mandated and widely acknowledged legitimacy to set norms and standards, its institutional reach and representation at country level through offices in most states, and its universal membership.

Despite its many problems,[62] the WHO is likely to remain a crucial integrative force in an increasingly plural world order. It has the support of major incumbent and new powers. For the former, support for the WHO is part of wider attempts to keep in place the multilateral system they helped create. The latter appreciate the multilateral system as an expression of state sovereignty and as a source of stability, which facilitated their economic development in the first place and remains crucial for further growth and expansion. The WHO represents this multilateral system in the field of health and is, therefore, likely to remain an important platform of collaboration for all major powers.

Suggested reading

Tim Eckmanns, Henning Fueller, and Stephen L. Roberts, "Digital Epidemiology and Global Health Security: An Interdisciplinary Conversation," *Life Sciences, Society and Policy* 15, no. 2 (2019): 1–13.

David Fidler, "Asia's Participation in Global Health Diplomacy and Global Health Governance," *Asian Journal of WTO and International Health Law and Policy* 5, no. 2 (2010): 269–300.

Lewis Husain and Gerry Bloom, "Understanding China's Growing Involvement in Global Health and Managing Processes of Change," *Globalization and Health* 16, no. 39 (2020): 1–10.

Colin McInnes and Kelley Lee, *Global Health and International Relations* (Cambridge: Polity Press, 2012).

Michael Moran, *Private Foundations and Development Partnerships: American Philanthropy and Global Development Agendas* (London: Routledge, 2014).

Anne Roemer-Mahler and Stefan Elbe, "The Race for Ebola Drugs: Pharmaceuticals, Security and Global Health Governance," *Third World Quarterly* 37, no. 3 (2016): 487–506.

Notes

1 First introduced in 2006 by the UN secretary-general's special envoy for tsunami recovery, former US president Bill Clinton, "building back better" became integrated into the Sendai Framework for Disaster Risk Reduction 2015–2030.

2 WHO, "Review Committee on the Functioning of the International Health Regulations (2005) During the COVID-19 Response," www.who.int/teams/ihr/ihr-review-committees/covid-19; WHO, "Independent Evaluation of Global COVID-19 Response Announced," *WHO News*, 9 July 2020, www.who.int/news/item/09-07-2020-independent-evaluation-of-global-covid-19-response-announced.

3 See, for example, Derek Yach and Douglas Bettcher, "The Globalization of Public Health I: Threats and Opportunities," *American Journal of Public Health* 88, no. 5 (1998): 735–738; and Kelley Lee, *Globalization and Health: An Introduction* (Basingstoke, UK: Palgrave Macmillan, 2003).

4 Andrew F. Cooper, John J. Kirton, and Ted Schrecker, eds., *Governing Global Health* (Aldershot, UK: Ashgate, 2009).

5 David P. Fidler, "From International Sanitary Conventions to Global Health Security: The New International Health Regulations," *Chinese Journal of International Law* 4, no. 2 (2005): 325–392.

6 WHO, *International Health Regulations (2005)*, 3rd ed. (Geneva: WHO, 2016).

7 Steven J. Hoffman, Clarke B. Cole, and Mark Pearcey, *Mapping Global Health Architecture to Inform the Future* (London: The Royal Institute of International Affairs, 2015); Sanjana J. Ravi, Michael R. Snyder, and Caitlin Rivers, "Review of International Efforts to Strengthen the Global Outbreak Response System Since the 2014–16 West Africa Ebola Epidemic," *Health Policy and Planning* 34, no. 1 (2019): 47–54.

8 Institute for Health Metrics and Evaluation, *Financing Global Health 2019: Tracking Health Spending in a Time of Crisis* (Seattle, WA: Institute for Health Metrics and Evaluation – University of Washington, 2020).

9 Hoffman, Cole, and Pearcey, *Mapping Global Health Architecture to Inform the Future.*

10 In the mid-1990s, a considerable body of literature was produced on global health threats: Stephen S. Morse, "Factors in the Emergence of Infectious Diseases," *Emerging Infectious Diseases* 1, no. 1 (1995): 7–15; Institute of Medicine, *America's Vital Interest in Global Health: Protecting Our People, Enhancing Our Economy, and Advancing Our International Interests* (Washington, DC: National Academy Press, 1997); and Philip S. Brachman, Heather C. O'Maonaigh, and Richard N. Miller, eds., *Perspectives on the Department of Defense Global Emerging Infections Surveillance and Response System* (Washington, DC: National Academy Press, 2001). On the emergence of the idea of "health security," see also: Stefan Elbe, Anne Roemer-Mahler, and Christopher Long, "Medical Countermeasures for National Security: A New Government Role in the Pharmaceuticalization of Society," *Social Science & Medicine* 131 (2015): 263–271; and Susan Wright, "Terrorists and Biological Weapons," *Politics and the Life Sciences* 25, no. 1 (2007): 57–115.

11 Simon Rushton, "Global Health Security: Security for Whom? Security from What?" *Political Studies* 59, no. 4 (2011): 779–796.

12 Anne Roemer-Mahler, "The Rise of Companies from Emerging Markets in Global Health Governance: Opportunities and Challenges," *Review of International Studies* 40, no. 5 (2014): 897–918.

13 Lewis Husain and Gerry Bloom, "Understanding China's Growing Involvement in Global Health and Managing Processes of Change," *Globalization and Health* 16, no. 39 (2020): 1–10.

14 Kirk Lancaster, Michael Rubin, and Mira Rapp-Hooper, *Mapping China's Health Silk Road* (Washington, DC: Council on Foreign Relations, 10 April 2020), www.cfr.org/blog/mapping-chinas-health-silk-road.

15 Statement by H. E. Xi Jinping, President of the People's Republic of China, at Virtual Event of Opening of the 73rd World Health Assembly, Beijing, 18 May 2020, www.fmprc.gov.cn/mfa_eng/zxxx_662805/t1780221.shtml; Gao Zugui, "Building a Global Health Community for All," *China Today*, 24 July 2020, www.chinatoday.com.cn/ctenglish/2018/commentaries/202007/t20200724_800215555.html.

16 Justin Y. Lin and Yan Wang, *Going Beyond Aid: Development Cooperation for Structural Transformation* (Cambridge: Cambridge University Press, 2017). On health, in particular, see, for instance: Gerry Bloom, "Building Institutions for an Effective Health System: Lessons from China's Experience with Rural Health Reform," *Social Science and Medicine* 72, no. 8 (2011): 1302–1309; Qingyue Meng et al., "What Can We Learn from China's Health System Reform?" *British Medical Journal* 365 (2019): 12349.

17 For an overview of the debate, see Mark Beeson, *Rethinking Global Governance* (London: Palgrave Macmillan, 2019), chapter 4.

18 Shaun Breslin, "The 'China Model' and the Global Crisis: From Friedrich List to a Chinese Mode of Governance?" *International Affairs* 89, no. 6 (2011): 1323–1343. Specifically, on China's health reform, see Lewis Husain, "Logics of Government Innovation and Reform Management in China," *STEPS Centre Working Paper* No. 85, STEPS

Centre, Brighton, 2015, http://steps-centre.org/publication/logics-of-governmentinnova-tion-and-reform-management-in-china/?referralDomain=workingpaper; and Lewis Husain, "Policy Experimentation and Innovation as a Response to Complexity in China's Management of Health Reforms," *Globalization and Health* 13, no. 54 (2017): 1–13.

19 Breslin, "The 'China Model,'" 1328.

20 Husain and Bloom, "Understanding China's Growing," 7.

21 Ibid.; and Lewis Husain, Gerry Bloom, and Sam McPherson, "The China-UK Global Health Support Programme: Looking for New Roles and Partnerships in Changing Times," *Global Health Research and Policy* 5, no. 26 (2020): 1–8.

22 Jeffrey P. Koplan et al., "Towards a Common Definition of Global Health," *The Lancet* 373 (2009): 1993–1995.

23 Gerry Stoker, "Governance as Theory: Five Propositions," *International Social Science Journal* 50, no. 155 (1998): 17–28; and Thomas G. Weiss and Rorden Wilkinson, *Rethinking Global Governance* (Cambridge: Polity Press, 2019). For global health governance see: Kelley Lee and A. Kamradt-Scott, "The Multiple Meanings of Global Health Governance: A Call for Conceptual Clarity," *Globalization and Health* 10, no. 28 (2014): 1–10.

24 Julio Frenk and Suerie Moon, "Governance Challenges in Global Health," *New England Journal of Medicine* 368 (2013): 936–942; Neil Spicer et al., " 'It's Far Too Complicated': Why Fragmentation Persists in Global Health," *Globalization and Health* 16, no. 60 (2020): 1–13.

25 On trade, see Kenneth C. Shadlen, Bhaven N. Sampat, and Amy Kapczynski, "Patents, Trade and Medicines: Past, Present and Future," *Review of International Political Economy* 27, no. 1 (2020): 75–97; Anne Roemer-Mahler, "Business Conflict and Global Politics: The Pharmaceutical Industry and the Global Protection of Intellectual Property Rights," *Review of International Political Economy* 20, no. 1 (2013): 121–152. On security, see Stefan Elbe, *Security and Global Health: Towards the Medicalization of Insecurity* (Cambridge: Polity Press, 2010); and Sara E. Davies, "Securitizing Infectious Disease," *International Affairs* 84, no. 2 (2008): 295–313.

26 David P. Fidler, "Emerging Trends in International Law Concerning Global Infectious Disease Control," *Emerging Infectious Diseases* 9, no. 3 (2003): 285–290.

27 WHO, *International Health Regulations (2005)*.

28 Roemer-Mahler, "The Rise of Companies from Emerging Markets"; Tim Eckmanns, Henning Fueller, and Stephen L. Roberts, "Digital Epidemiology and Global Health Security: An Interdisciplinary Conversation," *Life Sciences, Society and Policy* 15, no. 2 (2019): 1–13; and Rebecca J. Hester, "Bioveillance: A Techno-Security Infrastructure to Preempt the Dangers of Informationalized Biology," *Science as Culture* 29, no. 1 (2020): 153–176.

29 Colin McInnes and Kelley Lee, "Health, Security and Foreign Policy," *Review of International Studies* 32, no. 1 (2006): 5–23.

30 Wright, "Terrorists and Biological Weapons."

31 Anne Roemer-Mahler and Stefan Elbe, "The Race for Ebola Drugs: Pharmaceuticals, Security and Global Health Governance," *Third World Quarterly* 37, no. 3 (2016): 487–506.

32 William Aldis, "Health Security as a Public Health Concept: A Critical Analysis," *Health Policy and Planning* 23, no. 6 (2008): 369–375.

33 Susan Sell and Aseem Prakash, "Using Ideas Strategically: The Contest Between Business and NGO Networks in Intellectual Property Rights," *International Studies Quarterly* 48, no. 1 (2004): 143–175.

34 Stefan Elbe, Anne Roemer-Mahler, and Christopher Long, "Medical Countermeasures for National Security: A New Government Role in the Pharmaceuticalization of Society," *Social Science & Medicine* 131 (April 2015): 263–271.

35 Katrina Manson and David Pilling, "US Warns Over Chinese 'Spying' on African Disease Control Centre," *Financial Times*, 6 February 2020.

36 Kai Kupferschmidt, "'Vaccine Nationalism' Threatens Global Plan to Distribute COVID-19 Shots Fairly," *Science*, 28 July 2020.

37 Eric Olander, "China and the Race to Supply C19 Vaccines in Africa," *The China-Africa Project*, 2 December 2020, https://chinaafricaproject.com/analysis/china-and-the-race-to-supply-c19-vaccines-in-africa.

38 The concept of "weaponized interdependence" is relevant here, as well as Farrell and Newman's observation that only the United States, the EU, and, increasingly, China can enjoy the benefits of weaponized interdependence. Henry Farrell and Abraham L. Newman, "Weaponized Interdependence: How Global Economic Networks Shape State Coercion," *International Security* 44, no. 1 (2019): 42–79.

39 Adam Segal, "The Coming Tech Cold War with China," *Foreign Affairs*, 9 September 2020, www.foreignaffairs.com/articles/north-america/2020-09-09/coming-tech-cold-war-china.

40 Benedicte Bull and Desmond McNeill, *Development Issues in Global Governance: Public-Private Partnerships and Market Multilateralism* (New York: Routledge, 2007), 87.

41 Jan Kooiman, *Modern Governance: New Government-society Interactions* (London: Sage Publications, 1993).

42 Atul Kohli, *State-directed Development: Political Power and Industrialization in the Global Periphery* (Cambridge: Cambridge University Press, 2004); and Robert Wade, *Governing the Market: Economic Theory and the Role of Government in East Asian Industrialization* (Princeton, NJ: Princeton University Press, 1990).

43 Susan Strange, *The Retreat of the State: The Diffusion of Power in the World Economy* (Cambridge: Cambridge University Press, 1996); and Philip G. Cerny, *Rethinking World Politics: A Theory of Transnational Neopluralism* (Oxford: Oxford University Press, 2010).

44 Beeson, *Rethinking Global Governance*, 40 (emphasis in the original).

45 Bull and McNeill, *Development Issues in Global Governance*, 87.

46 David Fidler, "SARS: Political Pathology of the First Post-Westphalian Pathogen," *Journal of Law, Medicine & Ethics* 31, no. 4 (2003): 486.

47 Ibid.

48 Fidler, "SARS."

49 William Muraskin, "Origins of the Children's Vaccine Initiative: The Political Foundations," *Social Science & Medicine* 42, no. 12 (1996): 1721–1734.

50 Michael Moran, *Private Foundations and Development Partnerships: American Philanthropy and Global Development Agendas* (London: Routledge, 2014), 44.

51 Michael Moran, J. Guzman, A. L. Ropars, and A. Illmer, "The Role of Product Development Partnerships in Research and Development for Neglected Diseases," *International Health* 2, no. 2 (2010): 114–122.

52 Moran, *Private Foundation and Development Partnerships*.

53 Ibid.

54 Robert Heilbroner and William Milberg, *The Making of Economic Society* (London: Pearson, 2012).

55 Beeson, *Rethinking Global Governance*, 31.

56 World Bank, *The East Asian Miracle: Economic Growth and Public Policy* (Oxford: Oxford University Press, 1993).

57 Roselyn Hsueh, "State Capitalism Chinese Style: Strategic Value of Sectors, Sectoral Characteristics, and Globalization," *Governance* 29, no. 1 (2016): 85–102; and Deborah Bräutigam and Xiaoyang Tang, "Going Global in Groups: Structural Transformation and China's Special Economic Zones," *World Development* 63 (November 2014): 78–91.

58 Husain and Bloom, "Understanding China's Growing."

59 Paul Arthur Berkman, "Could Science Diplomacy Be the Key to Stabilising International Relations?" *The Conversation*, 12 June 2018, https://theconversation.com/could-science-diplomacy-be-the-key-to-stabilizing-international-relations-87836.

60 Africa CDC, *Africa CDC Receives Third Donation of Medical Supplies from Jack Ma Foundation, Co-hosts Global MediXChange Webinar on COVID-19*, 27 April 2020, https://africacdc.org/news-item/africa-cdc-receives-third-donation-of-medical-supplies-from-jack-ma-foundation-co-hosts-global-medixchange-webinar-on-covid-19; UN Secretary-General's High-Level Panel on Digital Cooperation, *The Age of Digital Interdependence*, June 2019, https://digitalcooperation.org/wp-content/uploads/2019/06/DigitalCooperation-report-web-FINAL-1.pdf.

61 Jules Crétois and Olivier Marbot, "Coronavirus: Tedros Ghebreyesus of WHO Faces Firestorm of Criticism," *The Africa Report*, 14 June 2020, www.theafricareport.com/29554/coronavirus-tedros-ghebreyesus-of-who-faces-firestorm-of-criticism.

62 Tine Hanrieder, *International Organization in Time: Fragmentation and Reform* (Oxford: Oxford University Press, 2015).

CONTENTS

Climate action

Beyond the Paris Agreement

Adriana Erthal Abdenur

In September 2018, United Nations Secretary-General António Guterres referred to climate change as the "defining issue of our time." In phrasing the challenge this way, Guterres not only acknowledged the centrality of climate change on the international agenda but also stressed its crosscutting and relentless nature. As he noted, climate change affects every aspect of human life; it is already taking place; and, at current rates, it poses an existential threat to humanity. On the same occasion, the Secretary-General sounded a second alarm: even after the negotiation and ratification of the 2015 Paris Agreement, "what we still lack . . . is the leadership and the ambition to do what is needed."[1] Guterres's comments hint at some of the major tasks facing climate governance post-Paris, which include not only rallying political momentum to implement the commitments made but also filling in major thematic gaps, especially with respect to three pivotal issues: adaptation, forests, and migration.

While it is true that the lack of climate leadership has left a glaring hole in climate governance, broader factors also help explain the inadequacy of action even when humanity is faced with record-breaking temperatures, increasingly unpredictable weather patterns, and sea-level rise, to mention only three. Simply put, there is a major mismatch between global governance – primarily, in this instance, those formal intergovernmental institutions and responses operating under the UN umbrella – and the demands and challenges of the period in which we

DOI: 10.4324/9781003139836-18

live. The existing climate regime has been built on the assumption that people, including policymakers, will change their behavior in the face of scientific evidence, but we live in an age of unprecedented science-bashing and climate denialism. Global governance has been far too slow in catching up to this fact. As a result, even as the planet transitions into the Anthropocene – a new geological epoch marked by significant human impact on the earth's ecosystems and geology – the slow wheels of global governance, beset not only by lack of leadership but also by harsh attacks on multilateralism and widespread science denialism, creak along too slowly.[2]

What does public global climate governance – whose entire history spans no more than 40 years – hold for the next quarter century? This chapter analyzes the main gaps and challenges of global governance with respect to climate change, situating major landmarks against the backdrop of broader changes in world order. Despite its brief history, climate change continues to generate sharp debate about the potential and limitations of state-centric regimes; the role of science and evidence; and the role of civil society, private sector actors, and subnational governments. Among the many governance challenges ahead are those relating to topics that have "fallen between the cracks" of climate governance negotiations.

The chapter begins with a brief overview of the scholarship on climate and governance. It then analyzes major landmarks in the history of global climate governance, including key achievements and remaining gaps. Finally, the chapter assesses the current state of global climate governance following debates around the 75th anniversary of the United Nations, as well as three major gaps that will have to be addressed to shore up the Paris Agreement and extend climate commitments in new, urgent directions.

Where are we?

Global governance, as we know it, emerged during the tail-end of the Holocene, when the impacts of human action already had global significance, especially because of greenhouse gas emissions and the destruction of critical global commons such as forests and ocean habitats. Contemporary political and administrative systems essentially evolved in response to the global challenges perceived by world leaders in the second half of the twentieth century: avoiding another world war, curbing nuclear proliferation, ending colonialism, and boosting women's rights.

Even as the gamut of global risks has broadened and as prominent members of the global scientific community underscore the significance of an increasingly unstable ecological environment, states have not shown the level of proactiveness required to anticipate and address emerging threats at the scale and intensity projected in climate change models. Without concerted action, the future of both the planet and what passes for global climate governance looks bleak. It is no wonder that youth leaders like Greta Thunberg, David Naibei, and Yolanda Joab Mori voice new levels of frustration at the snail's pace of global climate action.[3] Older generations, and the institutions they have relied upon, are failing not only to mitigate climate change but also to address increasingly glaring climate injustices, including intergenerational impacts and the differential effects on vulnerable populations and developing countries.

Despite decades of evidence-based warnings and considerable activism, too many stakeholders remain reluctant to prevent global warming from exceeding the 1.5°C goal set by the Intergovernmental Panel on Climate Change (IPCC).[4] As greenhouse gas emissions accumulate and the planet careers toward an increasingly uncertain future, marked by new risks and uncertainty levels – now superimposed onto older challenges – why has global governance been unable to develop adequate mechanisms for climate change? What major gaps remain for us to have a solid global climate governance, and what does this mean for the next 25 years or so?

Climate change has been thought of as a "super-wicked problem" – a set of multidimensional challenges that are extremely difficult to solve and for which tried and tested solutions do not currently exist.[5] While knowledge of climate change and its general effects has increased tremendously over the past four decades, we are only beginning to scratch the surface when it comes to understanding its finer-grained impacts in specific contexts. While we know that sea levels are rising, for many places the particular effects on coastal populations or food security, for example, are still unknown or are understood only for a specific (and typically long) time horizon.

Moreover, unlike many other international challenges, climate change cannot be pigeonholed into a particular niche; it must be tackled alongside many other challenges. Although it is linked to, and affects, every dimension of life – from disasters to public health, food security, and social inequality – its local impacts are highly variable. This means that risk assessments for development, humanitarian, and security efforts must incorporate climate variables and projections and that no quick fix or cookie-cutter approach will solve the problems posed by climate change.

Climate change also requires a radically different notion of time in the development of diagnostics and solutions. As Richard Lazarus has written, it demands "restraining the present to liberate the future."[6] In other words, more than any other area of international relations, climate governance requires humanity to take into account the well-being of youth and future generations. This intergenerational aspect of climate governance, in turn, demands greater participation by those whose futures are being compromised by present development models and behavioral patterns: youth.

Therefore, climate change demands unprecedented levels of action which, because of the global scope of the problem, entail not only concerted efforts by national and subnational actors but also international cooperation, exchange, and coordination. The infamous and well-known bureaucratic silos of the UN system,[7] through which policy-making is compartmentalized into themes that seldom dialogue with each other, remain a major impediment to the multidisciplinary, cross-area thinking that climate change demands. Eduardo Viola, Matias Franchini, and Thaís Ribeiro capture the scope of the task ahead when they refer to climate change as "a central civilizational driver of our time," essential to the maintenance of sustainability at a planetary level.[8] The transformations required of economic, political, and cultural systems are correspondingly monumental, involving all sectors of the economy and, indeed, of human life. This massive change also demands robust global climate governance that is capable of handling existential risks.[9]

Climate governance and the changing world order

How should we define global climate governance? Sverker Jagers and Johannes Strippe refer to global climate governance as the set of diplomatic, political, and institutional mechanisms, policies, and responses designed to steer social systems toward prevention, mitigation, or adaptation to the risks posed by climate change.[10] Thomas G. Weiss and Rorden Wilkinson remind us that myriad actors – often far beyond traditional conceptualizations – are involved in global governance.[11] This means that a complex web of actors are involved in, positively and negatively, climate governance but also that effective responses must also be multi-scale – from the local to the regional and the global – as well as multi-actor, involving not only states but also subnational governments, civil society organizations, and private sector companies.

Any international regime must be understood not only with respect to its formal and informal rules but also within the broader geopolitical context in which it emerged. The problem of climate change – and, alongside it, the imperative for global climate governance – emerged during a context of deep transformation in world order. The topic first appeared in international scientific debates in the 1960s, when the first advanced computer models began to predict possible outcomes of the rise in CO_2. These discussions took place during the Cold War, especially in the lead-up to the 1972 UN Conference on the Human Environment in Stockholm, but they only began to gain importance and appear systematically in key global policy discussions in the late 1980s, after the dissolution of the Soviet Union.[12]

The so-called unipolar moment, marked by unprecedented US hegemony – whether real or perceived – featured a single, momentarily unchallenged superpower interacting with "second-rank powers" such as Germany, Britain, France, and Japan.[13] Whereas the Cold War had been deeply marked by ideological disputes between the East and West – as well as the geopolitical disputes and arms races to which they gave rise – once the Iron Curtain came down, discussions of global governance changed in tone and, to some extent, in substance. For the first time since the aftermath of World War II, a wave of optimism swept through the international community regarding the capacity of international organizations, especially the UN, to tackle the complex challenges of a rapidly globalizing world. Mostly for political reasons, those issues had been left unaddressed during the Cold War as the global powers became caught up in geopolitical disputes and as developing countries tried to band together through regional blocs or coalitions such as the Group of 77 (G77) and the Non-Aligned Movement (NAM).

Alongside the surge in confidence about the capacity of global institutions to solve common problems, the international environmental movements that had been launched in the 1960s became more consolidated, although they tended to focus on local issues rather than climate change as a planetary problem. While concern with nuclear weapons has not subsided, within this changing context, climate change began to be seen as the "new Armageddon," which helped catalyze the first major steps toward global climate governance – and rather swiftly by the standards of other global governance challenges. Even so, the first report issued by the IPCC – which stated not only that the world had been warming but that further warming was likely[14] – faced a steep uphill battle in garnering political commitments from a broader set of member states and, more generally, the public.

Thus, the climate regimes and mechanisms that began to take shape in the aftermath of the Cold War fit squarely within the liberal world order that the United States and its Western allies had championed – one in which the idea of a rules-based international order was promoted as paramount and firmly anchored in the established organizations of the post–World War II period. If, at first, the centrality of the United States within this system helped launch initial attempts at building up global climate governance, this same centrality would ultimately prove its Achilles' heel, at least until major new changes began to occur in the international order.

One consequence of this optimism was that states sought to deal with the challenges of climate change by engaging the UN system – and, more specifically, by resorting to multilateral agreements. Recognizing the transboundary nature of climate change and its impacts, political leaders and policymakers prioritized getting all states on board to agree on shared objectives. Yet this choice often came at the expense of firmly binding commitments and enforcement mechanisms.

The 1992 Earth Summit in Rio de Janeiro reflected both the optimism about the role of states in addressing sustainable development and the limitations of this top-down approach. The summit gave rise to three conventions, all linked to scientific advisory boards and expert groups whose research and advice guided the implementation process. The United Nations Framework Convention on Climate Change (UNFCCC) – the major outcome of the Rio Summit – was hailed as a major landmark in the expansion of engagement by member states in climate action; it was signed by 154 countries (having, since then, attained near-universal ratification among states).[15] This broad adherence reflected not only that a near consensus had emerged within the global scientific community about global warming but also that scientists had been able – to some degree – to communicate to national leaderships and policymakers the need for immediate action. The convention laid the basis for later climate instruments, such as the Kyoto Protocol and the Paris Agreement.

The Rio Summit also opened for signature the Convention on Biological Diversity (CBD).[16] However, the CDB has been criticized on the grounds that Western countries' resistance to the implementation of the provisions favored by developing countries weakened the convention.[17] Others have criticized the CBD for losing steam during implementation. There are also reservations with respect to the protocols, for instance because of the perception that some of the provisions may hamper conservation and disease prevention.

The third instrument was the United Nations Convention to Combat Desertification (UNCCD), which has been ratified by 197 states and is designed to combat desertification and mitigate the impacts of drought through national action programs that incorporate long-term strategies supported by international cooperation. The convention suffered a momentary blow when Canada withdrew in March 2013 before returning in December 2016.

It is worth noting that a fourth big idea failed to gain enough momentum to deliver an agreement. A global forest convention to curb deforestation had first been proposed in 1990 in the IPCC's São Paulo Declaration and in a review of the Tropical Forests Action Plan. Despite support from the United States and the Group of 7 (G7), at the 1992 Earth Summit, a binding agreement could not be reached, partly because of discourses of national sovereignty common among heavily forested states. Instead, a softer compromise was reached on a "non-binding authoritative statement on forest principles."[18]

Over the five years that followed the Earth Summit, a broader recognition emerged that climate change poses challenges at a planetary level, and this led to the signing of the 1997 Kyoto Protocol, which represented a significant leap in intergovernmental climate cooperation through an effort to create a binding agreement among states. A total of 38 industrialized countries agreed to cut greenhouse gas (GHG) emissions by an average of 5.2 percent below 1990 levels during the period 2008–2012. The Kyoto Protocol categorized different countries into annexes, with each annex having its own responsibility for emission reductions based on historic GHG emissions and, thus, on historic contribution to global climate change. Another innovation accompanying the protocol was the Global Reporting Initiative (GRI), which represented an important step in the incorporation of non-government actors into global climate governance. By 2000, when the UN launched the Millennium Development Goals (MDGs), more attempts were made to link the emerging climate regime to the UN's key development frameworks – at that moment, an especially promising step because MDG 7 revolved around "ensuring environmental sustainability."[19]

However, deteriorating political trends soon affected the Kyoto Protocol. In 2001, shortly after George W. Bush was elected president, the United States, whose Senate had refused to ratify the Kyoto Protocol during the preceding Clinton administration, announced the withdrawal of the United States – at that time, the world's biggest polluter – from the agreement on the grounds that the protocol was unfair to American interests. President Obama ended up rejecting the Kyoto Protocol, drawing on similar justifications.

This example illustrates how one major spoiler can severely weaken a budding international regime that is built from the top down. US resistance created hurdles not only for the protocol itself but also for the negotiation of what would come after Kyoto. While there was no immediate bandwagoning by other states hoping to curry favor with the US government, in 2011, Canada, Japan, and Russia stated they would not take on further Kyoto targets, and later that year, the Canadian government announced its withdrawal.

One of the consequences of these reversals was that, barring the Kyoto Protocol, no other multilateral environmental agreement has managed to establish legally binding emissions targets for signatories. This is partly because confidence in the top-down, state-centric approach declined and partly because political and geopolitical cleavages had widened. Diplomatic efforts before and during the 15th Conference of the Parties (COP) to the UNFCCC, held in 2009, failed to negotiate a successor agreement to the Kyoto Protocol. The Copenhagen Accord that was the outcome of COP15 endorsed the continuation of the Kyoto Protocol, which ended in 2012; recognized that deep cuts were needed to stem rising GHG emissions; and underscored the importance of both adaptation and mitigation. Yet the agreement was non-binding, and the rules set for implementation of the accord established few obligations for states to execute ambitious climate action at the domestic level.

However, some novel trends are worth noting. The Copenhagen negotiations featured new attempts at policy coordination by rising powers, especially through the BASIC (Brazil, South Africa, India, and China) bloc, which was formally constituted in November 2009 and ended up brokering the final Copenhagen with the United States. Even as it worked to rally support for the climate change regime, the BASIC bloc underscored the need to address the difference in responsibility for climate change between the developed and developing world – the common but differentiated responsibilities (CBDR) enshrined as Principle 7 of the Rio Declaration – and the particular demands of the latter.[20] The proactiveness of this coalition marked a significant change in the geopolitics of climate governance, especially because of the emerging protagonism of China.

At the same time, the shift away from a strictly top-down approach opened up space for a greater variety of responses and discourses against climate change – including bottom-up approaches – and by a broader gamut of actors becoming engaged in climate governance efforts. In other words, not just states but also regional organizations, businesses, and civil society entities began to be viewed as necessary participants. This also meant that, in comparison to the earlier, state-centric period, global climate governance became more decentralized across multilateral technology partnerships, regimes regulating environmental areas such as ozone or biological diversity, and the world trade regime.[21]

Another result of the relative loss of momentum in the intergovernmental climate regime was a growing reliance by national and subnational actors on market-based solutions to climate governance – part and parcel of the rise of neoliberalism. Proposed solutions included carbon tax, cap-and-trade programs (in which the government sets an upper limit on emissions, allowing emission allowances that equal the cap to be distributed, either freely or through action, to regular sources), public-private partnerships, and self-regulation by industry. Around half the countries that signed the Paris Agreement signaled the intention to use market-based approaches to help achieve their emissions pledges. These measures, many of them pioneered in the United States, have spread to European countries, Canada, and several Chinese cities and provinces.[22]

Thus, despite the role of the United States, in particular, as a repeat climate spoiler, the issue of climate change slowly migrated to the center of the global agenda. This shift took place in part because of changes in world order. By the early 2000s, the shift in global power toward East Asia, and especially China, was becoming more evident – even beyond its role in the BASIC bloc. Along with the expansion of the Chinese economy and the spread of Chinese influence globally, other rising powers began to contest the liberal order more openly, including through loose configurations such as the BRICS (Brazil, Russia, India, China, and South Africa) coalition. It was in this context – the accelerating rivalry between the United States and China and increasingly vocal questioning of US hegemony and institutions perceived to be Western dominated – that negotiations leading up to the Paris Agreement took place. This was vastly different geopolitical terrain from the post-Cold War period that had incubated the first multilateral climate agreements.

In 2015, negotiations had gone into overtime, with the possibility that competing interests would torpedo the Paris Agreement altogether. Partly as a result of the prolonged cliffhanger, the agreement was hailed as a major diplomatic success – even though, next to the Kyoto Protocol, it is quite modest in the goals established for signatories. In addition to maintaining the increase in global average temperature to well below 2°C above preindustrial levels, the parties agreed to work toward limiting the increase to 1.5°C, recognizing that such a decrease would significantly reduce the risks and impacts of climate change. Through the Paris Agreement the parties also agreed to a long-term goal for adaptation – to increase the ability to adapt to the adverse impacts of climate change and foster climate resilience and low GHG emissions development, without threatening food production.

Rafael Leal-Arcas and Antonio Morelli consider the Paris Agreement a compromise between soft and hard law, relying on both binding and non-binding international legal provisions.[23] To Daniel Bodansky, the softer approach of the Paris Agreement actually provides a firmer foundation on which to build when compared to the more ambitious predecessor agreement, the Kyoto Protocol.[24] Indeed, the agreement was presented as a system that evolves over time and alters state behavior so as to encourage increasingly ambitious emissions reductions from signatory states.[25] It is also viewed as important to the achievement of the 2030 development agenda, with synergies built with most of the Sustainable Development Goals (SDGs), especially SDG 7 (affordable and clean energy), SDG 15 (life on land), and SDG 2 (zero hunger).[26]

Other developing countries also played a key role in shaping the Paris Agreement. During negotiations, the Small Island Developing States (SIDS) pooled their diplomatic resources to punch above their individual capacities – for instance, advancing the complex debate on loss and damage.[27] As of December 2020, a total of 189 states out of the 197 parties to the UNFCCC have ratified the Paris Agreement.[28]

However, the "Paris spirit" was achieved at the expense of a comprehensively binding agreement that could weather significant political and geopolitical winds. Since it is up to each state to establish, plan, and regularly report its contribution to the mitigation of global warming and its approaches to adaptation, there are no mechanisms in place to force signatories to set a specific emissions target by a specific date or to compel a concrete increase in climate ambition. In other words, much of the agreement was anchored in vague promises and ambiguous exhortations rather than firm commitments and enforceable goals. Tougher language such as decarbonization and zero emissions was left out altogether, and the promise by rich countries to allocate a minimum of $100 billion each year starting in 2020 to help climate-vulnerable countries was absent from the legally binding portion of the agreement.

The structural limitations of the Paris Agreement became clear in 2017, once again reflecting US politics. President Donald Trump, who promoted climate denialism, announced that the United States would leave the agreement – an action reversed on the first day of the Biden administration. Another climate denier – Brazil's president, Jair Bolsonaro – did not officially declare Brazil's intention to leave the agreement.

However, in practice, he implemented policies – including those leading to rampant destruction of the Amazon rainforest – that ran contrary to the goals of the Paris Agreement (and, indeed, to ambitions that Brazil had previously assumed under prior governments). The fossil fuel industry, too, has consistently worked to undermine the Paris Agreement. Despite growing calls for an energy transition and despite the boost provided by the agreement to renewable energy, the oil and gas lobby still holds enormous power, and vested interests continuously pull leaderships and institutions back from enacting major change, whether nationally or internationally.

In the late 2010s, these climate spoilers sparked a new wave of pessimism around global climate governance – a pessimism that abated only partially with new pledges of net-zero emissions targets, especially from China, the European Union (EU), and the United Kingdom as well as the United States after Joe Biden became president in 2021. At the same time, these promises were made against the backdrop of a global health catastrophe – the COVID-19 pandemic – whose implications for global climate governance remain uncertain.

The crisis has underscored the complex links among climate change, environmental destruction, and the risk of pandemics. At a time when tree clearing and forest fires reached new peaks in the Brazilian Amazon, scientists called attention to how habitat loss forces wildlife to migrate and potentially contact other animals or people, sharing germs. Debates also emerged over the impact of the pandemic on greenhouse gas emissions. Despite a temporary reduction in daily global CO_2 emissions,[29] the pandemic presented new challenges to climate cooperation as many countries turned inward, closing their borders in an attempt to prevent the virus from spreading.

Climate financing, too, took a hit as priorities shifted, with calls to address sharp increases in poverty, widespread hunger, climbing debt, and the sharp reduction in trade and investment. The pandemic proved truly disruptive to climate governance, which had, since its inception, relied on massive conferences and other events. The 2020 COP, set to be hosted by Glasgow, was expected to advance the ambitions of the accord, helping states adopt net-zero emissions, but the event was postponed to 2021. Some climate activists adopted a tone of optimism, calling post-pandemic recovery efforts a strategic opportunity to "build back better" – for instance, through the incorporation of green transitions and jobs into national and regional planning instruments – a movement that gained strength as numerous states and organizations, including Germany and the EU, announced major new initiatives in this direction.

Three climate gaps: Adaptation, forests, migration

As the UN commemorated its 75th anniversary in 2020, many observers noted the fragmented nature of global climate governance. While climate action has loosely coalesced around the Paris Agreement, and more broadly the UNFCCC, different aspects have been pigeonholed into separate conventions, agreements, and mechanisms – as had happened with biodiversity and desertification. Other areas of climate action, including local initiatives, exist altogether separately from the global frameworks – which encompass the climate norms of the World Trade Organization

(WTO) and many initiatives by regional organizations. In response to the perceived lack of policy coherence in global climate governance, some have called on the UN to make sustainable development – or climate, more specifically – a separate "fourth pillar" alongside the traditional trio of international peace and security, human rights and humanitarian action, and development. At the same time, critics of the system's excessive compartmentalization underscore the need to mainstream climate change throughout the UN system. Some observers have argued for a strong centralizing institution in which to anchor the climate regime,[30] while others have noted that fragmentation has both pitfalls and promises, including greater agility in policy-making.[31]

Regardless of the solutions for "anchoring" climate governance, there is broad consensus about the need for better enforcement of existing agreements and conventions. Spoiler states like the United States and Brazil have shown that the political costs of non-compliance with the Paris Agreement and other climate regimes are still low, with disastrous effects for the planet. While the toolkit of proven and proposed solutions being offered is broad, from REDD+ (which stands for "reducing emissions from deforestation and forest degradation, conservation of existing forest carbon stocks, sustainable forest management and enhancement of forest carbon stocks") to climate geoengineering (for instance, through atmospheric carbon dioxide removal),[32] rallying political backing from key leadership remains a sine qua non for ensuring that mitigation and adaptation commitments are met. Generally, persistent political divergences and lack of political willpower present an even greater challenge than technical problems, even though many previous impasses have been more or less hammered out during agreement negotiations. For instance, most issues related to CBDR, but other topics, such as technology transfer, climate assistance and cooperation, adequate climate financing, and payments for environmental services remain sticking points and will reemerge in any future global climate governance efforts as climate injustices deepen.

Equally essential to the future of global climate governance is the ability to reach and win over populations that have been heavily influenced by science denialism. Persuading them of the immense problems and of possible solutions will require innovations in communications that reach beyond the simplistic and apocalyptic framing of climate change as a wicked problem or solutions that focus narrowly on mitigation goals rather than concrete actions that seem more relevant in the daily lives of people around the world. Yet, even with innovations in the architecture of global climate governance, better implementation of the existing toolkit, and more effective communications about climate change and climate action, major thematic gaps remain in global climate governance.

First, adaptation presents serious challenges ahead, not only because the topic has received far less attention than mitigation in climate agreements but also because there is a serious lag in rich countries' delivery of promised support to developing countries, including those most vulnerable to climate change. As Asa Persson has noted, the Paris Agreement breathed new life into discussions and initiatives for adaptation, but the theme has yet to be operationalized.[33] The lack of adaptation governance is a result not only of the ambiguity surrounding the concept of adaptation but also of the lack of open recognition of adaptation as a global public good, which has fed into a chronic scarcity of adaptation financing. Unless climate governance incorporates new mechanisms for adaptation, this weakness means that low-income populations, marginalized communities, and vulnerable states will fall back even further as climate change intensifies.

However, adaptation governance requires a different approach than mitigation. Whereas mitigation addresses a global issue and is perceived as requiring a global and national approach, adaptation has multiple jurisdictional levels and is often understood as a set of actions that must take place at the local or regional level, perhaps with some facilitation or assistance from higher levels. The Global Adaptation Center, established by the government of the Netherlands ahead of the Global Adaptation Summit (held virtually in February 2021), may serve as one focal point for thinking about how to boost adaptation in normative frameworks, as well as in concrete policies and responses.

Second, the issue of forests remains a glaring hole in current climate governance. With the failure to negotiate a global forest convention, forests appear in intermittent fashion in existing agreements, without binding commitments on the part of member states. Although there is some reluctance to frame this topic under the umbrella of climate change, illegal deforestation accounts for approximately 10 percent of global greenhouse gas emissions and possibly three times as much if the activities permitted by illegal deforestation, including agriculture and ranching in deforested areas, are taken into account.[34] Yet the surge in forest fires, illegal deforestation, and other environmental crimes in the Brazilian Amazon in 2019 and 2020 has called renewed attention to the need to develop more effective mechanisms, at all levels of governance, to protect these critical global commons and the people who depend on them.

Third, despite the growing attention paid to and research on climate migration, the issue remains politically sensitive, not least because many member states are reluctant to endorse any frameworks that would lead to claims of compensation by people who are forcibly displaced by climate change – for instance, by extreme weather events or slow-onset impacts, such as soil erosion or loss of productivity.[35] Part of the challenge relates to the broader difficulties in establishing a global pact for migration and other worldwide frameworks that seek to coordinate policies on migration and enhance cooperation around this topic. Yet, without effective governance of climate migration, neither preventive nor adaptive measures can be properly designed and put into place. As a result of this gap, deep climate injustices – not only between states but also within countries – will continue to grow precisely at a time when migratory flows have reached an all-time high since World War II and when xenophobia and anti-migration sentiments are fed by nationalist populist leaders.

Conclusion

What will the next quarter century bring for global climate governance? If any hints can be gleaned from the past, it is that, over time, multilateral agreements have ceded space to a somewhat less top-down approach. In turn, the fragmentation of this governance has generated new challenges and new opportunities. As non-state actors, especially civil society and the private sector, have gained space, they have increasingly helped shape climate norms and frameworks. That said, their place within a system that remains heavily state centric is uncertain.

In addition, numerous weaknesses remain, including the difficulty in forging binding commitments and inadequate policy coordination. These weaknesses also encompass many thematic gaps that must be addressed in the next quarter century, including issues pertaining to adaptation, forests, and climate migration. All three are areas which, if left unaddressed, will widen the gap between rich and poor and between those who are relatively safe and those who are not.

The Paris Agreement lays out very clearly what is needed by the middle of this century, even if through a quantified mitigation goal. But we are still missing complementary frameworks and initiatives that will bring climate change, as well as climate action, closer to people and local actors.

The road ahead will depend not only on decision-making by world leaders and pressure from civil society but also on the rough winds of geopolitics. As world order transitions deeper into an asymmetrical multipolarity, in which the rivalry between the old superpower, the United States, and the emerging global rival, China, increasingly shapes relations of cooperation worldwide, climate has emerged as a strategic site for geopolitical competition. Will the United Nations remain the central pillar of global climate governance, or will alternative arrangements led by China overlap with and perhaps even erode this space? For now, China seems to be betting heavily on the UN system, but its sharpening rivalry with the United States could lead Beijing to pursue its climate diplomacy through other channels, including through South-South cooperation.

Some hints about the road ahead can also be gleaned from the COVID-19 pandemic. The scientific response to the crisis, with unprecedented speed in the development of multiple vaccines, shows that humanity possesses a remarkable ability to find technical solutions when urgency is perceived. However, the crisis also shows that politics and geopolitics can all too easily frustrate the effective and equitable implementation of scientific breakthroughs and technocratic responses. It thus remains to be seen whether growing climate activism – including efforts by youth, indigenous communities, migrants, residents of SIDS and other climate-vulnerable countries, and others – will provide the necessary impetus for the improvement and consolidation of global climate governance within this critical period.

Suggested reading

Elise Harrington, *The Fragmentation of Global Climate Governance* (Cambridge: MIT Press., 2019).

Rafael Leal-Arcas and Antonio Morelli, "The Resilience of the Paris Agreement: Negotiating and Implementing the Climate Regime," *The Georgetown Environmental Law Review* 31, no. 1 (2018), www.law.georgetown.edu/environmental-law-review/wp-content/uploads/sites/18/2019/01/Rafael-Leal-Arcas-Antonio-Morelli.pdf

Augusto López-Claros, Arthur L. Dahl, and Maja Groff, *Global Governance and the Emergence of Global Institutions for the 21st Century* (Cambridge: Cambridge University Press, 2020).

Timothée Ourback and Alexandre K. Magnan, "The Paris Agreement and Climate Change Negotiations: Small Islands, Big Players," *Regional Environmental Change* 18 (2017): 2201–2207.

Eduardo Viola, Matías Franchini, and Thaís Lemos Ribeiro, "Climate Governance in an International System Under Conservative Hegemony: The Role of Major Powers," *Revista Brasileira de Política Internacional* 55 (2012): 9–29.

Notes

1 United Nations Secretary-General, "Secretary-General Remarks on Climate Change," 10 September 2018, www.un.org/sg/en/content/sg/statement/2018-09-10/secretary-generals-remarks-climate-change-delivered

2 John S. Dryzek and Jonathan Pickering, *Politics of the Anthropocene* (Oxford: Oxford University Press, 2018).

3 One Young World, "Ten Young Leaders Championing Climate Action," 2020, www.oneyoungworld.com/news-item/ten-young-leaders-championing-climate-action

4 IPCC, "Global Warming of 1.5°C: An IPCC Special Report on the Impacts of Global Warming of 1.5°C Above Pre-Industrial Levels and Related Global Greenhouse Gas Emission Pathways, in the Context of Strengthening the Global Response to the Threat of Climate Change, Sustainable Development, and Efforts to Eradicate Poverty," 2018, www.ipcc.ch/site/assets/uploads/sites/2/2019/06/SR15_Full_Report_Low_Res.pdf

5 Anne Saab, "The Super Wicked Problem of Climate Change Action," *IDEID*, 2 September 2019, www.graduateinstitute.ch/communications/news/super-wicked-problem-climate-change-action. Hulme criticizes this idea, arguing that climate change should not be thought of as "a problem" waiting for "a solution" but rather as an environmental, cultural, and political phenomenon that is reshaping the way people think about humanity and the planet. David Hulme, *Why We Disagree About Climate Change: Understanding Controversy, Inaction and Opportunity* (London: Cambridge University Press, 2009).

6 Richard J. Lazarus, "Super Wicked Problems and Climate Change: Restraining the Present to Liberate the Future," *Cornell Law Review* 94 (2009): 1153–1234.

7 Tatiana Carayannis and Thomas G. Weiss, *The "Third" United Nations: How a Knowledge Ecology Helps the UN Think* (Oxford: Oxford University Press, 2021).

8 Eduardo Viola, Matías Franchini, and Thaís Lemos Ribeiro, "Climate Governance in an International System Under Conservative Hegemony: The Role of Major Powers," *Revista Brasileira de Política Internacional* 55 (2012): 9–29.

9 Nick Bostrom, "Existential Risk Prevention as Global Priority," *Global Policy* 4, no. 1 (2013): 15–31.

10 Sverker C. Jagers and Johannes Stripple, "Climate Governance Beyond the State," *Global Governance* 9, no. 3 (2003): 385–400.

11 Thomas G. Weiss and Rorden Wilkinson, *Rethinking Global Governance* (Cambridge: Polity Press, 2019).

12 Another important landmark was the 1979 World Climate Conference, organized by the World Meteorological Organization (WMO).

13 Charles Krauthammer, "The Unipolar Moment," *Foreign Affairs* 70, no. 1 (1990–1991): 23–33.

14 IPCC, "First Assessment Report," 1990, www.ipcc.ch/assessment-report/ar1/

15 As of February 2021, 197 countries have ratified the UNFCCC. United Nations Climate Change, "What Is the United Nations Framework Convention on Climate Change?," 2021, https://unfccc.int/process-and-meetings/the-convention/what-is-the-united-nations-framework-convention-on-climate-change#:~:text=The%20197%20countries%20that%20have,called%20Parties%20to%20the%20Convention

16 The CBD, which entered into force on 29 December 1993, was built around three key goals: (i) conserving biodiversity, (ii) the sustainable use of its components, and (iii) the fair sharing of benefits arising from genetic resources. It yielded two supplementary agreements, the Cartagena Protocol (governing the movements of living modified organisms, or LMOs) and the Nagoya Protocol, which provides a legal framework for the implementation of the fair sharing of benefits arising from genetic resources.

17 S. Faizi, "The Unmaking of a Treaty," *Biodiversity* 5, no. 3 (2004): 43–44.

18 David Humphreys, "The Elusive Quest for a Global Forest Convention," *Review of European, Comparative and International Environmental Law (RECIEL)* 14, no. 1 (2005): 1–10.

19 Marcos A. Orellana, "Climate Change and the Millennium Development Goals: The Right to Development, International Cooperation and the Clean Development Mechanism," *Sur* 7, no. 12 (2010), https://sur.conectas.org/en/climate-change-millennium-development-goals/

20 Common but differentiated responsibility is a principle of international environmental law establishing that all states are responsible for addressing global environmental destruction – yet not equally responsible. At the Earth Summit, states came to an agreement that developed countries contributed more to environmental degradation and should bear greater responsibility than developing countries.

21 Zelli Fariborz, "The Fragmentation of the Global Climate Governance Architecture," *WIREs Climate Change* 2, no. 2 (2011): 255–270, https://onlinelibrary.wiley.com/doi/abs/10.1002/wcc.104

22 C2ES, "Market-based Strategies," 2020, www.c2es.org/content/market-based-strategies/

23 Rafael Leal-Arcas and Antonio Morelli, "The Resilience of the Paris Agreement: Negotiating and Implementing the Climate Regime," *The Georgetown Environmental Law Review* 31, no. 1 (2018), www.law.georgetown.edu/environmental-law-review/wp-content/uploads/sites/18/2019/01/Rafael-Leal-Arcas-Antonio-Morelli.pdf

24 Daniel Bodansky, "The Paris Climate Change Agreement: A New Hope?" *American Journal of International Law* 110, no. 20 (2017), www.cambridge.org/core/journals/american-journal-of-international-law/article/abs/paris-climate-change-agreement-a-new-hope/413CC22E95E284C80541707F80B85252

25 Luke Kemp, "A Systems Critique of the 2015 Paris Agreement on Climate," in *Pathways to a Sustainable Economy*, ed. Moazzem Hossain, Robert Hales, and Tapan Sarker (New York: Springer, 2018), 25–41.

26 Adis Dzebo, Hannah Janetschek, Clara Brandi, and Gabriela Iacobuta, "Connections Between the Paris Agreement and the 2030 Agenda: The Case for Policy Coherence," *SEI Working Paper*, Stockholm Environment Institute, Stockholm, 4 September 2019, https://cdn.sei.org/wp-content/uploads/2019/08/connections-between-the-paris-agreement-and-the-2030-agenda.pdf

27 Timothée Ourback and Alexandre K. Magnan, "The Paris Agreement and Climate Change Negotiations: Small Islands, Big Players," *Regional Environmental Change* 18 (2017): 2201–2207.

28 UNFCCC, "Paris Agreement – Status of Ratification," 2021, https://unfccc.int/process/the-paris-agreement/status-of-ratification

29 Corinne Le Quéré et al., "Temporary Reduction in Daily Global CO_2 Emissions During the COVID019 Forced Confinement," *Nature Climate Change* 10 (2020): 647–653, www.nature.com/articles/s41558-020-0797-x

30 Augusto López-Claros, Arthur L. Dahl, and Maja Groff, *Global Governance and the Emergence of Global Institutions for the 21st Century* (Cambridge: Cambridge University Press, 2020).

31 Elise Harrington, *The Fragmentation of Global Climate Governance* (Cambridge, MA: Massachusetts Institute of Technology Press, 2019).

32 See, for instance, Mark G. Lawrence et al., "Evaluating Climate Geoengineering Proposals in the Context of the Paris Agreement Temperature Goals," *Nature Communications* 9, no. 13 (2018), www.nature.com/articles/s41467-018-05938-3

33 Asa Persson, "Global Adaptation Governance: An Emerging but Contested Domain," *WIREs Climate Change* 10, no. 6 (2019), https://onlinelibrary.wiley.com/doi/full/10.1002/wcc.618

34 IUCN, "Forests and Greenhouse Gas Emissions," 2021, www.iucn.org/resources/issues-briefs/forests-and-climate-change#:~:text=Forests'%20role%20in%20climate%20change,emissions%20after%20the%20energy%20sector

35 World Bank, "Groundswell: Preparing for International Climate Migration," 2018, http://documents1.worldbank.org/curated/en/983921522304806221/pdf/124724-BRI-PUBLIC-NEWSERIES-Groundswell-note-PN3.pdf

Biodiversity

Protecting the planetary web of life

Maria Ivanova and Natalia Escobar-Pemberthy

Natural resources are central to the survival of humanity. Mountains, forests, and rivers have undergone rapid and extensive conversion into environments providing direct value to the human enterprise. The inevitable result is that biological diversity has been and is being depleted and degraded faster than ever before in human history. Much like with climate change, "humans are the main culprit in biodiversity loss."[1] Global and local changes in the diversity and extent of nature's biological assets pose serious challenges to the stability of the earth's systems and to human health.

The COVID-19 pandemic brought into stark relief the importance of the relationship between people and nature. "We are reminded that when we destroy and degrade biodiversity," the UN General Assembly noted in 2020, "we undermine the web of life and increase the risk of disease spillover from wildlife to people."[2] Responses to the pandemic require intentional investment in the health of the planet as a prerequisite for ensuring public health.

Traditionally, concerns about the planetary web of life and its biological resources revolved around the distribution of such resources and the jurisdiction over their use and management. Since the late 1960s and early 1970s, however, global efforts have also focused on protection and sustainable use. Multiple multilateral governance processes focus on

DOI: 10.4324/9781003139836-19

biological and genetic resources, including species, forests, land, and ecosystems. The protection, restoration, and promotion of the sustainable use of terrestrial ecosystems is one of the key Sustainable Development Goals (SDGs) in the 2030 Agenda for Sustainable Development.[3]

In particular, SDG 15, "life on land," aims to reduce natural resources depletion and the degradation of natural habitats. Specific targets include the protection of wetlands, forests, natural habitats, mountain ecosystems, and endangered species and the sustainable management of land resources and invasive alien species. Many of these issues have a specific global environmental convention with a corresponding set of goals and mechanisms for action. If the implementation of SDG 15 integrates with the specific goals and targets of global environmental conventions, monitoring and assessment will be streamlined and countries' capacity could be augmented to achieve the different goals and protect the planetary web of life.

This chapter examines the evolution and potential futures of global governance efforts around biodiversity, ecosystems, species, and land resources. As the world embarks on a trajectory to progress on the protection of "life on land," including the definition of the post-2020 global biodiversity framework, the relationship between biodiversity and sustainable development becomes critical. We therefore analyze how the path that led to the definition of SDG 15 integrates different mechanisms supporting the implementation of the "life on land" goal and examine the potential for integration of the various governance instruments for biodiversity. We draw lessons from the successes and challenges of past governance efforts with a view toward a future where the powerful impacts of human activities on the environment do not backfire and are addressed in ways that promote both planetary and human health. The effectiveness of the environmental conventions, the SDGs, and the global biodiversity framework will hinge on implementation. Attaining planetary health, however, will require more profound transformation of the economic system and of values, attitudes, and ideologies.

Life on land

Only about 40 percent of the earth's surface is covered by land, and much of it is uninhabitable. Protecting the diversity of life on land has become a common global goal. Article 2 of the Convention on Biological Diversity (CBD) specifies the "variability among living organisms from all sources, including the diversity of genes, people, species, communities and ecosystems." Biological resources provide utilitarian value to human well-being through essential services and contribute to food security, human health, clean air and water, livelihoods, and economic development – all factors critical to poverty reduction and sustainability.[4] They also represent cultural and spiritual values deeply embedded in community traditions, knowledge, and identities.[5]

During the United Nations Decade on Biodiversity 2011–2020, countries sought to address the impacts of population growth, socio-economic development, and scientific and technological progress, including pollution, overexploitation of natural resources, climate change, and the presence of alien invasive species.[6] Serious challenges persist, however. The extent of natural habitats has declined 20 percent or more since 1980, and valuable ecosystem services have been lost. Wilderness and wetlands, for example, continue to decline globally at a dramatic rate.

Overexploitation of ecosystems has been the foundation for much economic growth and has resulted in the reduction of ecosystem services the value of which is difficult to measure in monetary terms alone. In 2020, the updated assessment of the International Union for the Conservation of Nature (IUCN) Red List established that of the more than 120,000 species evaluated, some 32,000 – about 27 percent – are threatened with extinction.[7] According to IUCN, 26 percent of mammals, 14 percent of birds, 41 percent of amphibians, 33 percent of reef-forming corals, and 63 percent of cycads are at risk of extinction.[8] The impact of such loss will be catastrophic but is not immediate. Ultimately, all forms of biodiversity loss result in new risks to the numerous benefits that humans receive from biodiversity.

Land conversion, deforestation, infrastructure development, changes in water temperatures, and invasion by alien species have decreased the area of world wetlands by 35 percent since 1970, costing more than US$20 trillion annually in ecosystem services.[9] Effective and equitable management of protected areas and their connectivity with ecosystem services require improvement. By 2020, 15 percent of the world's terrestrial and freshwater environments were covered by protected area agreements, which is below the goal of at least 17 percent set by the Aichi Targets – 20 ambitious conservation goals to safeguard global biodiversity that governments set out to achieve by 2020.

Approaches to the management of biological resources have evolved over time, connecting also with changes in the balance between environmental considerations and economic activities. From a very basic consideration in the allocation of resources among states, concepts have evolved into approaches such as protection, preservation, conservation, and sustainable use.[10] These concepts figure prominently in international regulatory frameworks. The evolution of the system of global environmental governance offered various perspectives to address the different components of biodiversity.[11] For the past five decades since the 1972 UN Conference on the Human Environment (UNCHE) in Stockholm, governments have adopted international regulations to address such challenges as species extinction, biodiversity conservation and sustainable use, and wetlands conservation and sustainable use to protect the benefits that these resources provide for humanity. The two key instruments and strategic approaches to protect biodiversity that led to the formulation of SDG 15 and the post-2020 global biodiversity framework are presented in the next section.

The legal regime for biodiversity: Ecosystems, species, use, and benefits

Concerns about the "ecological balance of the biosphere" and the "destruction and depletion of replaceable resources" have been core drivers for making collective action on the environment a central aspect of the international agenda.[12] In the past five decades, collective approaches to managing biological resources have resulted in the adoption of a series of international environmental agreements and have been part of the discussions and decisions at environmental governance summits since the 1972 UNCHE.

Efforts to raise awareness and establish mechanisms for the protection of specific ecosystems and species led to the signing of several global environmental conventions that recognized the importance and value of biodiversity, the role of people and states in the protection of biological resources, and the need for international cooperation to prevent the overexploitation of nature. The 1971 Ramsar Convention on the Protection of Wetlands of International Importance was followed by the 1973 Convention on International Trade in Endangered Species of Wild Flora and Fauna (CITES) and the 1979 Convention on Migratory Species (CMS). Governing biological resources is complex, requires explicit balance between environment and development priorities and policies, and takes time. The 1977 Plan of Action to Combat Desertification, for example, resulted in the formal adoption of the UN Convention to Combat Desertification as late as 1994.

The 1992 UN Conference on Environment and Development took place in Rio de Janeiro and is also known as the Rio Earth Summit. It focused political attention on the conservation and sustainable use of natural resources, establishing specific measures to address the issues that impact the viability of life on land.[13] Governments adopted the CBD with the explicit goal to conserve biodiversity and ensure the fair and equitable use of benefits from the use of genetic resources. Countries also adopted the "Non-legally Binding Authoritative Statement of Principles for a Global Consensus on the Management, Conservation and Sustainable Development of All Types of Forests," also known as the Forest Principles, to fulfill the mandate included in Agenda 21 to combat deforestation. Table 16.1 presents these global environmental agreements and summarizes their objectives.

Over time, governments have reaffirmed their commitments to the protection of biodiversity and created a range of additional goals. The Millennium Development Goals (MDGs) adopted in 2000 included an all-encompassing environmental aspiration, "ensure environmental sustainability." This goal, MDG 7, was explicitly targeted at reducing biodiversity loss. The 2005 Millennium Ecosystem Assessment developed this concept into a mechanism to promote reduction in biodiversity loss.[16]

Over the following two decades, the UN declared years and decades of various ecosystems and of biodiversity as one means of seeking political commitment and action on issues relating to the biosphere. The year 2006 was the International Year of Deserts and Desertification, and 2010 started the UN Decade on Desertification and the Protection of Drylands, including efforts to connect these issues with sustainable agriculture and land management. The International Year of Biodiversity was 2010, and 2010–2020 was the Decade on Biodiversity. The International Year of Forests was 2011, and since 2013, the UN has celebrated the International Day of Forests with tree planting and community-related activities. In the context of the Decade on Biodiversity, the adoption in 2010 of the Strategic

Table 16.1 Environmental agreements for biodiversity conservation[14]

	Year	Parties[15]	Main objectives
Ramsar Convention	1971	171	• The conservation and wise use of wetlands through actions at the international, national, and local levels, as a contribution to achieving sustainable development. • Cooperate internationally on transboundary wetlands, shared wetlands systems, and shared species.
CITES	1973	183	• Ensure that the international trade in specimens of wild animals and plants at risk of extinction does not threaten their survival. • Establish certain controls for the export, import, and reexport of species that have been identified as threatened. Controls are based on three lists or appendices for which there are different trade regulations.
CMS	1979	131	• Provision of a global platform for the conservation and sustainable use of migratory species and their habitats. • Bring together the states through which migratory animals pass—the Range States—and establish the international mechanisms for coordinated conservation measures throughout this passage. • Promote, cooperate in, and support research relating to migratory species.
CBD	1992	196	• Conservation of biological diversity. • Sustainable use of the components of biodiversity. • Fair and equitable sharing of the benefits arising out of the utilization of genetic resources.
United Nations Convention to Combat Desertification (UNCCD)	1994	197	• Combat desertification and mitigate the effects of drought in countries experiencing serious drought and/or desertification, particularly in Africa, considering the special needs and circumstances of affected developing country parties. • Develop long-term strategies that focus simultaneously, in affected areas, on improved productivity of land and the rehabilitation, conservation, and sustainable management of land and water resources. • Include populations and local communities in strategies and programs. • Improve cooperation and coordination at sub-regional, regional, and international levels, as well as resources mobilization.

(Continued)

Table16.1 (Continued)

	Year	Parties[15]	Main objectives
United Nations Forum on Forests (UNFF)	2000	193	• eements and of a common understanding on sustainable forest management. • Continue policy development and dialogue to address forest issues and emerging areas of concern. • Cooperate and coordinate on policies and programs on forest-related issues. • Monitor, assess, and report on the definition of forest-related policies. • Strengthen political commitment to the management, conservation, and sustainable development of all types of forests.

Plan for Biodiversity 2011–2020 represented an effort to provide an overarching framework for the entire UN system around biodiversity management and policy development. This framework includes the Aichi Biodiversity Targets, a set of 20 goals to address the underlying causes of biodiversity loss to ensure the provision of ecosystem services, enhance the benefits to all, and improve implementation through capacity building and knowledge management.

In the meantime, the 2012 UN Conference on Sustainable Development, also held in Brazil and called Rio+20, reaffirmed the value of biodiversity and its role in socio-economic development. Ecosystem services, the outcome document said, "are critical foundations for sustainable development and human well-being."[17] Furthermore, the conference reiterated the importance of implementing the strategic frameworks established by the different conventions, in particular the Convention on Biological Diversity. Member states also recognized the importance of addressing natural resource depletion and the adverse impacts of environmental degradation. This framework was used in SDG 15 to "protect, restore and promote sustainable use of terrestrial ecosystems, sustainably manage forests, combat desertification, and halt and reverse land degradation and halt biodiversity loss."

Human pressure on biodiversity puts species and humans at risk as it influences the emergence, incidence, and distribution of infectious diseases. The rapid rate of expansion of human activities, such as intensifying agriculture, logging, infrastructure development, and wildlife exploitation, has brought humans in closer proximity to wildlife and at greater risk of zoonotic disease. Indeed, the global health crisis of 2020 has brought to the fore the critical linkages between biodiversity loss and infectious diseases and the importance of biodiversity for society and the economy. Scheduled to take place in October 2020 in Kunming, China, the 15th Conference of the Parties of CBD was postponed because of the COVID-19 pandemic. The 2020 meeting of the UN General Assembly included the UN Summit on Biodiversity under the theme of "urgent action on biodiversity for sustainable development." The summit convened virtually a record number of countries (150 countries and 72 heads of state or government) to build political momentum around the conservation and sustainable management of biodiversity.[18]

The conventions and SDG 15

There are clear linkages between the biodiversity conventions and SDG 15. The 2030 sustainable development agenda continues the path established 15 years earlier by the MDGs and by the global summits that led to Rio+20, the 2012 UN Conference on Sustainable Development. However, there are important distinctions. Specifically, the evolution from the MDGs to the SDGs sought a transition from a goal for environmental sustainability into a more integrated approach that covers different policy areas and recognizes the linkages between the sustainable management of natural resources and social and economic development. The integration of environmental, social, and economic issues and the presence of the environment as a crosscutting factor in many other goals is critical to connect the different policy areas and guarantee balancing people, planet, prosperity, peace, and partnerships. In addition, member states have a clear responsibility in the implementation of the 2030 sustainable development agenda, implementing the different goals and targets, measuring the associated indicators, and providing the means for their implementation.[19]

Among these means of implementation, global environmental conventions have a critical role.[20] The Rio+20 outcome document, "The Future We Want," specifically recognized "the significant contributions to sustainable development made by the multilateral environmental agreements."[21] Considering that there is a clear connection between biodiversity and the sustainable development agenda,[22] SDG 15 maintains the spirit behind the biodiversity-related conventions to regulate conservation and sustainable use, reduce the threat of extinction, and guarantee the benefits that biodiversity provides for humankind. This goal – and other SDGs – incorporates specific targets to sustainably manage terrestrial ecosystems; regulate harvesting and over-fishing; ensure the conservation, restoration, and sustainable use of ecosystems; and take action to end poaching and the traffic of protected species, among many other targets.[23] These linkages are strengthened by the fact that the conventions constitute the international legal basis to address global environmental issues. In addition, in recent years the conventions have made efforts to link their mandates to these global initiatives for development. This has led to the identification of specific linkages between the conventions and the targets and indicators that are being defined to assess the implementation of the SDGs. However, besides the actual linkages between the policy areas established by each of these global agendas, it is important to understand how the conventions interact with the SDGs to constitute stronger, more effective governance instruments.

Implementing sustainable development

Once policy goals have been established, the main challenge is their implementation. As the international community of states has broadened the range of global goals through international agreements and development agendas, attention has shifted to the extent that countries are implementing their commitments. The adoption of domestic regulations and policies that facilitate and enable the fulfillment of the biodiversity agreements is critical to countries' ability to address these global problems and to the achievement of other global goals, including SDG 15 and the post-2020 global biodiversity framework.[24] However, evidence of the low implementation of global environmental conventions raises serious questions about the conditions required for the optimal implementation of an integrated global biodiversity agenda and its contribution to sustainable development. The conventions, therefore, provide insights for biodiversity governance.

Strategic targets and measurement for implementation

Targets and indicators are critical to the ability of countries to plan and implement their obligations. This is perhaps the main lesson from both the MDGs and the environmental conventions for the implementation of SDG 15 and the post-2020 global biodiversity framework.[25] Concrete measurement strategies and mechanisms provide governments and international organizations with the necessary data and science-based information to evaluate advancement in the development agenda and take corrective measures as required. Despite concerns about the extent to which metrics reflected the real speed of progress, the use of concrete targets and indicators for the MDGs proved to be an effective instrument for focusing the efforts of numerous actors, monitoring the evolution of the different strategies, and prompting global political mobilization around concrete targets for development.[26] Targets and indicators also helped create a culture of monitoring and evaluation that, despite the need for further improvement, brought to the international community more and better data.[27]

Until the adoption of the Aichi Biodiversity Targets in 2010, the biodiversity-related conventions had not articulated a set of specific targets and indicators to measure progress. Most of the biodiversity-related conventions provide rather vague obligations. To translate them into national policies to protect biological resources and improve their conservation, governments have to define concrete objectives and targets, metrics, and assessment mechanisms to evaluate progress. Measuring the implementation of the conventions is a difficult task. Nonetheless, evidence from efforts to measure implementation of selected conventions shows that there are still important gaps in terms of the extent to which countries are translating their commitments to agreements such as the Ramsar Convention and CITES and that data collection and the processing of national reports are persistent challenges.[28]

States parties have consistently discussed the need for better strategic frameworks to achieve the goals defined by each agreement. Different instruments have been defined with specific targets, indicators, and in some cases metrics to evaluate progress (see Table 16.2). Under these mechanisms, governments have been encouraged to develop, implement, assess, and report on national outcomes for biodiversity. In addition, the conventions have been working on connecting these instruments to the sustainable development agenda, since their outcomes can provide data and baselines for the implementation of the SDGs and guarantee that all national policy efforts point to the same results. The successful implementation of SDG 15 also requires synergies across the biodiversity-related conventions, and between this goal and other forms of governance, in order to respond to the complex challenges that biodiversity faces.

Furthermore, all the conventions contribute to the definition of the post-2020 global biodiversity framework. The CMS, for example, developed a connectivity framework to guarantee that the conservation needs of migratory species were represented in the new governance instrument. CITES has also considered the need for synchronization, particularly as the convention is also preparing an update of its strategic vision for the 2021–2030 period. The UN Convention to Combat Desertification (UNCCD) presented a specific proposal for a spatially explicit framework that allows for area-based targets for the post-2020 global biodiversity framework, taking into account the structure of its own Land Degradation Neutrality targets.

In this context, it is critical that the framework, as a new governance mechanism, has a clear definition of expectations from state parties and of measurement standards for assessing countries' progress. Monitoring, measuring, and assessing progress become indispensable as countries seek to implement the sustainable development agenda and avoid the crossing of planetary boundaries.[29] As we become increasingly aware of the implications of living in the Anthropocene and our interconnected actions, implementation of global commitments will be critical. To this end, conceptual and practical lessons from previous sets of global goals are important to ensure that progress will be achieved.

Lessons for better governance

Environmental conventions offer lessons for the post-2020 global biodiversity framework and for SDG 15 to articulate and implement a consistent, coherent, and ambitious vision for the protection of life on land. The SDGs could motivate political will and improve the ability of countries to deliver on core development priorities. In light of the COVID-19 crisis, the post-2020 framework is expected to secure more ambitious policies and new perspectives about the relation between humans and nature. In addition, conventions set agendas, proscribe behavior, prescribe actions, contribute to the socialization of policy issues, reduce uncertainty around regulation, and generate domestic policy responses.[30] Understanding how they work as governance instruments – independently and jointly – reflects on the importance of setting policy goals to generating positive outcomes and changing policy behavior. More robust efforts for the protection of biodiversity would reflect the following five elements:

Integration: Synergies are required among existing mechanisms within the biodiversity cluster and with other policy areas. Furthermore, efforts for implementation have to recognize and account for the socio-economic role of biodiversity. Convention secretariats have initiated joint activities on common issues. Specifically, governments need to integrate policies toward the achievement of

Table 16.2 Strategic mechanisms from biodiversity-related conventions

Strategic instrument	*Strategic approach, mission, and objectives*
Strategic Plan for Biodiversity 2011–2020 (CBD, Ramsar Convention, CITES, and CMS)	• Overarching framework for the UN system, including the CBD, all the biodiversity-related conventions, and other agencies engaged in biodiversity management. • The main goal is to guarantee that by 2050, "biodiversity is valued, conserved, restored and wisely used, maintaining ecosystem services, sustaining a healthy planet and delivering benefits essential for all people." • Efforts are constructed around the 2020 Aichi Biodiversity Targets: – Address the underlying causes of biodiversity loss by mainstreaming biodiversity across government and society. – Reduce the direct pressures on biodiversity and promote sustainable use. – Improve the status of biodiversity by safeguarding ecosystems, species, and genetic diversity. – Enhance the benefits to all from biodiversity and ecosystem services. – Enhance implementation through participatory planning, knowledge management, and capacity building.
Strategic Vision 2008–2020 (CITES)	• Characterizes CITES contribution to the achievement of the Strategic Plan for Biodiversity 2011–2020 and the relevant Aichi Targets and to the SDGs. • Aims at improving the work of the convention to guarantee that international trade in wild fauna and flora is conducted at sustainable levels. • Establishes three goals: – Ensure compliance with and implementation and enforcement of the convention. – Secure financial resources and means for the operation and implementation of the convention. – Contribute to reduce the rate of biodiversity loss and achieve other goals and targets by supporting other multilateral instruments.
Strategic Plan 2015–2023 (CMS)	• The overall goal is to ensure the favorable conservation status of migratory species, thereby contributing to global sustainability. • To achieve this, four specific objectives were established: – To ensure that the conservation and management of migratory species are based on the best available information. – To ensure that migratory species benefit from the best possible conservation measures. – To broaden awareness and enhance engagement in the conservation of migratory species among key actors. – To reinforce CMS's overarching and unifying role in the conservation and management of migratory species.
Strategic Plan 2016–2024 (Ramsar Convention)	• Aims at the conservation and wise use of all wetlands through local and national actions and international cooperation, as a contribution toward achieving sustainable development throughout the world.

Strategic instrument	Strategic approach, mission, and objectives
	• It is based on priority focus areas that include the prevention and reverse of the loss and degradation of wetlands, the provision of science-based advice and guidance, the connection with the definition of ecosystem services, the implementation of the convention, the wise use of wetlands, and the identification of Ramsar sites participation, synergies, and means of implementation, among other factors.
10-year strategy (UNCCD)	• Aims at forging a global partnership to reverse and prevent desertification/land degradation and to mitigate the effects of drought in affected areas in order to support poverty reduction and environmental sustainability. • The strategy provides a global framework for the development and implementation of national and regional policies. • Includes four strategic objectives: – To improve the living conditions of affected populations. – To improve the condition of affected ecosystems. – To generate global benefits through effective implementation of the UNCCD. – To mobilize resources to support implementation of the convention through building effective partnerships between national and international actors.
Land Degradation Neutrality Goals (UNCCD)	• Achieve a balance between three processes: degradation, rehabilitation/restoration, and sustainable land management.
Global Forest Goals (UNFF)	• Part of the UN Strategic Plan for Forests 2017–2030 that provides a global framework for actions at all levels to sustainably manage all types of forests and trees and halt deforestation and forest degradation. • The goals are connected to the implementation of the SDGs: – Reverse the loss of forest cover worldwide through sustainable forest management and increase efforts to prevent forest degradation and contribute to the global effort of addressing climate change. • Enhance forest-based economic, social, and environmental benefits. – Increase significantly the area of protected forests worldwide and other areas of sustainably managed forests, as well as the proportion of forest products from sustainably managed forests. – Mobilize significantly increased, new, and additional financial resources from all sources for the implementation of sustainable forest management, and strengthen scientific and technical cooperation and partnerships. – Promote governance frameworks to implement sustainable forest management, including through the UN Forest Instrument, and enhance the contribution of forests to the 2030 Agenda. – Enhance cooperation, coordination, coherence, and synergies on forest-related issues at all levels, as well as across sectors and relevant stakeholders.

the different goals and include these linkages as part of their measurement, monitoring, and assessment efforts.

Differentiation of responsibility: Conventions and the SDGs are universal instruments – that is, they are applicable to most if not all countries. Responsibility for action, however, is "common but differentiated," as enshrined in the 1992 Rio Declaration. This principle recognizes the responsibility of all states for the protection of the environment but acknowledges differing national abilities to prevent, reduce, or control the threat as well as the various contributions to environmental problems. It has been criticized for creating a problematic binary categorization of developed and developing states and ignoring the differing capacities within these categories. In this context, effective implementation of the post-2020 global biodiversity framework will require that the specific circumstances and needs of countries be considered, specifically around the means for implementation and the mobilization of resources for the new set of goals that it proposes.

Capacity building: Environmental conventions have established specific mechanisms to address capacity building and provide technical and financial assistance to support developing countries in implementation. Learning from these challenges, the sustainable development agenda was designed to be applicable for all, taking into account different national conditions and priorities. The post-2020 global biodiversity framework should assess the requirements of developing countries and provide the mechanisms that address their specific capacity needs.

National ownership: Environmental conventions request, through different mechanisms, that state parties define national implementation plans, strategies, and legislation that incorporate international agreements into domestic policies to guarantee ownership and implementation. Progress in national strategies has also required the support of donor countries and international funds. In the case of the post-2020 global biodiversity framework, national ownership is critical for sustainable development and guarantees implementation, follow-up, monitoring, and review.

Engagement: The environmental agenda has been successful in engaging civil society. Political and social engagement will be critical for the implementation of the post-2020 global biodiversity framework. Governmental actors involved in the implementation of the different biodiversity governance instruments should design political processes that also involve international organizations and other stakeholders, including civil society, the scientific community, and all the relevant agencies from the UN system.

Conclusion

In 2015, SDG 15 expanded goals and targets beyond the concept of protected areas and environmental sustainability and incorporated targets related to all the biodiversity-related agreements. Five years later, the negotiations for the post-2020 global biodiversity framework aim at establishing a mutually reinforcing relationship with the sustainable development agenda that also contributes to the objectives of the biodiversity-related global environmental conventions. In addition, the facilitation mechanisms created by each convention, and the strategies they define, are important for the effective translation of international environmental agreements into national policies and the consequent achievement of the SDG 15 and the global biodiversity framework.

However, environmental conventions also face important structural constraints, including vague obligations, multiplicity of targets across the various agreements, independent governance mechanisms, and limited financial resources; these short-comings affect their role within the post-2020 global biodiversity framework as instruments that articulate the specific actions countries are expected to undertake for biodiversity conservation. The challenges of operationalizing the new set of goals that will be developed around the framework will certainly require enhanced cap-acity, resources, flexibility, and leadership from the conventions. As synergies have not developed and conventions work independently, coordination and collaboration among the secretariats of the biodiversity-related conventions is a challenge, as silos persist, and yet it is an important precondition for delivery. Clear roles have to be defined in order for the conventions to integrate their different targets and indicators into their operations, understanding their contribution to sustainable development as well as to the other 16 SDGs.

The post-2020 global biodiversity framework represents an integrated and indivisible approach to the protection of biodiversity. It needs to communicate clearly to countries and stakeholders the importance of protecting, restoring, and promoting the sustainable use of terrestrial ecosystems. In addition, the COVID-19 crisis has highlighted the interconnectedness of planetary and human health. Three-quarters of new and emerging diseases originate in wildlife, and as natural habitats for wildlife shrink because of increasing pressure from human activity, the risk of spillover events increases. The COVID-19 pandemic made that risk a reality with unprecedented deleterious impact on public health across the world. The biodiversity-related conventions, SDG 15, and the post-2020 bio-diversity framework are instruments to manage the interaction between humans and nature.

Effective integration within the system of biodiversity governance will be critical to ensure that environment and human activities coexist to promote sustainability, biodiversity conservation, and public health. As we move toward the middle of the twenty-first century, a concrete and formal connection among the biodiversity instruments will be essential for progress measurement, engagement, and improved governance.

Suggested reading

Maria Ivanova, *The Untold Story of the World's Leading Environmental Institution: UNEP at Fifty* (Cambridge, MA: MIT Press, 2021).
Philippe G. Le Prestre, ed., *Governing Global Biodiversity: The Evolution and Implementation of the Convention on Biological Diversity* (London: Routledge, 2017).

Philipp Pattberg, Oscar Widerberg, and Marcel T. Kok, "Towards a Global Biodiversity Action Agenda," *Global Policy* 10, no. 3 (2019): 385–390.

Sui C. Phang, Pierre Failler, and Peter Bridgewater, "Addressing the Implementation Challenge of the Global Biodiversity Framework," *Biodiversity and Conservation* 29, no. 9 (2020): 3061–3066.

Maria Schultz, Tristan D. Tyrrell, and Torbjörn Ebenhard, *The 2030 Agenda and Ecosystems-A Discussion Paper on the Links Between the Aichi Biodiversity Targets and the Sustainable Development Goals* (Stockholm, Sweden: SwedBio at Stockholm Resilience Centre, 2016).

Esther Turnhout, Katja Neves, and Elisa De Lijster, " 'Measurementality' in Biodiversity Governance: Knowledge, Transparency, and the Intergovernmental Science-Policy Platform on Biodiversity and Ecosystem Services (IPBES)," *Environment and Planning A* 46, no. 3 (2014): 581–597.

Rogalla von Bieberstein et al., "Improving Collaboration in the Implementation of Global Biodiversity Conventions," *Conservation Biology* 33, no. 4 (2019): 821–831.

Notes

1 Ehsan Masood, "The Battle for the Soul of Biodiversity," *Nature* 560, no. 7719 (2018): 423–426.

2 UN, "United Nations Summit on Biodiversity," 2020, www.un.org/pga/75/united-nations-summit-on-biodiversity/

3 UN, *Transforming Our World: The 2030 Agenda for Sustainable Development* (New York: UN, 2015), UN document A/RES/70/1.

4 CBD, *Biodiversity, Development and Poverty Alleviation: Recognizing the Role of Biodiversity for Human Well-being* (New York: UN, 2009); MEA, "Millennium Ecosystem Assessment," in *Ecosystems and Human Well-being: Biodiversity Synthesis* (Washington, DC: World Research Institute, 2005); and Michael Bowman and Catherine Redgwell, eds., *International Law and the Conservation of Biological Diversity* (Dordrecht, The Netherlands: Kluwer Law International, 1996).

5 CBD, *Biodiversity, Development and Poverty Alleviation*.

6 Secretariat of the Convention on Biological Diversity, *Global Biodiversity Outlook 4* (Montreal: CBD, 2014); *Global Biodiversity Outlook 5* (Montreal: CBD, 2020); and UNEP, *Global Environmental Outlook 5* (Nairobi: UN, 2012).

7 IUCN, "The IUCN Red List of Threatened Species: Version 2020–2," 2020, www.iucn-redlist.org

8 Ibid.

9 Ramsar Convention on Wetlands, *Global Wetland Outlook: State of the World's Wetlands and Their Services to People* (Gland, Switzerland: Ramsar Convention Secretariat, 2018).

10 Rosemary Rayfuse, "Biological Resources," in *The Oxford Handbook of International Environmental Law*, ed. Daniel Bodansky, Jutta Brunnée, and Ellen Hey (Oxford: Oxford University Press, 2007), 362–393.

11 CBD, *The Strategic Plan for Biodiversity 2011–2020 and the Aichi Biodiversity Targets* (Nagoya, Japan: UNEP, 2010); United Nations Conference on Environment and Development (UNCED), *Agenda 21* (New York: UN, 1992); UN, "Declaration of the United Nations Conference on the Human Environment" (Stockholm Declaration), UN document 1972 A/CONF.48/14; and UN, "Johannesburg Declaration on Sustainable Development," UN document A/CONF.199/20, 2002.

12 Stockholm Declaration, para. 3.

13 UNCED, *Agenda 21*.

14 CMS, *Convention on the Conservation of Migratory Species of Wild Animals* (Bonn, Germany: UNEP, 1979); Economic and Social Council (ECOSOC), "Report on the Fourth Session of the Intergovernmental Forum on Forests," UN document 2000 E/RES/2000/35; IUCN, *Convention on International Trade in Endangered Species of Wild Fauna and Flora* (Washington, DC: IUCN, 1973); UNESCO, *Convention on Wetlands of International Importance Especially as Waterfowl Habitat* (Ramsar, Iran: UNESCO, 1972); UN, *Convention on Biological Diversity* (Paris: UN, 1994).

15 The data are updated through November 2020.

16 MEA, "Millennium Ecosystem Assessment," para. 2.

17 UN, "The Future We Want – Outcome Document from Rio+20, United Nations Conference on Sustainable Development, Rio de Janeiro," UN document A/RES/66/288, 2002, para. 197.

18 UN, *Scope, Modalities, Format and Organization of the Summit on Biodiversity* (New York: UN, 2019), UN document A/RES/74/269.

19 UN, *Critical Milestones Towards Coherent, Efficient and Inclusive Follow-up and Review at the Global Level* (New York: UN, 2016), UN document A/70/684.

20 UNEP, *Role of Multilateral Environmental Agreements (MEAs) in Achieving the Sustainable Development Goals* (Nairobi: UNEP, 2016).

21 UN, "The Future We Want," para. 9.

22 Hasrat Arjjumend, Konstantia Koutouki, and Sabiha Alam, "Evolution of International Governance of Biodiversity," *Journal of Global Resource* 3 (2016): 1–15; and Pisupati Balakrishna, *Biodiversity Governance: Lessons for International Environment Governance* (Chennai, India: National Biodiversity Authority, 2012).

23 UN, *Transforming Our World*.

24 Harold K. Jacobson and Edith Brown-Weiss, "Strengthening Compliance with International Environmental Accords: Preliminary Observations from Collaborative Project," *Global Governance* 1, no. 2 (1995): 119; Ronald B. Mitchell, "Institutional Aspects of Implementation, Compliance, and Effectiveness," in *International Relations and Global Climate Change*, ed. Urs Luterbacher and Detlef F. Sprinz (Cambridge, MA: Massachusetts Institute of Technology Press, 2001), 221–244; Sui C. Phang, Pierre Failler, and Peter Bridgewater, "Addressing the Implementation Challenge of the Global Biodiversity Framework," *Biodiversity and Conservation* 29, no. 9 (2020): 3061–3066; Beth A. Simmons, "Compliance with International Agreements," *Annual Review of Political Science* 1, no. 1 (1998): 75–93; and Oran R. Young, *Compliance and Public Authority: A Theory with International Applications* (Baltimore, MD: Johns Hopkins University Press, 1979).

25 Maria Ivanova and Natalia Escobar-Pemberthy, "The Quest for Sustainable Development: The Power and Perils of Global Development Goals," in *Poverty & the Millennium Development Goals (MDGs): A Critical Assessment and a Look Forward*, ed. Thomas Pogge, Gabriele Köhler, and Alberto D. Cimadamore (London: CROP/Zed Books, 2016), 83–111; and Open Working Group on Sustainable Development Goals, *Programme of Work 2013–2014* (New York: UN, 2013).

26 Pogge, Köhler, and Cimadamore, eds., *Poverty & the Millennium Development Goals*.

27 CROP, *Mobilizing Critical Research for Preventing and Eradicating Poverty* (Bergen, Norway: International Social Science Council, University of Bergen, and UN, 2015), Brief No. 13.

28 Natalia Escobar-Pemberthy and Maria Ivanova, "Implementation of Multilateral Environmental Agreements: Rationale and Design of the Environmental Conventions Index," *Sustainability* 12, no. 17 (2020): 7098.

29 Secretariat of the Convention on Biological Diversity, *Global Biodiversity Outlook 5*.

30 Jutta Brunée, "Enforcement Mechanisms in International Law and International Environmental Law," in *Ensuring Compliance with Multilateral Environmental Agreements: A Dialogue Between Practitioners and Academia*, ed. Ulrich Beyerlin, Peter-Tobias Stoll, and Rüdiger Wolfrum (Leiden, The Netherlands: Martinus Nijhoff Publishers, 2006), 1–24; Peter M. Haas, Robert O. Keohane, and Marion A. Levy, *Institutions for the Earth: Sources of Effective International Environmental Protection* (Cambridge, MA: Massachusetts Institute of Technology Press, 1993); Ronald B. Mitchell, *International Politics and the Environment* (London: Sage Publications Limited, 2010); Achim Steiner, Lee A. Kimball, and John Scanlon, "Global Governance for the Environment and the Role of Multilateral Environmental Agreements in Conservation," *Oryx* 37, no. 2 (2003): 227–237.

CONTENTS

Aid

The COVID-19 crisis and beyond

Catherine Weaver and Rachel Rosenberg

In the wake of the Great Recession in 2007–2008, international relations scholar Daniel Drezner proclaimed that the "system worked."[1] In doing so, he acknowledged that the set of international institutions designed to prevent and mitigate global crises had somehow managed to muddle through an unprecedented financial meltdown that was ignited in the so-called Global North. These institutions, including the International Monetary Fund (IMF) and the various G-clubs (such as the G20), were deemed resilient and even successful, if only because the crisis did not manage to cast enough doubt on their relevance to result in widespread demand for their dismantlement. In the midst of the 2020 COVID-19 global pandemic, can we say the same?

This chapter assesses the contemporary governance of international development and humanitarian aid (hereafter simply "aid"). We define the aid system as a complex set of principles and principals – that is, the ideas and institutions or key actors – that govern global aid. Most often, aid is officially tabulated as "official development assistance" (ODA) in authoritative reports about grant and concessional flows from the Development Assistance Committee of the Organisation for Economic Co-operation and Development (DAC/OECD). We treat aid more broadly to include ODA and the myriad sources of development finance provided to emerging and

DOI: 10.4324/9781003139836-20

developing country economics from non-DAC donors (such as China), the non-government sector, and the private sector. Before the COVID-19 pandemic spread in early 2020, the aid system was already suffering from tripartite challenges related to the relevance, legitimacy, and effectiveness of governance and – as we discuss in the conclusions – widespread fragmentation in the sources and actors that provide aid.[2] In many ways, this system continues to lumber through incremental institutional adaptation, but with growing evidence of a greater need for more fundamental reform to the rules and norms that govern aid.[3]

Yet, as in all matters political, such systemic change is inherently difficult because of vested political interests, economic constraints, and institutional and ideational inertia. Specific organizational reforms – in such aging institutions as the World Bank, the International Monetary Fund (IMF), and the United Nations – invariably prove daunting, with persistent democratic deficits in global development governance. More critically, the very landscape of development and humanitarian financing as well as the actors involved in aid implementation are changing much more quickly than the institutions meant to govern them.

This is an incredibly complex issue to unpack and address in a short chapter. Nonetheless, we try to do so using the COVID-19 crisis as a means of framing the discussion. The first section examines the empirical crises that the aid system faces today with respect to the global pandemic, characterized recently by many global leaders as the "lost decade of development" – a refrain we first heard in the 1980s. We examine COVID-19 issues as they relate to three critical areas of aid – health, food security, and education – as well as cross-sectional issues with gender. The chapter then turns to the linkages between COVID-19 and the looming debt crisis, using this topic to illuminate some of the broader weaknesses in the contemporary governance of aid and development. Thereafter, we offer three observations about fragmentation in the global aid system, the lack of transparency, and the sustained commitment to traditional aid structures. We conclude with two big takeaway messages: the need to "Go Global" and the need to "Go Local" when thinking about future global aid governance for development and humanitarianism.

Global development aid and the COVID-19 pandemic: The lost decade of development?

About half a year after the World Health Organization declared a pandemic, the number of COVID-19 cases worldwide was some 40 million.[4] Nearly one-fifth were in a single leading advanced industrial economy – the United States. Yet the real and potential consequences of the pandemic are likely to be far more extensive, lethal, and long term in emerging markets and developing economies (EMDEs).

By many accounts, the pandemic may set back progress in alleviating global poverty by at least 20 years.[5] Numerous estimates published by the IMF, the UN, and World Bank predict GDP (gross domestic product) growth to contract anywhere from 3.8 to 7.6 percent, under the rather hopeful assumption that a COVID vaccine is approved and ready for distribution by the end of 2020. In turn, the International Labour Organization (ILO) estimates that nearly half the global workforce – close to 1.5 billion people – may become unemployed because of the "great lockdown."[6]

Key sectors in development have been – and will continue to be – particularly hard hit by the COVID-19 pandemic. The starkest failings of development are observed in the health sector. Health-care-worker density varies significantly across states. India has 2.1 nurses per 1,000 people compared to Germany's 13.2 nurses per 1,000 people. A similar disparity exists in terms of resources and equipment – India has 0.7 hospital beds per 1,000 people compared to Germany's 8.3 hospital beds per 1,000 people.[7] In May 2020, there were fewer than 2,000 working ventilators to serve people in public hospitals across 41 African countries, compared to more than 170,000 in the United States.[8]

Disparities in the health sector have a disproportionately gendered effect. While, statistically speaking, women are not necessarily more likely to catch COVID-19, their socio-economic roles and responsibilities put them at higher risk of exposure. Women are more likely to be nurses and other frontline medical workers and bear the brunt of home care for the elderly and the sick. Many women also risk the loss of sustainable livelihoods. They are faced with tough decisions to exit the formal workforce to take care of, and educate, children when school and childcare facilities are closed and when families can no longer offer viable support systems because of social distancing guidelines and travel restrictions.

COVID-19 has also created a "shadow pandemic" of domestic violence against women and girls.[9] Lockdowns, unemployment, and disparities in internet and phone access limit critical access to victim support resources, with a disproportionate effect on poor women.[10] Reporting from different countries shows alarming rises in domestic violence.[11] A local source in Brazil reported a 40 percent to 50 percent rise in domestic violence.[12] One study found that 54 percent of vulnerable women surveyed in Lebanon reported an increase in violence and harassment during the pandemic, with 44 percent saying they felt less safe at home.[13] The World Health Organization (WHO) reported a 60 percent increase in emergency calls from women subjected to violence by their intimate partner among European Union states.[14] Overall, gender intersects the pandemic's destructive effects across issue areas like health, food security, and education.

General Assembly resolution 70/1 agreed in October 2015 to the 2030 Sustainable Development Goals (SDGs), which aim to ambitiously "transform our world for the better" by 2030.[15] Even before COVID-19, these UN-set goals seemed out of reach, at best. Prior to the pandemic, the population affected by food insecurity had risen between 2014 and 2018, undermining SDG 2 on hunger and global food security. COVID-19 has severely set back progress in alleviating global hunger and addressing the root causes of food security as the pandemic's effects further stress global supply chains and household incomes, with a disproportionate effect on the poorest.[16] By some estimates, nearly 250 million people could face severe food insecurity or famine because of these effects.[17] In East Africa alone, the World Food Programme (WFP) estimated that the number of acutely food-insecure people could increase by 73 percent in 2020.[18]

SDG 2 is also intimately related to the goal for quality education, SDG 4. The UN reports that nearly 369 million children rely on school meals and must find other sources of nutrition.[19] An article in the *Lancet* in the middle of the pandemic warns of the mortal and long-term consequences that disruptions in nutrition and health services are creating. As the authors argue:

> With an estimated 47 million children younger than 5 years affected by wasting globally before the COVID-19 pandemic, this would translate to an estimated additional 6.7 million children with wasting during the first 12 months of the pandemic – 80 percent of them in sub-Saharan Africa and south Asia – and more than 10,000 additional child deaths per month during this same period.[20]

UN projections prior to the pandemic showed that more than 200 million children would be out of school and that only 60 percent of young people would be completing upper secondary education in 2030.[21] In the first months of the pandemic, nearly 30 percent of the world's children were unable to access schooling either in person or remotely.[22] The lack of access to education poses the multiple risks of lost or delayed learning, increased hunger because of the absence of free school meals, and increased risk of forced child labor or early marriage.[23]

Remote learning is a prime example of inequality across households and among countries. In 2019, 78 percent of European households owned a computer compared to 11 percent in Africa.[24] Although "leaving no one behind" is a recurring and overarching objective of the SDGs,[25] the pandemic highlights and exacerbates preexisting inequalities that impede this objective.[26] While donors have promised to "do whatever it takes," the allocation of ODA has not reflected this rhetoric.[27] A study of International Aid Transparency Initiative (IATI) data found that bilateral donors decreased aid commitments by 17 percent between 2019 and 2020.[28] Additionally, the study concluded that neither bilateral donors nor international financial institutions are increasing the share of aid to low-income countries. There is little evidence to suggest that these numbers will bounce back because of COVID-19, bar extraordinary one-off funds that (as discussed in the following) donors have only slowly and unevenly disbursed.

Setbacks in education spill over in gender equality goals, SDG 5. Such lessons were already apparent with the Ebola outbreak, which illuminated the harm of school closures and demonstrated that the probability of returning to school greatly diminishes the longer girls are kept away.[29] School closures and travel restrictions limit access to reproductive services, potentially triggering a rise in teen pregnancy and threatening girls' long-term access to education.[30] Unemployment and stress on household incomes may lead to early marriages that also threaten long-term access to education. The United Nations Population Fund (UNFPA) estimates that 13 million more girls will be forced into early marriages between 2020 and 2030.[31] These aftershocks exacerbate the preexisting gender disparities that SDGs 4 and 5 aim to address.[32]

Overall, the threat to global development is severe: between 130 million and 500 million people worldwide may fall back into extreme poverty this year, defined as living on less than $1.90 per day.[33] As a result, numerous experts predict that progress toward the SDGs is not only slowing but may be moving in reverse.[34] Even in the most optimistic scenarios, COVID-19 will, as it did Africa and Latin America in the 1980s, likely result in "lost decades of development."[35]

COVID-19 and the new debt trap

One of the most serious systemic threats related to the pandemic and global development is the looming debt crisis. Nearly half of emerging and developing market economies were already at high risk of debt crises before COVID-19 was declared a global pandemic by the WHO in March 2020.[36] Since then, the debt situation has worsened. The IMF projects that the average 2021 debt-to-GDP ratios will rise by 7–10 percent in these countries.[37]

While the debt-to-GDP ratio projection is even worse for advanced industrialized economies such as the United States (with projections near 20 percent increases), developing countries do not have the same capacity to carry additional debt. This is largely because developing countries lack access to the capital necessary to service debts. This economic stress is exacerbated by capital flight out of developing countries into "safe haven" economies, limited access to hard currencies necessary to service debt payments, and slowing economic growth resulting from declining commodity prices, falling remittance inflows, and disruptions in global trade and tourism.[38] In March 2020 alone, foreign investors withdrew more than $83 billion from low-income countries (LICs) and lower-middle-income countries (LMICs), the largest capital flow ever recorded.[39]

One example of the looming debt crisis is Uganda. While it has a remarkably low number of reported COVID cases, Uganda has suffered tremendously from the economic dislocations caused by the pandemic. According to a study by Development Initiatives, a UK-based think tank, Uganda's domestic job losses and declining remittances resulted in significant loss of tax revenues.[40] Without export earnings or domestic resources, it is difficult for the Ugandan government to address key gaps in its health infrastructure, much less address enduring problems in poverty, education, and food insecurity. Scarce resources have been reallocated toward COVID-19 prevention and treatment, but at the cost of reduced spending on malaria prevention and treatment. Public debt in Uganda is roughly equal to 41 percent of its GDP, and debt servicing accounts for near 12 percent of the annual government budget. Uganda's struggle with COVID-19 demonstrates the extent to which the pandemic is not simply a public health crisis but rather a threat to the long-term sustainable development of most LICs and LMICs.

Debt burdens in developing countries limit fiscal resources and the policy space needed to address immediate crises in their health-care and other social policy systems, as shortfalls in inward investments and high debt payments curtail spending on other sectors. This is particularly debilitating in least developed countries where health-care infrastructure was weak prior to the pandemic. The WHO estimates that 83 countries[41] currently do not meet the basic threshold for health workers (defined as 23 skilled professionals per 10,000 people) and that, globally, we will need an additional 9 million nurses and midwives by 2030.[42] As a result, developing countries are not only at higher risk for COVID-19-related illness and death, they are also vulnerable to rapid increases in maternal and infant mortality, the spread of untreated diseases like malaria, and an inability to sustain critical vaccination campaigns against preventable diseases like polio and tuberculosis.[43] Globally, weak health-care systems are further threatened as political support wanes for institutions such as the WHO, from which former US president Trump threatened to withdraw the United States in July 2020.[44]

In October 2020, at the fall annual meetings of the IMF and World Bank, the UN director of financing for sustainable development warned finance ministers and central bank governors of "protracted fiscal paralysis" and the "worst global crisis since WWII" if developing countries do not receive significant debt relief.[45] Yet debt relief initiatives led by the G20 so far have fallen short for three key reasons.

First, global aid has fallen in the past several years, as aid from many major donor countries (including the United States) has stagnated or declined in the face of domestic economic downturns and the rise of right-wing, ethno-nationalist opposition to foreign aid.[46] Multilateral financial institutions, including the IMF and World Bank, had promised to deliver on the estimated $2.5 trillion in financing needed to combat COVID-19.[47] Yet, as detailed by financial experts, many of these institutions have been slow to tap all their available resources, and disbursement of funds has been painfully slow.[48] By August 2020, the IMF and multilateral development banks had approved just under $175 billion, despite having the legal authority to mobilize and allocate nearly $1 trillion from existing resources.[49] According to one of these reports, as of September 2020, only about $90 billion had been disbursed – less than 12.6 percent of available multilateral and bilateral financing.[50] This may largely be because of fundamental disagreements between major donors over the conditions placed on debt relief, debt suspensions, and debt restructuring. For example, while China supported the expansion of IMF Special Drawing Rights (SDRs) in April 2020, the United States and India blocked this in the G20.[51] Overall, while the G20 agreed at the IMF and World Bank annual meetings in 2020 to extend the Debt Services Suspension Initiative (DSSI), the forum has been very slow to come to an agreement on the terms of debt relief and to disburse needed funds.[52] Moreover, the IMF and World Bank may be hesitant to overextend themselves on debt relief because of concerns that they themselves might lose their "preferred creditor status" and face degrading of their own bond credit ratings.[53]

In October 2020, the G20 announced a "Common Framework for Debt Treatments" beyond the DSSI that was agreed at the Riyadh G20 Leaders' Summit in November 2020.[54] This approach reaffirms the practice of "case-by-case" debt restructuring, which does not ensure comparability among cases and does not create open accountability that offsets some of the asymmetrically powerful political and economic interests of creditors. Some experts have been critical of the interim lack of transparency.[55] For example, the countries most affected by this framework (e.g., the debtors) and most vulnerable to a "lost decade of development" are not included in these negotiations. Likely, powerful actors (e.g., the IMF, World Bank, and G20) will not reform traditional debt restructuring at the expense of excluded countries most plagued by the status quo framework's inimical effects.[56]

More crucially, other current programs such as the IMF's Catastrophe Containment and Relief Trust (CCRT) do not adequately address the structural problems inherent to contemporary debt restructuring and relief initiatives. Instead, these initiatives repeat historical mistakes in placing the burden of adjustment more squarely on borrowers without redressing the moral hazards that perpetuate bad lending on the creditor's side. While the DSSI and previous debt relief programs have actively solicited creditor cooperation, with innovative options such as green debt swaps and buyouts to encourage action on climate change, private creditors are rarely forced to realize the risks of their behavior. They are the first to be "bailed out" when countries receive debt relief, as emerging and developing country economies are eager to maintain critical credit ratings and access international credit markets.[57] As a result, private sector cooperation in the DSSI and other debt relief programs has been slow, uneven, and only on a voluntary basis. This problem grows as the overall percentage of private sector debt grows relative to public sector debt offered via multilateral and bilateral sovereign channels. In 2018 alone, EMDEs (excluding China) had a collective external debt of $5.9 trillion, of which $2.1 trillion was in private sector debt (e.g., loans from commercial banks) and $1.7 billion in public sector debt to private creditors (e.g., bondholders).[58] Debt relief or restructuring programs without full buy-in from private creditors are unlikely to succeed and may even exacerbate the crisis if debt relief stimulates developing countries' sale of new high-yield sovereign bonds to private creditors or, worse, triggers a new round of private capital flight.

Moreover, unlike past debt crises, today's overwhelming balance of bilateral debt held by these countries is owed to China, which has largely eschewed multilateral debt relief in favor of direct negotiations about bilateral debt agreements.[59] In June 2020, China suspended some debt repayments for 77 countries, and President Xi pledged to provide $2 billion over the next two years to aid developing countries in responding to the COVID-19 crises within their borders.[60] However, many critics point out that China primarily offers debt relief in the form of cancellation of zero-interest loans or loans that were already in default.[61] These loans only represent a small portion of China's aid. This inadequate form of debt relief may leave many developing countries (especially those participating in the Belt and Road Initiative, BRI) still responsible for existing and new non-concessional loans – a form of "debt trap" diplomacy that may exacerbate, rather than alleviate, the looming debt crisis.[62] At the same time, as Carol Wise argues, many of China's recent interactions on debt renegotiations have resulted in debt write-offs, deferments, and refinancing. As a result, "with no conditionality, China has little choice but to work with its debtors, some of which have drawn China into a creditor trap."[63]

Overall, an effective global response to the pandemic will require a well-coordinated and ambitious effort by multilateral and private sector donors. These actors must quickly offer debt relief and suspension packages on conditions that do not undermine the ability of borrowing countries to service existing debt. More critically, debt programs need to enable countries to attract new sources of capital, which allows them to reallocate financial resources to address the immediate public health crisis. In the long term, aid and global finance for development more broadly need to be reimagined to avoid the inevitable debt traps that we have seen repeatedly in history. Without such steps, the developing world is not just going to suffer from the lost decade of development. They are likely to be living with the consequence of the COVID-19 crisis for decades to come.

The future of global development aid?

This analysis provokes three immediate observations about weaknesses in the current governance of development and humanitarian assistance and how this informs our two big takeaways about the future of aid. The first observation is that the COVID-19 crisis highlights the challenges and opportunities posed by an increasingly fragmented system of institutions and actors. We see fragmentation to include the proliferation of formal and often competing institutions providing development finance (including non-governmental and private sector actors), coupled with a loss of centralization or focality in aid governance. Only about 30 percent of ODA is disbursed multilaterally.[64] Potentially, lower transaction costs and greater political ease motivate donors to channel their resources through decentralized, bilateral systems or non-traditional relationships.[65] This has been most strongly evident in the rise of new emerging donors such as China and related trends in "South-South cooperation."[66] Yet it also includes the growing share of private and non-profit investments in development financing. In 2016, Development Initiatives found that private development assistance is equivalent to over a quarter of ODA.[67]

Normatively speaking, in normal times, system fragmentation and decentralization may not necessarily be bad with respect to the legitimacy and effectiveness of the system. Such contested multilateralism may spur a healthy diversity in ideas and usher in a new age of choice that creates critical and long-desired policy space for aid recipients.[68] Competition may also eventually provide the necessary stimulus for deeper institutional reform, especially with a rebalancing of voice and votes between rising and waning powers in the Bretton Woods institutions (BWIs).

In the meantime, as revealed in the previous discussion of COVID-19 and the looming debt crisis, aid governance during crises can be a different beast. As Nancy Birdsall, former president of the Center for Global Development, argues, "the coronavirus is the poster child for the need for global cooperation."[69] Yet, how well does the current system of aid governance work to quickly resolve collective action problems and achieve needed cooperation in times of crisis? Rapid, coordinated responses are both more necessary and more difficult with the diffusion of power and the plurality of voices and interests, in addition to the growing number of influential actors from the private and non-governmental sectors who do not have formal seats at the table in forums like the G20. When and if consensus is reached and commitments are made, can decisions be implemented in a timely and effective manner?

The second observation is that the aid governance system continues to suffer from a debilitating lack of transparency which, in turn, inhibits aid accountability and our ability to measure aid effectiveness. Aid transparency has been a major focus of development and humanitarian reform for over a decade. Yet today, despite significant improvement in donor data reporting via efforts such as the International Aid Transparency Initiative and the Grand Bargain for humanitarianism, we still lack the means to collect and report critical information on sectoral and geographical allocation or COVID-19 funds. Only at the end of 2020, for instance, nearly eight months after the WHO declared the novel coronavirus a pandemic, has data on aid reached a consistent and timely critical mass, according to analysis by Development Initiatives.[70] Prior to the pandemic, reports argued that the quality, timeliness, and granularity of data needed to be addressed to be usable at the global level – demonstrating the need for more support and participation within the Grand Bargain transparency work-stream.[71] Amplifying the importance of transparency and global aid governance, resources previously devoted to collecting data on gender and food security have disappeared, as funds have been diverted to other COVID-19 programs. As a consequence, the information to better understand and redress COVID-19's impact on these sectors is directly undermined by the absence of robust data.

The third observation, related to the fragmentation and the lack of transparency, is that the aid system as a whole is increasingly struggling to sustain commitment to, and financial investments in, development and humanitarian aid. Aid fatigue is real, as is evident in data on declining and stagnating donor aid commitments. Moreover, aid skepticism is in many ways rightly justified when we consider concerns about the development aid system and the dangers of aid dependency. Yet now is not the time for major donor countries to turn away their global responsibilities any more than the middle of a pandemic is the moment to discuss the overdue reform of the WHO. Nonetheless, this is exactly what we have seen, as donor countries turn inward out of a sense of economic necessity but also out of political necessity in an age of waning domestic support for foreign aid and rising ethno-nationalism.[72]

This is not a surprising observation. Always subject to tensions between self-interest and altruism, the aid system as a whole is always vulnerable to the ebb and flow of major donor support. Today, the system lacks resilience because of its dependence on outdated multilateral and bilateral government-based funding models, something that many experts have illuminated in calling for the diversification away from government-sponsored to domestic resource mobilization, the greater role of philanthropic groups and non-governmental organization (NGOs), and even, in some cases, the privatization of aid.

Aid as a percent of overall development finance is rapidly shrinking, with foreign direct investment (FDI) and remittances accounting, respectively, for 41 percent and 33 percent of financial flows to developing countries versus only 15 percent by ODA specifically.[73] Hence, our thinking about governance of development finance must adjust to a new reality where non-state actors will have much more voice and influence. This challenge is aptly captured in the earlier discussion of COVID-19 and the looming debt crisis, which exemplifies politics and need for cooperation among multilateral, bilateral, and private sectors sources of development finance.

Conclusion

Overall, these observations reify our general belief that aid governance needs to become more inclusive and focused on system effectiveness and resilience for a vastly different twenty-first century. To this end, we offer two bold prescriptions for the future of aid.

The first is "Go Global." The assessment of aid in the COVID-19 era reinforces our view that aid governed primarily through state-led bilateral and multilateral frameworks is outdated and ineffective. We need to rethink global aid governance to acknowledge just how different the world of 2020 is from the world of 1945 or 1995 or even 2015. The global order has changed, and not solely in terms of the balance of power between states but also in terms of the balance of power and influence between states and non-state actors. Rethinking global aid governance requires looking beyond the accommodation of such rising state powers as China and toward the inclusion of increasingly important voices from civil society and the for-profit private sector. Continued reliance on exclusive, state-centric decision-making forums such as the G20 is precarious at best. They may even reinforce the very weaknesses in the global development system by reinforcing the interests and ideas of status quo powers.

So, our recommendation to "Go Global" coincides with contemporary arguments that we need to move away from thinking about governance through a lens of *international* development to a framework based on *global* development.[74] In practical terms, this entails investing more in global public funds that are designed to deal with cross-border issues, nimbler in funding disbursements, and better able to work directly with partners on the ground rather than multiple layers of sovereign hierarchies.

The second prescription is "Go Local." The pandemic – perhaps more than any other global crisis that preceded it – demonstrates the need to localize aid governance and practice.[75] COVID-19 is an external threat to existing development practices that prioritize the work of researchers and practitioners in the Global North over local experts in the Global South.[76] At the same time, by introducing an exogenous shock that leads to the removal of expatriate aid workers in many developing areas, the COVID-19 era drives decision-makers to acknowledge not just the value, but also the necessity, of truly locally driven aid implementation and oversight.

This localization agenda also reflects a collective desire to decolonize aid and create the aforementioned "policy space" for alternative theories and approaches to development; they would be based not on "first developer" Western historical experiences but on the varied contexts of developing countries.[77] This is entirely consistent with the espoused goal of numerous high-level forums on aid effectiveness, including the commitment to more borrower "ownership" in development expressed in the 2005 Paris Agreement and the 2008 Accra Agenda,[78] and more tolerance for deviation from Western models of development. More generally, going local means flipping the approach away from top-down, elite-driven processes and blueprint approaches to development. This "new normal"[79] is an opportunity to move vigorously toward localization[80] and alternative use of aid by recipients in the Global South. Moreover, going local has the potential to renew global aid governance in inclusive and effective ways that will help the system recapture its legitimacy, relevance, and effectiveness.

Suggested readings

Romily Greenhill, Annalisa Prizzon, and Andrew Rogerson, "The Age of Choice: Developing Countries in the New Aid Landscape," *ODI Working Paper* 364, Overseas Development Institute, 2013.

Rebecca M. Nelson and Martin A. Weiss, *COVID-19: Role of the International Financial Institutions* (Washington, DC: Congressional Research Service, May 4, 2020).

UN Inter-agency Task Force on Financing for Development, *Financing for Sustainable Development Report 2020* (New York: UN, 2020).

Jakob Vestergaard and Robert Wade, "Protecting Power: How Western States Retain the Dominant Voice in the World Bank's Governance," *World Development* 46 (2013): 153–164.

Carol Wise, *Dragonomics: How Latin America Is Maximizing (or Missing Out on) China's International Development Strategy* (New Haven, CT: Yale University Press, 2020).

Notes

1 Daniel Drezner, *The System Worked: How the World Stopped Another Great Depression* (Oxford: Oxford University Press, 2016).

2 Ngaire Woods, "Global Governance After the Financial Crisis: A New Multilateralism or the Last Gasp of the Great Powers?" *Global Policy* 1 (January 2010): 51–63, DOI:10.1111/j.1758–5899.2009.00013.x; and Manuella Moschella and Catherine Weaver, eds., *Handbook of Global Economic Governance* (London: Routledge, 2014).

3 Jakob Vestergaard and Robert Wade, "Protecting Power: How Western States Retain the Dominant Voice in the World Bank's Governance," *World Development* 46 (June 2013): 153–164, DOI:10.1016/j.worlddev.2013.01.031; Rob Clark, "Quotas Operandi: Examining the Distribution of Voting Power at the IMF and World Bank," *The Sociological Quarterly* 58 (August 2017): 595–621, DOI:10.1080/00380253.2017.1354735; and Catherine Weaver and Manuella Moschella, "Bounded Reform in Global Economic Governance at the IMF and World Bank," in *International Politics and Institutions in Time*, ed. Orfeo Fioretos (Oxford: Oxford University Press, 2017), chapter 13.

4 See "COVID-19 Dashboard by the Center for Systems Science and Engineering (CSSE) at Johns Hopkins University," https://coronavirus.jhu.edu/map.html

5 "The Great Reversal," *The Economist*, 23 May 2020, www.economist.com/international/2020/05/23/covid-19-is-undoing-years-of-progress-in-curbing-global-poverty.

6 Andy Harman, *ILO Warns of Massive Unemployment* (Bonn: Deutsche Welle, 2020), www.dw.com/en/ilo-warns-of-massive-unemployment/av-53286327; and *From the Great Lockdown to the Great Meltdown: Developing Country Debt in the Time of Covid-19* (United Nations Conference on Trade and Development [UNCTAD] document UNCTAD/GDS/INF/2020/3), 23 April 2020.

7 Colm Quinn, "Coronavirus Disproportionately Affects Health Workers: Here Are the Countries Most at Risk," *Foreign Policy*, 4 May 2020, https://foreignpolicy.com/2020/05/04/coronavirus-disproportionately-affects-health-workers-here-are-the-countries-most-at-risk/.

8 Ruth Maclean and Simon Marks, "10 African Countries Have No Ventilators: That's Only Part of the Problem," *The New York Times*, 17 May 2020.

9 "The Shadow Pandemic: Violence Against Women During COVID-19," *UN Women*, www.unwomen.org/news/in-focus/in-focus-gender-equality-in-covid-19-response/violence-against-women-during-covid-19.

10 Andrew M. Campbell, "An Increasing Risk of Family Violence During the Covid-19 Pandemic: Strengthening Community Collaborations to Save Lives," *Forensic Science International: Reports* 2 (December 2020): 100089, DOI:10.1016/j.fsir.2020.100089.

11 Caroline Bradbury-Jones and Louise Isham, "The Pandemic Paradox: The Consequences of COVID-19 on Domestic Violence," *Journal of Clinical Nursing* 29 (April 2020): 2047–2049, DOI:10.1111/jocn.15296; and Emma Graham-Harrison, Angela Giuffrida, Helena Smith, and Liz Ford, "Lockdowns Around the World Bring Rise in Domestic Violence," *The Guardian*, 28 March 2020.

12 Graham-Harrison, Giuffrida, Smith, and Ford, "Lockdowns Around the World Bring Rise in Domestic Violence."

13 UN Women, "Access to Justice and Gender-Based Violence," *Gender Alert on COVID-19 in Lebanon*, 3 June 2020, https://arabstates.unwomen.org/en/digital-library/publications/2020/04/gender-alert-on-covid-19-lebanon.

14 Elisabeth Mahase, "Covid-19: EU States Report 60% Rise in Emergency Calls About Domestic Violence," *British Medical Journal* 369 (May 2020), DOI:10.1136/bmj.m1872.

15 UN, "Transforming Our World: The 2030 Agenda for Sustainable Development," UN General Assembly Resolution 70/1, 21 October 2015. UN, *The Sustainable Development Goals Report 2020* (New York: UN, 2020), https://doi.org/10.18356/214e6642-en.

16 "Will the COVID-19 Pandemic Threaten the SDGs?," *The Lancet Public Health* 5 (September 2020): e460, DOI:10.1016/S2468–2667(20)30189–4.

17 "The Food Miracle," *The Economist*, 9 May 2020, www.economist.com/leaders/2020/05/09/the-global-food-supply-chain-is-passing-a-severe-test; and Peter S. Goodman, Abdi Latif Dahir, and Karan Deep Singh, "The Other Way COVID Will Kill: Hunger," *The New York Times*, 14 September 2020.

18 *COVID-19 L3 Emergency, External Situation Report #13* (Rome: WFP, 2020), https://reliefweb.int/report/world/covid-19-l3-emergency-external-situation-report-13-20-august-2020.

19 UN, *The Impact of COVID-19 on Children* (New York: UN, 2020), www.un.org/sites/un2.un.org/files/policy_brief_on_covid_impact_on_children_16_april_2020.pdf.

20 Henrietta H. Fore et al., "Child Malnutrition and COVID-19: The Time to Act Is Now," *The Lancet* 396 (July 2020): 517–518, DOI:10.1016/S0140-6736(20)31648-2.

21 UN, *The Sustainable Development Goals Report 2020*.

22 *COVID-19 and School Closures: Are Children Able to Continue Learning?* (New York: UNICEF, 2020), https://data.unicef.org/resources/remote-learning-reachability-factsheet/.

23 Emma Batha, "'COVID Generation' Risks Child Marriage, Forced Labour, Ex-Leaders Warn," *Reuters*, 17 August 2020, www.reuters.com/article/us-health-coronavirus-education-childlab-idUSKCN25D2P3.

24 UN, *The Sustainable Development Goals Report 2020*.

25 See Stephen Browne and Thomas G. Weiss, eds., *Routledge Handbook on the UN and Development* (London: Routledge, 2021).

26 UNDP, *What Does It Mean to Leave No One Behind?* (New York: UNDP, 2018), www.undp.org/content/dam/undp/library/Sustainable%20Development/2030%20Agenda/Discussion_Paper_LNOB_EN_lres.pdf.

27 G20, "Extraordinary G20 Leaders' Summit Statement on COVID-19," *Communiqué*, 26 March 2020.

28 Amy Dodd, Dean Breed, and Daniel Coppard, *How Is Aid Changing in the Covid-19 Pandemic?* (Bristol: Development Initiatives, 2020), https://devinit.org/resources/how-aid-changing-covid-19-pandemic/.

29 *COVID-19 and Child, Early and Forced Marriage: An Agenda for Action* (London: Girls Not Brides, 2020), https://beta.girlsnotbrides.org/learning-resources/resource-centre/covid-19-and-child-early-and-forced-marriage-an-agenda-for-action/.

30 "COVID-19: Lockdown Linked to High Number of Unintended Teen Pregnancies in Kenya," *Plan International*, 25 June 2020, https://plan-international.org/news/2020-06-25-covid-19-lockdown-linked-high-number-unintended-teen-pregnancies-kenya.

31 UNFPA, *Impact of the COVID-19 Pandemic on Family Planning and Ending Gender-Based Violence, Female Genital Mutilation and Child Marriage* (New York: UNFPA, 2020), www.unfpa.org/resources/impact-covid-19-pandemic-family-planning-and-ending-gender-based-violence-female-genital.

32 *COVID-19 Aftershocks: Access Denied* (Uxbridge: World Vision International, 2020), www.wvi.org/publications/report/coronavirus-health-crisis/covid-19-aftershocks-access-denied.

33 Amy Lieberman, "COVID-19 Will Push 130 Million into Poverty by 2030, UN Report Shows," *Devex*, 14 May 2020, www.devex.com/news/sponsored/covid-19-will-push-130-million-into-poverty-by-2030-un-report-shows-97232; Andy Sumner, Chris Hoy, and Eduardo Ortiz-Juarez, "Estimates of the Impact of Covid-19 on Global Poverty," *WIDER Working Paper* 2020/43, UNU-WIDER, Helsinki, 2020; Andy Sumner, Chris Hoy, and Eduardo Ortiz-Juarez, "Will COVID-19 Lead to Half a Billion More People Living in Poverty in Developing Countries?" *WiderAngle* (blog), 3 April 2020, www.wider.unu.edu/publication/will-covid-19-lead-half-billion-more-people-living-poverty-developing-countries; and David Laborde, Will Martin, and Rob Vos, "Estimating the Poverty Impact of COVID-19 the MIRAGRODEP and POVANA Frameworks 1," June 2020, DOI:10.13140/RG.2.2.36562.58560.

34 Masoon Ahmed, "Act Now to Preserve Development Gains in a Post-COVID World," *Center for Global Development* (blog), 14 September 2020, www.cgdev.org/blog/act-now-preserve-development-gains-post-covid-world; Nurith Aizenman, "Gates Foundation Says World Not on Track to Meet Goal of Ending Poverty by 2030," *NPR*, 17 September 2019, www.npr.org/sections/goatsandsoda/2019/09/17/761548939/gates-foundation-says-world-not-on-track-to-meet-goal-of-ending-poverty-by-2030; and UN Department of Economic and Social Affairs (DESA), *Achieving the SDGs Through the COVID-19 Response and Recovery* (New York: UN/DESA, 2020), www.un.org/development/desa/dpad/publication/un-desa-policy-brief-78-achieving-the-sdgs-through-the-covid-19-response-and-recovery/.

35 Kevin Watkins, "Can We Avoid a Lost Decade of Development?," *Future Development* (blog), 9 July 2020, www.brookings.edu/blog/future-development/2020/07/09/can-we-avoid-a-lost-decade-of-development/.

36 UN/DESA, *2020 Financing for Sustainable Development Report* (New York: UN/DESA, 2020), https://developmentfinance.un.org/fsdr2020.

37 Kristalina Georgieva, Ceyla Pazarbasioglu, and Rhoda Weeks-Brown, "Reform of the International Debt Architecture Is Urgently Needed," *IMF Blog* (blog), 1 October 2020, https://blogs.imf.org/2020/10/01/reform-of-the-international-debt-architecture-is-urgently-needed/.

38 Rabah Arezki and Shanta Devarajan, "Fiscal Policy for COVID-19 and Beyond," *Future Development* (blog), 29 May 2020, www.brookings.edu/blog/future-development/2020/05/29/fiscal-policy-for-covid-19-and-beyond/; *COVID-19 and Sovereign Debt* (New York: UN/DESA, 2020), www.un.org/development/desa/dpad/publication/un-desa-policy-brief-72-covid-19-and-sovereign-debt/; and Amy Dodd, Rob Tew, and Anna Hope, *Covid-19 and Financing Projections for Developing Countries* (Bristol: Development Initiatives, 2020), https://devinit.org/publications/covid-19-and-financing-projections-developing-countries/.

39 Alexander Kentikelenis et al., "Softening the Blow of the Pandemic: Will the International Monetary Fund and World Bank Make Things Worse?," *The Lancet Global Health* 8 (April 2020): e758–759, DOI:10.1016/S2214-109X(20)30135-2.

40 Moses Owori, *Socioeconomic Impact of Covid-19 in Uganda: How Has the Government Allocated Public Expenditure for FY2020/21?* (Bristol: Development Initiatives, 2020), https://devinit.org/resources/socioeconomic-impact-of-covid-19-in-uganda/.

41 Jim Campbell et al., *A Universal Truth: No Health Without a Workforce* (Geneva: Global Health Workforce and WHO, 2013), www.who.int/workforcealliance/knowledge/resources/GHWA_AUniversalTruthReport.pdf.

42 "Nursing and Midwifery," *WHO*, 9 January 2020, www.who.int/news-room/fact-sheets/detail/nursing-and-midwifery.

43 Watkins, "Can We Avoid?"

44 Eliza Relman and John Haltiwanger, "Trump Announces He's 'Terminating' the US's Relationship with the World Health Organization," *Business Insider*, 29 May 2020, www.businessinsider.com/trump-says-hes-terminating-us-relationship-with-world-health-organization-2020–5.

45 "UN Calls for Comprehensive Debt Standstill in All Developing Countries," *UNDP*, 15 October 2020, www.undp.org/content/undp/en/home/news-centre/news/2020/UN_calls_comprehensive_debt_standstill_developing_countries.html.

46 UN/DESA, *2020 Financing for Sustainable Development Report.*

47 Mickaël Sallent, "External Debt Complicates Africa's COVID-19 Recovery, Debt Relief Needed," *Africa Renewal*, 30 July 2020, www.un.org/africarenewal/magazine/july-2020/external-debt-complicates-africas-post-covid-19-recovery-mitigating-efforts.

48 Rebecca M. Nelson and Martin A. Weiss, *COVID-19: Role of the International Financial Institutions* (Washington, DC: Congressional Research Service, 2020), https://crsreports.congress.gov/product/pdf/R/R46342#:~:text=The%20international%20financial%20institutions%20(IFIs,economic%20consequences%20of%20the%20COVID%2D.

49 Stephanie Segal and Olivia Negus, "International Financial Institutions' Ongoing Response to the Covid-19 Crisis," *Center for Strategic International Studies*, 24 August 2020, www.csis.org/analysis/international-financial-institutions-ongoing-response-covid-19-crisis.

50 Thomas Stubbs et al., "Whatever It Takes? The Global Financial Safety Net, Covid-19, and Developing Countries," *World Development* 137 (January 2021): 105171, DOI:10.1016/j.worlddev.2020.105171.

51 Nancy Lee et al., "Calling All Official Bilateral Creditors to Poor Countries: Switch to IDA Concessional Terms as Part of COVID-19 Response," *Center For Global Development* (blog), 8 April 2020, www.cgdev.org/blog/calling-all-official-bilateral-creditors-poor-countries-switch-ida-concessional-terms-part; and Sallent, "External Debt Complicates Africa's COVID-19 Recovery, Debt Relief Needed."

52 Jevans Nyabiage, "Coronavirus: China Under Pressure to Detail Debt Relief Before G20 Talks," *South China Morning Post*, 22 August 2020, www.scmp.com/news/china/diplomacy/article/3098431/coronavirus-china-under-pressure-detail-debt-relief-g20-talks.

53 Vasuki Shastry and Jeremy Mark, "Credit Rating Agencies Could Resolve African Debt Impasse," *Atlantic Council* (blog), 8 September 2020, www.atlanticcouncil.org/blogs/new-atlanticist/credit-rating-agencies-could-resolve-african-debt-impasse/.

54 G20, "G20 Finance Ministers & Central Bank Governors Meeting 14 October 2020," *Communiqué*, 14 October 2020.

55 Daniel Munevar, "The G20 'Common Framework for Debt Treatments Beyond the DSSI': Is It Bound to Fail? Part 1," *Eurodad* (blog), 22 October 2020, www.eurodad.org/the_g20_common_framework_for_debt_treatments_beyond_the_dssi_is_it_bound_to_fail.

56 Daniel Munevar, "The G20 'Common Framework for Debt Treatments Beyond the DSSI': Is It Bound to Fail? (II)," *Eurodad* (blog), 28 October 2020, www.eurodad.org/the_g20_common_framework_for_debt_treatments_beyond_the_dssi_is_it_bound_to_fail_2.

57 Marc Jones, "Debt Relief for Poorest Countries Will Not Penalise MDB's 'Preferred Creditor' Status -Moody's," *Reuters*, 14 May 2020, www.reuters.com/article/health-coronavirus-developmentbanks-idUSL8N2CW7PQ.

58 Patrick Bolton et al., *Born Out of Necessity: A Debt Standstill for COVID-19* (Washington, DC: Center for Economic Policy Research, 2020), https://papers.ssrn.com/sol3/papers.cfm?abstract_id=3586785.

59 Nyabiage, "Coronavirus."

60 "China Announces Suspension of Debt Repayments for 77 Developing Nations Due to COVID-19," *China Banking News*, 8 June 2020, www.chinabankingnews.com/2020/06/08/china-announces-suspension-of-debt-repayments-for-77-developing-nations-due-to-covid-19/.

61 Jevans Nyabiage, "China's Loan Write-Offs 'Does Not Fix Africa's Bigger Debt Crisis,'" *South China Morning Post*, 20 June 2020, www.scmp.com/news/china/diplomacy/article/3089856/chinas-promise-loan-write-offs-distressed-african-nations; and Mercy A. Kuo, "COVID-19: The Impact on China-Africa Debt," *The Diplomat*, 2 June 2020, https://thediplomat.com/2020/06/covid-19-the-impact-on-china-africa-debt/.

62 Yun Sun, "China's Debt Relief for Africa: Emerging Deliberations," *Africa in Focus* (blog), 9 June 2020, www.brookings.edu/blog/africa-in-focus/2020/06/09/chinas-debt-relief-for-africa-emerging-deliberations/.

63 Carol Wise, *Dragonomics: How Latin America Is Maximizing (or Missing Out on) China's International Development Strategy* (New Haven, CT: Yale University Press, 2020), 13.

64 Pierre E. Biscaye, Travis W. Reynolds, and C. Leigh Anderson, "Relative Effectiveness of Bilateral and Multilateral Aid on Development Outcomes," *Review of Development Economics* 21 (November 2016): 1425–1447, DOI:10.1111/rode.12303.

65 Homi Kharas, "What to Do About the Coming Debt Crisis in Developing Countries," *Future Development* (blog), 13 April 2020, www.brookings.edu/blog/future-development/2020/04/13/what-to-do-about-the-coming-debt-crisis-in-developing-countries/.

66 Allen S. Alexandroff and Andrew F. Cooper, eds., *Rising States, Rising Institutions: Challenges for Global Governance* (Washington, DC and Waterloo, CA: Brookings Institution and CIGI, 2010); and see also www.unsouthsouth.org/about/about-sstc/.

67 "Private Development Assistance: Key Facts and Global Estimates," *Development Initiatives*, 15 August 2016, https://devinit.org/resources/private-development-assistance-key-facts-and-global-estimates/.

68 Julia Morse and Robert O. Keohane, "Contested Multilateralism," *Review of International Organizations* (March 2014): 385–412, DOI:10.1007/s11558-014-9188-2; Diego Hernandez, "Are 'New' Donors Challenging World Bank Conditionality?" *World Development* 96 (August 2017): 529–549; Ilene Grabel, *Financial Architectures and Development: Resilience, Policy Space, and Human Development in the Global South* (Amherst: Political Economy Research Institute, 2012), www.peri.umass.edu/fileadmin/pdf/working_papers/working_papers_251-300/WP281_revised.pdf; Homi Kharas and Andrew Rogerson, *Global Development Trends and Challenges: Horizon 2025 Revisited* (London: Overseas Development Initiatives, 2017), www.odi.org/sites/odi.org.uk/files/resource-documents/11873.pdf; Romilly Greenhill, Annalisa Prizzon, and Andrew Rogerson, *The Age of Choice: Developing Countries in the New Aid Landscape* (London: Overseas Development Initiatives, 2013), www.odi.org/sites/odi.org.uk/files/odi-assets/publications-opinion-files/8188.pdf; and Chris Humphrey and Katharina Michaelowa, "Shopping for Development: Multilateral Lending, Shareholder Composition and Borrower Preferences," *World Development* (April 2013): 142–155, DOI:10.1016/j.worlddev.2012.12.007.

69 Nancy Birdsall, Karen Greenberg, and John Berger, "Resilience in Developing Nations," *Center For Global Development* (blog), 8 June 2020, www.cgdev.org/blog/resilience-developing-nations.

70 Amy Dodd, Dean Breed, and Daniel Coppard, *How Is Aid Changing in the Covid-19 Pandemic?* (Bristol: Development Initiatives, 2020), https://devinit.org/resources/how-aid-changing-covid-19-pandemic/.

71 Ibid.

72 Yoshirharu Kobayashi, Tobias Heinrich, and Kristin Bryant, "Public Support for Development Aid During the COVID Pandemic," *World Development* 138 (October 2020): 105248, DOI:10.1016/j.worlddev.2020.105248.

73 OECD, "Big Picture of Total Receipts by Year," *Tableua Data Visualization*, 2020, available at https://public.tableau.com/views/Bigpictureoftotalresourcereceiptsbyyear/Byyear?:embed=y&:display_count=yes&publish=yes&:showVizHome=no#1.

74 Johan A. Oldekop et al., "COVID-19 and the Case for Global Development," *World Development* 134 (June 2020): 105044, DOI:10.1016/j.worlddev.2020.105044.

75 Lisa Cornish, "Putting Localization at the Center of the Humanitarian Future," *DevEx*, 31 May 2019, www.devex.com/news/putting-localization-at-the-center-of-the-humanitarian-future-94997

76 Carmen Leon-Himmelstine and Melanie Pinet, "How Can Covid-19 Be the Catalyst to Decolonise Development Research?," *From Poverty to Power* (blog), 4 June 2020, https://oxfamblogs.org/fp2p/how-can-covid-19-be-the-catalyst-to-decolonise-development-research/.

77 Dani Rodrik, *The Globalization Paradox: Democracy and the Future of the World Economy* (New York: W.W. Norton, 2011).

78 The Paris Accords resulted from the Second High Level Forum on Aid Effectiveness (2005) and the Accra Agenda for Action resulted from the Third High Level Forum on Aid Effectiveness. For further information, see www.oecd.org/dac/effectiveness/

parisdeclarationandaccraagendaforaction.htm#:~:text=At%20the%20Second%20 High%20Level,does%20not%20work%20with%20aid.

79 "A New Normal: UN Lays Out Roadmap to Lift Economies and Save Jobs After COVID-19 – World," *ReliefWeb*, 27 April 2020, https://reliefweb.int/report/world/ new-normal-un-lays-out-roadmap-lift-economies-and-save-jobs-after-covid-19.

80 John Bryant, "All Eyes Are on Local Humanitarian Responders During Covid-19 – Now They Need Support," *Overseas Development Institute* (blog), 29 May 2020, www.odi.org/ blogs/16998-all-eyes-are-local-humanitarian-responders-during-covid-19-now-they-need-support.

CONTENTS

Data

Global governance challenges

Madeline Carr and Jose Tomas Llanos

As we embark upon the Fourth Industrial Revolution, many questions arise that reflect the social, political, cultural, and economic implications of the first (steam power) and second (electricity) industrial revolutions. While many of the changes and achievements that emerged from those two technological bursts of innovation have been positive, there have also been negative consequences such as environmental degradation, resource depletion, and social fragmentation. With hindsight, we may have made different decisions about how to manage the shift from agrarian to industrial labor, about the responsibility and accountability of industrialists, and about urban planning and transport systems. Over the period following the first two industrial revolutions, successive generations of scholars and analysts have had time to study these unintended consequences – both positive and negative. Building on this work, we are well placed to think through how to avoid the worst and maximize the best outcomes of digital technologies as we leave the Third Industrial Revolution (digital technologies like the Internet) and embark upon the Fourth (the Internet of Things, IoT).

Data are the essential ingredient of many emerging technologies and systems like artificial intelligence, machine learning, and the IoT. It is increasingly common to hear data referred to as the "new oil," and certainly it will be fundamental to many aspects of our future economy – directly or indirectly. We are only at the very beginning of thinking through how to govern data locally and globally.

DOI: 10.4324/9781003139836-21

If we get this right, there is huge potential to use data flows to improve the human condition and implement sustainable, healthy, and equitable frameworks that will allow us to maximize the full benefit of this transformative period while mitigating common and differentiated threats. Indeed, an approach to data governance that unlocks this potential will be a central challenge of our time. But it is, in many ways, new territory, and the road map is humanity's to make.

This chapter explores the tensions in efforts to balance competing interests and values when it comes to data and its (global) governance. It argues that the challenges of getting data governance right may well be a catalyst for much-needed innovation in the global governance of digital technologies more broadly. The following pages outline three main, high-level approaches to governing personally identifiable data that have emerged over the past two decades: a US approach of governance by and for the private sector; a Chinese approach based on governing through data; and a European Union (EU) approach that promotes a global governance role based on the protection of human rights. But first, it is useful to lay out some of the reasons why data (and its governance) are of such significance.

The significance of data flows

The global governance of digital technologies is too complex to discuss as a coherent process or system. Digital technologies are controlled and managed at local, national, and international levels through markets, regulatory and legislative frameworks, technical standards, voluntary codes of conduct, trade agreements, international treaties, manufacturing supply chains, and other mechanisms. The actors involved in these governance practices are diverse and varied and range well beyond governments, industry, and the policy community. Focusing on data governance helps us narrow the scope of the problem while also encompassing these diverse factors.

One class of data raises unique governance complexities. Personally identifiable – or personal – data forges a very direct link among corporate actors that typically collect and use this data, governments that both draw benefit from that data and are also responsible for protecting citizens from harm, the individuals who produce the data, and those that attempt to acquire data for nefarious purposes. From the macro to the micro, personally identifiable data blends a growing global economic sector with deeply personal preferences about identity, privacy, safety, and security – for the assurance of which, we typically look to governments. Tolerance for the collection, use, and reuse of personal data is not homogenous and varies widely among individuals, which complicates governance in a way that balances competing (and sometimes conflicting) interests and values among relevant actors. There are a number of factors that make the governance of data a challenge.

First, we are seeing a huge increase in the volume of data. The growth of systems like the IoT, smart cities, connected infrastructure, and consumer devices that collect and share data has been dramatic over the last five years and will continue to increase. The World Economic Forum (WEF), for instance, has predicted that the global volume of data will double between 2018 and 2022 and double again between 2022 and 2025.[1] There is a concentration of innovation and investment in how to maximize the potential of that data through analysis, security, and aggregation tools. But there is less attention paid to how to resolve the problems of ownership and use of that data in diverse political cultures.

Second, some of these data flows will be local, and others will be global. Some data can remain local and be locally governed, but too much localization can introduce complications for those who collect and use data across jurisdictional boundaries. Business systems need to be compliant with numerous frameworks that do not align. The WEF has identified more than 120 data privacy laws currently in place globally.[2] Interrupting the global supply chain for data by implementing conflicting regulatory frameworks can impede the benefits of sharing data or making it available to researchers, developers, and innovators. For example, urban planners could benefit from comparing traffic, footfall, and pollution levels in very different locations to test the outcomes of proposed initiatives in their own municipalities. How weather conditions combine with emissions from diesel- and gas-powered vehicles to affect people on bicycles who suffer from asthma can be studied globally and have very useful outcomes for global health.

Third, data need to have a high level of integrity. Data flows are becoming a new international critical infrastructure as the range of applications and systems that rely upon them grows. Consequently, assurances that the data flows have not been compromised or altered (accidentally or intentionally) will be necessary to ensuring safety, privacy, and security. The demands of access control, giving and obtaining consent, and verification of data flows all need to be managed by appropriate actors with a degree of legitimacy. Providing these assurances requires some form of governance – possibly through standards, guidelines, or regulation.

Data have an innate commercial value, they can be used to promote worldviews, they impact directly and tangentially on human rights, and they are developing into a global critical infrastructure upon which many systems rely. For all these reasons and more, data require governance and input from (among others) those policymakers responsible for ensuring the public interest – however that is perceived. Governing data is inherently political. While collecting, aggregating, sharing, and using data will continue to involve a wide range of actors, doing so in a sustainable way that accommodates a wide range of interests also requires government and governance.

Over the past few decades, we have seen the emergence of three main approaches to governing data that currently coexist alongside one another: (1) a US approach, (2) a Chinese approach, and (3) an EU approach. While they currently coexist, they do so promoting different interests and pursuing different goals.

The US approach: Individuals as data farms

Anti-governance narratives have dominated the last two decades of the digital revolution – predominantly in a deadlock between the United States and China. Building on Bill Clinton and Al Gore's early vision for how the Internet would enhance its power, the US approach to data governance privileges the interests of its own commercial sector above all else. This approach has led to huge growth, the emergence of a few wildly wealthy individuals, and a lack of investment in some critical future data technology (5G, for example). In this framework, human rights and public goods are portrayed as protected by the private sector against the ills of government. To some extent, this narrative was sharply underscored by the 2013 leakage of classified documents by former US National Security Agency (NSA) employee Edward Snowden, which revealed large-scale collection and use of data by the US government intelligence community – although the fact that the data were provided by the private sector was neatly tucked away. In reality, data collected by US data giants have not promoted human rights with any consistency and have not been intentionally directed toward solving global challenges like the Sustainable Development Goals (SDGs).

Since the first wave of mainstream computerization in the 1970s, the United States has implemented a market-driven policy for the protection of personal data (known in the US context as personally identifying information). This has featured a liberal, business-friendly data privacy regulatory framework composed of narrow sectoral laws focusing on specific industries and contexts where personal data are used.[3] Any regulatory gaps are filled with self-regulation: in the absence of statutory rights, the protection of privacy is left to industry standards, codes of conduct, terms of service, or contracts.[4] In this regard, data privacy is understood as a market issue rather than a fundamental rights concern, with individuals being "consumers" or "users" instead of citizens.

The US approach leads to fragmented and inconsistent data protection. For example, data held by an entity subject to the Health Information Portability and Accountability Act of 1996 (HIPPA) or by a school regulated by the Family Educational Rights and Privacy Act of 1974 (FERPA) are subject to different sets of rules, some more strict than others. If data do not fall within the scope of any of these laws or other sectoral rules, they may not be protected at all.[5] Moreover, the threshold for the application of privacy laws is lower than that seen in other leading data protection frameworks, such as the EU's General Data Protection Regulation (GDPR). US laws typically focus on actual identification of individuals; information pertaining to people who are not currently identified, yet may *allow* for identification, typically falls outside their scope.[6]

As a general rule, processing of personal information is allowed unless it causes legal harm or is otherwise restricted by laws.[7] Thus, the US approach gives companies significant freedom to experiment with new ways of data processing. This is particularly the case for tech companies that are free from regulation under a sectoral regime, as they face virtually no restriction on developing innovative methods and techniques that may increase efficiency and revenues but come at a high privacy cost for their consumers. Coupled with a "risk-taking culture,"[8] a lax data protection regime likely facilitated the birth, growth, and dominance of highly innovative data-driven platforms like Google, Amazon, Facebook, and Apple (collectively known as GAFA), along with Twitter, eBay, and Uber – and all have established a global presence.

The reach and data collection capabilities of US-based platforms made them irresistible targets of governments' requests to access data about their users in the context of law enforcement and national security investigations. The Snowden leak revealed a number of surveillance activities carried out by the US and UK governments in partnership with US platforms which involved bulk, ongoing, and sometimes real-time access to phone and Internet metadata, as well as to the content of communications,[9] raising substantial privacy concerns and causing public outcry.

Companies responded by publishing detailed reports about government demands for user data, seeking to enhance transparency and accountability in their data handling practices and show a true commitment to prevent privacy intrusions from governments.[10] Facebook, Google, LinkedIn, Microsoft, and Yahoo sued and reached a settlement in 2014 with the US Department of Justice (DoJ)[11] to be able to report meaningful information on national security–related requests for data, thus paving the way for transparency reforms in the USA Freedom Act of 2015. Companies like Twitter have implemented a policy to always request judicial review of non-disclosure or "gag" orders accompanying user data requests[12] – that is, government or court orders that prohibit request recipients from disclosing any information about the request – and Apple has consistently resisted demands from the US Federal Bureau of Investigation (FBI) to create a backdoor on iPhones to access data about suspects in law enforcement investigations.[13]

Thus, a market-driven privacy dichotomy characterizes the US approach: individuals have very few protections against commercial surveillance, but major online platforms deploy substantial efforts to ensure that they are not subject to governmental surveillance.

The combination of a poor data protection culture with the worldwide reach of major US-based platforms has had far-reaching ramifications both in the United States and worldwide. The imperative of maximizing "user engagement" at all costs and the data-driven philosophy which encourages data sharing and repurposing to extract hidden value has given major online platforms the power "to track, target and segment people into audiences that are highly susceptible to manipulation."[14]

Misuse of this power by third parties through the dissemination of "fake news" and the unlawful access and mining of personal data of millions of Facebook users by Cambridge Analytica to promote a political agenda enabled the exploitation of people's ideological biases to try to influence the 2016 US presidential election and the UK's EU referendum. Having attracted significant public and political discontent with their size, data handling practices, their role in elections, and need for stringent regulation, including privacy regulation, are becoming increasingly acknowledged in Washington. It is unclear, however, whether this regulatory momentum will materialize in anything concrete. In a bid to ward off regulations, Amazon, Apple, Facebook, and Google reportedly spent a combined $55 million on lobbying in 2018, more than doubling their combined spending in 2016.

In many developing countries with populations new to both democracy and social media, fake stories can also be widely believed. And in some of these countries, Facebook exercises significant control over the information infrastructure by offering free smartphone data connections to basic public online services, some news sites, and Facebook itself but limiting access to broader sources that could help debunk fake news. One such place is the Philippines, where a spokes-man for its populist president, Rodrigo Duterte, shared on Facebook an image of a corpse of a young girl believed to have been raped and killed by a drug dealer. Fact checkers later revealed that the photo had come from Brazil. Despite the debunking, proponents of Duterte's bloody crackdown on reported drug dealers and addicts still cite the image in his defense.[15]

The key players in the US data governance framework include market actors (particularly big tech companies) and the US government. While there are tensions between these actors, they essentially drive toward the same goal: mass data col-lection for economic growth of the US private sector and continued global market dominance. These governance arrangements rely on individuals within and beyond the US territory being "farmed" for data to fuel this growth. These are the "invisibly governed" – they do not participate in the commercial transaction arising from their data, and they have little scope to opt out given the prevalence of these systems. Power is concentrated in the hands of a small number of individuals and their com-panies that have amassed unprecedented wealth and have, thus far, skirted between regulatory frameworks that would otherwise extract the public benefits of this (un) natural resource.

The Chinese approach: Governing *through* data

There are a number of similarities between the Chinese and US approaches to governing data. The end goals, however, differ. While the US approach is geared toward market dominance for its own private sector, the Chinese approach is oriented toward governance *through* data. This manifests in a number of ways: systems, power dynamics, and relevant actors.

China did not have a data protection regulatory framework per se until 2018, when the Personal Information Security Standard ("2018 Standard") was imple-mented. Until then, data protection provisions were found in Chinese criminal and civil laws and in an array of instruments passed by China's second-highest legis-lative body, the Standing Committee of China's National People's Congress.[16] Under this liberal data protection regulatory approach – which resembled that followed by the United States – a number of Chinese tech companies emerged, grew exponentially, and established an international presence: Baidu, Alibaba, and Tencent (commonly referred to as "BAT") are the most famous examples. The latter two, which were featured in the top ten most valuable companies in the world in 2020,[17] own AliPay and WePay, two online payment apps that have enabled China's transformation from a cash-only society to a close-to-mobile-payment-only society. Many offline and online services are integrated in the Ali-baba and Tencent ecosystems – including hotel and flight bookings, train and taxi rides, grocery shops, restaurants, utility bills, video streaming sites, and mortgage payments. They can be seamlessly managed within their respective payment apps. Given people's increased reliance on AliPay and WePay, Alibaba and Tencent have gained the ability to collect, process, and combine unprecedented volumes of data about individuals' lives.

While Chinese data governance follows the US model in terms of the widespread collection of personal data through consumer apps, there is a stronger narrative of utilizing that data for governance purposes and for delivering a "public good." Alibaba's data troves were used to calculate individuals' credit scores based on their activities in a program called Zhima Credit (translated as Sesame Credit). This solved a long-standing issue in China, which has historically lacked a well-functioning credit system – largely because of cash being the preferred payment method until recently – let alone a reliable third-party, credit-scoring entity. This data-driven approach opened up the financial system to people who had been left out, such as students and inhabitants of rural locations. It was also used by the Chinese government to implement a "social credit system." This resembles the credit score systems used in Western countries, such as FICO scores in the United States or Experian in the United Kingdom. Sesame Credit takes into account financial information as well as broader aspects of individuals' lives, such as their purchase history, political activities, and interactions with others.[18] Every company and citizen in China is intended to have a dynamically generated social credit score that fluctuates through constant evaluation and monitoring of subjects' behavior across digital networks.

The introduction of the Personal Information Security Standard in 2018 created a comprehensive framework for collecting, storing, handling, and sharing personal information. For example, it features detailed provisions on user consent, as well as requirements that data must be de-identified before sharing. It also imposes strict limits on "secondary uses" of data beyond the original purpose. Third-party vendors involved in the handling of these data must undergo extensive security assessments.[19] With the passing of this standard, China has established a data protection regime which – at least in principle – aligns with that championed by the EU. Although strict on paper, the standard is intended to be more business friendly than the GDPR, partly with an aim not to undermine developing fields crucial for China's economy – like artificial intelligence (AI), which relies on access to massive data sets.[20] In fact, standards in China are not legally binding and are best understood as policy guidelines. Nonetheless, the 2018 standard also sought to make Chinese companies more accountable stewards of data because of rising public concerns over fraud and misappropriation of personal information by private sector actors.[21]

As a result, a Chinese privacy dichotomy is emerging, which is inverse to that seen in the United States: Chinese people are increasingly concerned about their data privacy and have broad protections against commercial surveillance, yet they are bound to continue experiencing relatively unrestrained government surveillance. Although the Chinese government portrays the social credit system as a tool to foster honesty among Chinese people, in Western countries this is seen as a mass surveillance system that facilitates social and political control.[22] Thus, for both the United States and China, there are significant national security and political stability implications for the collection and analysis of personal data. Hence, data governance is unlikely to move too far beyond the purview of governments, regardless of how big a role market actors play.

The EU approach: Squaring a circle

Data protection, as a field of law and policy, is the product of early European discussions on the privacy-related threats posed by information communication technologies (ICT).[23] Largely influenced by the relatively recent experience of authoritarian states in Europe, data protection is linked to the protection of dignity, autonomy, personal integrity, and the German notion of "informational self-determination" (*informationelle Selbstbestimmung*) – that is, the ability of individuals to control for themselves the release and use of their own personal data. After the entry into force of the Treaty of Lisbon in 2009, the right to data protection was enshrined as a fundamental right in the EU legal order. At the same time, the free flow of personal data is important for cross-border trade and, by extension, the development of the EU internal market. As a result, EU data protection has historically sought to achieve a dual objective, as seen in the title of first EU-wide data protection instrument, the 1995 Data Protection Directive (DPD): the "protection of individuals with regard to the processing of personal data" and ensuring "the free movement of such data."[24]

The EU has an omnibus and stringent data protection regime that applies to the processing of personal data, which is "any information that relates to an identified or identifiable person." Given the state-of-the-art data processing technologies and the amounts of data available, most data that have undergone a process of anonymization can be reverse engineered and linked back to an individual.[25] For this reason, most data are personal, and therefore the scope of the EU data protection law is broad. The DPD was built on the principles set out in the 1980 Guidelines on the Protection of Privacy and Transborder Flows of Personal Data of the Organisation for Economic Co-operation and Development (OECD).[26] As such, it requires the consent of the data subject or another basis laid down by law to legitimize personal data processing, as well as observance of a number of data protection principles such as, inter alia, purpose limitation (i.e., data must be collected for specified, explicit, and legitimate purposes and not further processed in a manner that is incompatible with those purposes); data minimization (i.e., the processing of personal data must be limited to what is necessary in relation to the purposes for which they are processed); and storage limitation (i.e., personal data must be kept for no longer than is necessary for the purposes for which they are processed). Overall, these requirements and principles seek to afford individuals some degree of control over their personal data and prevent unnecessary, unwarranted personal data collection, so they may not be unduly singled out for unauthorized purposes.

With the advent of the digital revolution, the DPD was increasingly perceived as outdated. In the year of its adoption (1995), only 1 percent of the EU population was using the Internet, Amazon and eBay were still being launched, the founder of Facebook was 11 years old, and Google did not exist.[27] Thus, the GDPR was developed and passed to address the challenges around the protection of personal data posed by new and increasingly pervasive data collection methods.[28] Yet, despite what was already understood to be a dysfunctional transaction between individuals and the data giants that collect and on-sell their personal data, the GDPR maintained the DPD's core data protection tools, including the role of giving and obtaining consent and the aforementioned data protection principles, albeit in a somewhat more elaborated fashion. This regulatory choice has led to two consequences. First, individuals are constantly bombarded with consent requests online, causing disruption and annoyance. As a result, most people almost automatically consent to whatever terms are presented to them, and user consent as a data protection tool remains as devoid of any meaningful effect as ever. Second, with the GDPR's core principles incompatible with the tenets of a big data economy,[29] the GDPR makes it more challenging for businesses to use their users' personal data to engage in data-driven innovation.

This is likely to be particularly harmful to the EU digital economy and thus a factor in future global approaches. Since no EU firm has been able to replicate the success of non-EU platforms, they would benefit from fewer – rather than more – restrictions on their ability to experiment and innovate with data in their efforts to attain market penetration. The GDPR effect on firms' ability to engage in data-driven innovation is largely the result of the tension between the EU data protection law's goals mentioned prior. Just like the DPD, the GDPR seeks to strike a balance between the protection of individuals and the free flow of personal data. However, in the current AI race, where the EU's competitors – the United States and China – are home to data giants and have significantly less strict data protection laws,[30] this balance may prove insufficient to foster the competitiveness of EU firms.

At any rate, the GDPR is innovative in some respects and will have implications not only for EU data governance but for global data governance to some extent, and this is an important factor for this discussion. The GDPR stipulates that any firm offering goods or services to EU residents or monitoring individual behavior taking place in the EU must abide by its rules, regardless of their place of establishment. Since the GDPR amounts to the most comprehensive and strict data protection framework worldwide, companies with global presence can use GDPR compliance as a competitive advantage – by applying the GDPR standards to all their customers located in different jurisdictions, the processes for handling data protection issues can be streamlined, generating efficiencies and lowering compliance costs.[31] Therefore, the GDPR may also stimulate the improvement of data protection standards internationally.

The future of global data governance

These three different approaches to data governance – particularly of personally identifiable, or personal, data – provide a starting point for consideration of what might lie ahead and what changes could be implemented now to ensure maximizing the relevant benefits and minimizing the risks. The US approach, which sees the individual as a data farm that generates commodifiable data for exploitation by its own private sector, would have to be transformed in some important ways in order to continue to dominate the next decade as it has the past two. First, the channeling of unprecedented wealth into private and individual pockets of US entrepreneurs will increasingly be challenged by states that recognize data as a national or (un) natural resource. Second, concerns about the extent to which important democratic institutions like elections are being undermined by the opaque manipulation of private data flows will dissuade some states from pursing this model but attract others. And finally, the growth in data-facilitated crimes like abuse and theft is shifting the public discourse away from "no government intervention" toward one more based on governmental responsibility for mitigating online harms.

The Chinese approach of bolstering their online economy and using data as a governance mechanism to uphold a form of social and political stability will appeal to some states and be readily adopted by them. It will also impede strong relations with other states that have human rights concerns about the level of government surveillance and concerns over Chinese technological hegemony. The 5G conflict between the United States and China highlights the very significant implications for Washington's failure to reinvest in next-generation technology – despite the obvious benefits of having done this in the latter half of the twentieth century. The extent to which technological dominance shapes the international ecosystem cannot be underestimated, and dominance in data-driven systems will be a huge part of that hegemonic renovation.

The EU is attempting to do what neither the United States nor China has been able to do – stimulate innovation while protecting human rights in the data economy. As pointed out, these can be seen as irresolvable goals that threaten to cancel each other out. If the GDPR is effective in shaping the global market, it may be enough to carve out space for a data governance framework that accommodates human rights. If not, the EU will have to turn to other instruments beyond the market to shape international order in this dimension. However, by failing to attend to the preferences of individuals – to the invisible "globally governed," to adopt the notion of our editors[32] – both Washington and Beijing may find their own data governance approaches undermined. The greatest risk to future innovation is an interruption to the supply of data. The growing market for privacy-enhancing technologies (PETs) can be understood as a response to dissatisfaction with a lack of personal control over one's data and digital footprint.

Realizing the full potential of the next stage of digital technologies will require finding ways to share personal data as widely as possible while fostering conditions that will increasingly shape citizens' preferences for giving consent. In this regard, the EU approach comes closest, but both the Chinese and US approaches are fashioned to develop at least some period of continued or future hegemony for those states that will fuel their own economic growth and control over local and global political power dynamics.

In an effort to align competing systems, there is much emphasis on developing legal frameworks that respect what might come to be understood as the "property rights" of data owners in order to maintain a kind of digital social contract and avoid the kind of Hobbesian anarchy that might stem from the flow of data critical to all. However, others are thinking through potentially disruptive and innovative ideas of how the commodification of data could be completely reoriented to benefit individuals rather than organizations.

This one issue of governing personal data brings human beings into the global governance equation in a very direct and represented way that is driving regulatory frameworks. In particular, the EU's innovation in making the GDPR extraterritorial is a step toward rethinking how we arrange actors, interests, and outcomes in a way that is human centric. It shifts power (to some degree, and not yet perfectly) away from the large corporate actors that have thus far "governed" data through market monopolies and toward the individuals who generate that data. This may prove a catalyst for innovation in the coordination and management of digital technologies.

Conclusion

Data governance is going to be a defining issue for future innovation. Through very deliberate and strategic moves, data have been firmly established as a commodity in a highly dysfunctional transaction between a small number of data giants and billions of individuals. The public good is not consistently extracted or passed on in any meaningful way, and there is no evidence of a business case that would allow the current data economy to address the Sustainable Development Goals (SDGs), for example, that are supposedly providing guidance for the 2030 development agenda.[33] Returning to the metaphor of data as the "new oil," there are some critical distinctions that need to be made. Unlike fossil fuels, data do not come from the ground. They rely on a transaction with individual citizens, and those citizens will have to find benefit in the way their data are collected and shared, or they may begin to withdraw their consent.

Critically, though, those citizens are individuals, and their perceptions of what constitutes "benefit" will remain diverse. Consequently, accommodating differences will be as important as finding common ground. Each of the three approaches outlined in this chapter has flaws. Rather than propose a "fourth way" that improves on these, what is really needed is a commitment to focusing on the long-term implications of decisions that we make now. What is prioritized in these decisions about data governance will have lasting implications for generations – just as decisions made in the past industrial revolutions about governing resources, labor, property, and knowledge. It is essential, at this moment, to be critical, questioning, creative, and reflexive. If not, we are at great risk of setting in stone arrangements that we may sorely regret later.

The successful global governance of data will be about striking a bargain between all actors that is sustainable, supports innovation, and incentivizes citizens to continue to contribute to the data pool. And the challenge of doing that – driven in large part by our reliance on a data economy – may very well push us to the kind of innovation in governance that is so badly needed to address the opportunities and challenges that we face in the Fourth Industrial Revolution.

Suggested readings

Lee A. Bygrave, *Data Privacy Law, an International Perspective* (Oxford: Oxford University Press, 2014).

Min Jiang and King Wa-Fu, "Chinese Social Media and Big Data: Big Data, Big Brother, Big Profit?," *Policy & Internet* 10, no. 4 (2018): 372–392.

OECD, *Revised Guidelines on the Protection of Privacy and Transborder Flows of Personal Data* (Paris: OECD, 2013).

Tal Z. Zarsky, "The Privacy-Innovation Conundrum," *Lewis & Clark Law Review* 19, no. 1 (2015): 115–168.

Shoshana Zuboff, "Big Other: Surveillance Capitalism and the Prospects of an Information Civilization," *Journal of Information Technology* 30, no. 1 (2015): 75–89.

Notes

1 World Economic Forum, "Shaping the Future of Technology Governance: Data Policy," www.weforum.org/platforms/shaping-the-future-of-technology-governance-data-policy.

2 Ibid.

3 Paul M. Schwartz and Daniel J. Solove, "Reconciling Personal Information in the United States and European Union," *California Law Review* 102, no. 4 (2014): 877, 881.

4 Joel R. Reidenberg, "Resolving Conflicting International Data Privacy Rules in Cyberspace," *Stanford Law Review* 52, no. 5 (2000): 1315, 1331.

5 Paul M. Schwartz, "The EU-US Privacy Collision: A Turn to Institutions and Procedures," *Harvard Law Review* 126, no. 7 (2013): 1966, 1974–1975.

6 Schwartz and Solove, "Reconciling Personal Information," 880.

7 Ibid., 881.

8 Adam Thierer, *Embracing a Culture of Permissionless Innovation* (Washington, DC: Cato Institute, 2014), www.cato.org/publications/cato-online-forum/embracing-culture-permissionless-innovation.

9 Ira Rubinstein, Greg Nojeim, and Ronald Lee, "Systematic Government Access to Personal Data: A Comparative Analysis," *International Data Privacy Law* 4, no. 2 (2014): 100–102.

10 New America, "Case Study #3: Transparency Reporting," http://newamerica.org/in-depth/getting-internet-companies-do-right-thing/case-study-3-transparency-reporting/.

11 *Letter dated 27 January 2014, from the Office of the Deputy Attorney General of Washington D.C. to Facebook, Google, LinkedIn, Microsoft and Yahoo!*, 27 January 2014, www.justice.gov/iso/opa/resources/366201412716018407143.pdf

12 See Twitter Transparency Report – Information Requests – United States, headings "User Notice" and "National Security Requests," https://transparency.twitter.com/en/reports/countries/us.html#2019-jul-dec

13 Jack Nicas and Katie Benner, "F.B.I. Asks Apple to Help Unlock Two IPhones," *The New York Times*, 7 January 2020, www.nytimes.com/2020/01/07/technology/apple-fbi-iphone-encryption.html.

14 Dipayan Ghosh and Ben Scott, "Digital Deceit II: A Policy Agenda to Fight Disinformation on the Internet," 2018, www.newamerica.org/public-interest-technology/reports/digital-deceit-ii/.

15 Alicia Parlapiano and Jasmine C. Lee, "The Propaganda Tools Used by Russians to Influence the 2016 Election," *The New York Times*, 16 February 2018, https://www.nytimes.com/interactive/2018/02/16/us/politics/russia-propaganda-election-2016.html; Paul Mozur and Mark Scott, "Fake News in U.S. Election? Elsewhere, That's Nothing New," *The New York Times*, 22 December 2017, https://www.nytimes.com/2016/11/18/technology/fake-news-on-facebook-in-foreign-elections-thats-not-new.html.

16 Ibid.

17 "Most Valuable Companies in the World – 2020," *FXSSI – Forex Sentiment Board*, 6 February 2021, https://fxssi.com/top-10-most-valuable-companies-in-the-world.

18 Karen Li Xan Wong and Amy Shields Dobson, "We're Just Data: Exploring China's Social Credit System in Relation to Digital Platform Ratings Cultures in Westernised Democracies," *Global Media and China* 4, no. 2 (2019): 221.

19 Samm Sacks, *New China Data Privacy Standard Looks More Far-Reaching than GDPR* (Washington, DC: Center for Strategic & International Studies, 29 January 2018), www.csis.org/analysis/new-china-data-privacy-standard-looks-more-far-reaching-gdpr.

20 Ibid.

21 Center for Strategic and International Studies, "China's Emerging Data Privacy System and GDPR," 2019, www.csis.org/analysis/chinas-emerging-data-privacy-system-and-gdpr.

22 Wong and Dobson, "We're Just Data," 221.

23 Lee A. Bygrave, "Privacy and Data Protection in an International Perspective," *Scandinavian Studies in Law* 56, no. 8 (2010): 165, 168.

24 *Directive 95/46/EC of 24 October 1995 on the Protection of Individuals with Regard to the Processing of Personal Data and on the Free Movement of Such Data.*

25 Paul Ohm, "Broken Promises of Privacy: Responding to the Surprising Failure of Anonymization," *UCLA Law Review* 57, no. 6 (2009): 1701, 1742; Paul M. Schwartz and Daniel J. Solove, "The PII Problem: Privacy and a New Concept of Personally Identifiable Information," *NYU Law Review* 86, no. 6 (2011): 1814, 1877; and Omer Tene and Jules Polonetsky, "Big Data for All: Privacy and User Control in the Age of Analytics," *Northwestern Journal of Technological and Intellectual Property* 11, no. 5 (2012): 258.

26 OECD, *OECD Guidelines on the Protection of Privacy and Transborder Flows of Personal Data*, (C 58 final), Organisation for Economic Co-operation and Development, Paris, France, 1 October 1980.

27 *Speech by Viviane Reding at Digital Enlightenment Forum*, "Outdoing Huxley: Forging a High Level of Data Protection for Europe in the Brave New Digital World," 18 June 2012, www.identityblog.com/wp-content/images/2012/06/Viviane_Reding_Digital_Enlightenment_Forum.pdf

28 European Commission, "Communication from the Commission to the European Parliament, the Council, the Economic and Social Committee and the Committee of the Regions – A Comprehensive Approach on Personal Data Protection in the European Union," (COM(2010) 609 final: 2), Official communication from the European Commission to the European Parliament.

29 Tal Z. Zarsky, "Incompatible: The GDPR in the Age of Big Data," *Seton Hall Law Review* 47, no. 4 (2016): 995, 996.

30 Daniel Castro, "Who Is Winning the AI Race: China, the EU or the United States?," *Center for Data Innovation*, 19 August 2019, www.datainnovation.org/2019/08/who-is-winning-the-ai-race-china-the-eu-or-the-united-states/.

31 W. Gregory Voss and Kimberly A. Houser, "Personal Data and the GDPR: Providing a Competitive Advantage for US Companies," *American Business Law Journal* 56, no. 2 (2019): 287.

32 Thomas G. Weiss and Rorden Wilkinson, "The Globally Governed: Everyday Global Governance," *Global Governance* 24, no. 2 (2018): 193–210.

33 Stephen Browne and Thomas G. Weiss, eds., *Routledge Handbook on the UN and Development* (London: Routledge, 2021).

CONTENTS

Illicit drugs

Prohibition and the international drug-control regime

Mónica Serrano

Future global governance will undoubtedly continue to face a significant challenge in the area of illicit drugs. In 2017, 35 million people worldwide (almost Canada's population) suffered from drug-use disorders. Of them, only one in seven was receiving treatment and care. The rest were left unprotected, resulting in 585,000 lives lost. Today's most pressing drug challenge developed as consumers turned to opioids, a class of drugs including both natural and synthetic chemical compounds (the best known include heroin, fentanyl, and several prescription medications). The number of opioid users has increased by nearly 60 percent in recent years, reaching 58 million by 2018. Roughly half the lives lost to drugs each year are now attributed to opioids.[1]

While these fatalities pale in comparison to those of other global epidemics, the addictive power of drugs makes them extraordinarily destructive. First-time cannabis users have a 10 percent probability of addiction. The risk increases by a third for cocaine. For opioids it more than doubles, leaving users with a 25 percent risk.[2] Illicit drugs pose a global challenge to public health.

The International Drug Control Regime (IDCR) was established to provide a global governance solution to the drug problem. Yet the

DOI: 10.4324/9781003139836-22

drug-prohibition norm has been problematic in practice. The IDCR rests on three pillars: the 1961 UN Single Convention in Narcotic Drugs (as amended by the 1972 Protocol), the 1971 Convention in Psychotropic Substances, and the 1988 Convention against Illicit Traffic in Narcotic Drugs and Psychotropic Substances. In their respective preambles, they all express concern for the "health and well-being" of humankind, but only the 1988 Convention against Illicit Traffic in Narcotic Drugs refers to human rights.[3] This reference aside, in combination these three pillars uphold a prohibitionist penal approach to the issue of illicit drugs, one isolated from other global governance priorities, especially human rights. And they reflect the century-long role of the United States in building and policing the regime.

The practice of drug control has resulted in a number of significant negative, if somewhat unintended, consequences – as was recognized in an unprecedented 2008 report by the executive director of the United Nations Office on Drugs and Crime (UNODC). Notable among these is growth of a large black market, many attendant human rights abuses, including the denial of the right to health and infringements of civil liberties, the casualties of coercive police and military drug-control operations as well as criminal violence, and executions for drug-related offences in some states.[4] Despite these violations, for over six decades, UN drug-control agencies have shown little or no interest in human rights.[5]

How did this situation come to pass? The purpose of this chapter is to examine how the prohibition-based system embodied in the IDCR came about, highlight the consequences that such an approach has had, and survey the prospects for and benefits of an alternative human rights–centered approach to drug control. The chapter begins with a glimpse of the prelapsarian land. It then explores the drug-control regime's mounting failures, coming as they did in tandem with Washington's efforts to tighten the legal framework and rigidly align national and international practices and subsequently bolstered by strident support from prohibitionist-authoritarian states. Thereafter, the chapter turns to those forces of change that exist. The harm-reduction treatment campaign led by Europe has offered one possible new path, above all by bringing human rights into global drug-control debates. Soft defection from the regime over marijuana use, not least within the United States, has also been an important trend. But as we cast ahead to the middle of the twenty-first century, it remains to be seen whether these quiet "opt-outs" are more than just the stirrings of unease.

Life before prohibition

In a long durée, psychoactive drugs and narcotic substances have been essential elements of "drug cultures" and "subcultures" in societies around the world in which they have often assumed a host of religious and medicinal uses. Well into modern times, for instance, they have kept up the stamina of soldiers. Psychoactive substances and stimulants have also long been important commodities in the global economy: many of those widely used in Western societies – from tea, cacao, and coffee to tobacco and rum – became truly global commodities. So, too, did opium, in a manner worth recalling in a discussion of the moral vagaries of drug prohibition.

Opium smoking became a staple of nineteenth-century Western stereotypes of China – but only after the two Opium Wars waged by Britain with the purpose of breaking China's attempts to prohibit the drug, cultivated in British India. This was a shameless but successful campaign by the world's then superpower to force open a market for an addictive but highly lucrative drug (and, in the process, correct Britain's long-standing trade imbalance with China). Imperial Britain's forcing of opium onto China casts a shadow over much of the later story of global drug control.

Opium addiction increased significantly in the United States during the Civil War. Morphine salts had been manufactured since the 1830s, while heroin, introduced by the Bayer Company in 1898, remained commercially available. By 1915, heroin had emerged as the drug of recreational choice among young males in New York. Until then, opium imports into the United States faced practically no restrictions beyond at-the-border taxation (tariffs). In fact, drug use remained virtually unregulated in the United States through most of the nineteenth century. In the 1880s, two decades after cocaine was isolated from coca leaf, physicians welcomed its power to mitigate depression, not to mention its use as a local anesthetic. Coca and cocaine use soon became popular in both Europe and the United States. In soft drinks like Coca-Cola, in "elixirs" like French Vin Mariani, in syrups to help fatigue, or sniffed for the treatment of sinusitis and hay fever, the consumption of coca and cocaine-related products saw a legal boom. Cocaine enthusiasm was high on both sides of the Atlantic. In Britain, Sigmund Freud was a fervent champion of its "magic" virtues, and in the United States, a wide variety of cocaine products were produced by Parke Davis Company. The pope also endorsed his own favorite cocaine brand.[6]

The story turned with the twentieth century, when Western societies woke up to the need for some form of regulation. The level and type of regulation, however, remained an open question. In the United States, society had gained better knowledge about the harm of drugs, beginning with widespread morphine addiction, which prompted federal government action, most notably a drop in crude-opium imports. Yet proper concern for social well-being was also whipped up into a panic, and scaremongers entered the picture. With them came a fatal connection between drugs and race, with the perils of one lumped with those supposed of the other. Addicts were given the face not of white suburban American housewives but of opium-smoking Chinese, followed by African Americans and Mexican minorities. The origin of the evil was held to be beyond US borders, and early drug legislation was directed at both users and suppliers.

Even so, there were realistic views in the first debates about narcotics control in the United States. While many in the medical profession counseled against morphine overuse and for cuts in the use of narcotics in patent medicines, they also questioned the prospect of eliminating both the craving of addicts and the overall supply of narcotics. This approach did not last long. The more restrictive law enforcement perspectives of some of the pharmaceutical as well as medical professions prevailed, reinforced by a nascent US drug diplomacy. By 1906, when Washington embarked on building the IDCR, the enactment of strict national legislation became both an expression of domestic commitment to narcotics control and a banner of US drug diplomacy. This converged around a goal of total control at home and abroad and brushed aside franker assessments of appropriate levels and types of regulation – with significant, lasting consequences.

Prohibition and the international drug-control regime: How did we get here?

The actions of two universal organizations, first the League of Nations and then the United Nations, forged the essential components of the contemporary IDCR.

The League of Nations

Many factors, including chance, were behind the swift ascent of the drug-prohibition norm and the IDCR in the last century. Two stand out, nonetheless. The first factor was the role of "moral entrepreneurs" intent on securing US government commitment to prohibition at home and locking Washington into the role of patron of an emerging international norm. The second factor was the exceptional circumstances created by two world wars.

The regime's founders were Hamilton Wright, Dr. Charles C. Tenney, and Bishop Charles Brent. Wright was recognized as the champion of US domestic federal drug legislation. Brent, who had witnessed the ravaging effects of opium in the Philippines, in particular pursued the goal of an international meeting on the opium question. By 1906, his personal political contacts, including with William H. Taft and Theodore Roosevelt, helped him win State Department support. Washington's own interest was in stealing a march over the European powers in gaining access to the Chinese market. China itself was eager to see some international control over the scourge of opium. Preparations for the first international opium meeting, held in Shanghai in 1909, were entrusted to Brent, Wright, and Tenney, with their unabashed puritanically moralistic approach to drugs.[7] Fully backed by President Taft, an International Opium Conference to consider an international drug-control treaty ensued in The Hague in December 1911. The US vision of international drug control took form, resting on two tenets: the notion of legitimate medical and scientific uses, a notion both strict and vague; and an international agenda of stringent supply control.[8]

Conflicting international trade interests and diverging views about opium use forced Washington to keep the agenda open but were not enough to hinder the negotiation of the 1912 Opium Convention.[9] Although US ratification of the Hague Convention in 1913 and the enactment of the 1914 domestic Harrison Narcotics Act were testimony to its commitment to stringent drug control, high ratification standards – reflecting the doubts of both producing countries and colonial powers – delayed the convention's entry into force. The outcome of the World War I would change this fact.

Two articles of the Treaty of Versailles provided a solid basis to the regime. Article 23 entrusted the League of Nations with supervising the execution of agreements with regard to traffic in opium and other "dangerous drugs." Article 295 bound signatories of the peace treaty to the 1912 Opium Convention. It was the League that provided the framework of the international drug-control regime. The one country that most wanted it, the United States, pushed for these articles but did not subsequently become a member of the League of Nations.

Washington's presence in the organization's machinery was nonetheless constant and "ruthlessly energetic."[10] In 1920, one of three assessors appointed to the new Opium Advisory Committee was Elizabeth Washburn Wright, widow of US Opium Commissioner Hamilton Wright. In 1928, the new Permanent Central Opium Board included Herbert L. May, an expert in international laws on opium traffic. And in 1931, Harry J. Anslinger, commissioner of the Federal Bureau of Narcotics, joined the US delegation, and Washington's policeman-like role surged. Anslinger was the original moral entrepreneur's dream come true, a crusader set on both reinforcing prohibition and punitive enforcement at home while also exporting US drug-control priorities abroad. Eventually he became "de facto global drug Czar," and to him is due the "Americanization" of international drug-control policies and the enduring primacy of prohibition and the supply-control paradigm.[11]

Together, the drug-control treaties established during the interwar period under Washington's leadership bolted down the main planks of the IDCR. The first of these was the Geneva Opium Convention of 1925, issued by the League of Nations. The convention implemented proposals originally advanced at the Shanghai 1909 meeting but expanded the scope of control to coca and cannabis and their derivatives as well as opium. The basis was laid for an international system regulating trade in these now controlled substances, which required signatories to produce authorized import-export certificates. At the same time, the system's Achilles' heel showed: disagreement over vaguely defined legitimate drug uses. The result was US withdrawal from the convention.

Second, the 1931 Convention for Limiting the Manufacture and Regulating the Distribution of Narcotic Drugs introduced restrictions on the manufacture of cocaine, heroin, and morphine. The United States now conceded that this should be according to medical and scientific needs, but it also made country estimates binding. The 1931 convention enshrined the practice of naming and shaming reporting countries and – most anomalously – claimed to require only the ratification of 25 countries to be universally binding.

Finally, the 1936 Convention for the Suppression of the Illicit Traffic in Dangerous Drugs did not come into force. It nonetheless cemented a penal precedent. In addition to making the illicit transportation and sale of narcotics an international crime, the convention requested signatories to introduce changes in their domestic legislations to severely punish drug offences.[12]

The United Nations

The UN Charter did not explicitly refer to international drug control, but reactivating it remained a US priority. The League's drug-control machinery was swiftly transferred to the newly created United Nations organization. In February 1946, in its first session, the UN's Economic and Social Council established the Commission on Narcotic Drugs (CND) with a view to ensuring the continuity of the League's drug-control system, developing capacities to monitor international drug-control efforts, and revalidating the interwar conventions. Efforts to amalgamate these instruments in a single convention started at once.

This occurred alongside a key disjuncture between norm and fact. The global illicit drug trade had been boosted by World War II. Consumer non-medical drug demand rose sharply, as did economic incentives for both criminals and poorer producer countries scouring for sources of foreign exchange. Smaller, contained markets were swept aside by far larger illicit circuits in the hands of a new class of international criminals. By the end of the war, estimates of heroin addiction in the United States pointed to a decline, but scarcity had boosted heroin prices to $1,200 per pound for crude opium and $600 per ounce for the refined product. The United States represented a hugely profitable illicit heroin market, as the Mafia quickly recognized.

Could all this be ended by edict? The transfer of the League's drug-control system to the UN proceeded with the unrealistic conviction that it could. With the 1948 Paris Synthetic Narcotics Protocol, the goal of widening the net of control substances to include synthetic opiates was achieved. Drug control became a police matter as Anslinger campaigned to keep the CND an insulated body of enforcement officials rather than public health experts. The CND was steered toward a radical supply-control agenda with opium, coca, and to a lesser extent marijuana as top priorities. Decolonization, which saw imperial powers giving up opium-producing possessions, helped secure a long-envisaged goal: the dismantling of opium monopolies. Yet decolonization also undermined global supply control: many of the new states had no means, even if they had the will, to meet enforcement demands.

Efforts to bring together eight international treaties and conventions, including the Paris Protocol, into the Single Convention, and to expand the scope of drug control, started in 1948 and continued for over a decade. In the event, Anslinger was distracted by a parallel project to create an international opium monopoly, a quixotic attempt to form a cartel of legal opium-producing countries (with quotas and inspections) that ironically included India but excluded China.[13]

The Single Convention that emerged in January 1961 partly reflected the rise of a new generation of more professional drug-control diplomats more willing to challenge the thinking behind the quixotic project's monument, the 1953 Opium Protocol. At the same time, the over 70 delegations at the UN in New York showed how there had been a mutation in the global drug scene: not only were many more countries involved, but they had clearly divided between drug-producing and drug-manufacturing countries, with competing interests. The drug-producing countries were keen on restricting synthetic narcotics but not keen on restricting opium, cannabis, and coca. The drug-manufacturing countries pleaded (successfully) that synthetic and psychotropic substances were – if they were at all – far less addictive. Both groups scored victories, but the drug-producing countries had more – the manufacturers, after all, did not want opium scarcity and higher prices. The Opium Protocol and its exclusive club were thus finally killed off (its budget had, in any case, failed to materialize). Producing countries got looser restrictions – no inspections or embargoes – but also stricter requirements to report their legal needs to the new International Narcotics Control Board (INCB) and, of course, to reduce production, conditions at which both Bolivia and Peru balked.[14]

Even as it wobbled in practice, the Single Convention hardened the regime. The restrictive supply-control ethos of its predecessors was sanctified. Drawing explicitly on the 1936 Convention, Article 36 of the Single Convention established as "punishable offences" the cultivation, production, extraction, preparation, possession, offering, offering for sale, distribution, importation, exportation, and sale of "drugs contrary to the provisions of this Convention" and called on the parties to punish them "particularly by imprisonment or other penalties of deprivation of liberty."[15] Its preamble even revived the earliest crusading rhetoric, casting "addiction to narcotic drugs" as a "serious evil for the individual . . . fraught with social and economic danger to mankind" and calling on the duty of the parties "to prevent and combat this evil."[16] In fall 1962, over 80 countries supported the resolution in favor of the convention's crusade.

Nor was the practical side of the story over. After opium came a surge in consumption of newer and mostly synthetic drugs – amphetamines, analgesics, sedatives, tranquilizers, stimulants, anti-depressants, barbiturates, and hallucinogens such as LSD (lysergic acid diethylamide), particularly in the United States and Europe – and with it the pillars upon which today's IDCR rests. The 1971 Psychotropic Treaty (Vienna Convention) sought to tackle this booming synthetic drug market while the 1972 Conference to Strengthen the 1961 Single Convention again emphasized controls at source for traditional narcotics.

Manufacturing countries and pharmaceutical companies had long resisted robust international controls on psychotropic substances and, mostly through national regulatory systems, drew a line between hallucinogens and amphetamines, on the one hand, and tranquilizers and barbiturates, on the other, with a view to safeguarding the latter's market. Although they managed to limit the number of prohibited controlled substances in the short term, over time, informal practices by the UN and pro-control Scandinavian and Soviet states closed some of the loopholes.

In the United States, the heroin epidemic propelled by the Vietnam War and rising marijuana consumption provided the backdrop for the first war on drugs and President Richard Nixon's campaign to strengthen the Single Convention. The aim was simultaneously to bolster the regulatory and investigatory powers of the INCB and to beef up international restrictions on narcotics. The resulting 1972 Protocol paid attention to education, treatment, and rehabilitation, but it also reinforced the regime's punitive supply-control approach. Led by Washington, the regime also embraced diagnoses that cast the problem as alien to the United States and an evil sent by producing countries. Opiates, cannabis, and coca thus remained the main targets, and the doctrine of controlling the problem "at source" endured. The vital relevance of demand and the vexing links between repressive control and criminality were, in practice, ignored.

The third pillar of the IDCR, the 1988 Convention against Illicit Traffic in Narcotic Drugs and Psychotropic Substances, was negotiated in the midst of a wave of drug consumption in the United States and Europe and massive cocaine trafficking bound to the United States. The 1988 Convention was also an offshoot of the two Nixon-Reagan drug wars, the latter based on an assessment of global narcotic trafficking as a threat to the national security of the United States. As in prior negotiations – as it did in many post–World War II intergovernmental forums – Washington set the terms. Various aspects of illicit trafficking were considered serious offences, and a number of provisions already part of the US drug-control arsenal were adopted and internationalized. The upshot was the universalization of a penal approach and the widening of penalization resulting from new provisions on money laundering, asset seizure, and the diversion of precursor chemicals. The 1988 Convention also introduced the potential criminalization of individuals and groups. Thus, in addition to large-scale traffickers, individuals linked to the illicit market chain – from peasants and manufacturers to couriers, dealers, and consumers – were also targeted.

The dark side of prohibition and drug control

From the regime's early days, critics warned that strict national and international regulations would encourage – rather than attenuate – illegal manufacture, trafficking, and criminality. As had been the case with alcohol prohibition, drug use would not disappear but go underground, while the preferences of consumers would simply move around the barriers of punitive enforcement. Punitive drug control would exacerbate the very problem it sought to solve.[17]

If this had been the only objection to the regime, the historical verdict might have remained open – unintended consequences arguably weighing less than noble intentions. However, the record of prohibition is a litany of perversities and disasters. Notably, even though monopolies of illicit drugs had been dismantled, global drug trafficking intensified. In cases like that of the French colonial administration in Indochina, this was because of official protection. Despite the US lead in creating the drug-control regime, protection was also extended by the Central Intelligence Agency (CIA). As the international scene was shaped by the Cold War, the crusade against illicit drugs came second to the crusade against communism. Mafia leaders had already provided useful intelligence to the US Navy for the wartime Allied occupation of Sicily and Italy; as postwar Italy bent alarmingly, for the United States, toward communism, the CIA lent backing to the Mafia as it built an international narcotics syndicate. The CIA's logistical protection was also behind Burma's rise to the world's number one opium producer in the 1960s.[18]

This perverse interaction between prohibition and protection boosted the regional and global illicit drug trade. The "balloon effect," in turn, also quickly demonstrated the elusiveness of the regime's goal of simultaneously controlling all the world's production zones, along with its own role in fostering black markets. Cocaine industrialization and the transformation of family enterprises into transnational criminal organizations in Bolivia can be traced back to General Manuel Odría's 1949–1950 war on Peru's drug traffickers. Mexico's entry into the big drug league was the result of Turkey's 1972 ban on opium poppy cultivation and the consequent disruption of the famous French Connection (the Turkish-French heroin smuggling network from Marseilles into the United States). The proverbial balloon's endless capacity for popping up in one place after being squeezed in another defeated the purposes of the global drug governance regime.

The United States continued to drive the regime at the same time as it grew as the world's single largest market for illegal drugs. Was the problem really only a matter of exogenous supply? Those behind the rise of punitive drug control, including the IDCR architects, rarely considered questions related to demand, they had little knowledge of addicts, and they were predisposed to disregard them as criminals. The challenges faced by addicts and the intractable nature of addiction barely featured in the calculations about what policies were necessary. The expectation was that once licit drug production was properly defined and regulated, the regime's penal control measures would take care of illicit production. The intended result was that illicit supply and consumption would then fade. These were the assumptions of an era that, in the United States, ended with the 1960s. The rise of a mass youth counterculture in which drugs were central, along with the far-from-negligible impact of heroin and marijuana consumption by American soldiers in Vietnam, marked an epochal turn. From then until today, despite both the health and legal risks, millions of US citizens would experience drug dependency as an integral part of their lives. The neat calculations of a previous generation were blown away. Here was a demand that could not be turned off. And, because prohibition drove the black market's profits ever upward, the United States became the most lucrative as well as the largest illicit drug market, estimated at $150 billion in 2016.[19]

Grimly, the United States showcased the flaws in the supply-control paradigm that it had long promoted. Cutting the supply, so it had been thought, would drive up street prices, taking drugs beyond users' reach. Despite significant seizures of illegal drug shipments, though, supply control proved no match for the endlessly replaceable drugs. US import drug prices, from the second half of the 1980s, in fact fell, but this did not deter traffickers. The huge differentials between dirt-cheap production costs and entry-point prices still guaranteed enormous dividends and were more than sufficient to absorb the costs of interdicted cargoes. Without prohibition, commodities like coca leaf would have been next to worthless. With prohibition, handsome profits were guaranteed, which, in turn, accounted for the increasing professionalization and ruthlessness of transnational criminal organizations. In the United States, they had a market that could not be flooded.

Forces of inertia

The global rise of the "narco" has also been grim, for all the tawdry glamor of the current brand. For the weak democracies of Colombia and Mexico, the upsurge in the value of the cocaine market from the 1980s was a catastrophe, empowering criminals to kill with impunity and corrupt judicial, political, and military institutions. Within a few decades, as narco violence broke through all constraints, Latin America as a whole came to account for 30 percent of total world homicides, many drug related. Full-scale humanitarian crises like mass population displacements also were in evidence. They were inconsequential for the global drug-control regime. The imperviousness of the enforcers of a global governance regime to the havoc and suffering for which it is so responsible is sobering.

A paradigm that had always been an article of faith – that the evil of illicit drugs lay in their supply from abroad – had progressively entrenched itself. On that basis, the United States deployed a set of costly tools for Latin America, from bilateral law enforcement operations and military aid transfers to coca eradication programs. Illicit drug cultivation, production, and trafficking only expanded. Thus, within two decades following the 1999 Plan Colombia (the joint US-Colombian effort to eliminate drug trafficking as well as end Colombia's armed conflict and promote its development), and after the US Congress approved $10 billion for these goals, Colombia's total coca cultivation area had almost doubled – from 122,500 hectares to 212,000.[20]

By this point the pretense that enforcement of a global drug-control regime was anything more than a unilateral US prerogative had been dropped. At the behest of another US agency, the Drug Enforcement Agency (DEA), Colombia and Mexico adopted the so-called Kingpin strategy, which involved the arrest and extradition to the United States of high-profile drug cartel leaders. In Mexico, the strategy unleashed yet further waves of violence and mass atrocities as cartels fragmented and reorganized, but the DEA won the media victories, justifying its sumptuous budget.

The DEA had emerged as the rightful heir to Harry J. Anslinger and had become the emblematic case of bureaucratic inertia as regime sustainer. Yet, bitter as it may be to admit, a regime so identified with the United States had finally won wider global support. Authoritarian countries, with little or no restrictions on extreme repressive measures, had grown comfortable with enforcing the prohibition norm. States in Asia and the Middle East were eager to seize on the norm's justification of their use of the death penalty, responsible for the executions of over 1,000 people a year for drug offenses mostly among the seven "high application" countries of China, Indonesia, Iran, Malaysia, Saudi Arabia, Singapore, and Vietnam.[21] When a Special Session of the UN General Assembly was convened on the world drug problem in 2016, authoritarian governments, led by China and Russia, were the regime's strongest supporters.

It had taken a very long time, but the long-buried dissonance between the drug-control regime and human rights was at last coming into the open. In retrospect, the ascendance of the drug-control regime is inexplicable without its predating of the advance of human rights as a global governance priority. Invidious as it may seem, it remains the case that human rights non-governmental organizations (NGOs), while protesting the death penalty, continued to show a remarkable deference to drug-control orthodoxy in the face of clear evidence of its wide human rights abusiveness, accepted as collateral damage.

The drug-control regime inculcated imperviousness to the casualties of interminable drug wars in Latin America – blame lay with its corrupt or craven governments. And in the country that had championed the regime, the United States was indifferent to the incarceration of millions on petty drugs charges, which fell disproportionately on African Americans. Puritanical righteousness was satisfied, as were the needs of the prison industrial complex. A harsh verdict is hard to avoid: if the global drug-control regime works well in authoritarian settings where human rights have little or no bearing, it is because it was always working toward authoritarian outcomes. Can this change?

Forces of change

Change can never be ruled out. What is notable about approaches to changing the drug-control regime are their obliquity. Slow, water-like erosion has been the course of change in this regime.

The first moves to the legalization of marijuana, the first sapper of the regime, date back to special commission reports of the 1960s – simultaneously in the United States, a few European countries including the Netherlands and Britain, and Australia. The findings were that the psychoactive dangers of marijuana were exaggerated and that the costs of criminalization outweighed the benefits. In the 1970s, an early wave toward more tolerant cannabis use started in the United States, when 11 states softened their legal responses. In Alaska, a spatially confined legalization of personal possession and use was created. This was followed in the 1980s in the Netherlands, where the pioneering coffee-shop system allowed Dutch authorities to establish a framework to regulate quasi-legal cannabis sales.

The second wave of marijuana and drug toleration expanded in Europe, with Spain, Portugal, and Switzerland in the lead, reaching Australia and New Zealand, Israel, and parts of the Americas. The persuasive forces were the economic costs of mass incarceration, the more intangible social and democratic costs of criminalizing substantial numbers of the population, and the benefits of erecting a barrier between relatively harmless and more dangerous drug markets. This second wave relied on ingenious interpretations of the conventions but did not yield a uniform trend. Policy choices varied along a spectrum running from depenalization and decriminalization to partial or de facto legalization. No common front emerged to challenge the regime.

Washington's role as the regime's guardian could not check subnational trends favoring marijuana regulation in the United States. By the end of 2020, 35 US states had legalized medical marijuana. In 15 states (in addition to the District of Columbia), recreational adult use had been approved. And in Oregon, the possession of hard drugs has been decriminalized.[22]

Washington's displeasure at this change may be gauged by its previous loud condemnations of marijuana initiatives in Canada, Jamaica, and Mexico and its extraordinary denunciation of the Netherlands as a "narco-state."[23] At the national level, the US federal government maintained its deterrent/law enforcement approach. With no changes in the federal Controlled Substances Act, flexibilization was left to the discretion of the executive branch. Under the Obama administration, the Justice Department eased up on marijuana possession enforcement, but under the Trump administration, this was reversed by Attorney General Jeff Sessions's instruction to enforce federal marijuana law. The result was a patchwork of federal and state laws in which federal agencies, especially the DEA, have been left free to launch federal operations, including raids on medical marijuana clubs.[24]

Following marijuana, harm reduction entered the policy equation in favor of change. Long coming, it was propelled by the impact of the HIV (human immuno-deficiency virus)/AIDS (acquired immunodeficiency syndrome) pandemic in the 1980s. Originating in public health, harm reduction refers to interventions to mini-mize health risks, ranging from opium substitution therapy to controlled heroin prescription, syringe distribution, and safe drug-consumption locales. A broader definition extends to policies that seek to mitigate the negative health, social, and economic consequences of punitive prohibition. The opening here was in the room for leeway over the meaning of the "medical and scientific" drug uses still allowed by the Single Convention. As with marijuana legalization, the results have been mixed.

Harm reduction did become part of the drug-control agenda of an increasing num-ber of advanced countries (over 70 by the end of the first decade of the twenty-first century) and was championed by the European Union (EU). But soft defection failed to drive reform of the IDCR, and the United States continued to affirm the centrality of punitive prohibition. As with marijuana, there was pushback from Washington against harm reduction, concretely manifested in the congressional ban in 1988 that has blocked federal funds for syringe programs, whether at home or abroad. Between 2005 and 2015, harm reduction became a battleground at the UN Commission on Narcotic Drugs. As energetic as ever, US delegates successfully bullied to make harm reduction a taboo, as it is in the Outcome Document of the 2016 Special Session of the United Nations General Assembly on the world drug problem.

Pushback denoted defensiveness. This change was more of a menace, bringing forth the EU as an actor ready to assume a leading role in drug diplomacy, manifested in the enshrining of the right to health in its Drugs Strategy and European Practice. Conspicuously, too, the battle over harm reduction opened a rift among different UN bodies. The traditional bastions of the IDCR – the INCB and the UN Office on Drugs and Crime – stood firm, whereas the World Health Organization, the United Nations Development Program, and the Joint United Nations Programme on HIV/ AID (UNAIDS) broke ranks, as (significantly) did the Office of the High Commis-sioner on Human Rights. A public health wedge seemed to be heading toward the long-missing component of human rights.

In important ways, this was the case, but perversity continued to be a feature of the story: while democratic countries often fell short when it came to funding harm-reduction programs, countries like Iran and China enthusiastically implemented forced treatment programs in mass detention "rehabilitation" centers. Even in this backhanded manner, however, human rights were now the elephant in the drug-con-trol-regime room. In 2012, the closure of compulsory detention-rehabilitation cen-ters was called for by a dozen UN agencies, including all the advocates of harm reduction.[25] This was a decade after the UN special rapporteur on violence against women, together with the UN Working Group on arbitrary detention, had highlighted the preponderance of drug users in prisons[26] and a few years after Mandred Nowak, special rapporteur on torture and other cruel, inhuman, or degrading treatment or punishment, had voiced concern at the disconnect between the IDCR and the UN human rights protocols.[27] In 2015, the Office of the High Commissioner on Human Rights called for protection of the right to life of persons convicted for drug-related offenses.[28] Opposition to the practices enabled by the UN drug-control regime was coming from within the UN. The time seemed ripe for broader efforts to humanize the regime.

In 2008, the resolution "Proper Integration of the UN Human Rights System within International Drug Control Policy" was put to the Commission on Narcotic Drugs by Uruguay, Bolivia, Argentina, and Switzerland.[29] China complained at any requirement to bring drug policy into line with human rights law; the secretary of the International Narcotics Control Board objected to any involvement of the board with human rights.

In 2012, Colombia, Guatemala, and Mexico requested the Special Session of the General Assembly, which eventually met in 2016, in the hope of reforming the drug-control regime.[30] The session revealed that many African countries were ready to admit to facing the same intractable drug-control problems as Latin America. Moreover, in the strong counter-reactions of prohibitionist countries, the deliberations revealed that, for the foreseeable future, adjusting global drug control to democratic and human rights standards is implausible.

Conclusion

As this chapter has argued, from a global governance perspective, the drug-prohibition norm and the resulting IDCR have proven to be dysfunctional. On the one hand, they have generated illicit drug markets, assisting the rise of a new league of powerful criminals. On the other, they have become embroiled in an increasingly intractable conflict with other global governance priorities, above all human rights. The regime's puritanical approach denied the reality of millions of addicts, and it was painfully at odds with democratic and human rights standards.

The late development of the human rights regime in relation to the IDCR led to its subordination to drug-control priorities. In a human rights void, millions of people were incarcerated on petty possession charges, and the lives of thousands, if not millions, were claimed by punitive enforcement in authoritarian countries and endless drug wars in Latin America. The record of mass incarceration in the United States, the vindication and enactment of the death penalty in Asia and the Middle East, and the casualties of militarized drug control in Latin American all lay bare the tensions between drug control and human rights.

Through harm reduction and regulation, European countries sought to bring addicts into the fold and reconcile drug control and civil liberties. These trends were soon echoed by health and human rights actors, including within the UN system, which creatively exploited the core medical ambiguities of the drug regime to alter it. Such insufficient modifications meant that a better future will demand courageous reassessment of the regime's own role in unleashing malignly powerful illicit drug markets and, with them, the conditions for state capture and failure. These developments have been particularly marked among weak democracies, not just in Latin

America but increasingly Africa. The experience of these realities lay behind the Latin American plea to address the regime's flaws. It may not have succeeded, but one of the morals of the story is that precedents count.

Global drug governance is likely to remain both a reality and a goal over the next quarter century. To work properly, in a manner consistent with democratic standards and human rights, it needs to bring in public health from the margins to the center. The creation of such a regime will require decades and, in all likelihood, a crusade – two things, after all, that the regime needed to impose itself in the first place.

Suggested reading

David R. Bewley-Taylor, *International Drug Control: Consensus Fractured* (Cambridge: Cambridge University Press, 2012).

William B. McAllister, *Drug Diplomacy in the Twentieth Century: An International History* (London: Routledge, 2000).

Alfred W. McCoy, *The Politics of Heroin: CIA Complicity in the Global Drug Trade* (Chicago, IL: Lawrence Hill Books, 2003).

David Musto, *The American Disease: Origins of Narcotic Control*, 3rd ed. (Oxford: Oxford University Press, 1999).

Ethan A. Nadelmann, "Global Prohibition Regimes: The Evolution of Norms in International Society," *International Organization* 44, no. 4 (1990): 479–526.

Notes

1 *World Drug Report 2020*, Booklet 1 (United Nations publication, Sales No. E.20.XI.6, 2020), 17; *World Drug Report 2019* (United Nations publication, Sales No. E.19.XI.8, 2019), 7.

2 American Society of Addiction Medicine, "Opioid Addiction 2016 Facts & Figures," www.asam.org/docs/default-source/advocacy/opioid-addiction-disease-facts-figures.pdf; Robert J. MacCoun and Peter Reuter, *Drug War Heresies* (Cambridge: Cambridge University Press, 2001), 19; Beckley Foundation, *The Global Cannabis Commission Report*, 2008, http://fileserver.idpc.net/library/BF_Cannabis_Commission_Rpt2008_EN.pdf

3 Article 14, (2) requests the parties to respect fundamental rights in the context of eradication and control of illicit cultivation and to take into account traditional licit uses. United Nations Convention against Illicit Traffic in Narcotic Drugs and Psychotropic Substances, 19 December 1988, www.incb.org/documents/PRECURSORS/1988_CONVENTION/1988Convention_E.pdf

4 Commission on Narcotic Drugs, "Making Drug Control 'Fit for Purpose': Building on the UNGASS Decade," UN document E/CN.7/2008/CRP.17, 7 March 2008, www.unodc.org/documents/commissions/CND/CND_Sessions/CND_51/1_CRPs/E-CN7-2008-CRP17_E.pdf.

5 Damon Barrett and Manfred Nowak, "The United Nations and Drug Policy: Towards a Human Rights-Based Approach," in *The Diversity of International Law: Essays in Honour of Professor Kalliopi K. Koufa*, ed. Aristotle Constantinides and Nikos Zaikos (Leiden, The Netherlands: Martinus Nijhoff, 2009), 449–478; Richard Lines, *Drug Control and Human Rights in International Law* (Cambridge: Cambridge University Press, 2017).

6 Paul Goootenberg, *Andean Cocaine: The Making of a Global Drug* (Chapel Hill, NC: University of North Carolina Press, 2008), 23–29.

7 David Musto, *The American Disease: Origins of Narcotic Control*, 3rd ed. (Oxford: Oxford University Press, 1999), 31, 36.

8 The literature on the IDCR has thoroughly documented the key role played by these and other entrepreneurs, including Stephen G. Porter, chief US representative in interwar negotiations, and Harry J. Anslinger, US CND representative (1946–1970), in shaping US drug control and establishing an international regime modeled on US preferences. See Ethan B. Nadelmann, "Global Prohibition Regimes: The Evolution of Norms in International Society," *International Organization* 44, no. 4 (1990): 479–526; Musto, *The American Disease*; William B. McAllister, *Drug Diplomacy in the Twentieth Century: An International History* (London: Routledge, 2000); William O. Walker, III, *Drug Control in the Americas*, 2nd ed. (Albuquerque: University of New Mexico Press, 1989).

9 This convention called upon the parties to restrict trade in opium; refrain from exporting it to states that prohibited its import, including China; and gradually suppress opium smoking. Manufactured drugs – morphine, heroin, cocaine – were also considered, but, through vague control provisions on licensing, manufacturing, and distribution, Germany managed to protect its industry.

10 Norman Ansley, "International Efforts to Control Narcotics," *Journal of Criminal Law and Criminology* 50, no. 2 (1950): 107.

11 McAllister, *Drug Diplomacy*, 144.

12 Arnold H. Taylor, *American Diplomacy and the Narcotics Traffic, 1900–1939: A Study in International Humanitarian Reforms* (Durham, NC: Duke University Press, 1969), 33–34; Walker, *Drug Control in the Americas*, 47–51; Ansley, "International Efforts to Control Narcotics," 108.

13 Also included were Bulgaria, Czechoslovakia, Greece, Iran, Turkey, and Yugoslavia. See McAllister, *Drug Diplomacy*, 179, 205.

14 Walker, *Drug Control in the Americas*, 197.

15 Single Convention on Narcotic Drugs, as amended by the Protocol amending the Single Convention on Narcotic Drugs, 1961, https://treaties.un.org/doc/Treaties/1975/08/19750808%2006-05%20PM/Ch_VI_18p.pdf. As with many other norms and regimes, enforcement was envisaged as largely a domestic matter for signatory states. See Andrew Hurrell, "International Society and the Study of Regimes: A Reflective Approach," in *Regime Theory and International Relations*, ed. Wolker Rittberger (Oxford: Oxford University Press, 1993), 49–72.

16 Single Convention on Narcotic Drugs, 1961.

17 McAllister, *Drug Diplomacy*, 33; Lisa McGirr, *The War on Alcohol: Prohibition and the Rise of the American State* (New York: W.W. Norton & Company, 2016), 51–53.

18 Alfred W. McCoy, *The Politics of Heroin: CIA Complicity in the Global Drug Trade* (Chicago, IL: Lawrence Hill Books, 2003), 32–39.

19 Estimates for cocaine, heroin, marijuana, and methamphetamine. Gregory Midgette, Steven Davenport, Jonathan P. Caulkins, and Beau Kilmer, *What America's Users Spend on Illegal Drugs, 2006–2016* (Santa Monica, CA: RAND Corporation, 2019).

20 "Cocaine Production in Colombia Is at Historic Highs," *The Economist*, 6 July 2019; "Colombia: Background and U.S. Relations," *Congressional Research Service*, 29 November 2019, https://fas.org/sgp/crs/row/R43813.pdf

21 At least 35 countries (divided into high, low, and symbolic users) maintain the death penalty for drug offences, with China and Vietnam keeping figures as a state secret. In 2018, 149 people were sentenced in 13 countries; over 7, 000 are currently on death row.

Giada Girelli, "The Death Penalty for Drug Offences: Global Overview 2018," *Harm Reduction International*, February 2019, http://fileserver.idpc.net/library/HRI_DeathPenaltyReport_2019.pdf

22 "Oregon Becomes First US State to Decriminalise Hard Drugs," *BBC News*, 4 November 2020, www.bbc.com/news/world-us-canada-54809825

23 This slur was attributed to David Murray, a special assistant and chief scientists at the US Office of National Drug Control (2001–2009). Spinning information has been a long-established and documented practice among orthodox US drug officials. Marijuana decriminalization initiatives in Canada, the Caribbean, Mexico, and Central America were condemned by both the Bush and Clinton administrations. David R. Bewley-Taylor, *International Drug Control: Consensus Fractured* (Cambridge: Cambridge University Press, 2012), 108, 171; Mónica Serrano, *El debate de la Sesión Especial de la Asamblea General de la ONU sobre el problema mundial de las drogas de 2016* (Mexico City: Mexico's Senate, Instituto Belisario Dominguez, 2018).

24 Christopher Ingraham, "Obama Says Marijuana Should Be Treated Like Cigarettes or Alcohol," *The Washington Post*, 30 November 2016; Ryan Lucas, "Attorney General Rescinds Obama-Era Marijuana Guidelines," *NPR*, 4 January 2018.

25 Joint Statement, "Compulsory Drug Detention and Rehabilitation Centres," March 2012, www.unodc.org/documents/southeastasiaandpacific/2012/03/drug-detention-centre/JC2310_Joint_Statement6March12FINAL_En.pdf

26 Radhika Coomaraswamy, "Report of the Special Rapporteur on Violence Against Women, Its Causes and Consequences: Mission to the United States of America on the Issue of Violence Against Women in State and Federal Prisons," UN document E/CN.4/1999/68/Add.2, 4 January 1999, www.hr-dp.org/contents/1192; Report of the Working Group on Arbitrary Detention, "Civil and Political Rights Including the Question of Torture and Detention," UN document E/CN/.4/2006/7, 12 December 2005, https://documents-dds-ny.un.org/doc/UNDOC/GEN/G05/166/48/PDF/G0516648.pdf?OpenElement

27 Manfred Nowak, "Report of the Special Rapporteur on Torture and Other Cruel, Inhuman or Degrading Treatment or Punishment," UN document A/HRC/7/3/Add.7, 10 March 2008, https://digitallibrary.un.org/record/623649?ln=en; Barrett and Nowak, "The United Nations and Drug Policy."

28 Office of the UN High Commissioner for Human Rights, "Study on the Impact of the World Drug Problem on the Enjoyment of Human Rights," UN Document A/HRC/30/65, 4 September 2015, https://digitallibrary.un.org/record/804342?ln=en.

29 UN Commission on Narcotics, "Strengthening Cooperation Between the United Nations Office on Drugs and Crime and other United Nations Entities for the Promotion of Human Rights in the Implementation of the International Drug Control Treaties," UN document Res 51/12, www.unodc.org/documents/commissions/CND/Drug_Resolutions/2000-2009/2008/CND_Res-2008-12e.pdf.

30 Mónica Serrano, "A Forward March Halted. Latin America and the UNGASS 2016 Process," in *Transforming the War on Drugs: Warriors, Victims, and Vulnerable Regions*, ed. Annette Idler and Juan Carlos Garzón (London: Hurst & Co., Publishers, forthcoming).

INDEX

Note: Numbers in **bold** indicate a table. Numbers in *italics* indicate a figure on the corresponding page.

Wandel durch Handel 61
Wang Yi 58
war and war governance 40–49
water rights 35–36
WEF *see* World Economic Forum (WEF)
Weiss, Thomas G. 241
Wellcome Trust 230
WePay 291
Westphalian order 9, 43, 66, 91, 102
Westphalia, Treaty of 55
"West to the Rest, the" 81
WFP *see* World Food Programme (WFP)
WHO *see* World Health Organization
Wilkinson, Rorden 241
Williams, Bernard 124
WIPO *see* World Intellectual Property
 Organization (WIPO)
Wise, Carol 275
WMO *see* World Meteorological
 Organization (WMO)
Wolf, Martin 73, 77
"woman," ontological definition of 130
women's rights 190, 121
World Economic Forum (WEF) 162,
 287–288
World Food Programme (WFP) 271
World Health Organization (WHO) Geneva
 Assembly 74
World Intellectual Property Organization
 (WIPO) 79
World Meteorological Organization (WMO)
 250n12

world order 55–56; changing 241–246; four
 main features 87; new 5
World Trade Organization (WTO) 29, 71,
 98, 121; Agreement on Agriculture,
 failure to reform 212; Doha Declaration
 89, 227; global trade rules 211
World War I 54, 55, 121
World War II 54, 55, 57; migration since
 248; optimism in wake of 241; post-War
 global governance 152
Wright, Elizabeth Washburn 303
Wright, Hamilton 302
WTO *see* World Trade Organization (WTO)
Wuhan, China 1

xenophobia 2, 138, 248
Xi Jinping 58, 93
Xinjiang 58, 59, 78

Yalta Agreement 65
Yan Xuetong 58–59
Yazidi refugees 110
Yi, Wang *see* Wang Yi
Yoshide, Suga 62
Yukio, Hatoyama 62

ZANU 183
Zhima Credit *see* Sesame Credit
Zhu, Min 162
Zimbabwe 177, 178, 184
Zukerberg, Mark 166
Zuma, Jacob 1